Praise for *Letters from Black America*

"There can't be a better way to salute Black History Month than to read this collection. It gathers everything from the desperate letters of 19th century slaves—spouses who'd been sold, never to see each other again—to expressions of friendship between poets. . . . Drawn from two centuries, these letters are a lesson drawn from the heart of African-American history."

—ANNE STEPHENSON, *Arizona Republic*

"*Letters from Black America* . . . presents the pantheon of the African-American experience in a unique and intimate format, through the heartfelt correspondence of both the ordinary and extraordinary men and women who lived it."

—JOY T. BENNETT, *Ebony*

"This collection offers an intimate look at the joys and concerns in the lives of ordinary and famous black Americans."

—VANESSA BUSH, *Booklist*

"What makes this book powerful is not only the letters of famous people—Martin Luther King, Booker T. Washington, Alice Walker—but the missives of ordinary folks. Annie Davis, for example, wrote President Lincoln a year after the Emancipation Proclamation, 'It is my desire to go free . . . my mistress won't let me. You will please let me know if we are free and what I can do. I write to you for advice.'"

—BILLY HELTON, *New York Post*

"Ah, the lure and lore of the letter! Nowadays we turn to cell phones, e-mail and instant messaging to connect, but when you crack open Pamela Newkirk's *Letters from Black America* you'll see that the pen is mightier than the thumb."
— MIKA ONO, *Essence*

"An instructive, moving—even delightful—primer on the myriad facets of African-American private and public life."
— *Publishers Weekly*

"This long-overdue collection by writers from all walks of life is moving, illuminating, and difficult to put down."
— MARIAN WRIGHT EDELMAN, president, Children's Defense Fund

"When we think of great memorials and monuments, we often envision structures crafted out of steel or stone. But I believe the letters in Pamela Newkirk's tremendous collection represent perhaps the most powerful and enduring legacy to the strength, creativity, genius, and resilience of the African American community. *Letters from Black America* is itself a work of art."
— ANDREW CARROLL, editor of *Letters of a Nation* and *War Letters*

"Seldom has the intimate life of a people been more variously revealed. Think of the day when there may only be downloaded e-mail, and then thank Pamela Newkirk for the enduring significance, poignancy, and delight of her *Letters from Black America*."

— DAVID LEVERING LEWIS, Julius Silver University Professor, New York University, and author of *W.E.B. Du Bois*

"From slavery to post-9/11, from Phillis Wheatley to Barack Obama, the book gathers correspondence from politicians, writers, and academics, as well as slaves, sharecroppers, servicemen, and domestic workers. . . . The most moving entries are the barely literate and astonishingly painful pleas for family, and for simple justice, by otherwise nameless individuals of the Jim Crow era. Here are people with no hope left other than the belief that death will bring the reunion in Heaven of husband and wife, mother and son. . . . Each section has a brief introduction by Newkirk, just enough to set the stage."

— ROBERT SAUNDERSON, *School Library Journal*

"A unique look at the inner thoughts of many of the most notable African Americans in history. The format enables a reader to pick up the book for just a minute or two to read a particular letter. But the entries can also hold one's interest for hours if an entire section or the whole book is read in one sitting."

— *Journal of Blacks in Higher Education*

Letters from Black America

ALSO BY PAMELA NEWKIRK

A Love No Less

Within the Veil: Black Journalists, White Media

Letters from Black America

Edited by

PAMELA NEWKIRK

Beacon Press

Boston

Beacon Press
Boston, Massachusetts
www.beacon.org

Beacon Press books
are published under the auspices of
the Unitarian Universalist Association of Congregations.

This book is printed on acid-free paper that meets the uncoated paper ANSI/NISO
specifications for permanence as revised in 1992.

Owing to limitations of space, acknowledgments for permission to reprint
previously published and unpublished material can be found starting on page 365.

Designed by Jonathan D. Lippincott

Library of Congress Cataloging-in-Publication Data
Letters from Black America / edited by Pamela Newkirk.—1st ed.
p.   cm.
Includes index.
ISBN-13: 978-0-8070-0115-8 (paperback : alk. paper)
1. African Americans—Correspondence.   2. American letters—African
American authors.   3. African Americans—Attitudes—Sources.   4. African
Americans—Social conditions—Sources.   5. African Americans—Intellectual
life—Sources.   6. African Americans—Politics and government—Sources.
7. African Americans—Race identity—Sources.   I. Newkirk, Pamela.

E184.6.L49 2009
305.896′07300922—dc22
2008041265

This book was originally published in hardcover by Farrar, Straus and Giroux.
It is here reprinted by permission of Farrar, Straus and Giroux,
18 West 18th Street, New York, New York 10011.

Credits for front cover photos: Dr. James Arthur Kennedy and A'Lelia Walker cour-
tesy of A'Lelia Bundles; Alice Walker courtesy of Emory University; Lewis Douglass
from Moorland-Spingarn Research Center, Howard University; Paul Laurence
Dunbar from General Research and Reference Division, Schomburg Center for
Research in Black Culture, The New York Public Library, Astor, Lenox and Tilden
Foundations; W.E.B. Du Bois and Alice Ruth Moore (Alice Dunbar Nelson) from
Photographs and Prints Division, Schomburg Center for Research in Black Culture,
The New York Public Library, Astor, Lenox and Tilden Foundations

To the memory of my mother

Contents

PART II: *Courtship and Romance*

PART III: *Politics and Social Justice*

PART IV: *Education and the Art of Scholarship*

PART V: *War*

PART VI: **Art and Culture**

Introduction

The popular enchantment with the art of letter writing can be traced back to the 1730s, when the poet Alexander Pope published his correspondence as literary works. Since then, hundreds of epistolary anthologies have been compiled, attesting to the enduring power of letters to satisfy our voyeuristic yearnings while animating and explicating facts. As linguistic snapshots of bygone eras, letters anchor us in the past with unparalleled intimacy and spontaneity, lighting the dark crevices of our private and public history. But despite their importance as historical markers and as literature, the letters of African Americans—like so much of Black history—have historically been undervalued or ignored. Until recent decades, an African American epistolary tradition was considered an anomaly given the relatively low literacy rates during slavery and the century following Emancipation.*

This collection is an attempt to help fill this literary and historical void by presenting a multidimensional portrait of African American life from the eighteenth to the twenty-first century through the illuminating letters of ordinary and exceptional African Americans. The correspondents—enslaved and free, powerless and privileged—explore the social, religious, artistic, political, civic, and domestic lives of a people over the course of three centuries, providing a sweeping narrative history of the Black American experience.

The letters—particularly those written before the latter part of the twentieth century—provide a stark contrast to today's rapid-fire correspondence facilitated by cell phones, PDAs, text messaging, and e-mail. While we have gained the ability to bridge our physical distances

---

*See Janet Duitsman Cornelius, *"When I Can Read My Title Clear": Literacy, Slavery, and Religion in the Antebellum South* (Columbia: University of South Carolina Press, 1991).

with the speed of light, we often write without the benefit of the quiet reflection that is evident in many of the letters contained here. Our gratification may be instant, but perusing these missives from the past invites us to contemplate what has been diminished in the name of velocity: the art of penmanship, the poetry of language, the enduring value of letters as historic objects, the sentimental connotations of a postmark and a loved one's handiwork, the contemplative act, and the anticipation and yearning tucked into an envelope.

While wide-ranging, this volume represents a mere fraction of the correspondence of African Americans deposited in archives or held in private collections. Many of the letters included here were selected from thousands culled from archives around the country, while others were unearthed through the African-American Life in Letters Project, launched in 2003. The project, initiated with a grant from the New York University Graduate School of Arts and Science fund and then sponsored by a New York University Research Challenge Fund grant, supported research and clerical assistance, travel, and a wide appeal through direct letters and e-mail to some of the most celebrated individuals in African American life. Outreach also involved Listserv announcements to civic organizations and veterans' groups, lectures, newspaper notices, and word-of-mouth. The project was intended not only to prepare this volume but also to encourage the preservation of these important historical papers at archives. The Schomburg Center for Research in Black Culture agreed to serve as a repository for letters deemed historically significant and not cataloged elsewhere.

When I embarked on this project, I did not anticipate how difficult it would be to secure contemporary letters or to obtain permission to publish correspondence already deposited in archives. In retrospect, I appreciate the wish of contemporary correspondents to keep private what are, in fact, intimate artifacts. A history of disparaging portrayals in popular culture has surely contributed to the reluctance by African Americans to expose their inner lives. This reticence poses a challenge for scholars seeking to depict the fullness of African American life and makes all the more precious the contributors to these pages.

What emerges from the more than 200 letters in this volume is a textured, compelling, and unvarnished portrait of African American life that highlights our shared humanity. Laid bare are the public and private musings of some of the giants in American life: the letters of

Rev. Dr. Martin Luther King, Jr., reveal both a romantic and a rebel; W.E.B. Du Bois shifts from a public intellectual impatient with the pace of progress to a doting father. We experience the pride of a father as his son goes to war, and the turmoil of a son explaining his decision to convert from the Christianity of his family to Buddhism. A gay activist poignantly describes his quest for acceptance, and young lovers revel in the poetry of their affections, with all its passion, pain, and pleasure.

It is my hope that this volume will contribute to the growing recognition of African American letters as historical treasures while inspiring those in possession of these irreplaceable relics to preserve them—whether in local or national archives, or in well-cared-for family libraries—for future generations.

A Note on the Text

While I have attempted to preserve the original texts as faithfully as possible, I have at times placed in brackets correct spelling or grammar, or contextual information, if they are needed to grasp fully the meaning of a letter. I particularly struggled with the letters written by barely literate slaves but in the end decided to allow the letters to retain their original character. I believe the poignancy of the writers' plight overshadows their grammatical shortcomings. Unbracketed ellipses are the writers' own, while those in brackets indicate the omission of passages that are immaterial to the essence of the letter or that contain personal information such as telephone numbers or addresses. In a few instances I have omitted passages to protect the privacy of one or both of the correspondents. I have, when the information is provided, indicated where and when the letter was written. When the date is not provided, I have, when possible, noted the date of the postmark.

PART I

Family

For more than two centuries slavery would test the ability of Africans in the Americas to sustain family ties. Children were sold away from their parents and husbands torn from wives. Many slaves tried in vain to retain bonds with family members dispersed across the country, but their efforts were often undermined by their legally mandated illiteracy, the inability to locate or maintain contact with loved ones, and society's overarching disregard for black family life.

The legacy of slavery, followed by a century of legal segregation and discrimination, still resonates today as African American families are disproportionately beset by high levels of poverty, unemployment, out-of-wedlock births, divorce, and male incarceration. In 1965 *The Negro Family: The Case for National Action,* a controversial report by U.S. Assistant Secretary of Labor Daniel Patrick Moynihan, highlighted the growing number of African American female-headed homes and out-of-wedlock births, and an increasing reliance on welfare. According to the report, nearly 23 percent of black homes had absent fathers, compared with 8 percent for whites. While divorce rates for blacks and whites were equal in 1940, by 1964 the rate for blacks was 40 percent higher. Moynihan attributed many of the problems to a legacy of slavery and discrimination, high black unemployment, and inferior education, but also to the destabilization of the black nuclear family and a federal welfare system that eclipsed the role of the black male.

While many civil rights leaders accused Moynihan of blaming the victim, the findings in the widely condemned report would compare favorably with the portrait of the black family at the dawn of the twenty-first century, when some 70 percent of black children are born out of wedlock, compared with 23 percent in 1964. And while nearly

80 percent of black families were headed by married couples in 1950, only 48 percent were in 2000. The disintegration of the nuclear family has had a profound impact on the economic well-being of African Americans. The 2006 National Urban League's State of Black America report said the median net worth of the average black family is ten times less than that of a white one.

Still, as the letters in this part poignantly demonstrate, throughout history many African American families have found a way to prevail over even the worst adversity. A portrait of African Americans' dysfunction and crisis has often overshadowed the reality of the many blessed with nurturing families, whether headed by two parents or one. The following letters are testaments to the viability—and possibility—of the black family.

Hannah Grover to Her Son Cato

Caldwell, [?]
June 3d 1805

My dear Son Cato

I long to see you in my old age   I live in Caldwell with Mr. Grover the Minister of that place   now my dear son I pray you to come and see your dear old Mother—Or send me twenty dollar and I will come and see you in Philadelphia—And if you cant come to see your old Mother pray send me a letter and tell me where you live what family you have and what you do for a living—I am a poor old servant   I long for freedom—And my Master will free me if any body will ingage to maintain me so that I do not come upon him—I love you Cato you love your Mother—You are my only son

This from your affectionate Mother—
Hannah Van Buskerk now—
Hannah Grover

P.S. My dear son I have not seen you since I saw you at Staten Island   At Addee Barker's 20 years ago—If you send any money send it by Dotr. Bonr and he will give it to me—If you have any love for your poor old Mother pray come or send to me   My dear son I love you with all my heart—
Hannah Van Buskerk—

George Pleasant to Agnes Hobbs

George Pleasant and Agnes Hobbs were the parents of Elizabeth Keckley (1818–1907), a slave who became the seamstress for Mary Todd Lincoln

while she was First Lady. Keckley kept the letters written by her father after his master on a nearby plantation in Virginia relocated to Tennessee, forever separating him from his wife and child. Keckley published the following letter in her autobiography, Behind the Scenes; or, Thirty Years a Slave, and Four Years in the White House *(1868).*

Shelbyville, [Tennessee]
Sept. 6, 1833

Mrs. Agnes Hobbs,
Dear Wife:

My dear beloved wife I am more than glad to meet with opportunity writee thes few lines to you by my Mistress who ar now about starterng to Virginia, and sevl others of my old friends are with her; in compeney Mrs. Ann Rus the wie of mster Thos Rus and Dan Woodiard and his family and I am very sorry that I havn the chance to go with them as I feele Determid to see you If life last again. I am now here and out at this pleace so I am not able to get of at this time. I am write well and hearty and all the rest of masters family. I heard this eveng by Mistress that ar just from theree all sends love to you and all my old frends. I am a living in a town called Shelbvlle and I have wroe a greate many letters since Ive beene here and almost been reeady to my selfe that its out of the question to write any more at tall: my dear wife I don't feeld no whys like giving out writing to you as yet and I hope when you get this letter that you be Inncougege to write me a letter. I am well satisfied at my living at this place I am a making money for my own benefit and I hope that its to yours also. If I live to see Nexct year I shall heve my own time from master by giving him 100 and twenty Dollars a year and I thinke I shall be doing good bisness at that and heve something more thean all that. I hope with gods helpe that I may be abble to rejoys with you on the earth and In heaven lets meet when will I am determnid to nuver stop praying, not in this earth and I hope to praise god In glory there weel meet to part no more forever. So my dear wife I hope to meet you In paradase to prase god forever. I want Elizabeth to be a good girl and not thinke that because I am bound so fare that Gods not abble to open the way.

George Pleasant,
Hobbs a servant of Grum.

Lucy Smith to Sarah Boon

Fayetteville, North Carolina
May 1, 1842

My Dear Sister

We received your letter last Saturday that contained the distressing news of our dear Mother Death   we did not know until we received it that she had moved   it gave us grate pleasure to hear that she was with her Daughter when she died   it greeved us much to hear that she was no more and to know we should see her no more   but we sorrow not as those who have no hope for we know our loss is her eternal gain   we wanted very much to go up and see her last Christamass but were disappointed   I have nursed Miss Della Baby ever since it was born that was one reason why I could not go   I have no news to tell you   I am glad to hear tat times is the same with you as when we were there the Methodist Preacher Mr Mood Emersed two yesterday in the creek   there was great rejoiseing

Your Brother sends his love to you   he received your letter but has neglected to answer it   his son garner is married to Jacob Harrises Daughter and has got a son   his health had improved very much   my health is not good   Estra has been in bad health all the winter   your Brother sends his love to you and all your family give our love to Sister, Brother your Mother husband and al your family. Accept a portion for your self prey for us

your Affectionate Sister Lucy Smith

Abream Scriven to Dinah Jones

New Orleans, Louisiana
September 19, 1858

My Dear Wife.

I take the pleasure of writing you these few with much regret to inform you that I am sold to a man by the name of Peterson [a trader] and stay in New Orleans. I am here yet. But I expect to go before long but when I get there I will write you and let you know where I am. My Dear I want to send you some things but I don't know who to send them by but I will try to get them to you and my children. Give my love to my father and mother and tell them good Bye for me and if we shall not meet in this world I hope to meet in heaven. My dear wife for you and my children my pen cannot express the griffe I feel to be parted from you all. I remain your truly husband until death.

Abream Scriven

James Tate to His Wife

West Point, Georgia
February 4, 1863

My Dear Wife,

I received your very welcome letter two weeks ago. You must not think hard of me for not answering it sooner— I have been getting Miss Maria to write for me ever since I have been living here at home this year and Master found out three or four weeks ago that she was writing letters for me and he told her to stop it at once and not to write any more for me that it was just keeping you and me miserable to be writing letters to each other for he said that your [Master] John would never let you come to see me and that he never expected to let me go to see you, that Mobile was too far off for him to ever let me go there and that he was going to try to persuade me to marry another woman that is living here and that he wants you to marry some other man that is living in Mobile, now I am just telling you what my Master said it is not what I say for I can assure you my dear wife I have not thought or said any thing like that yet. I can not think of any thing more to write to you now my dear wife. You must kiss Jimmie and little Mary Olivia for me and tell them their Papa would give any thing he had in this world to see them both. Give my love to John too.

If I ever do take a notion to marry again my dear wife I shall write and let you know all about it but I do not think I shall ever take such a notion again directly not if I always feel like I do now. For I can not think of any other woman nor love any other but <u>you</u> my <u>dear wife.</u>

Your devoted Husband
James Tate

Ann Valentine to Andrew Valentine

The following letter from a Missouri slave was written to her husband, Andrew Valentine, an enlisted soldier, and addressed to his barracks in St. Louis, Missouri.

January 19, 1864

My Dear Husband,

I r'ecd your letter dated Jan. 9th also one dated Jan'y 1st but have got no one till now to write for me. You do not know how bad I am treated. They are treating me worse and worse every day. Our child cries for you. Send me some money as soon as you can for me and my child are almost naked. My cloth is yet in the loom and there is no telling when it will be out. Do not send any of your letters to Hogsett especially those having money in them as Hogsett will keep the money. George Combs went to Hannibal soon after you did so I did not get that money from him. Do the best you can and do not fret too much for me for it wont be long before I will be free and then all we make will be ours.

Your affectionate wife,
Ann

P.S. Please send our little girl a string of beads in your next letter to remember you by. Ann

Mandy McCinny to George McCinny

Jefferson City, Missouri
May 11, 1864

Dear husban—

It is with pleasure that I take the opportunity of riting these few lines to you to let you no that I am well and hope these few lines reach you—they may find you the same. I want you to answer this letter as soon as you get it—my baby was born on Easter Monday the 28th—it is a girl. Its name is Mary Easter—it looks like you. I should like to see you very much. Fanny is well and the baby is well and I am well. I long to see the day that we will meet again. I have seen a great deal of trouble since you left. I want to no where cousin Dave is and if you can get together or not. He left the Monday after you did. Tell Jim I heard from his girl. She is well and at his old home [. . .] I am in Jefferson City and times are very hard hear. I wish that you would send som money as soon as you can as I need it so much. I want you to rite where you are and how you are. I heard you was sick.* Direct your letter to Mr. Prince. No more at this time but I remain your Dear wife,

    Mandy McCinny

Susanah Hart to Mark Hart

Harrisburg, Pennsylvania
February 23, 1865

My dear Husband,

    I take my pen in hand to rite a few lines to you to let you no that I have bin very sick and not bin able to go out. I want you to come as soon as you can and see about me and the children. I am out of money and I am very poor an if you don't come home or send some help to me, I and the children have to go to the poor house. My friends is no count to me. George went and put himself in the army on no word to me and I had hard work to get him out and had to promise to let him go with a Captain and I am afraid that he will run off yet—he is very bad and is very head strong. I received the letter you sent—I was very glad to hear from you. I have sent you 4 letters I got but one letter from you for some time. I would like to see you—I want you to come and see to getting places to put the children—I can't keep them—I have no money—I would like to see you once more—so no more, but remain your dear wife,

    Susanah Hart write soon

Martha Bruce to John Edward Bruce

An ailing Martha Bruce wrote this letter to her son John Edward Bruce (1856–1924), a prominent New York–based journalist and activist whose pen name was Bruce Grit. Born a slave in Maryland, the self-educated Bruce founded the Argus *in Washington, D.C., and was a contributing writer to numerous publications, including* The Boston Tribune *and* The Albany Argus. *In 1908 he launched the* Weekly Standard *in New York, and he later served as an American correspondent for* The African Times Orient Review *in London. A staunch believer in Pan-African nationalism, he belonged to Marcus Garvey's Universal Negro Improvement Association and wrote for that organization's* Negro World *and the* Daily Negro Times.

---

*George was indeed ill and died of pneumonia about a month after this letter was written. He never received it.

September 23, 1887

Dear Son,

I were more than pleased to hear from you this morning that you were well and your prospects were so bright. I have been very much worried about you owing to bad dreams as well as bad thought. I have been expecting Marion to have called on me but expect her non-appearance has been caused by illness on her part or her family. Am in need of nothing but Gods blessing and the use of my limbs [illegible] I trust the worst part is over although I have not the use of my foot or being able to walk.

I have been three days at Mrs. Smoots and they were very kind and good to me and I was very sorry . . . I were sick, very sick, the whole time I were there. You need not hurry yourselves to come home to me if your remaining away is to your betterment if it is for a month to come. Marion has been expecting to hear from you. Your letter and P.C. did not reach me till this morning as Mr. C has been out to work for over two weeks and he has brought them to me to day. He says that he sent word to me on last Tuesday but his messenger never made his appearance. He and his wife joins me in love to you and wish you all success.

Answer soon as possible and do not worry about me. I trust that I will be able to be about soon. [T]o hear from you today is worth more to my mind than five dollars and am certain that the news from you helps me more than medicine. Be sure if you have no other business to call you here except seeing me do not come until you settle your business. Do not come until you settle your business. The medicine did me a great deal of good as long as it lasted. Best love to you [illegible] George. Sorry to hear that he has had such a pull back but sickness is the lot of us all.

Your affectionate mother,
Martha Bruce

Paul Laurence Dunbar to Matilda Dunbar

The following letters are between the poet Paul Laurence Dunbar (1872–1906) and his mother, Matilda Dunbar, who was born into slavery in Kentucky. Paul was one of two children Matilda had with Joshua, a Civil War veteran who served in the legendary 55th Massachusetts Volunteer Infantry.

Matilda also had two children from a previous marriage. After her divorce from Joshua in 1874, she supported her children by working as a washer-woman in Dayton, Ohio.

Chicago, Illinois
June 6, 1893

My Dear Mother,

I thought I would write you again and let you know how things are going with me and of the evening I spent with Frederick Douglass; You know Eugene Griffin made the remark in Dayton that I had never met any great men like Frederick Douglass, and that they wouldn't know anything about me. Well, Mr. Douglass had known of me for about a year and Sunday night his nephew took me to call upon him. We went where he staid at Lawyer and Mrs. Williams had found the old man gone home. [H]e had expected us earlier in the day and was much provoked because we did not come & had to leave and go out to dinner. Well after staying here a good while & making a pleasant call, meeting another writer, Mrs. Grimke* of Washington, D.C., we went to the house where Mr. Douglass was taking dinner. The old man was just finishing dinner. He got up and came tottering into the room, "and this is Paul Dunbar," he said shaking hands and patting me on the shoulder. "Paul, how do you do, I've been knowing you for some time and you're one of my boys." He said so much Ma that I must wait until I am with you before I can tell you all. He had me read to him my "Ode to Ethiopia" and he himself read to us with much spirit "The Ol' Tunes" with which he seemed delighted.† I gave him a book, although he insisted on buying it. "Well," he said, "if you give me this I will buy others," so I expect to sell him two or three anyhow. I am in the very highest and best society that Chicago affords. Mrs. Jarvis who owns a seven story building down in the heart of the city, is over seventy years old and with over $20,000.

---

*This is most likely a reference to Charlotte Forten Grimké (1838–1914), who was born into a wealthy African American family in Philadelphia. She was a teacher and writer whose articles were published in *The Atlantic Monthly*. She married Francis Grimké, a graduate of Princeton Theological Seminary, who hailed from a prominent family in Washington, D.C., where for six decades he was pastor of the Fifteenth Street Presbyterian Church.

†Both of these poems were included in *Oak and Ivy* (1893), Dunbar's first collection of poetry.

After all her boasting Eugenia Griffin is not in it. I am invited to attend a reception tonight at this Miss James' house given to five distinguished Englishmen who want to see some of the representative colored people in this country and think Mamma your poor little ugly black boy has been chosen as one of the representative colored people after being in Chicago only five weeks. I forgot to say that Mr. Douglass invited me to visit him at his home in Washington City next winter and stay awhile. He says, "It would do my heart good just to have you there and take care of you. I have got one fiddle there (his son) and now I want a poet; and it would do me good to have you up there in my old study, just working away at your poetry."

[. . .] Your little room will cost me only seven dollars a month and you will have it to yourself. Let me know what you think of my plans and when you think best to come out.

[. . .] Hoping [to] hear from you very soon, I am with love

Your affectionate Son,

Paul

Matilda Dunbar to Paul Laurence Dunbar

Dayton, Ohio
June 8, 1895

Paul My Son,

I received your kind letter and was glad to here from you. I am having very good health just now but I am [lonesome] I should like to come and see you and my sister. I am trying to make the very best of things I can but it is very hard for me to be [alone]. I try to write Sunday but I could not settle my mine to do so I got a letter from rob* and he sad that he would let me know in a few days about coming to Chicago but I cant go any why without aranet, I sent you some roses and hope they will be nice when you get them.

I must close   write as soon as you get and obligd your

Mother

---

*A reference to Paul's brother Robert Murphy.

Paul Laurence Dunbar to Matilda Dunbar

Washington, D.C.
Nov. 25th, 1897

My Dear Mother:—

I thought I would write to you on the type-writer this afternoon so that the people could read it. It is Thanksgiving Day and I have a holiday from the library of course. I am getting along all right and getting some of the things in the house. I will be glad when you come. I want so much to be settled. You need not give the carpenters any of that money unless you have so much over your fare that you can spare it. I have no idea what the things are going to cost: but start them on as soon as possible. The house is very beautiful and my parlor suite is very swell. My sideboard and extension tables are beautiful. The floors in the parlor, dining-room and my study which is just off the parlor are all polished, and I have a Japanese rug on my study floor, I have a new book case under a fine big Morris chair. The parlor suite is in dark green plush and cherry colored inlaid wood. Of course I do not know anything about curtains and I cannot fit up the bedrooms until you come. Send the things I think I told you to me at 1924 Fourth St. northwest and let me know when and by what road they come. You had better take either the Pennsylvania or the Big Four that leaves Dayton about five o'clock in the afternoon, and telegraph me from one of the way stations when you will get in. This will be easier than having me tell you what train to leave on. Let me know first by what road you are coming before you start and if I should happen to miss you, don't feel afraid, but take a cab and go to your own house 1924 Fourth St. Northwest. If I am not there or a girl, get the key next door and go in there will be fire and a comfortable chair. Does Mr. Samson understand how I am to pay him? I can send him fifty dollars for his men as soon as you come or would you rather have me send it before. Of course I am making a good deal of money just now, but I am also spending a good deal as it takes no little bit to furnish a house.

I am sorry to say that Alice [his wife] who was to have been here to-day is very sick in New York. Mrs. Curtis is here from Chicago and I am going there to call in a few minutes. But Burns is up in New Jersey and will probably go South this winter with his employers. Let me hear from you at once and get here as soon as you can.

Ever Your Devoted Son,
Paul

Bring Lucy with you if she will come as it will be very lonesome for you. I am away all day but shall have to be out of the city a good deal this month at night. I should be willing to pay her way if she would come and help you get settled. If she won't, bring someone else.

Matilda Dunbar to Paul Laurence Dunbar

Washington, D.C.
July 5, 1901

Paul, my dear son,

I received your letter this morning and I am so glad I hasten to answer right away. I have felt better in the last three days than I have felt since you left. I have failed in either of my other letters to let you know how hot it is here it is roasting. It is impossible to keep cool. I don't use anything but ice water and cold lemonade but very little [illegible] since you left. I shall be so glad when you come home. The folks next door are going to leave tomorrow and it will be very lonesome. Give my love to Alice and all of the family and say to her that I am going to answer her letter when I get cool enough. I will close. Write soon again.

From your mother

Mary Church Terrell to Robert H. Terrell

Mary Church Terrell (1863–1954), a popular lecturer, cofounder of the Colored Woman's League, and the first president of the National Association of Colored Women, was born in Memphis, Tennessee. She met her husband, Robert H. Terrell (1857–1925), while teaching at M Street High School in Washington, D.C. In 1901, Terrell, a graduate of Harvard University and Howard University Law School, was appointed justice of the peace by President Theodore Roosevelt. That same year his wife became the first African American woman appointed to the District of Columbia Board of Education. The couple wed in 1891 and had two children, Phyllis and Mary.

Chicago, Illinois
Windsor Clifton Hotel Co.
Sat., July 9, 1902

My own Sweetheart:

(It is so blessed to <u>own</u> a man like you). As I was about to say—a knock, loud and imperative and shocking in its suddenness just made me jump out of my skin fairly and rush to the door. It was a special delivery from the one being in all this crowded universe from whom I should rather hear than from any of the other millions of its swarming human kind. My watch says its twenty minutes past twelve and that means it is really twenty minutes past eleven by Chicago time. I [illegible] change my watch from the Washington time. It is a comfort to me to know exactly what time it is at home, and I don't seem so far away. [. . .] If I had been at the coronation in the flesh today and had sat with the beautiful sweet womanly queen, I should have preferred to be with you and Phyllis, my dear—The more I roam the wide world over, the sweeter and more desirable my own home becomes to me. The more other people praise me and seem to appreciate my company, the more satisfying to my comfort and happiness are you and Phyllis. Even tho' I think that remaining in Chicago will mean $20 extra in money, still I have been asking myself whether an extra ten days or an extra seven days from home are not worth a great deal more than that—whether earning $20 should have tempted me to stay away from you seven whole days, when we might have lived together—But perhaps this separation, only casual and, as a rule, very short—will work out for both of us a more exceeding and abundant joy—A company of three women and one man occupied the room next to mine for a few hours this evening—I'll tell you all about them when I come home. The world is so full of prostitutes. I am deeply impressed with that. And really there is such temptation in the way of some poor women. We should really be charitable to such poor creatures and frown down upon the rich women who go wrong and are unfaithful for the fun of the thing—But the rich women have all the best of it—Nobody makes them suffer—Today I went to another luncheon given by the president of the Chicago Woman's Club, Mrs. Fred Pelham, whose husband is the manager of the Central Lyceum Bureau—At least two distinguished people were there, one—a Miss Elinor Smith, a composer of songs, and the other an Englishman, Mr. [illegible] who was a classmate of Samuel Coleridge Taylor,* in the Royal College of Music—He sings divinely and I marched right up to him, of course, after I found he knew Taylor—I think of you and Phyllis all the time. The company, the singing, the luncheon, the house itself—everything this afternoon was ideal, but there was an undertone of sadness and dissat-

*Samuel Coleridge-Taylor (1875–1912), a well-known composer, studied at the Royal College of Music in London. His most famous work, the cantata *Hiawatha's Wedding Feast*, first performed in 1898, was widely acclaimed in the United States and England.

isfaction to me through it all, because I was not home—Yesterday at Miss Addam's luncheon I sat by the wealthy Mrs. Heurotin whose son in Cape Town, South Africa, is manager of the [illegible] Diamond mines— Mrs. Heurotin will entertain me the next time I come to Chicago, for she insisted that I visit [. . .] When Miss Addams introduced me to her, she said "Oh—I remember Mrs. Terrell very well—When the National Association of Colored Women were in Chicago three years ago, I spoke after Mrs. Terrell delivered her address—a wonderful eloquent speech— Mr. Heurotin said it was the first address he ever heard—and the next day I received an anonymous letter saying "How on earth did you have the nerve to get up in [illegible] Chapel and get off those common place remarks you made last night, after Mrs. Terrell had delivered that marvelous address?" And there was Heurotin just rhapsodized over the speech herself. It was very embarrassing to me, I must confess—I could write all night. It's the only way I can be with you all night but as I am to leave here tomorrow morning I suppose I should go to bed and get some rest. How much better I could rest with you tonight. I hope I shall do as well in Columbus Junction, Iowa as I did in Decatur—Try to keep Phyllis from eating too much meat and have her eat lightly at night [. . .] Kiss her and yourself thousands of times for me and give my love to Mother,
    Yours always
    Mollie

Robert H. Terrell to Mary Church Terrell

Treasury Department
Office of the Register
Washington, D.C.
[Undated]

My Darling:

Enclosed you will find notice of my appt. from NY paper. The *Times* of this city has a fine sketch of me, but I have not a copy. [. . .] I was sworn in this morning and took charge of the office. I am simply overwhelmed with telephone and letters of congratulations. Not a word from Pinch. He is dead in his shock. The girl is doing very well. She is keeping an account of her expenditures to submit to you on your return. Booker Washington telegraphs that he will be here at 10:30 tonight. I shall go to the depot to meet him and take him home with me.

[. . .] I am anxious to hear from Grandma. I hope she is not as ill as we supposed. I am getting card this morning.

Excuse this rambling letter. I am trying to get it off in the 7:30 p.m. mail.

Oceans of love from your devoted husband,

Berto

Robert H. Terrell to Mary Church Terrell

Municipal Court of the District of Columbia
Dec. 30, 1913

My dearest Wife:—

I wish you and the girls a joyful New Year and I trust that your whole Christmas holidays have been all that you would wish them to be at any time. I have spent a quiet time and about as pleasantly as I could have under the circumstances. I have only attended one function of any consequence and that was the dancing class last night. I took Mrs. Arthur Brooks with me. Her husband is with the President in [illegible]. Everyone enjoyed himself. There was a good dancing crowd present and the men and women were equally divided. Of course there were many inquiries for you as well as expressions of deep regret that you could not be with us. The young set of people have had several nice functions during the week, so I was informed last night. I take it that our girls know all about them. The big party at New Auditorium Hall I scheduled for tomorrow under the auspices of Mrs. Bruce and other ladies has fallen through because there was some mix up as to the renting of the place. The boss had rented it to one part and the janitor to another. The orchestra and printing must be paid for by the ladies at a loss. The ladies are very much chagrined.

I saw Mrs. Bruce yesterday. She informed me that she had been sick abed for fifteen days with the grippe. She doesn't look well.

In the *New York Age* which I mailed to you a few days ago you will find page three or four, subsidized by Robert Church, carrying that editorial from the *Memphis Sun* on the mill trouble that says nothing at all. He paid well for that space. He seems daffy on Roscoe, if one may judge from his correspondence with the *Age*. You told me, by the way, that hearing in the Court of Appeals would take place about January 1. Are you going down again? It will hardly be necessary unless you simply wish to listen to the arguments. There will be testimony taken again unless the court of Appeals agrees with Judge Galloway. Then the real mill contest will be on.

Nagi [the dog] is well and wishes to be most affectionately remembered to you and the girls. I have had to change his soap because that [other] brand seemed to chafe him so much. I am using "Surgeons and Physicians Soap" now and it makes a beautiful lather. He insists on his talcum powder. He enjoys it so much. I have to keep him clean because he gets right under the cover with me.

Where is Tom living in New York? I never hear from him but I should like to know just where to reach him.

I hope it will not be long before I shall be with you again even for a few days.

With lots of love,
Berto

W.E.B. Du Bois to Yolande Du Bois

W.E.B. Du Bois (1868–1963), the eminent scholar, journalist, activist, and author of The Souls of Black Folk *(1903), wrote to his daughter Nina Yolande Du Bois (1900–1961), who later was briefly married to Countee Cullen (1903–1946), the well-known Harlem Renaissance poet.*

Atlanta, Georgia
March 13, 1907

Dear Little Yolande—

This is Sunday night and papa has talked all his letters into the graphophone and he has half of one of the records left, so he is going to talk a little while to you. I wonder what you are doing—I suppose you must be in bed. How do you like sliding down hill? Papa used to slide down hills when he was a little boy and used to think that it was great fun. We are having nice sunny weather here now, the grass is green, little buds are coming out on the trees, while you up there are all ice and snow. Everybody asks about you. Miss Ware wants to know how you are getting on and Miss Thomas wants you to write to her and Miss Clifford thinks of you and Mrs. Herndon speaks of you and Miss Pingree, especially misses you. But most of all I think papa misses you when he comes in and has nobody to disturb him and nobody to interrupt his work. He'd be very glad to have you interrupt his work a little while now. I suppose you are being a very good girl and helping mama to get well. You must hurry up and write me a nice letter. Now good night.

    Papa

W.E.B. Du Bois to Yolande Du Bois

The fourteen-year-old Yolande was in her first year at The Bedales School, a boarding school in Great Britain, when this letter was written.

New York
October 29, 1914

Dear Little Daughter:

    I have waited for you to get well settled before writing. By this time I hope some of the strangeness has worn off and that my little girl is working hard and regularly.

    Of course, everything is new and unusual. You miss the newness and smartness of America. Gradually, however, you are going to sense the beauty of the old world: its calm and eternity and you will grow to love it.

    Above all remember, dear, that you have a great opportunity. You are in one of the world's best schools, in one of the world's greatest modern empires. Millions of boys and girls all over this world would give almost anything they possess to be where you are. You are there by no desert or merit of yours, but only by lucky chance.

    Deserve it, then. Study, do your work. Be honest, frank and fearless and get some grasp of the real values of life. You will meet, of course, curious little annoyances. People will wonder at your dear brown and the sweet crinkly hair. But that simply is of no importance and will be soon forgotten. Remember that most folk laugh at anything unusual whether it is beautiful, fine or not. You, however, must not laugh at yourself. You must know that brown is as pretty as white or prettier and crinkly hair as straight even though it is harder to comb. The main thing is the YOU beneath the clothes and skin—the ability to do, the will to conquer, the determination to understand and know this great, wonderful, curious world. Don't shrink from new experiences and custom. Take the cold bath bravely. Enter into the spirit of your big bedroom. Enjoy what is and not pine for what is not. Read some good, heavy, serious books just for discipline: Take yourself in hand and master yourself. Make yourself do unpleasant things, so as to gain the upper hand of your soul.

Above all remember: your father loves you and believes in you and expects you to be a wonderful woman.

I shall write each week and expect a weekly letter from you.

Lovingly yours,

Papa

Dr. William R. R. Granger, Sr., to Son

The Grangers were a prominent family in Newport News, Virginia, and later Newark, New Jersey, that included Dr. William R. R. Granger, Sr., a physician, and his wife, Violet, a teacher. Among their six sons were three physicians, two dentists, and the civic leader Lester B. Granger (1896–1976), who served as executive director of the National Urban League from 1941 to 1961. This letter is from William R. R. Granger, Sr., to one of his sons.

Newark, New Jersey
October 8, 1911

Dear Son,

I read your letter to your mother and am prouder of you than ever. That's right! Dig deep and stick to it, it will grow easier as you get accustomed to the task. Just remember that you have a father who has traversed the entire journey—with this difference—that he had no loving father and mother to spur him on. I am proud of your expressed sentiments regarding women. Let your mother be ever your ideal of womanhood . . . Whatever you do, join neither man nor boy in maligning or casting aspersions on womanhood. Do not neglect the "Thrown of Grace" in all your doings. There's strength there . . .

Keep yourself in prime by at least one substantial feed a day. Any retrograde just now might be disastrous for all time. A well nourished body brings a well balanced mind and active mind. Therefore eat! . . . All are fairly well. Your mother will write soon.

With affection and Pride—

Your loving father

Dr. William R. R. Granger, Sr., to W.R.R. Granger, Jr.

Newark, New Jersey

September 30, 1914

My dear Son Rudolph,

I am in receipt of your letter and have read it carefully. I know that in many respects I must appear a stranger father and rather disinterested, but that is not the case. There is more of the Indian stoicism in me than the Negro loquacity. When I am deeply moved I am least demonstrative. You were exactly about my age when you made your choice. I have not tried to dominate your selection in any way. I have taken the girl only on what your mother has said. She intimated the probability of this last year, and seemed satisfied. I therefore made myself satisfied. I hope your choice will be all you desire and as you have expressed it, she may prove as noble a wife as your mother is. I suppose really that I should have interested myself in Isabel* when she was here last. But to tell the truth, it did not occur to me. Just tell her for me that she must take me as she finds me. Make herself at home whenever she comes around me and do not look for any gushing over as it is not my way. Let her know that I will take her to my bosom just as warmly as either of you boys and would do as much for her as for any of you.

All I ask is that you boys will not neglect your mother, for, hale and active as I appear, my time is fast approaching and I feel that my [illegible] is not far off . . .

Wishing you the best,

Your loving father

Dr. A. T. Granger to Dr. W.R.R. Granger, Jr.

Harrisburg, Pa.

August 5, 1917

Dear Ran—:

I suppose that you are down there having a grand time lording it over the nurses part of the time and flirting with the same the rest of the time! Tis a great life, I assure you! I had a short turn at it you know.

Really though you should be having quite a nice and interesting time. There are so many things to see in a hospital. Things that you have never seen and perhaps never will see again. All kinds of odd cases. When

*His future wife, Dr. Isabella Vandervall, was a gynecologist.

I was up at Dr. Mudgett's I almost wished that I was a physician, so I could take an active part in all the work. You have the interesting profession, while I have the money profession. About even isn't it?

Things are a little slow here around now. Perhaps on account of the time of the year, and perhaps on account of the draft. A good many young fellows are refusing to have their mouths fixed to allow a chance of being refused on account of their teeth. Things will pick up soon I hope. As it is I have cleared expenses since the first month. My expenses are about sixty dollars a month. At least sixty. I think that I am doing very well, don't you?

Kat is well and sends her love. She is getting along fine here. She doesn't like the place, but we manage. Perhaps we will get used to it after a while. There is a little fun once in a while. There is always the river for swimming and rowing. We are just going out now; Sunday is our only free day, you see.

When you get hard up, don't forget that I am down here. I am perfectly willing to share what little I have with you. I am sending enc. a dollar bill and two or three stamps. Use one of the stamps to write to me. Wish that I had more to spare, but perhaps things will be better next time.

Say, just where are you on the draft list? I am around eight thousand. That doesn't look much like I shall be called. At least not soon. Who in the family is first on the list? If one is drafted, I think that I shall enlist.

Much love to you and to Isie* when you next write. Let me hear from you soon

Your devoted brother

Gus

P.S. Best regards to Aldrich. Tell him not to shoot all the Germans, leave some for me.

Lester B. Granger to Dr. W.R.R. Granger, Jr.

Between 1922 and 1934 Lester B. Granger, a Dartmouth graduate, was an extension worker with the State of New Jersey Manual Training School for African American youth in Bordentown, New Jersey. In 1930 he went to Los Angeles to organize that city's chapter of the National Urban League. Ten

---

*Isie is Dr. Isabella Vandervall, W.R.R. Granger's wife.

years later he became the National Urban League's executive director, a position he held until 1961. The World War I veteran also received the Navy's Distinguished Civilian Service Medal and the Presidential Medal for Merit from President Harry S. Truman. President Franklin Roosevelt appointed him a special adviser to the secretary of the Navy on Negro Personnel.

Los Angeles, California
July 15, 1930

Dear Ran,

California is nice and in fact is wonderful, but I'd give a whole lot to be able to cut myself a large slice of New Jersey just now.

Of course I'm tickled to death with the weather and the climate. It hasn't rained yet, and folks tell me that I won't see rain before October. The days are comfortably warm and the nights are delightfully cool. All in all, it comes pretty close to being a Negro's paradise of weather.

I miss a lot of things, however. I miss the smooth routine of my work at Bordentown, the tennis tournaments that you and I have enjoyed so much together, and most of all, the Family . . . I have been lonesome. The two weeks of coming, and the two weeks of getting acquainted certainly gave me a chance to have plenty of my own company, and I got thoroughly sick of it.

I had absolutely no trouble on the way here, and heartily recommend the trip for your first long vacation. Such sights I've never seen before, and am ever now looking forward to the return drive, when I can take more time and enjoy it.

My love to Isie and the young scamp.

Yours affectionately,

Lester

Lester B. Granger to Dr. W.R.R. Granger, Jr.

Bordentown, New Jersey
February 23, 1932

Dear Ran:

I know you've been calling me this, that, and several other things, and I have probably deserved it all. However, don't think too harshly of your poor little younger brother who loves you in spite of his seeming neglect.

I've been sticking closer to base than usual since basketball season opened up. The fact that basketball breaks into my spare time, coupled with my loss of stenographic services for four days in the week, plus the fact that my traveling allowance has been cut fifty percent, "due to the depression,"—all these factors have been responsible for my growing a real hard shell, and staying in it.

However, I am positively going to be in your city within the next week or so, and I am positively going to give you the rare pleasure of having my feet under your table and my elbow in your victuals.

What do you think of the tennis rating? Are the Granger Brothers hot, or are they not? It's too bad we won't appear in the national ratings to any advantage, but we'll make up for that this summer. If my condition this winter is any criterion, then I'm due to be in fine shape for the summer months. My feet aren't bothering me any to speak of, my legs are standing up under an hour of basketball without getting cramps, and my wind is all that it should be for an aged gentleman of 35. If you can say as much for yourself, then the famous team of Granger and Granger is due to set new altitude records this summer. Give Isie, big and little, my love. Watch yourself. Be good. Your affectionate, though somewhat dilatory brother.

　　　Les

Madam C. J. Walker to A'Lelia Walker

Madam C. J. Walker (1867–1919), the child of former slaves born on a plantation in Delta, Louisiana, made a fortune creating hair products for black women. Born Sarah Breedlove, she was an orphan by age seven and married at fourteen to escape the home of an abusive brother-in-law. In 1905 she moved to Denver as a sales agent for a black entrepreneur; she changed her name and founded her own business selling hair products. By 1910 she had relocated to Indianapolis, where she built a factory, salon, and training school. She wrote this letter to her daughter A'Lelia (1885–1931) upon learning she planned to marry James Arthur Kennedy, a future surgeon. By then Madam Walker was living in Villa Lewaro, her mansion in upstate New York.

My Darling Baby:—

Lou and Edna just read me your letters and you made me very happy to know that at last you have decided to marry Kennedy. Altho I have never let you know this—it has been my wish ever since I met Wylie in Wash. I never thought he would make you happy, but I do believe Kennedy will. Let me know what time in Aug. you will return and at what time you will marry. If you think best I will announce the engagement while you are away. My wish is for you to have a very quiet wedding out here and leave shortly afterward for France. You may get your chateau and I will follow. Then I will take my contemplated trip around the world. Let Kennedy study abroad for a year. I will make France my headquarters. I never want you to leave me to go this far again.

Nettie is here with Frank and your little namesake. You will love her, she is too sweet and dear for anything. I am so happy having them with me. Alice is coming too for a few days. She was to spend her vacation here next summer, but this has been a particularly busy season with her and I feel she needs a rest and so I am having her come now instead.

Nettie and the girls join me in love to you and Mae and I send with my love, kisses and kisses and kisses.

Your Devoted,
Mother

Grace Nail Johnson to James Weldon Johnson

James Weldon Johnson (1871–1938) was a novelist, poet, journalist, lyricist, lawyer, diplomat, activist, and educator, and a leading figure in the Harlem Renaissance, known for his guidance of many younger artists and writers. He is perhaps best known for his critically acclaimed novel The Autobiography of an Ex-Colored Man *(1912) and* God's Trombones: Seven Negro Sermons in Verse *(1927). He also wrote* Black Manhattan *(1930), a history of African Americans in New York, and penned the lyrics to "Lift Every Voice and Sing." Johnson was a field officer and later general secretary of the NAACP. From 1906 to 1913 he served as U.S. consul to Venezuela and Nicaragua. His wife, Grace Nail Johnson, was an artist who hailed from a prosperous family in Harlem, where her father was a real es-*

tate developer. They were married from 1910 until James Weldon Johnson's sudden death in an automobile accident in 1938.

Great Barrington, Massachusetts
June 19, 1929

Dearest Sonny,

The report of the heat wave in New York is anything but comforting. Do take it carefully and should you need me to help with some of the running about, I'll be glad to come down. Be sure to catch Dorothy Peterson* right away because school will be closing and you can't tell what will become of the pictures in her absence.

This, your birthday—I do hope that it will mark the turning point in that you may sincerely realize some of the present dreams and time to fulfill the immediate ideas that are running riot in your mind. To me it seems possible and probable.

My love and every wish for a happy birthday. Don't wait until the end of the week to do everything. Eat carefully and continue your early to bed program.

So long. Lots of love.

Your devoted wife.

Leigh Whipper to Dr. Ionia Whipper

Leigh Whipper (1876–1975) was a leading stage and screen character actor whose career spanned sixty-five years. He graduated from Howard University Law School in 1895 but immediately turned to the theater. His Broadway credits include Of Mice and Men *and* Abraham's Bosom. *He also appeared in many films, including* The Oxbow Incident, *which was nominated for an Academy Award;* The Harder They Fall; *and* Mission to Moscow. *He wrote the following letter to his sister, Washington physician Ionia Rollin Whipper. Their mother, Frances Anne Rollin, was the author of* The Life and Public Service of Martin R. Delany, *and their father, Judge William J. Whipper, was a circuit court judge and a member of two Constitutional Conventions during the Reconstruction era.*

---

*Dorothy Peterson (1897–1978) was a teacher and arts patron closely associated with the Harlem Renaissance writers and artists. She cofounded the Harlem Experimental Theater in 1929 and was influential in helping establish the James Weldon Johnson Collection of Negro Arts and Letters at Yale University.

My Dear Onie:—

I never know if your Birthday is the 8th or 9th but as one is as close to the other it does not matter as long as I let you know that you have a Birthday to me.

So if you were not here on the 8th you should have been to keep up with my Telegrams.

Now for a little REMINISCENSES.

I recall a Large house in a very big yard The Harris house a good Father (that I did not understand until I learned myself) The Finest Mother that ever lived and a Big Brother Bud.

Later a trip to Charleston, to Nanna's where I met a pair of sisters, Rebecca, Lefman Uncle and a host of Children that Nanna used to teach. While there uncle was stabbed very mysteriously.

Later my sisters at home in Beaufort where I got a ducking and Onie tried to save me from it.

Pap's dog Guess dying and then I don't remember seeing my sisters again until we started for Washington.

Well do I remember their coming there for it has been from that time on that I really knew them.

When we went to housekeeping on 17th street and were taking the preserves home and you broke one of the jars. How Fred Bruce and the boys ate the preserves regardless of it having glass in it.

All of these things pass and repass in my mind because it is your Birthday and I am thankful that we are spared another year. I guess at times we both are thankful that God sent us to the Family he did, and also proud of it. Yet I think we could pass up the proud part and just be thankful for those things are gifts and not to our choosing. So all of the background we are able to boast of is only a gift.

Well Old Scout I hope that you will live to see many more and that you may enjoy such health as you are enjoying now to say nothing about the prosperity. You know I always wish you much of that. For your success is mine. That is I enjoy the thought of any success of yours.

Strange that all of my life you have been [the] one that has been my inspiration and I your hope. I have not measured up to your ideals but it has not been for the lack of inspiration, only to my own neglect. I think you will feel your duty finished when you plead for me at the throne of God.

With such a sister how can one help but be proud of her, how can one help but adore her. If there are ties stronger than the metal wrought into the statues of Ancient Kings, I feel that it is the tie that binds our hearts together. And why? Just because God was good enough to leave us at old man Whipper's Home and because Old Man Whipper was no Fool when he picked our Mother for his wife.

God Bless you sweetheart and may he save you for me another year.

Your loving brother

Leigh

Robert Murphy to Matilda Dunbar

Robert and William Murphy were the half brothers of the poet Paul Laurence Dunbar. Little is known about William and Robert, who were their mother, Matilda's children from a previous marriage, to Wilson Murphy.

October 30, 1933

Dear Mother,

One year ago you lost a son and I a brother and on this day memories make our minds bleed afresh but we can comfort ourselves this way. But a few more days and we too shall pass into that land of shadows. Will was amiable, lovable, sympathetic, and kind and very few people knew him well enough to appreciate these qualities in him but to those who did, they realize that the world was bettered by him having lived in it . . .

Sorrowing on this day with you is

Your Loving Son

Rob

Ralph Ellison to Ida Millsap Ellison

Ralph Ellison (1913–1994) is famous for his acclaimed novel Invisible Man *(1952), which won the National Book Award in 1953. Born in Oklahoma City, he attended Tuskegee Institute on a music scholarship. His father, Lewis Ellison, a construction foreman, died when he was three, and his mother, Ida Millsap, worked as a domestic to support Ralph and his younger brother, Herbert. After moving to Harlem, Ralph was influenced by friendships with writers such as Richard Wright (1908–1960) and*

*Langston Hughes (1902–1967), whom he met on 125th Street the morn-
ing after he arrived in July 1936.*

New York
April 20, 1937

Dear Mama,

It seems the Spring has come to New York at last, and no one seems
to object to its arrival, though for myself I feel it will be a very uncomfortable time. Closed up in a factory nine hours out of twenty-four is
bad enough when there is the frost, the wind and rain outside, but to
stand inside and look out at the ships sailing up the East river as it
sparkles in the sunlight, and all the birds flying and birds singing, and
with memories burning in my head like melted lead, it's apt to be
a hellish season. Sometimes I wish I had the nerve to go on and take a
boat and go until I grow tired. Daddy no doubt felt the same way when
he ran off to the army, and so did Langston [Hughes]. I don't think it's
lack of nerve that holds me back for I find myself fighting to stay put.
Nor is it only in the Spring I feel these impulses, but in the dead of
winter, at parties, when walking along the streets, early in the morning
and in the dead of night. Especially in the night. Nights on which the
skies remind me of southern moons which used to turn me soft inside.
Sometimes I wonder if I shall ever grow out of this way of feeling about
things. For so far there seems to be no hope. I had a long talk with
Langston about it, in fact we had many talks and he tells me there is
no use, and isn't even to be desired. He said he had the same trouble
and was surprised to discover I was going through the same experiences. I suppose this has made us friends, all for which I am very glad.
You see in spite of my confidence in desiring to become a musician, so
many things happened in school and here that I've become a little bewildered. And the urge I feel within seems not to fade away but becomes
more insistent for expression, and I have yet to discover just what form
it will take. Let us hope I shall soon find myself. This state of things
leaves me very worried and unhappy . . .

Try and answer soon and forgive me if I don't write as often as before because this job takes quite a bit from me. Nights find me asleep
as soon as I enter my room.

Good bye and watch out for the spring fever.

Ralph

Ralph Ellison to Ida Millsap Ellison

August 30, 1937

Dear Mama,

I haven't written because there really hasn't been anything new to write about. I am still living with Lang's aunt, but since her fall season has started I fear I'll have to find another place to stay. She is a very busy dressmaker, and people come in at all hours making my presence somewhat an inconvenience. They thought I would have had the job on the boat long before now, so I can't impose on them much longer. The job has failed to materialize due to the strike situation and I have no idea as to when it will. In the meantime I am trying to go on relief in order to get a job on the W.P.A. This has its own set of difficulties, the most important of which is to establish residence. I received your letter with the dollar which certainly was needed but you must not try to send me anything as long as you yourself are unable to work . . .

I am very disgusted with things as they are and the whole system in which we live. This system which offers a poor person practically nothing but work for a low wage from birth to death; and thousands of us are hungry half of our lives. I find myself wishing that the whole thing would explode so the world could start again from scratch. Now one must have an education in order to get most any job, yet they don't give us opportunities to go to school. Look at your own life. You've lived these years since Dad died toiling from morning to night, toiling and praying from morning to night. From Okla. City to Gary, to Okla., only there was no work in Gary, only prayer and those dimes with the holes which we filled with lead, then to McAlister where things were about as bad, and then back to Okla. City, and now it's Dayton. You've seen Herbert and myself grow up, and neither of us has a job. All those years and all that work, and not even a job to bring a dollar a week. The people in Spain are fighting right now because of just this kind of thing, the people of Russia got tired of seeing the rich have everything and the poor nothing and now they are building a new system. I wish we could live there. And these rich bastards here are trying to take the W.P.A. away from us. They would deny a poor man the right to live in this country for which we have fought and died. You should see New York with its millions of unemployed, the people who sleep in the parks and in doorways. The rich old women strolling down Fifth Avenue carrying their dogs which are better cared for than most human beings. Big cars and money to burn and right now I couldn't buy a hot dog. I'm sick thinking of the whole mess and I hope something happens to change it all.

It is rainy weather here and for the last few days the skies have been gray with mist falling whenever it isn't raining. The water lies in puddles and you have to pick your way if the soles of your shoes are not the best. The Fall is coming and the boys will soon be returning to school and I hope they leave a few jobs behind. I would like to be in a car riding up through Ill. just now while the trees are beginning to turn deep red, and yellow, and purple and you can see the birds flying southward in the distance, soaring away, soaring away, and the apples on the trees, and the hay stacks in the fields. You can see the sun rise in the early morning blending the color of all this foliage into one sparkling mass of natural beauty with the dew upon it all. Sometimes you can see the harvesters already working in the fields and you think of the stories of the big meals they are supposed to serve and eat, and you visualize the big prize pies and home cooked breads, and sometimes you become hungry thinking about it all. Especially when you are hungry as I am now, I missed my lunch.

The city is no different in the Fall. The only change here is in the skies which on some days are grey and misty and rainy; and you wonder where the people who sleep in the parks will spend the long night to come, the cold nights to come, and if you'll have to join them.

The kids are now flying kites but they haven't started playing marbles. Those who can afford them are still wearing summer clothing and there is some talk and much talk of hope of buying new overcoats. Over the tops of flats and buildings you can see the kites sailing, and dipping, and rising like gulls riding the wind over a blue gulf, and you can hear the cries of the boys floating down, floating down to the street, like when you were around Look Out Mountain and you heard people climbing above you. On the streets are picket lines of people fighting for higher wages and shorter hours, and when you walk down some of the streets you wonder how some of the people are able to eat. If you walk down Eighth Avenue you can see the curb markets and fruit stores and sea food joints and if you come by around meal time when the poor people are eating you can smell the fish frying and the hog maws and home fries. On the stands you see plenty of tropical fruit: mangoes, guavas and plantains, melons and yams. And on the corners you can buy bananas and fresh fish from vendors of push carts. All the fruit and fruit smells and fruit colors become all mixed with smells of washed and unwashed bodies and perfume and hair grease and liquor and the bright and drab colors of dresses and overalls, and that which the dogs leave on the side-walk. I like to walk on such streets. Life on them is right out in the open and they make no pretence of being what they are not. The whore, the pimp, the ditch digger, the likker head, and the down-and-outer are all here trying to get along. It makes me very angry to think of the causes behind all the misery in the world, and the way it's all concentrated here in Harlem. I hope something happens to change it all.

Please let me hear from you soon, and you must remember not to worry about me. Tell me how your hip is doing and if you are able to walk.

Tonight's the night of the fight between Joe and Farr.* Already you can see the excitement rising and the police gathering. Just now a regiment of patrol passed all in blue and yellow-trimmed uniforms and you can hear the horses' feet going cloppity clop, cloppity clop on the asphalt sounding all out of place and the smacking whirr, smack, smack whirr of the rubber tires. Tonight there will be hundreds of cops in Harlem and much shouting of excited Negroes and most of the whites will stay out if Joe loses and if he wins, they'll come up to see the fun. I'll write of it later. So until next time—

Love Ralph

The Watson Children to Justice James S. Watson

James S. Watson (1882–1952) was born in Spanish Town, Jamaica, where his father, James Michael Watson, was a sergeant in the Jamaica Constabulary and a dispatcher for the Jamaica Railway Company. Watson immigrated to the United States in 1905 and attended Harlem Evening High School in New York. In 1913 he graduated from New York Law School. In 1930, Watson and his running mate, Charles E. Toney, became the first two black justices elected to judicial office in New York City. In 1950, the popular jurist resigned from the municipal court to become president of the Municipal Civil Service Commission. As this letter suggests, Watson, the father of two sons and two daughters, was a beloved family man. His eldest daughter, Barbara (1918–1983), served as U.S. ambassador to Malaysia, and his youngest son, James L. (1922–2001), was posthumously honored

---

*A reference to the legendary fight between world heavyweight champion Joe Louis (1914–1981), nicknamed the Brown Bomber, and Tommy Farr (1913–1986), a Welshman who held the British Empire heavyweight championship. Louis (born Joseph Louis Barow) retained his title in a close match that went fifteen rounds before some 35,000 people at Yankee Stadium in New York City.

when the Manhattan federal building where he served as a judge for thirty-six years was renamed the James L. Watson Court of International Trade Building. At the time of his death he was the most senior black judge in the country.

[Undated, 1937]

To the Sweetest Dad In the World

On this memorable day, the fifty-fifth anniversary of your birth, we want to look back over the past years and recall the many loving kindnesses which you have showered upon us unselfishly. The sole return you hoped to gain were our thoughtful appreciation and love. Perhaps we have failed in some degree to manifest the deepest and sincerest love we feel for both yourself and mother, our parents, but nevertheless we assure you it is not lacking.

We would like to take this opportunity to express a part, if not all of our heartfelt gratitude for these many years of your tender devotion and we earnestly hope that we may enjoy with you many more such anniversaries. May the coming years be filled with continued good health, happiness and prosperity.

Love,
The children

James L. Watson to Justice James S. Watson

James L. Watson (1922–2001), James S. Watson's youngest child, was born in Harlem. During World War II he fought with the Army in Italy and was awarded the Purple Heart.

Army Training Camp, Desert Training Center, Ca.
May 16, 1943

My dear Father,

I received your delightful letter last Sunday and as usual I was more than happy to hear from you. You really don't know just what your letters mean to me. As soon as I received your letter I wrote to you but just today I found out that I had forgotten to mail the letter. I hope that you shall forgive me for not doing so. Nevertheless I hope that this shall serve a double purpose. First to congratulate you on the splendid news which you related to me in your last letter and second. To . . . Well just to say that I miss you very much along with the rest of the family.

Dad many of the things which you have told me during the years and even now are coming back to me now. Those precious words of wisdom which you have often spoken to me and serve as a form of guidance to me during my Life: Dad, remember many times when you used to lecture to me and then you would say "You may pay no attention to me now but in later life you'll realize the significance of what I am saying." As usual you were right and I now full realize the significance and wisdom of your words and I find that I now also see them to good advantage.

Gee Dad, it sure made me feel proud to know that you're to receive the degree of Doctor of Law. Gee, that Watson Family is really coming on. What with you receiving the degree, Barbara going to get hers and Douglas conferring with all these Big Shots. I'm not doing so badly myself. I have been accepted to go to the Army Specialist School. Dad, I'll have to close now, my commanding officer has [ordered] me to go on a ration detail. I'll write soon again.

Your loving and devoted son,
"Skiz"

Doug Watson to Justice James S. Watson

Jamaica Station, NY
September 29, 1947

Dear Dad—

I feel quite ashamed about not having written you before this and especially so since there is really no excuse. However, I've been keeping abreast of your activities in Jamaica by reading your letters to mother and the girls. They have been masterpieces of reporting and are worthy of the case notes of Sherlock Holmes himself.

I received my check yesterday Dad, and I can't tell you how much I appreciate all you have done for me and the rest of the children by your untiring efforts in seeing that the matter was settled. It is very important from your letter that your trip has been less a vacation than a nightmarish treasure hunt with all its obstacles. I do hope that you will be able to get at least a few days complete rest before your return.

I was telling Bobbie last night that it is my sincerest hope that I will be as fine a father to our children as you are to yours. As you have been a pattern for me in my professional life, so shall you be in my home life. In short, Dad, I think you are the finest man I know.

For you to have made the sacrifice financially to take this trip, not for personal gain but just to make certain that your children got a square deal, and to have worked so untiringly in the face of myriad obstacles to finish the job, is a true indication of a devoted father's love for his children. Should that all other fathers were like you.

We've all missed you very much, Dad, and though we are separated physically we have a spiritual unity that brooks all distances and keeps us close together. Thus we are always with you and you with us.

Please give Dr. Plummer our regards and all the rest too. Barbara sends her fondest love and hopes you get some rest. God bless you, Dad.

Your devoted son,

Doug

Martin Luther King, Jr., to Martin Luther King, Sr.

Martin Luther King, Jr. (1929–1968) had just graduated from high school at the age of fifteen when he wrote his father this letter from Connecticut, where he spent the summer working on a tobacco farm to earn money before beginning his first year at Morehouse College.

Simsbury, Connecticut
June 15, 1944

Dear Father:

I am very sorry I am so long about writing but I have been working most of the time. We are really having a fine time here and the work is very easy. We have to get up every day at 6:00. We have very good food. And I am working kitchen so you see I get better food.

We have services here every Sunday about 8:00 and I am the religious leader. We have a boys choir here and we are going to sing on the air soon. Sunday I went to church in Simsbury. It was a white church. I could not get to Hartford to church but I am going next week. On our way home we saw some things I had never anticipated to see. After we passed Washington there was no discrimination at all. The white people here are very nice. We go to any place we want to and sit any where we want to.

Tell everybody I said hello and I am still thinking of the church and reading my bible. And I am not doing any thing that I would not do in front of you.

Your Son

Julia Davis Rustin to Bayard Rustin

Bayard Rustin (1912–1987), the civil rights activist, pacifist, and adviser to Rev. Dr. Martin Luther King, Jr., was sentenced to three years in federal prison for refusing to obey the Selective Service Act. His mother wrote this letter to him in anticipation of his release from federal prison in Lewisburg, Pennsylvania.

Jamaica, New York
April 15, 1946

Dearest Bayard:—

I am trusting that you received this note: It is just to say your room is ready and waiting for you. I am very happy here and we will all be happier to see your darling face. Shall I send some clothes to the cleaners for you. Anne Sylvia is standing alone almost walking and tries to talk. Mrs. Roberts paid me a visit. She is a lovely young woman. Wanted to take me to Columbus with her, but I am to wait and go with you at some future time. Helen is very sweet. May God bless you and speed the time of your coming. Bessie + Pierre, Ruth + Lucien send much love. It is a most beautiful place here. Write me if you are permitted to do so,

Love—Mamma

Martin Luther King, Jr., to Alberta King

Alberta King (1904–1974), the mother of Martin Luther King, Jr., was raised in Atlanta, Georgia, where her father was the pastor of Ebenezer Baptist Church. She earned a teaching certificate from Hampton Normal and Industrial Institute and then married Martin Luther King, Sr., who became pastor of Ebenezer Baptist in 1931, upon the death of Alberta's father. Alberta was the church's choir director and organist. Martin Luther King, Jr., would go on to serve as pastor of the church after his father. This letter was written during his first semester at Crozer Theological Seminary in Pennsylvania. In 1951 he graduated with a bachelor of divinity degree.

Chester, Pennsylvania
October 1948

Dear Mother,

Your letter was received this morning. I often tell the boys around the campus I have the best mother in the world. You will never know how I appreciate the many kind things you and daddy are doing for me. So far I have gotten the money (5 dollars) every week.

As to my wanting some clippings from the newspapers, I must answer yes. I wondered why you hadn't sent many, especially the *Atlanta World*.

You stated that my letters aren't newsy enough. Well I don't have much news. I never go anywhere much but in these books. Sometimes the professor comes in class and tells us to read our assignments in Hebrew, and that is really hard.

Do you know the girl I used to date at Spelman (Gloria Royster). She is in school at Temple and I have been to see her twice. Also I met a fine chick in Phila who has gone wild over the old boy. Since Barbor told the members of his church that my family was rich, the girls are running me down. Of course, I don't ever think about them. I am too busy studying.

I hear from Christine every week. I try to answer her as regularly as possible.

Well I guess I must go back to studying. Give everybody my regards,
Your son,
M.L.

Edith Braithwaite to William Stanley Braithwaite

William Stanley Braithwaite (1878–1962) was a self-educated writer, poet, and anthropologist who published two volumes of poetry, Lyrics of Life and Love *(1904) and* House of Falling Leaves *(1908). He also edited nineteen anthologies of British, Catholic, and wartime verse. The following letters are between Braithwaite and Edith, one of his seven children with his wife, Emma.*

3713 W. Adams Blvd.
Los Angeles, Cal.
Dec. 27, 1954

Dearest Papa:

It was certainly wonderful and a most welcome surprise to talk with all of you on Christmas day. I had not expected to hear from anyone which made it so much nicer. You had been in my thoughts and I didn't even attempt to put a call in since in the past it has always been difficult to get a wire through. The call came in the nick of time for a short time later I would have been gone.

I'm so happy that you are getting along so well after your siege of illness. It usually takes a long while to recover from operations and I think you are doing wonderfully well. Keep it up!

We had a nice day having spent the afternoon with Dorothy and her family where we had dinner. The turkey and all the fixings were very nice. I picked Aunt Lil up at work and from there went directly to Dorothy's. After we left, we went home to open our gifts. Aunt Lil had a small tree on the table but I did not bother with one this year.

Did Mama tell you that I had thought seriously of surprising you and coming home for the holidays? I went so far as to make reservations on the plane but after thinking it over thought it unwise since I could not afford it. I just longed to be home for the holidays since it has been so long but there are bills to get out of the way and I hope to be home another year.

I had quite a time with a tooth that I had pulled last week and finally had to go to an oral surgeon to let him finish the job. The tooth broke off and the dentist had such a time and I was so nervous from it all that he sent me to this other dentist. My face was terribly swollen which is nothing unusual inasmuch as I have so much trouble after an extraction. However, my face is about down to normal and I am feeling fine.

When Clarence gets back to New York, he will bring the tape recorder over for you to tape some poems etc. for me. I will be so happy to have the tape and I shall always treasure it.

The last few days it grew very cold and it is so nice for a change. We have so much warm weather, which is tiresome. Last night reminded me so much of weather at home. It is unusual for men to wear overcoats here but it was really needed the last couple of days.

I want to thank you and Mama for the lovely Christmas and birthday cards. They were both lovely. Also thank you so much for the sweepstake ticket. I do hope I'll have some luck so I can leave this place and we be together.

I hope you enjoyed the holiday. My only regret was that I could not be home and it saddens me when the holidays come around and I'm so far from you folks.

Must run along now but I'll be writing again soon. Give my love to Mama and Peter. Tell Brother the telegram was in the mailbox, a place I never expected to find it and I imagine it was there when I was talking with him. I shall write and thank him.

Much love,
Edith

William Stanley Braithwaite to Edith Braithwaite

409 Edgecombe Avenue
New York, New York
September 27th 1956

Dearest Edith:—

It doesn't seem possible that you have come and gone—leaving a terrible void and ache in my heart. When I saw you pass through the gate to the plane, I wanted to reach out and pull you back and keep you always here. We stood on the observation ramp, trying to catch another glimpse of you, but could not, and when the plane lifted and took off our hearts went with you. The next ten hours were hours of suspended heart and mind until the phone call came to inform us that you had arrived safely. And we sent our prayers to heaven that you were back safe. And now the long wait until you come again, and this time we hope to stay. We do hope you had a happy time with us, in spite of all the little ruffles which shouldn't be. I am only sad because there were so many little things I would have liked to do. The things I had hoped and worked for didn't come through, but they are there like a fruit to be ripened and harvested.

There were so many things I wanted to talk about, for you are the only one in the family I can talk them. My mind is now constantly full of these possibilities which may yield an income to Mama and you children when I am no longer about. One must think of these things when the years are shortening. I have worked hard and accumulated a lot of material that can be turned into books. Night and day I am haunted with the fear it might be neglected, or taken advantage of by others. But no more about that; I will inform you more in detail later on.

Fiona said she put the two clippings about you and Peter in your bag, and I hope you have found them by now. I tried to get another copy of the paper at the paper-store on the corner but they were all sold out; I will stop at the paper office on Eighth Avenue, when I go down town, for I think you ought to have an extra copy.

I am glad to know you found everything in shape at the office. I asked Billy if he missed you, and I think he understood, for he mentioned the plane.

A Mrs. Sears—I think that's the name she said, but I think you worked with her as Miss Jamison (?) in Washington and who had seen the item of your being here in the paper, called by on Monday. She had been in Los Angeles, also, she said, and now lives in the Bronx.

Peter's team plays its first game Saturday, and Paul says he is going to see it. He told me yesterday he is shifted from end to half back because of his speed. In his first literature test he got a hundred. It is a course, he said, in which only the smartest boys are allowed to take.

Your letter came yesterday, and we were so glad to have it, and I wanted to get this letter off you to let you know what memories it stirred. Do take care of yourself. Give my love to Aunt Lil. It was so nice that she had everything in such readiness for you. Lots of love, dear!

Papa

Adam Clayton Powell, Jr., to Hazel Scott Powell

In 1945, Adam Clayton Powell, Jr. (1908–1972) became the first African American from the Northeast elected to the U.S. Congress. The New York congressman and ordained minister, who also succeeded his father as pastor of the famed Abyssinian Baptist Church in Harlem, served in Congress until January 1971.* In 1961 he became chair of the House Education and Labor Committee, during which time he sponsored key legislation related to education and civil rights. His wife, Hazel Scott (1920–1981), was a famous classical and jazz singer and pianist and the first African American to have her own television show, The Hazel Scott Show, *which premiered in 1950. She and Powell married in 1945, and a year later they had their only child, Adam Clayton Powell III, who is referred to in this letter as Skipper.*

October 11, 1957

My dear Hazel:

None of us have heard from you and Skipper has been home for ten days. Did you receive our cable and my letter?

You must be very happy that you are not here. Asiatic flu, so far has cut one third of the school attendance. Skipper has had it, so have I, and after five days of fever he is now convalescing and will be back to school Monday. I hope to be out tomorrow. Fortunately he was stricken with it while he was being entertained at Sunday dinner at Dr. & Mrs. Freemen. Needless to say he received the best of attention. I was by myself, but there is nothing much you can do about Asiatic flu except stay in bed, drink liquids and take aspirin. It is pretty rough.

---

*Powell was excluded from membership in the Ninetieth Congress on February 28, 1967. He was then elected to that Congress by special election to fill the vacancy resulting from his exclusion. He was defeated for reelection in 1970.

Indications are that we are to go to see President Eisenhower Tuesday, take with me, so far, A. Phillip Randolph, Roy Wilkins and Martin Luther King. Trying to find some women to go, but frankly there isn't anyone of outstanding caliber since Ms. [Mary McLeod] Bethune passed on, except Nannie Burroughs.* She, of course is the President of the Baptist. It would be King, Burroughs, and myself, and it would be lopsided in terms of denominationalism. I did suggest Vivian Carter Mason, President of the National Council of Negro Women. She is leaving tomorrow for Europe to attend an International meeting of women.

The weather has been very bad . . . the World Series exciting. Everyone who has had Asiatic flu at least has been watching the series.

Fortunately I was stricken after church and will be able to be back in time for next Sunday. Nothing has been lost there, in regards to the church work. I don't know who is going to type this letter, because Howard is out, Hattie is out, and everything is operating on a skeleton basis . . . and that is no pun.

I have just had the dish washing machine fixed . . . very minor charge, but the furnace had to have a major overhaul with new parts. It refused to work at all. I have paid these two bills from my own funds, but for the sake of you having in your files, the record, I will send the receipted bills to Marshall.

Love to both of you,

Adam

Dr. Martin Luther King, Jr., to Coretta Scott King

In 1952 Martin Luther King, Jr., met Coretta Scott (1927–2006) in Boston, where she was a student at the New England Conservatory of Music and he was pursuing doctoral studies at Boston University's School of Theology. The couple wed on June 18, 1953. He wrote the following letter from a Georgia state prison.

---

*Nannie Burroughs (1883–1962) was a writer, educator, businesswoman, and activist who in 1909 founded a school for girls that in 1964 was renamed the Nannie Helen Burroughs School. Mary McLeod Bethune (1875–1955) was an educator and civil rights leader and founder of a school in Daytona Beach, Florida, that is now Bethune-Cookman University, where she served as president from 1923 to 1942, and 1946 to 1947.

Reidsville, Georgia
October 26, 1960

Hello Darling,

Today I find myself a long way from you and the children. I am at the State Prison in Reidsville which is about 230 miles from Atlanta. They picked me up from the DeKalb jail about 4 o'clock this morning. I know this whole experience is very difficult for you to adjust to, especially in your condition of pregnancy, but as I said to you yesterday this is the cross that we must bear for the freedom of our people. So I urge you to be strong in faith, and this will in turn strengthen me. I can assure you that it is extremely difficult for me to think of being away from you and my Yoki and Marty for four months, but I am asking God hourly to give me the power of endurance. I have the faith to believe that this excessive suffering that is now coming to our family will in some little way serve to make Atlanta a better city, Georgia a better state, and America a better country. Just how I do not yet know, but I have faith to believe it will. If I am correct then our suffering is not in vain.

I understand that I can have visitors twice a month—the second and fourth Sunday. However, I understand that everybody—white and colored—can have visitors this coming Sunday. I hope you can find some way to come down. I know it will be a terrible inconvenience in your condition, but I want to see you and the children very badly.

Eternally Yours,
Martin

Medgar Evers to Myrlie Evers and Children

Medgar Evers (1925–1963) was a civil rights activist from Mississippi, where he was the state's field secretary for the NAACP and helped to desegregate the University of Mississippi, which in 1954 denied him admission to its law school. On June 12, 1963, Evers was assassinated outside his home in Jackson after attending an integration meeting. A World War II veteran who fought in the Battle of Normandy, he was buried in Arlington National Cemetery before more than three thousand mourners. His murderer was convicted in 1994. Myrlie Evers (b. 1933) was born Myrlie Beasley in Vicksburg, Mississippi, and met Evers while both were attending Alcorn A & M College. They married in 1951 and had three children. Myrlie Evers would go on to become the first full-time chairperson of the NAACP, serving from 1995 to 1998.

November 27, 1962

My darling wife and children,

I love you dearly and miss you terribly! I am now aboard TWA's #54 for Idlewild Airport N.Y. City and the time is 12:50 p.m. Eastern Standard Time or 11:50 your time. It is a beautiful day with a slight overcast and bright sun coming through my cabin window.

Honey, tell the children daddy will be returning soon and that when Xmas comes, if it is in the Lord's will, we are all going to enjoy Santa Claus and a good Xmas.

You be sweet and take care of yourself. Be assured this trip can't end too soon.

Love,

Medgar

Urnestine Lewis to David Levering Lewis

David Levering Lewis (b. 1936), a noted historian whose two-volume biography of W.E.B. Du Bois each won a Pulitzer Prize, is Julius Silver university professor and professor of history at New York University. In this letter, his mother fills him in on racial news in America a week after the historic 1963 March in Washington and notes the passing of Du Bois. At the time Lewis, who had graduated in 1962 from the London School of Economics with a Ph.D. in modern European and French history, was teaching French history at the University of Ghana.

54 Ashby Street, N.W.
Atlanta 14, Georgia
September 7, 1963

Dearest David:

Warn you in advance that this is an ancient, resurrected typewriter with no margin control that I have yet been able to discover, so here's hoping you will be able to translate this.

Well, echoes of the Great March are still ringing. I read a very objective account in the *Manchester Guardian*—which no doubt you have seen. I am sending you a few of the many evaluations which have been published. The *Post*, *Newsweek*, *Time*, *Life*—all carry objective articles.

Another event which has quite disturbed the "Snopses" of Georgia, Mississippi, et al., is the announcement of the marriage of Charlayne

Hunter—first colored girl to matriculate at the University of Georgia, and a white classmate from Douglass, Georgia. Tempest in a teapot.*

The name [W.E.B.] Du Bois probably means little to you—he was active long before your time. I was fortunate enough to have him as a teacher many years ago at Atlanta University. You may know that he was living at Ghana at the time of his death.

You mentioned having seen [Julian] Bond pictured in the march. He is extremely active locally in the Student Non-violent movement, as are Jane and her new husband, Howard Moore—who, by the way, has been cited for contempt of court by a local judge in a sit-in case, suppose all of this is Greek to you. I was interested to read that Josephine Baker had left her beloved Paris long enough to participate in the march.†

I hope that, as the days pass and you are further and further away from your past Army experience, you will suffer less and less of the depression you describe. You may find the Ghana situation a challenge. What you need is something that one must have to live in peace with himself—something to believe in and work for—and that I am sure you will find. Maybe not in Ghana, who knows? And, somewhere, the girl who will be a partner in the realization of your life plans—whatever they may be. Your immediate job is, as you say, to go to Ghana primarily to teach.

So sorry to hear of Preston's accident. I hope it has been less serious than was thought.

By the way, did you ever receive the several letters I had written on my return? Let me ask you this? How are you fixed for clothing for your tropical habitat? What do you plan to do? Shop in Ghana for a suit, or in London? It seems to me that I remember reading in your brochures that it was advisable to shop before reaching Ghana. Will you be able to buy what you need. I can send you an additional $50—tho funds are somewhat depleted by the summer.

---

*After a two-year legal battle, Charlayne Hunter was one of the first two African American students admitted to the University of Georgia. She graduated in 1963 and went on to become an award-winning journalist at *The New Yorker*, *The New York Times*, the *MacNeil/Lehrer NewsHour*, National Public Radio, and CNN. In 1961 her marriage to a white student, Walter Stovall, sparked controversy. They divorced a few years later.

†Josephine Baker (1906–1975), a singer and dancer who became a citizen of France in 1957, spoke at the march in Washington and refused to perform in segregated venues. See p. 312.

Jerry is now either in Spain or on his way there, as the result of an appeal to his congressman about the raw deal he was getting. His racial identity was known, and he suffered because of the fact that many had been mistaken about it. This whole situation—this so called revolution—is challenging, exciting, and rewarding in results obtained. But, Lord, you get so very, very weary of having to fight for every concession made. To live in an African country—dominated by Africans—must be an interesting experience; yet, from what I can read about Ghana—it is far, far from approaching a democracy. I suppose, at this stage of its development, a strong hand is needed.

I shall never forget the wonderful experience of the past summer. It was such a joy to be with you—that apart from the enjoyment of the tour itself and the thrill of visiting ancient and historic spots, and the beauty of the Italian and French countryside. I do hope to see it all again before my final curtain falls.

The Yates, Bells, et al. send bushels of love. Drop a line to me when you find time. Under separate cover I am sending little notes to Henry and Keens-Soper, to whom I should have written "thank you's" long ago—but stupidly left their addresses in the car. I know that you will see that they get them.

Love as always,
Maman

Derrick Bell, Jr., to Derrick Bell, Sr.

Derrick Bell, Jr. (b. 1930), a prolific writer, educator, legal scholar, and civil rights activist, born and raised in Pittsburgh, Pennsylvania, played a lead role in the desegregation of public schools throughout the South following the Supreme Court's 1954 decision in Brown v. Board of Education of Topeka. *His many books include the bestselling* Faces at the Bottom of the Well *(1992). In 1971 Bell became the first tenured African American on the Harvard Law School faculty.*

Washington, D.C.
July 26, 1967

Dear Dad:

In the last several weeks I have had several painful and expensive indications that my 1961 VW is not going to last forever. I still think it can perform worthwhile service as a second car, and certainly Jewel [his wife] will never be a confident driver unless she has a car at her disposal whenever she needs it.

For all these reasons and despite being ready or willing to spend money, I have purchased a new car. As you might expect, I searched the market very carefully and while giving a lot of consideration to a Plymouth Valiant, finally decided on another foreign car, the Volvo 144-S.

I am enclosing some literature on the car, which was only introduced in this country a few months ago. The risks with any foreign car are substantial, but the Volvo company's record for building sturdy, reliable, and long-lived cars is most impressive. It is probably not as powerful as some of the American cars, but has good pep and is certainly far more stable on curves than most of the softer riding American products. I was particularly impressed with the attention to safety in this car. While it is not very long by American standards, it has more room inside than many much larger American cars. It will at least make it possible for our family to travel to Pittsburgh, and perhaps we will be able to do so before fall.

It certainly would have been nice if you had been able to give advice during the selection process, but I think you would agree with my final choice. I decided on the dark blue color as pictured in the brochure and while automatic transmission was available, I am staying with the standard shift. I shall keep you advised as to how this latest investment turns out.

Love,
Derrick

Joseph F. Beam to Mom and Dad

Joseph F. Beam (1954–1988) was a gay activist and writer in Philadelphia who edited In the Life: A Black Gay Anthology (1986), *a groundbreaking reflection on the lives of gay African American men. He died from complications related to AIDS in 1988.*

Sunday, May 29th, 1976

Hi Mom & Dad,

How are you? Are you happy?

(Before you read this letter, sit down and devote your full attention to it.)

I hope it's not upsetting, but it's all true.

Four years & the subsequent college degree have come between us.

Before this year, life in Franklin had been strange & different & fun, but this year has been just plain weird & quite difficult. Moving off campus was my idea, but I still wanted a roommate, but I couldn't find one with which I was compatible. Consequently I lived alone. My best friend dropped out of school [a] year & half ago and although I have a few good friends it's not the same. I don't have a girlfriend, so whenever I felt bad/depressed or just wanted to talk there was no one around. Sometimes I cried, other times I went to the darkroom and still other times I rode my bike. On an occasion I would talk to Buddy. Anyway, this year's been spent alone, and sometimes lonely. I go back to this, because your visit was important to me. Although it was short, it's been a long time since we've talked and I wanted so much to talk to both of you. Living alone does something to you, it's very easy to retreat into your self. Perhaps because you can really depend on yourself or something like that. I'm not quite sure. When I talk about living alone, I don't really mean it literally, the idea of living without a mate, be it blessed by marriage/the church or not. Or more simply that other person who <u>knows</u> you. The three of us are lonely, very lonely. We never had the good basis to form a solid relationship, so <u>now</u> instead of relating to each other, we react to each other. Think about this.

We pick at each other, in a cyclical kind of thing—where Daddy jumps on my shit for something & you Mom react to that to defend me or protecting me from my father. I either react to one or both of you. We argue—slammed doors, screaming, "I'm leaving!" The reason why I asked you to leave, was I wished to avoid this. We argued for years & years and it upsets me more than almost anything in the world. Although you left and we never argued I still felt like shit. (Excuse all these "curse"/"bad" words, but this letter is down-to-earth and quite like me.) All this week I've felt bad but I took the course of action I thought necessary. If I had left and not come back until time to take you to the airport it would have been just as hurting.

The time to play cards is over 'cause I'm laying mine on the table. Right now I'm quite freaked out—school acts as [a] motivating, progressive force in one's life, and then it's over. You get the school habit so to speak and you call yourself a student. Now I've graduated and I'm a cook at Pizza Hut. I have a new identity or role. College is like the womb and in many ways it comes to be just like home. Race is a topic of discussion but seldom is it an issue from which violence ensues as it is in the real world, which I have a foot in the door. College shields you from heartache & hardship. Franklin is a lad's school & most students here are being helped through school so one does not get a "reality-based" perspective so certain questions just don't have to be dealt with while in school. These questions need answers now, before I approach full adulthood. I'm finding myself in this gray world—somewhere between black & white, literally & figuratively. I'm black & anyone could see that. I like sharp clothes & I like to shake my ass & sing and all those stereotyped black folks "things," but I also get into white folks & those things which are traditionally white. Am I the city slicker or the countryman? I like the excitement of the city, but I also enjoy the quiet evenings, reading or just listening to music. I'd like to do more camping but . . . I'm trying to learn to appreciate all kinds of things and people. I like going to concerts & I like being able to go to the country. I like photography.

I don't like television, and watches, and most often the radio. I see the media as most often attempting to sell me a product or an idea. T.V. & radio "push" kinds of lifestyles, careers, ideologies. I don't want them. Watches keep us attentive to appointments & dates. I'm looking at the clock. When will this be over or when will he or she be here? Since I haven't worn a watch I can tell time usually by orienting my self toward time, just like one doesn't really think about walking up a flight of steps. Some of these are my idiosyncrasies but this is me.

Finally, the major consideration & motivating factor currently is my androgynous self—another "gray" matter. Androgyny is a new concept which was defined & formulated by Sandra Bern* in the early 70's. It seeks to name, and categorize those characteristics, which are both male and female in a given person such as sensitivity, loving children, aggressiveness. I'm almost 22 yrs old, and I'm beginning to know myself. I'm quite androgynous . . . In fact I'm so androgynous, I could be homosexually inclined, more likely to be bisexual, but most desired to be heterosexual, now I'm asexual. In other words, my whole sex thing is fucked up. I'm starting therapy on Tuesday, June 1. Recently, I've had no close male friends or female sex partners from which I can reflect my sexuality. The other identities are not important, because they'll fall into place once I

*Sandra Bern, PhD, is professor of psychology and women's studies at Cornell University, where from 1978 to 1985 she was director of the Women's Studies Program. She is the author of *The Lenses of Gender: Transforming the Debate on Sexual Inequality* (1993). She developed the Bern Sex Role Inventory (BSRI) personality test for androgyny.

get the sexuality thing straightened out. It affects my self confidence and about everything that I do, you can't imagine. It feels good to be loved by someone to someone. I've never had any homosexual experiences, what makes me feel effeminate is my inability to satisfy a woman and I have just not recently. In the past couple of months my fear of not satisfying a woman has kept me from maintaining an erection, because my body was just completely freaked out because of that fear. So I'm taking everything slow now. I work three days a week at Pizza Hut. I can handle this, therapy is going to be intense but I plan to devote as much energy, attention and anything it takes to resolve this problem. There's nothing either one of you can do, coming home won't do it, besides Franklin is home for me. I'd like to get out of here by December & start grad school in January but I have to see what happens. If I can conquer this problem, I feel I could get through anything, almost.

Sometimes I think I'm crazy, but I'm not. On occasion I've even contemplated suicide, but I have much too much in my favor to kill myself. Inside is a great deal of talent to do several things all I have to do is get myself together. I'm trying to do this now, before I move in to another role or lifestyle. All I ask of both of you is love & understanding and if you're inclined—an occasional prayer. I also ask for a car, a used one (insurance on a new car for me would be $500–$600 annually). I can't afford that. I don't ask for a car because I want it, or because I deserve it, but because I need one. Right now I'm trying to live as simply as possible only doing things which are positive (job at Pizza Hut) and fulfilling (photography) because anything which is even slightly negative will divert my attention from the problem at hand.

In a letter before, I mentioned that in the past you've bought things I've wanted; you can have them back in trade for the car. I'm not going to live in a big city soon & public transportation is nil around here. The only thing I would like to keep are my albums, they're very important to me. This is all I ask. I don't want you to pay my rent/or for my food or even my therapy. My health (mental & physical) is my responsibility. I'm making arrangements for my dental care etc, and I'll eventually get some medical insurance but now I can't afford it. If I'm hungry, sometimes—that's cool—I weigh 190 lbs or so. There are a number of people who really like or love me. The Kahans, Diantha & Linda, and there are people who are looking out for me, so I'll make [sic]. Life is hard sometimes but we all get through.

This is not saying I'm never coming back to Philly, or that I hate you for I love both of you very much. The time has come & I must do what I have to, which includes something I don't like, but it's all an intricate part of the whole life process.

I'll be home some time, it's cheaper if I drive. If I had had a car years ago I would have been able to come home more frequently. This not to say I'll be there every month but I'm only 12 hours & 20 away & you're only 2 hrs by plane. I feel free to come home when I want to maybe even surprise you sometimes. A large part of loving is recognizing the needs of another and trying to fulfill them. I ask myself, haven't we all been very selfish at times—our personal desires, needs overpowering what ever another wanted or needed.

[Quoted three lines from Neil Young's song "Pardon My Heart"]

I'm always your loving son,

Joe

Walter J. Leonard to Angela Leonard

Walter J. Leonard (b. 1929) was president of Fisk University from 1977 to 1984. He also served as assistant dean of the Howard and Harvard University law schools, and was founding chairman of the W.E.B. Du Bois Institute at Harvard. His daughter, Angela M. Leonard (b. 1954), is a history professor at Loyola College in Baltimore.

April 16, 1991
Ms. Angela M. Leonard
Lecturer
Department of History
Bowdoin College
Brunswick, ME 04011

Dear Angela,

Happy Spring! It is my hope that you are enjoying the natural beauty, the buoyancy of spirit, and the optimistic projection of the future that this season brings. I like to think of spring as that helping hand, that kind voice, and/or that warm smile that was, somehow, there to help one through hard times; that touch that said, Don't worry, we will get through this together.

So much for all of that.

When we last talked, you indicated a degree of ensuing involvement in several projects. How have they gone; have they progressed or have the results been as you expected; and, have you won the kind and level of support that often escapes the efforts of creative people? As we know, creativity is all too often viewed as ambitious behavior, particularly by persons who fear competition or may be disturbed by new ideas.

Hang in there, and "accept no limits" to your potential or to the possible level of personal achievement. It should be very clear to all that women of your vintage, reflecting the richness of your cultural and ethnic legacy, must and will continue to make _real_ differences in our reluctant society.

I would welcome an opportunity to hear about your efforts and your plans for future projects.

With every good wish, I remain,

Sincerely,

Walter Leonard/Daddy

Walter J. Leonard to Mamie K. Singleton

Chevy Chase, Maryland
November 10, 1992

Dear Mom,

On May 12, 1992, the Life Force of the universe, the Creator, the holder of the ultimate destiny of all things, the Lord God Almighty, made a dramatic and, for us, a traumatic decision: It was time for Richard Singleton, Sr., in the eighty-fourth year of his tenure on Earth, to rest; to go home. Richard Singleton the spirit, and Richard Singleton the body, had worked and served tirelessly and faithfully for so many years; it was now time for the reward of quiet repose and peaceful sleep to accommodate his transition from this world through twilight, infinity, and into eternity.

Those of us who love you, and who loved you both, try to imagine how hard it must be to lose someone with whom your thoughts, joys, fears, plans, past and future had been conjoined for more than sixty-four years. We try to understand, in shared bereavement, the sudden suspension of the settled course by which life was proceeding, and the laceration of anticipation and continuity of the daily affection, care and love that you so tenderly demonstrated toward each other.

Maybe we should know that Dad was required to go ahead of us such that he could do what he always did here: prepare a place for his loved ones. He had to be certain that there would be enough rooms for his children, grandchildren and great-grandchildren. And maybe, as always, he had to insist that you, his "Mamie," will never have to worry about basic comforts and necessities.

I am sure that in youth, when we are all charged with life and the fantasy of Earthly immortality, there were few, if any, thoughts that he would not always be here; that some day there would be silence where he stood or sat; that he would be off the scene. But we now know that our forever does not include a perpetual stay on Earth. So we happily express gratitude for the time he was with us, and we appreciate the good fortune of having shared with him a closeness and kinship of care and grace.

I am comfortable in the belief that Dad is looking down at his family with a smile, knowing that he did his best to leave a legacy of decency, family pride, self-reliance and dignity.

With love, affection, and every good wish, I remain,

Sincerely,

Walter

Queen Esther Gupton Cheatham Jones to Renée Cheatham Neblett

Queen Esther Gupton Cheatham Jones (1929–2000), a native of Boston, Massachusetts, wrote these two letters to her daughter Renée Cheatham Neblett (b. 1947), an artist and teacher who in 1989 moved to Ghana, where in 1992 she founded Kokrobitey Institute, an art and education center. In the second letter, Jones mentions Sukari and Sékou, Neblett's children.

March 1993

Dear Renée,

An institution is the lengthened shadow of one person.

Life gives nothing to mortals except earth's great labor.

In reference to your Kokrobitey School: The test of progress is not whether we add more to the abundance of those who have much; it is whether we provide enough for those who have too little.

This is sunshine for your cloudy days.

Always,

Mother

Queen Esther Gupton Cheatham Jones
to Renée Cheatham Neblett

[Undated, circa 1996]

Your correspondence has quite a flattering closing. However, there is no reason for you ever to feel inferior to anyone. Our relationship as mother and daughter is the same as yours and Sukari. Respect for motherhood and experience should be acknowledged, nothing else. All of us have a role in life as Shakespeare said, "We have our own entrances, and our exits." The role assigned can be embellished by one's own conscience and desire, or can be executed simply as duty. My decision to do what I did was because you were my responsibility. I owed you the best I could provide emotionally and financially. The exact same as you did for Sukari and Sékou. Mothers do this. I knew you would do something. Your job as mother is one already an accomplished task to be proud of. Your dream and work to build Kokrobitey is beyond what most people, including myself, could imagine. It's more than having a career. Renée, in some sense we function alike. If we decide to do something, we put it in motion, never stopping to think of any obstacles we will encounter in the process. But for me it is how things get done. If I had stopped to think, would I make class throughout the year because of lupus, it would never have happened. You are independent as I, and I, as independent as Dad. It is inherited—so we live with it. When all is done, it is done and it is done your way. Yes, I do get very frustrated by having limitations because of health problems. The reason for such solitude at times is because the separation provides me with not having to explain my lack of participation. Pity serves no one—only understanding.

This year hopefully will be better, even though my body is beginning to feel the presence of constant pain and the aging process. Yet, there is something within me that wants to continue living life as long as I am able. So maybe I am coming to Ghana October 4, [19]96 for 5 months, and returning for classes in 1997.

Renée, with Kokrobitey no one will ever see your clear vision as clearly as you. Even with input from others, the onus is on you. Well, I love you and have always been proud of you as a daughter and mother. Give Sukari & Sékou my love.

Love mum

Thomas Allen Harris to Lyle Ashton Harris

Thomas Allen Harris (b. 1962) is an award-winning filmmaker whose works include the critically acclaimed 2005 documentary Twelve Disciples of Mandela: A Son's Tribute to Unsung Heroes.* *He wrote this letter to his brother Lyle (b. 1965), a prominent artist and photographer whose work has been exhibited around the world and was included in the 2007 Venice Biennale. Both brothers were raised in New York City and Tanzania. This note was written while they collaborated on a show at the Corcoran Gallery of Art in Washington, D.C., in 1998. "Standing Tree" and "Flying Free" are names they were given by a Native American medicine man.*

[Undated, 1998]

Dear Lyle,

I deeply enjoy and benefit from this journey that we are on together. I feel the profundity. It anchors me and sets me free. From humor to tragedy, to love to exercise and repose, from standing tree to flying free.

Love,

Tommy

Michael Leon Thomas to Mom and Dad

Michael Leon Thomas (b. 1966), a dancer, choreographer, and director, was a principal dancer with the Alvin Ailey American Dance Theater from 1991 to 1997, and in 2001 was one of the three founders of RhythMEK, a critically acclaimed modern dance company. In the following letter to his parents, he explains his conversion from Christianity to Buddhism.

New York

October 12, 2000

Dear Dad and Mom:

I hope my letter finds you rested and well after your vacation. Certainly both of you deserve the opportunity to relax and enjoy the fruits of your labor. Forgive the type written letter, but you know how illegible my handwriting can be.

---

*The film, which had its world premiere at the 2005 Toronto International Film Festival, is Harris's tribute to his stepfather, Benjamin Pule Leinaeng, and his eleven comrades, who fled South Africa in 1960 after the banning of the African National Congress. For thirty years the twelve men waged a battle against apartheid from abroad.

You have been inquiring for some time now whether or not I attend church and read my bible. Your desire to read me scripture over the telephone and to mail materials has really touched me. I know that you and mom love me very much. I have always known that you both love and care for me deeply. I have attempted, in the past, to give you a glossy picture of my life, thereby neglecting, while growing up, to include you in my personal development.

I now feel there are issues I would like to discuss with you. The first is my religious practice. Dad, I have been practicing Nichiren Diashonin's Buddhism for over a year, and on May 7, 2000, I received my gohonzon and joined the SGI-USA (Soka Gakkia, International), the lay organization for this Buddhism, the American chapter being about 40 years in existence. Mom and I have already begun a dialogue about my practice—she believes that I am on the path to destruction. I don't agree—but have come to realize that my Buddhist faith and your Christian one is going to do exactly what I have been chanting for—to become closer to my family spiritually. Because I have neglected to share my thoughts with you in the past—you now have an unclear picture of who I am.

Mom says that she often sees a sadness in me—I believe that stems from my realization that you and she—indeed the majority of our family—don't know who Michael Leon Thomas really is. Why? Because I have rarely followed through with the dialogue when discussing my life, my career, my friends, difficulties, or intimate relationships. Dialogue is a Buddhist tradition—it is a nonviolent way of resolving conflicts and assumes the presence of frankness, openness and equality between the two parties involved. With that in mind, I would love to begin a dialogue with the two of you through letters. I feel it would be a great way for us to begin to learn more about each other. I would like to share with you the story of how I actually came to Buddhism—why it has become so important in my life. We can freely write our opinions to each other, share our views honestly, so that when we come together again it will be with a deeper awareness about who the other person is—what they are going through.

I realize that this is not easy to read. I do believe however that your questioning my spiritual practices means that it is time for this dialogue. You are both wonderful people—I am still learning a great deal from you most particularly your actions. The love that you pour out to people and your great causes are a marvelous example for me. There have been so many times when I hoped we had more in common—sports, political views, interests, etc—but we are very different. I have often wondered how could that be—they say the apple does not fall far—but I see you in me, especially when I am dealing with MEK* or children.

Dad, your ability to be an incredible salesman and people's immediate trust in you is a quality that is growing in me more every day. Mom, your capacity to speak effectively and your great leadership skills, not to mention your party planning expertise, is blossoming in me as well. Those attributes have played a direct role in my work as a director for RhythMEK. Nevertheless, it has been my Buddhist practice, which aided me with the focus and determination required to direct MEK. More importantly, it took away my fear that I would not be loved OR accepted for who I am.

Now I feel free to be me—and for a person who has always been "in the closet" to be able to come out of the dark tiny room—it is a liberating and marvelous feeling. I know that not only am I loved, but also I am protected. That knowing gives me the courage to advance toward my dreams.

I look forward to your response—I know these letters will be thought provoking and will take our relationship to an incredible level; because we will be able to truly discuss each other's feelings and views. If you have gotten this far in the letter, and not thrown it away, then we are all in for quite a spiritual journey. Thank you both for agreeing to take it with me—it would be easier to just walk away. I love letters—one has the chance to really choose carefully the words, the tone, so as to relay the message clearly. I hope I have chosen my words wisely, and that the tone is one filled with the incredible love I have for you both.

Your first,
Michael

Walter J. Leonard to Angela M. Leonard

Chevy Chase, Maryland
May 12, 2005

Dear Angela,

I have very much enjoyed your descriptive reports of the shades and bits and pieces of the "Old" and "New" England, as you observe them standing before, or passing by, you on your path of research and discovery.

---

*MEK is short for RhythMEK, a dance company founded in 2001 by Thomas, Karine Plantadit-Bageot, and Elizabeth Roxas, two other former members of the Alvin Ailey American Dance Theater.

And I am more than pleased that in this process your own sense of growth and value is enhanced by this opportunity to examine some of life through a different lens.

Having given some additional thought to areas of your research interest, I am persuaded that some of what you must be doing is instructing your hearers, and your readers, that these sites are what some describe as "settings of commemoration and reflection"; that they are, and should be, ". . . recognized as cultural landscapes . . . but also places of reverence and sacred ground."

We will talk of other things a little later.

May the sun catch you smiling.

With every good wish, I am,

Sincerely,

    Dad

PART II

Courtship and Romance

The romantic lives of African Americans have traditionally received scant attention in popular culture. Images of African Americans in books, in music videos, and on film and television have tended to glorify a mythologized hypersexuality and black male misogyny. However, as the previous part demonstrated, African Americans of all economic classes have, throughout their history, risen above personal circumstance to forge and maintain bonds of affection. Whether barely or highly literate, the correspondents in this part all express the rhapsody of romance, highlighting a feature of African American life that has for centuries been acutely underrepresented in and by the American media.

Nicey E. Bush to Harvey Moore

The courtship between Nicey E. Bush of Carthagena, Ohio, and Harvey Moore of Coldwater comes to a head in these letters written in September and October 1869. Little is known about the correspondents, whose letters have been transcribed almost verbatim.

Carthagena, Ohio
September 14, 1869

Dear Harvey,

I am well at present and hope these few lines may find you the same. There is something that compells me to write—yet something I have tried to keep which I cannot retain any longer that is love, yes, I love you. You have stolen my heart. Now I know that I have treated you wrong you said I had but I never thought so before. I know that if you was to treat me now like I did you my heart would almost break. I would even receive letters from you and not answer them for a long time and some times not at all but I know that you are tender hearted and will forgive me for so doing. If I have wrote any thing wrong you will forgive me for it. Am in a hurry. I don't expect you can read this if you cant I will read it for you Bostwick will take up school on the first of Oct. I am as ever
        Nicey

Harvey Moore to Nicey E. Bush

Coldwater, Ohio
October 26, 1869

Dear Nicey,

Your kind and affectionate letter of September 14th was received with much pleasure was read and reviewed more than once. I hope you will not be mad at me for my neglect. Pardon me if it be an offense. I would not knowingly wound your heart. [H]ow could I think that one whom I so ardently love when I read your [illegible] with that ameliorating influence to my mind confideing in you only I cannot [illegible]. I am not adequate to the task like two drops of water those sentiments run together. My heart has bin stolen and I believe it's you that has in it possession, would you be willing to give me yours in return or would you refuse or persist in refusing to speak on this most solemn subject, subject of matrimony. I have no doubt you will censure me of forcing this question. I hope you will forgive me. You know I am weak minded and you say I am tender hearted but I don't think so. I falt my self for being hard hearted and always need to return evil for evil but I need not informe you, you know to much already, although if I had not such implicit confidence I could not divulge the secret emotions of my heart with such freedom. I have something I call a condisional proposition that I wish to make to you. If it is agreeable in reference to our future destiny you I must informe did not say any thing wrong in my view in your communication. I hope you will forgive me if I have said anything wrong now. I must bid you good night, happy dreams attend you

And I will be your most

Devoted Harvey

Harvey Moore to Nicey E. Bush

Carthagena Ohio
Dec. 20th 1869

Dear Nicey,

I must call you by that little name. A poem has elapsed since our correspondence began, but what motives were we prompted and to what purpose shall we concede[.] I don't know why I can not cease to think of you, and to love you, you say I have stolen your heart. I can say this much you stole mine first and a fair exchange is no roberry. I think it was down right [illegible] for you to keep from me your real centiment. If those hearts are blended and linked together by the ties of affection so let it be [.] Never break or sever that vow, or promise you made in your last letter, as there is something I have tryed to retain I find I can not so I will present you my heart and hand to accompany it provided you will accept of them in return for the one that was stolen from you as you have implicated me or rather charged me as the guilty one so you see at once I am generous.

Well Nicey when shall that happy day bee, please decide the doubtful case, you may ask what day our wedding day, you must get your excuses ready, I shall be plain on this subject and short as I have not the talent to write a prolonged detail, think of this and tell me when I see you. Then I desire a private interview, then after I hear your decision, if you allow me I have something to tell you,——I don't see how you could afforde to attach your self to one so limited in point of education circumstances and every other material consideration remember that notwithstanding I have commended [*sic*] my self to you, willing to shear all the joys and sorrows of life with you—Christmas gift dear and then a sweet kiss good bye as ever

Harvey

Paul Laurence Dunbar to Alice Ruth Moore

Alice Ruth Moore (1875–1935) was born in New Orleans, Louisiana, the child of Joseph Moore, a sailor, and Patricia Wright Moore, a former slave who worked as a seamstress. Moore graduated from the teacher's training program at Straight College (now Dillard University) and worked as a teacher while developing her talent as a writer. In 1895 Violets and Other Tales, her first collection of essays, poetry, and short stories, was published. In 1898, after a courtship maintained through letters, she married Paul Laurence Dunbar and moved with him to Washington, D.C. Many of her poems, including "I Sit and Sew" and "Sonnet," were widely celebrated during the Harlem Renaissance.

3 Northcumberland Avenue
Trafalgar Square
[London, England]
March 7, 1897

Alice, My Darling,

Someday when I can hold you in my arms and punctuate every sentence with a kiss and an embrace, I may be able to tell you how happy your letter has made me, happy and yet unhappy from the very strength of my longing to be with you; a longing not to be satisfied it seems to so distant a day.

You love me, Alice, you say; ah yes but could you know the certainty with which I worship you, you would realize that your strongest feelings are weak beside. You gave me no time to think or to resist had I willed to do so! You took my heart captive at once. I yield bravely, weak coward that I am, without a struggle. And how glad I am of my full surrender. I would rather be your captive than another woman's king. You have made life a new thing to me—a precious and sacred trust.

Will I love you tenderly and faithfully? Darling, darling, can you ask! You who are my heart, my all, my life. I will love you as no man has ever loved before. Already I am living for you and working for you and through the gray days and the long nights I am longing and yearning for you;—for the sound of your voice, the touch of your hand, the magic of your presence, the heavenly thrill of your kiss.

You did wrong to kiss me? Oh sweet heart mine, does the flower that turns its golden face up to the amorous kisses of the moving wind do wrong? Does the cloud that clasps the mountain close to its dewy breast do wrong?

Do any of the eternal forces of nature do wrong? If so then you have done a wrong. But darling you could not have helped it. This love of ours was predestined. I had thought that I loved you before, and I had. I loved Alice Ruth Moore the writer of "Violets," but now I love Alice Ruth Moore, the woman,—and my queen. "All the current of my being runs to thee."

I am writing wildly my dear I know, but I am not stopping to think. My head has retired and it is my heart and my pen for it.

For your sake I will be true and pure. You will help me to be this for you are always in my thoughts. Last night as I started out upon a rather new undertaking or rather phase of action, I took your letter with me and read it as I drove down town. "It will give me heart," I said. It did and I have never had before such a brilliant success. It was at a dinner of the Savage Club, artists, literatures, scientists and actors, where every man could do some thing. I was an honored guest and held a unique position as the representative of a whole race. I took my turn with the rest and,—dear is this egotism?—was received with wonderful enthusiasm. You were with me all the time! You do not leave my thoughts. Alice, Alice, how I love you! Tell me over and over again that you love me. It will hearten me for the larger task that I have set myself here. I am so afraid that you may grow to care less for me. May God forbid! But if you do, let me know at once. I love you so that I am mindful only of your happiness. This is why I shall not complain about your being in New York although I do not like it. It is a <u>dangerous</u> place. But I know, darling that you will do me no injustice, and yourself no dishonor, so I am content. Go often to Miss Brown's but do not entirely usurp my place in the heart of that queen of women. Love me dear, and tell me so. Write to me often and believe me ever

> Your Devoted Lover, Paul

Roscoe Conkling Bruce to Clara Burrill

Roscoe Conkling Bruce (1879–1950) was the son of Blanche Kelso Bruce (1841–1898), a former slave who, during Reconstruction, was the second African American elected to the U.S. Senate and the first to serve a full six-year term.* The letters that follow were exchanged while the younger Bruce was an administrator at Tuskegee Institute and his fiancée, Clara Burrill, was a student at Radcliffe College. While Bruce and Burrill refer to each other as husband and wife, the two were still engaged when these letters were written. They wed in June 1903.

---

*In 1873, Pinckney B. S. Pinchback (1837–1921) of Louisiana became the first African American elected to the U.S. Senate, but he lost his seat when the election was contested. A year earlier he had been elected to Congress but was also denied the right to serve. Blanche Kelso Bruce was elected to the Senate from Mississippi in 1874 and began his term on March 4, 1875. Bruce settled in Washington, D.C., where he was among that city's social elite. In 1878 he married Josephine Wilson, the daughter of a Cleveland dentist. A year later they had Roscoe Conkling Bruce, their only child. The older Bruce later served as register of the treasury under Presidents Garfield, Arthur, and McKinley, and he also owned about three thousand acres of land in Mississippi and ran a successful real estate, insurance, and investment business, making him one of the capital's wealthiest men.

Josephine Bolivar County, Mississippi.

3 January 1903

My darling Wife—

Let me thank you with all my heart for the whisk broom & case that you sent me for Christmas & for the pin-cushion you made for your new Mama. Dear heart, I love you very much & I prize very highly the many gentle courtesies I receive at the hands of her I love. I'm awfully glad you did select the pin cushion for Mother; she will appreciate it deeply. And I needed a whisk broom & case very much. I am glad that your Mama liked the Bible & that Mama liked the sketch; I wanted to give them something they'd like. I'm sorry, dearie, that I wasn't able to send you a larger check but you realize our (not my) situation. You must regard the ring rather than the poor little books as your Christmas gift.

I'm afraid that the *Dynamic Sociology* had best be sent by express. Before the end of the year I'm going to send you a check to buy some other books that we'll need in our library.

Dear heart, I have missed you a very great deal—how much no mortal but me can quite realize (You, dearie, are an immortal!) I think of you literally all of the time. In my office my mind refuses to bind itself to routine duties & insists upon planning dresses & tomes & receptions & the Lord knows what for you. I love you, darling, with all my soul. My life you are. I pray that we may be always the creatures of poetry & romance that now we are; I pray that I may make you always happy; I pray that your life will not be narrowed by marriage but enlarged; I pray that we may be useful & worthy always. Let us, whatever comes, never forsake our scholarly interests; let us never degrade our ideals; let us always live on the summits of experience; & let us always be simple & noble & sensible & just.

I have been reading thse last few days Cardinal Jerome's *Idea of University.* His estimate of intellectual cultivation seems singularly just. Culture means enlargement of life; the scholar is the man of balance. But above intellectual cultivation Jerome would place noble feeling, pure aspiration. And more & more I am getting a similar point of view. Fine emotions give to life all its value; love gives even one a religion.

I hope you've written to Mama. The poor dear has written me a letter that would bring tears to your eyes. I love her, she loves you, & you must love her.

Your devoted,

Ros

Clara Burrill to Roscoe Conkling Bruce

[Cambridge, Massachusetts]
[Undated, 1903]

My darling:

The sweet letter that I received this morning from you I have read and re-read many times. It is perfectly true, dearie, that if I were not so deeply in love with my sweet Husband I could do ever so much better work at Radcliffe. Often when I should be studying I am writing a letter to you or I am holding my book in my hand, looking at the printed page while my thoughts, my heart, are in Tuskegee with you. I often sit for hours dreaming of you. But, dearie, what can one expect of a girl whose soul is at Tuskegee and whose body alone is in Cambridge?

Dear heart, I love you with all the strength of my being. Every day I long more and more to see you, to hear the voice that voice I love so well, to look into your eyes, and to kiss your lips. This has been a bittersweet year, dearie. Bitter because we must be physically apart; sweet because we know that the love we bear each other rises above the physical separation and keeps us one tho we are hundreds of miles apart. I love you, darling.

Write to me soon, dearie. Dear heart, I love you with all my heart.
Your
Clara

Roscoe Conkling Bruce to Clara Burrill

Tuskegee, Alabama
January 31, 1903

My darling—

Just four months & four days from today you will be made, in accordance with the traditions of our civilization, my wedded wife; you are, thank Heaven, morally my Wife this moment. I hope, dear heart, that my last two letters have not obscured the fact that if Eddie were to refuse to help financially or were to yield to your noble request, I should in some way raise the money to pay the bill. If I were disappointed in the hope that he has made my life full of joy, the hope that we will become man & wife in June 1903—my faith in my efficiency in the world would be shattered. Come, dearie, tell me once for all that whatever comes you will marry me this June. Here I have made you a beautiful home; my salary will support you in comfort; my heart yearns for your presence; you have promised. Never, never harbor the thought, darling, that it is <u>possible</u> for June 4 to pass without our marriage. I love you devotedly.

Ros

Roscoe Conkling Bruce to Clara Burrill

Tuskegee, Alabama
February 19, [1903]

My dear heart—

Yesterday & again today I was really disappointed in failing to hear from you. You, perhaps, don't realize that a letter from you is an event in my life. The nearer our wedding day approaches, the more dependent am I upon you & your love. Darling, I hope & pray that I may prove worthy of your beautiful & absolute devotion. Your photograph smiles upon me this moment. Although you are probably in the land of dreams, I can't help feeling that even the dreams are sometimes of your Husband. He loves you with all his heart & soul; his life is consecrated to your happiness.

What a splendid girl you are! You are never the least bit cross with me. You have learned from me—ahem!—never to flirt! Well, dearie, if you were here on my knee, I think I'd forgive just a wee bit of a flirtation; yes, I'd even let you kiss me!!!!! Alas! For space & time. Yet every moment brings our supreme happiness a step closer. I sometimes watch the little hand on my watch as it spins around & around bringing you closer, closer, closer to my arms. I love you.

Devotedly
Ros

Dr. James Arthur Kennedy to A'Lelia Walker

A'Lelia Walker (1885–1931) was the daughter of Madam C. J. Walker. During the Harlem Renaissance, A'Lelia hosted "The Dark Tower," a popular literary salon that was patronized by many of the leading lights of the movement, including Langston Hughes, James Weldon Johnson, and Countee Cullen. In 1926 she married Dr. James Arthur Kennedy, a Chicago physician. This letter was written by Kennedy while A'Lelia was on an extended trip to Europe, Africa, and the Middle East.

Chicago, Illinois
12/8/21

My Dear Darling Lelia:

I presume ere this you have received my first letter in which I expressed my very great pleasure in receiving your cablegram. Oh, how Old Father Time seems to drag at his slowest pace since your departure. I think of the whole of Europe in terms of you and I am praying and praying each day for your safety and pleasure; that your entire tour may be like unto a beautiful long road strewn with fragrant crimson flowers, its end of which terminates within the circumference of my arms.

I do hope that you are well and happy and shall remain in that ecstatic state every moment of your life. I am planning now to increase that state of happiness for my darling and make it permanent, while on this earth. There is no news of any special note since your departure in America—This Disarmament Conference looks rather favorable, but no special details have been hashed out as yet regarding the ratio and no specific system of reduction or elimination of ships and armies have been worked out by any of its experts.

Chicago is about the same, if I am to speak locally; except a strike at the Stock Yards is now in force, which resulted in a riot last night. Not a race riot; however I did hear of one colored person getting injured, two whites were killed and about thirty eight wounded; I think this constitutes the battle casualty list.

I presume everybody is looking forward to the wonderful Xmas tide, which is soon to flow in upon us, however I am not included with its number who are expecting wonderful pleasure and etc. because you, dear Heart, constitute my entire life and pleasure, Xmas included and of which I am now deprived, eliminates all ecstacies or even the elements which enter into the compound. Yet I shall exist until you return to me at which time my happiness will break the flood gates of melancholy and flow out into the beautiful field of life, turning with the golden sunshine of success and with it beautiful crimson fragrant flowers of achievement and ultimate victory.

Sincerely,
Jack

Dr. Henry Arthur Callis to Myra Colson

Dr. Henry Arthur Callis (1887–1974) was a physician and teacher at Tuskegee Institute's U.S. Veterans Hospital and Howard University's School of Medicine. Myra Colson (1892–1979) was a social worker and graduate of Fisk University and the University of Chicago. They wed in 1927 and had two children.

Chicago, Illinois
Christmas Eve, 1925

Myra, dear:

You are gone and yet there is no realization of the fact. I am more dazed than anything. It is as yet incomprehensible that in an hour or two I cannot talk to you over the telephone and then come speeding to you. I am glad for my stupidity at the last moment. The need for thought and effort to avert catastrophe took our minds off ourselves at least.

Your gift is a treasure. I have wanted to read it. To possess *Loon's Tolerance* from your hand is delightful. Next to people, I love books most. To have them near is to feel the presence of friends. To have this associated with loved ones makes them invaluable companions. Your gift shall travel with me to Detroit. To insure it good company I am taking the photograph of you Rosa gave me of [*sic*] also. My address in Detroit will be St. Antoine Street Branch Y.M.C.A. May I look for a letter on Monday?

One's never quite satisfied. There are always so many desirable things to do. Yet as I look from this Christmas to others that have passed, I am able to see a steady gain from year to year. In this introspective contentment more than in anything else comes the happiness of this season. It is the quiet, undemonstrative happiness of reflection. With this spirit is of course, the perennial hope. I hope greater things of the new year, but I am willing also to work for them.

Give my love to Rosa and advise her that my only insistence is that she watch over you carefully for you are a very much spoiled child.

With love,
Arthur

Dr. Henry Arthur Callis to Myra Colson

Thursday morning
January 7, 1926

Myra dear:

The love of you, the longing for you, makes me physically ill. I am unfit to attempt anything. Such absolute weakness seems incredible. Situations that require the utmost marshalling of reserves to approach, under other circumstances would be as nothing. In your absence I have found the keystone of my being, the center at once of my strength and my weakness.

I should be away from this spot. I am going. But how much easier it would be to sit here in silence with my eyes invited on space. Myra, I am miserable without you, dear.

With love,

Arthur

Robert Keyes to Hattie Haynes

This letter was written by an uncle of the renowned Los Angeles–based artist Betye Saar (b. 1926), who used some of the letters in a series of mixed media collages and assemblages in her 2006 series Migrations/Transformations, in which she constructed fictional biographies of nameless characters to represent the millions of Africans transported across the Atlantic during the Middle Passage.

Sunday Afternoon
April 15, 1928

Hattie! Dearest One,

With pleasure untold I write you. This beautiful, beautiful lonesome afternoon. I'm thinking of you all the while. The thought of you is all pleasure to me. In space we are quite some distance apart, but in Heart, we are near. In leaving you at night the time it takes me to get home is so short I cannot realize it; Why! Because I am thinking of you every bit of time. I'm running. Talking to myself to you. Oh! But you cannot imagine how happy you have made me. It worries me when I hear you say "Oh! I was a little blue today." I don't see how you can become <u>Blue</u> if you think of me the way I think of you. Of course my thoughts are so much of the future, as well as the present. You may be looking at the future with such doubt that it brings on "The Blues."

Look forward for Light and you will get it for there is no Darkness where there is Light. I Love You. Now if you can say the same, and be not from the Lips, but The Heart, then there will be Light. When there is Light there be <u>Happiness</u>. Sorrow and Happiness can not dwell together. I am asking you to Trust in, and Believe Me.

"I Will Not Deceive You."

<u>I think</u> I understand you in a way. You have seen and heard of so many fakes that you are afraid to trust. I can not blame you. It is wise to be careful but I can say truthfully have no worries, and that is a lot to say. You have made my life a real one of Happiness and I Love You. The Love I have for you I've never had for any one before. I never feel as if I want to <u>cheat</u> on you. I have been a cheatter in my time, but I have no desire to cheat on you. It seems as if I've come to the end of the road. I'm satisfied and contented. My only and longing desire is to make you Happy. Make you as you have made me. You need never worrie about me on our absence for I certainly will be good. Closing I'll say good by and may God bless you.

I remain as ever yours in love,

"Daddy"

Fredi Washington to Lawrence Brown

Fredi Washington (1903–1994), a native of Savannah, Georgia, moved to New York at age sixteen and began a successful show business career. Her stage credits include Shuffle Along; Black Boy *(1926), starring Paul Robeson; and* Singin' the Blues *(1931). Her film credits include* Black and Tan Fantasy *(1929), featuring Duke Ellington; and the role she is perhaps best known for, Peola in* Imitation of Life *(1934). In July 1933 Washington married Lawrence Brown, a trombone player in Duke Ellington's orchestra. Their first correspondence was a postcard.*

[Winston-Salem, North Carolina]
June 22, 1932

Hello Sweets,

They're having a little party tonight and they're playing soft love music and singing and I wish you were here with me. Just the sort of music I like to dance to with you. Would you hold me close? Be sweet my darling.

Love,

Fredi

Lawrence Brown to Fredi Washington

Western Union Telegram
New York, NY
[Undated]
Miss Fredi Washington=
Empire Theatre=
EASTER GREETINGS TO THE SWEETEST LIL EASTER BUNNY I KNOW=
ME

Fredi Washington to Lawrence Brown

New York, New York
Friday 12:20 p.m.
September 29, 1934

Dearest—

This time next week I shall be safe in your arms and I'm so excited I simply don't know what to do with myself. I leave here at 8:15 tomorrow night, arrive Chicago Tuesday morning and N.Y. Wed. morning at 8 so I shall join you some time on Thurs. It is probably afternoon. Have you a nice room in Hartford? I hope so. Gosh: darling just to think of being kissed again by you gives me goose pimples up and down my spine. I don't know how I'm going to be able to stay on that train for those four days. I'm so very, very happy dear. Can you hear my heart beating? Just think when you read this I'll probably be going through St. Louis or some hick town. You know I'm going on the Santa Fe California Limited. Leaves 8:45 p.m. I don't know, oh yes, car No. 45 Section 5. So there, you have all the particulars. I'll expect you to call me at home Wed. night. Make it kinda late because I'll probably be out late trying to see everybody in that one day. Isabel wants me to have dinner with them. I think they're going to meet me. I'm going to see if I can't get a hold of a little car for the day to do my running around in. I don't want to wear myself out with the subs and etc. I want to be nice and fresh for my sugar.

Well, I've got my teeth and you couldn't tell to save your life that they aren't mine. Dr. Hess Kirshner and Merdock stayed up all night, night before last in order to finish them so that I could get away tomorrow night. They've been so sweet and considerate of me. It's mighty nice to have friends like them. They both send their best to you and told me to tell you they hope it's true that you're coming back.

It's sorta dull and dreary here today but thank goodness cooler. So at least I can be cool and excited.

I've got everything all straightened out now. I go to the dentist, doctor, Pasadena, and dump the car tomorrow and then the train and you. So I'm all in readiness. I'm going now and have washed. I hope it doesn't get too dirty on the train because I want to look nice for my daddy. Oh! Dearest. I'll soon hear your very own voice in my very own ears. It thrills me just to think about it.

I guess I'd better try to come down to earth because if I don't I'll be a wreck by the time I get there instead [of] being rested.

Regards to the gang. Will write tomorrow again.

All my love to my sweetheart.

Yours

    Baby-dear

Charles Drew to Minnie Lenore Robbins

Charles Drew (1904–1950) was a surgeon, medical researcher, and teacher who is credited with saving many lives during World War II with his groundbreaking work in the preservation and transfusion of blood. He served as medical director of the American Red Cross and the Blood Transfusion Association's joint program for U.S. military forces but was asked to resign after he protested the racial segregation of banked blood.* In 1939, a year before receiving his degree in medical science from Columbia University, he married Minnie Lenore Robbins, a teacher.

Western Union Telegram
Washington, D.C.
April 9, 1939
Miss Lenore Robbins=
Spellman [*sic*] College Atlanta GA=

STILL IN A DREAM I WALK LIKE ONE ENTRANCED AND THINK OF YOU =

    CHARLIE

---

*In 1941 the military established a policy that forbade the donation of blood to whites by nonwhites.

Charles Drew to Minnie Lenore Robbins

Washington, D.C.
Easter Sunday at twilight
[1939]

Lenore,

With a heart that's full with a new found joy my thoughts turn to you as the day closes and a sigh rises as an evening prayer to ask whatever gods there be to keep you safe for me. Since first meeting you I have moved through the days as one in a dream, lost in reverie, awed by the speed with which the moving finger of fate has pointed out the way I should go. As the miles of countryside sped by on our return trip I sat silent and pondered on the power that lies in a smile to change the course of a life; the magic in the tilt of a head, the beauty of your carriage and the gentleness that struck so deeply.

Later when I become more coherent I shall say perhaps many things but tonight this one thing alone seems to ring clearly. I love you.
    Charles

Charles Drew to Minnie Lenore Robbins

Washington, D.C.
April 21, 1939

Lenore,

On my mother's birthday you wrote me the loveliest letter I've ever received, the kind I've always wanted from someone like you. It is symbolic for me joining you in my mind and heart, you about whom all my future revolves, to all that is finest, dearest, loveliest in the years that have passed, that part which has clung to at least a few ideals, has striven to be decent and achieve simply because it would please one of earth's sweetest souls, my mother. I should like to do things to make you proud, seek you out when I'm tired, tell you my stories of the day's work, the things I dream about. The Things there are which are necessary for happiness—someone to love, to be loved by someone, and a job to do. You can teach me to be those things which you'd have me be and my joy shall be in learning. What would you have me be? What are the things I can do that will make you most happy? It seems so strange that having been with you so little I could miss you so much, that days which are so terribly full could have so much of emptiness in them, that nights which should be spent in sleeping are wide eyed with a lingering loneliness.

I'm jittery with anticipation, impatient, that I can't get things going faster, that I can't find out just what plans have been laid out for me so that I may know what to tell you. Most of my bridges to the past have been destroyed without regret. The future seems to glow in the radiance of you. Lenore have you ever looked for anything for a long, long time and then suddenly found it and knew at once you had. It's indescribably grand. It changes one, changes the world and all that's in it, adds meaning, purpose and a new succession of goals. Up to now I have gone alone. I never want to again. Just thinking of you has helped so much, loving you means so much more.

Your last letter leaves me with almost a feeling of pure gratitude. It gave me a peep into your heart. You darling, I do thank you,
    Charles

Martin Luther King, Jr., to Coretta Scott

Martin Luther King, Jr., met Coretta Scott in January 1952 in Boston, where they were both students. King was pursuing doctoral studies at Boston University's School of Theology while Scott, a native of Marion, Alabama, was attending the New England Conservatory of Music, planning to pursue a career as a concert singer. The couple wed on June 18, 1953.

Atlanta
July 18, 1952

Darling, I miss you so much. In fact, much too much for my own good. I never realized that you were such an intimate part of my life. My life without you is like a year without a spring time which comes to give illumination and heat to the atmosphere saturated by the dark cold breeze of winter . . . O excuse me, my darling. I didn't mean to go off on such a poetical and romantic flight. But how else can we express the deep emotions of life other than in poetry? Isn't love too ineffable to be grasped by the cold calculating hands of intellect?

By the way (to turn to something more intellectual) I have just completed Bellamy's *Looking Backward*. It was both stimulating and fascinating. There can be no doubt about it. Bellamy had the insight of a social prophet as well as the fact finding mind of the social scientists. I welcomed the book because much of its content is in line with my basic ideas. I imagine you already know that I am much more socialistic in my economic theory than capitalistic. And yet I am not so opposed to capitalism that I have failed to see its relative merits. It started out with a noble and high motive, viz., to block the trade monopolies of nobles, but like most human systems it fell victim to the very thing it was revolting against. So today capitalism has out-lived its usefulness. It has brought about a system that takes necessities from the masses to give luxuries to the classes. So I think Bellamy is right in seeing the gradual decline of capitalism. I think you noticed that Bellamy emphasized that the change would be evolutionary rather than revolutionary. This, it seems to me, is the most sane and ethical way for social change to take place.

Eternally Yours,

Martin

Rev. Martin Luther King, Jr., to Coretta Scott King

King, who in 1955 received his Ph.D. from Boston University, sent this telegram to his wife from New Orleans, where he was inducted as president of the Southern Christian Leadership Conference.

New Orleans, Louisiana
Mrs. Coretta King
309 South Jackson St. Montgomery Ala
February 14, 1957

MY DARLING IT IS A PLEASURE FOR ME TO PAUSE WHILE ATTENDING TO IMPORTANT BUSINESS WHICH AFFECTS THE WELFARE OF THIS NATION AND ATTEND TO THE MOST IMPORTANT BUSINESS IN THE WORLD NAMELY CHOOSING AS MY VALENTINE THE SWEETEST AND MOST LOVELY WIFE AND MOTHER IN ALL THE WORLD. AS THE DAYS GO BY MY LOVE GROWS EVEN GREATER FOR YOU WILL ALWAYS BE MY VALENTINE.

MARTIN

Booker T. Washington III to Joyce Dodson Washington

Booker T. Washington III (1915–1994) was the grandson of his namesake, the legendary educator who was founding principal of Tuskegee Institute and one of the most prominent African American leaders of his day. The younger Washington graduated with a degree in architecture from Tuskegee

Institute. In 1966 he moved to New York, where he met Joyce Dodson, a native of Norfolk, Virginia. The couple married in 1967 and settled in New York, where she worked as an assistant superintendent of the New York City school system while he was involved in numerous architectural projects, including the Metropolitan Opera House at Lincoln Center, the Pan Am Building, and Rockefeller University. In 1968 Joyce was pursuing graduate studies in Norfolk, Virginia.

219 E. 44th St.
New York, N.Y.
Mon. 4 Feb. 68

My precious Wife—

Just a few more days and it will be over—the waiting—aching—longing to be with you.

Have a reservation for the flight that is scheduled to arrive at Norfolk at 8:10 this Friday night. Certainly hope there will be no delay.

Hope the accompanying reading material will interest you. I wish that I had majored in Political Science, economics and Sociology—and Psychology—and Law!—all of which it seems that I have been trying to do—anyway—on my own—for several years.

I love you <u>very</u> much—and hope that this tortuous time that we are both enduring—when apart—will not weaken, demoralize or destroy our high hope for a wonderful future together.

<u>Yours</u>—Booker

Walter D. Broadnax to Angel Wheelock Marshall

Walter D. Broadnax (b. 1944) is an educator who in 2002 became the second president of Clark Atlanta University in Atlanta, Georgia. He previously served as dean of the School of Public Affairs at American University and as assistant secretary of health under President Bill Clinton. He married Angel Wheelock, a statistician for the U.S. Census Bureau, in 1984.

Marrakech
March 28, 1984

My Dearest Angel,

We have arrived in Marrakech after departing Casablanca this afternoon. This is a most beautiful country. It is easy to understand why the French were not anxious to let the Moroccans have it back. Just this minute, outside, I can hear the evening prayers coming from the mosque just out my window.

This city is on the site of an oasis formerly developed in 1062 AD by the Berbers. Obviously, with the Sahara just to the south of us, water is at a premium.

We have been visiting all kinds of industrial and agricultural projects, e.g., phosphate mining, orange groves, olive groves, bean farms and ship yards. The people are gorgeous but very reserved (Moslems are very reserved at home).

Our group is having a marvelous time. I am eating myself to pieces and walking many miles each day. Hopefully, the walking will counterbalance my consumption of very fine food.

My darling lady, I miss you terribly. The only thing I would rather be doing with this time is spending it with you. Moreover, I would much prefer that this time here could have been spent with you. You would love it but credit cards are difficult to use outside of the big hotels. Seriously, the medinas (shops) are spectacular. I think I may become a professional snake charmer when I return to Cambridge. Or, is that what I do for a living now?

I love you. I am sure that I will have spoken with you by the time you receive this. I look forward to holding you again.

All my love,
    Walter

Francesca Momplaisir to Nnabu Gogoh

Francesca Momplaisir (b. 1973) is a native of Haiti who immigrated to the United States at the age of two. She grew up in New York City and earned her undergraduate and doctoral degrees in literature from New York University. Momplaisir met Nnabu Gogoh (b. 1970), a native of Nigeria, during an NAACP Youth Council event when she was seventeen and in high school and he was a sophomore in college. The two were married on Valentine's Day, 2002, and later that year had a son, Ife.

Queens, New York
Saturday, May 8, 1999

Hello, my love.

I hope you're feeling a little better. I just received your letter dated May 5th. And yes, I am smiling from ear to ear once again. I have to stop reading so that I don't feel overwhelmed. I love you so much and I am as fortunate as you are to be in this relationship. Loving you comes quite naturally. I couldn't stop myself if I tried. You'll probably receive this along with the Xeroxes from the Bible and the photograph. It's blurry, I know, but it's a copy of a copy. I took pictures today and they will be ready by Wednesday, so you'll have something clearer and more recent. When you return, we will take pictures together and you will smile.

I am looking forward to your return so that I can finally get a good night's sleep. No matter how early I go to bed, I wake up feeling tired partly because I wake up in the middle of the night wanting you and thinking about you. You are so important to me. I value you so much. I'm still smiling because of your letter. I'm so glad that you chose to be so expressive in writing. Yesterday I opened a fortune cookie that said, "You will be married within a year." I hope that that's the case. Actually, I know that that will be the case.

I wish that you had told me sooner how you felt about me all these years. It would have kept me from feeling that I was insane or obsessed with you. For a long time I didn't know that you felt the same for me and I just figured that I should give it up or cover up my feelings for you because nothing was going to come of it. Even if we couldn't get together back then, I still would have liked to know what you were thinking. There were times when I thought that you really didn't love me, or didn't love me enough. I questioned myself for a long time and tried to determine what was wrong with me that kept you from loving me. I wanted your love and acceptance so much that it's sometimes hard to believe that we are where we are in this relationship. I used to have what I referred to as "Gogoh cravings." There were times when I wanted to be with you so badly it was overwhelming. I remember being with someone (in the biblical sense) years ago and hearing myself in my mind just calling out to you. I could have killed that man for not being you.

Isn't it wonderful when things fall into place and come together. When I'm with you and when reading your letters I know that this was worth waiting for. You're the one, baby. If not for situations like these with you being away, I think we'd be living a fairytale. I guess we need something to keep us grounded. I could think of other, less painful ways of keeping us from getting outlandishly euphoric, but this is the method that has been chosen for us. But. Our "happily ever after" is yet to come. The stories we'll be able to tell. Our grandchildren or great grandchildren will someday discover our letters in an old attic covered with dust and read them and know that they are the products of an incredible love. I'm so happy to be loved by you. Now all we need to do is get you back home.

I just need to see you and touch you and really know that you're okay. D.C. sent me an email asking me in jest when you and I are planning to get married. He didn't expect me to have a timeframe so soon. I often think that if I had been in his shoes I would have let go a long time ago, years ago. If I knew that my mate had such strong feelings for someone else, I could never stay. I really believe that we all have "one true love." That's not to say that we can't love other people and be happy with them. But, at some point in our lives, usually early on, we all encounter one individual who is our one true love. I think that very few people actually end up with that person. I'm very fortunate to have that come back to me.

I love you, sweetie.

Francesca.

Nnabu Gogoh to Francesca Momplaisir

York, Pennsylvania
June 10, 2000
10:50 p.m.

Hey You—

How's my baby doing? I have to tell you that it hurts not to see you this weekend. Even though it's my own idea that you not come, I still feel the pinch of wanting to see you and not being able to. Sometimes I wonder just why it is that I punish myself. Lord only knows that if I had my way I would be with you every waking moment. I love to finish your sentences, I love to say "bless you" when you sneeze. I love to look into your eyes and make you blush. I just love you.

Although talking to you seems more personal, I feel as if I'm better able to express my feelings for you in writing a little more clearly. Through you, I am able to see my future and unlock my potential. Because you love me, I am able to return that love to you in ways that often surprise me. With you, I hope to be a part of a family, eternally bound by love and mutual admiration.

Even though you don't like to hear this, I will continue to thank you not only for your love. But also for your friendship. The friendship, built over the years on long conversations, arranged meetings and failed relationships, has not only strengthened our bond, but has given us the rare opportunity, often denied most, to try again. For your support, both from near and far, I am now and will always be eternally grateful. Just grin and bear the compliments. You are more than deserving of them and more. I promise to forever hold you dear to my heart and commit myself totally to loving you.

Forever yours

Nnabu

Nnabu Gogoh to Francesca Momplaisir

York, Pennsylvania

Sept. 28, 2000

Hey you,

I got your letter this morning and you would not like my reaction. It's been so long since I've smelled your perfume that I had to put the letter away for quite some time. I placed it under my pillow and cried myself back to sleep. I haven't had such a physical reaction to anything in quite a long time. It's amazing how much emotion can be contained in a scent. (I'm still shaking as I write this letter.)

I'm not entirely certain if you know how reassuring it is to hear you describe how you feel about me/us. To know that you don't just want to get married and have a child, but that it's me and my child that you want that has to be the greatest compliment that I have ever received. Thank you so much. I am also flattered by you saying that I make you feel beautiful. You have to be my absolute mirror. I see in you what you see in me, and you were right about that picture years ago, the love we shared was evident in that picture.

To the extent of your wondering about whether or not I love you baby, I can only hope that my prior actions have answered that question. I love you baby and have taken every opportunity to further explore it. Whether dressed or nude (preferably nude) I've often tried to figure out just what it is about you that I can't resist. (Another reason for those stolen glances that you always ask about.) The point is that I see you, have always seen you and can only see you through love. No matter how much you might disagree, you have a beautiful body. (So much so that even Akei knows.) You mentioned feeling like a china doll and a show piece. Although I would like nothing more than to put you on a pedestal, I also know that it is not a part of who you are or what you are. Being with you makes me proud and confident. I know that when we are together, you are with me and I with you. There is no insecurity, no question as to where your heart is. I have never experienced that with anyone other than you. When I smile, it's genuine; when I express my feelings to you, it's effortless; and when we embrace and make love, it's complete. There isn't any other way to explain it. Maybe that is why I could never say no to you when we were cheating on other people with each other or cheating on each other with other people. I love you Francesca. That's it. There is nothing else to say.

Always yours

Nnabu

PART III

Politics and Social Justice

The first recorded slave revolt in North America occurred in early 1526, when Spanish explorers brought Africans to build a fort in what is now the United States. Revolts became a common feature of slavery, at times encouraged by an eloquent cadre of African Americans who, in letters, speeches, and articles, articulated the plight of their enslaved brethren.

In 1863, the Emancipation Proclamation ushered in an unprecedented experiment in interracial democracy, during which African Americans could turn to electoral politics for racial redress.* From 1863 to 1877, the period known as Reconstruction, some one thousand African Americans served as delegates selected throughout the South to draft new state constitutions. One such delegate was Pinckney B. S. Pinchback of Louisiana, who in short order became president of the state senate, lieutenant governor, and then the nation's first black governor, following the impeachment in 1872 of Gov. Henry Clay Warmoth.

By the end of Reconstruction, nearly seven hundred African Americans had been elected to state legislatures and sixteen to the U.S. Congress, including two, Hiram Revels and Blanche Kelso Bruce, both of Mississippi, to the U.S. Senate.

However, Reconstruction policies were soon undermined by a campaign of terror led by Southern planters, merchants, and Democrats determined to stifle the gains made by newly enfranchised African Americans. The Ku Klux Klan held its first national convention in

*On January 1, 1863, President Abraham Lincoln issued the Emancipation Proclamation, which declared the freedom of slaves in the confederate states but which did not apply to slaves in the border or southern states under Union control. Nearly all slaves were finally emancipated by July 1865.

1867, and by 1871 a congressional investigating committee reported that in South Carolina alone the Klan had murdered 35 men, whipped another 262 men and women, and destroyed the property of 101 African Americans.

By 1873, a national economic depression preoccupied Republicans and weakened support for Reconstruction policies. Southern Democrats flaunted their control of the South by openly advocating violence against African Americans and their sympathizers. In 1877, with the inauguration of President Rutherford B. Hayes, Reconstruction screeched to a halt when, to appease Southern Democrats, he removed federal troops that had protected blacks from acts of terror.

While African Americans' political gains were significantly reversed, their legacy of activism was sustained through churches, schools, civic organizations, and families. A century after Reconstruction, the Civil Rights and Black Power movements effectively dismantled the remaining legal, if not sociocultural, barriers to equal opportunity for African Americans. Beginning in the 1960s, African Americans were elected in large numbers to high office for the first time since Reconstruction.

By the end of the twentieth century, African Americans had served in practically every level of government with the exception of the presidency. There were forty-three blacks in the 110th Congress, which began in January 2007. Among them was Barack Obama, the third African American elected to the U.S. Senate since Reconstruction. In 2008 he was the first African American to win a major party nomination for president, when he defeated former First Lady Hillary Clinton in the Democratic primary. On November 4, 2008, he was elected the forty-fourth president of the United States.

Phillis Wheatley to Rev. Samson Occom

Phillis Wheatley (c. 1753–1784) was born in Gambia (now Senegal) and brought to Boston on a slave ship at the age of seven or eight. Because of chronic illness, she was spared the most extreme hardships of slavery in the home of Susanna and John Wheatley, a prominent Boston merchant. The Wheatleys defied convention by teaching Phillis to read and write not only English but also Latin and Greek. Wheatley published her first poem in 1767 and gained international celebrity in 1773 upon publication of her book Poems on Various Subjects, Religious and Moral. *Wheatley's popularity in the United States and England helped secure her freedom in 1773, but she stayed with the Wheatley family until John's death in 1778, when she married John Peters, a free black Bostonian. Wheatley wrote this letter to her friend Rev. Samson Occom (1723–1792), a Mohegan Indian and ordained Presbyterian minister.*

February 11, 1774

Reverend and honoured Sir,

I have this Day received your obliging kind Epistle, and am greatly satisfied with your Reasons respecting the Negroes, and think highly reasonable what you offer in Vindication of their natural Rights: Those that invade them cannot be insensible that the divine Light is chasing away the thick Darkness which broods over the Land of Africa; and the Chaos which has reign'd so long, is converting into beautiful order, and reveals more and more clearly the glorious Dispensation of civil and religious Liberty, which are so inseparably Limited, that there is little or no Enjoyment of one Without the other: Otherwise, perhaps, the Israelites had been less solicitous for their Freedom from Egyptian slavery; I do not say they would have been contented without it, by no means, for in every human Breast, God has implanted a Principle, which we call Love of freedom; it is impatient of Oppression, and pants for Deliverance; and by the Leave of our modern Egyptians I will assert, that the same Principle lives in us. God grant deliverance in his own Way and Time, and get him honour upon all those whose Avarice impels them to countenance and help forward the Calamities of their fellow Creatures. This I desire not for their Hurt, but to convince them of the strange Absurdity of their Conduct whose Words and Actions are so diametrically opposite. How well the Cry for Liberty, and the reverse Disposition for the exercise of oppressive Power over others agree,—

I humbly think it does not require the Penetration of a Philosopher to determine.—

Benjamin Banneker to Secretary of State Thomas Jefferson

Benjamin Banneker (1731–1806) was born the son of freed parents in Baltimore County, Maryland, and distinguished himself as an amateur astronomer, mathematician, and inventor. In 1791 he was hired by George Ellicott, a local surveyor, and the French engineer Pierre L'Enfant, who were commissioned by President George Washington to survey the area in Virginia and Maryland that was to become the nation's capital. When L'Enfant abandoned the project over a dispute and left with his drafts, Banneker reproduced them from memory. That same year he began publication of his annual almanac, published under the title Benjamin Banneker's Pennsylvania, Delaware, Maryland and Virginia Almanack and Ephemeris. *Banneker sent this letter, along with his first almanac, to then Secretary of State Thomas Jefferson to protest slavery and challenge Jefferson's view that Africans were intellectually inferior to whites.*

[Baltimore County, Maryland]
August 19, 1791

Sir:

I am fully sensible of the greatness of that freedom, which I take with you on the present occasion, a liberty which seemed to me scarcely allowable, when I reflected on that distinguished and dignified station in which you stand, and the almost general prejudice and prepossession which is so prevalent in the world against those of my complexion.

I suppose it is a truth too well attested to you, to need a proof here, that we are a race of beings who have long labored under the abuse and censure of the world, that we have long been considered rather as brutish than human, and scarcely capable of mental endowments.

Sir, I hope I may safely admit, in consequence of that report which hath reached me, that you are a man far less inflexible in sentiments of this nature than many others, that you are measurably friendly and well disposed towards us, and that you are willing and ready to lend your aid and assistance to our relief from those many distresses and numerous calamities, to which we are reduced.

Now, sir, if this is founded in truth, I apprehend you will readily embrace every opportunity to eradicate that train of absurd and false ideas and opinions, which so generally prevails with respect to us, and that your sentiments are concurrent with mine, which are that one universal Father hath given Being to us all, and that he hath not only made us all of one flesh, but that he hath also without partiality afforded us all the same sensations, and endued us all with the same faculties, and that however variable we may be in society or religion, however diversified in situation or color, we are all the same family, and stand in the same relation to him.

Sir, if these are sentiments of which you are fully persuaded, I hope you cannot but acknowledge, that it is the indispensable duty of those who maintain for themselves the rights of human nature, and who profess the obligations of Christianity, to extend their power and influence to the relief of every part of the human race, from whatever burden or oppression they may unjustly labor under, and this I apprehend a full conviction of the truth and obligation of these principles should lead all to.

Sir, I have long been convinced that if your love for yourselves and for those inesteemable laws, which preserved to you the rights of human nature, was founded on sincerity, you could not but be solicitous that every individual of whatever rank or distinction, might with you equally enjoy the blessings thereof; neither could you rest satisfied, short of the most active diffusion of your exertions, in order to their promotion from any state of degradation to which the unjustifiable cruelty and barbarism of men have reduced them.

Sir, I freely and cheerfully acknowledge that I am of the African race, and in that color which is natural to them of the deepest dye; and it is under a sense of the most profound gratitude to the Supreme Ruler of the Universe that I now confess to you, that I am not under that state of tyrannical thraldom, and inhuman captivity, to which too many of my brethren are doomed, but that I have abundantly tasted of the fruition of those blessings, which proceed from that free and un-equalled liberty with which you are favored; and which, I hope, you will willingly allow you have mercifully received, from the immediate hand of that Being, from whom proceedeth every good and perfect Gift.

Sir, suffer me to recall to your mind that time, in which the arms and tyranny of the British crown were exerted, with every powerful ef-fort, in order to reduce you to a state of servitude: look back, I entreat you, on the variety of dangers to which you were exposed; reflect on that time, in which every human aid appeared unavailable, and in which even hope and fortitude wore the aspect of inability to the con-flict, and you cannot but be led to a serious and grateful sense of your miraculous and providential preservation; you cannot but acknowl-edge, that the present freedom and tranquility which you enjoy you have mercifully received, and that it is the peculiar blessing of Heaven.

This, Sir, was a time when you clearly saw into the injustice of a state of slavery, and in which you had just apprehensions of the horrors of its condition. It was now that your abhorrence thereof was so ex-cited, that you publicly held forth this true and invaluable doctrine, which is worthy to be recorded and remembered in all succeeding ages: "We hold these truths to be self-evident, that all men are created equal; that they are endowed by their Creator with certain inalienable rights, and that among these are, life, liberty, and the pursuit of happi-ness." Here was a time, in which your tender feelings for yourselves had engaged you thus to declare, you were then impressed with proper ideas of the great violation of liberty, and the free posession of those blessings, to which you were entitled by nature; but, Sir, how pitiable is it to reflect, that although you were so fully convinced of the benev-olence of the Father of Mankind, and of his equal and impartial distri-bution of these rights and privileges, which he hath conferred upon them, that you should at the same time counteract his mercies, in de-taining by fraud and violence so numerous a part of my brethren, un-der groaning captivity and cruel oppression, that you should at the same time be found guilty of that most criminal act, which you pro-fessedly detested in others, with respect to yourselves.

I suppose that your knowledge of the situation of my brethren is too extensive to need a recital here; neither shall I presume to prescribe methods by which they may be relieved, otherwise than by recommending to you and all others, to wean yourselves from those narrow prejudices which you have imbibed with respect to them, and as Job proposed to his friends, "put your soul in their souls' stead"; thus shall your hearts be enlarged with kindness and benevolence towards them; and thus shall you need neither the direction of myself or others, in what manner to proceed herein.

And now, Sir, I shall conclude, and subscribe myself, with the most profound respect,

Your most obedient humble servant,
Benjamin Banneker

Frederick Douglass to Captain Thomas Auld

Born into slavery in Talbot County, Maryland, Frederick Augustus Washington Bailey changed his name to Frederick Douglass after he escaped from bondage in 1838. Douglass (1817–1895) went on to become the most famous African American of his time, and one of the nineteenth century's most eloquent abolitionists, journalists, and orators, lecturing throughout the United States and Europe. His first autobiography, Narrative of the Life of Frederick Douglass, an American Slave *(1845), was a bestseller and was followed by* My Bondage and My Freedom *(1855) and* Life and Times of Frederick Douglass *(1881). Douglass also published several influential newspapers, most notably the* North Star *(1847–1851);* Frederick Douglass' Paper *(1851–1860); and the* New National Era *(1870–1874). Following the Civil War, Douglass held several important political posts, including president of the Freedmen's Savings Bank, U.S. minister of Haiti, and marshal of the District of Columbia. This letter to his former master was published in the* North Star *and* The Liberator *on September 8, 1848, and September 22, 1848, respectively.*

Rochester
September 3d, 1848

Sir:

The long and intimate, though by no means friendly relation which unhappily subsisted between you and myself, leads me to hope that you will easily account for the great liberty which I now take in addressing you in this open and public manner. The same fact may possibly remove any disagreeable surprise which you may experience on again finding your name coupled with mine, in any other way than in an advertisement, accurately describing my person, and offering a large sum for my arrest. In thus dragging you again before the public, I am aware that I shall subject myself to no inconsiderable amount of censure. I shall probably be charged with an unwarrantable, if not a wanton and reckless disregard of the rights and proprieties of private life. There are those North as well as South who entertain a much higher respect for rights which are merely conventional, than they do for rights which are personal and essential. Not a few there are in our country, who, while they have no scruples against robbing the laborer of the hard earned results of his patient industry, will be shocked by the extremely indelicate manner of bringing your name before the public. Believing this to be the case, and wishing to meet every reasonable or plausible objection to my conduct, I will frankly state the ground upon which I justify myself in this instance, as well as on former occasions when I have thought proper to mention your name in public. All will agree that a man guilty of theft, robbery, or murder, has forfeited the right to concealment and private life; that the community have a right to subject such persons to the most complete exposure. However much they may desire retirement, and aim to conceal themselves and their movements from the popular gaze, the public have a right to ferret them out, and bring their conduct before the proper tribunals of the country for investigation. Sir, you will undoubtedly make the proper application of these generally admitted principles, and will easily see the light in which you are regarded by me. I will not therefore manifest ill temper, by calling you hard names. I know you to be a man of some intelligence, and can readily determine the precise estimate which I entertain of your character. I may therefore indulge in language which may seem to others indirect and ambiguous, and yet be quite well understood by yourself.

I have selected this day on which to address you, because it is the anniversary of my emancipation; and knowing of no better way, I am led to this as the best mode of celebrating that truly important event. Just ten years ago this beautiful September morning, yon bright sun beheld me a slave—a poor, degraded chattel—trembling at the sound of your voice, lamenting that I was a man, and wishing myself a brute. The hopes, which I had treasured up for weeks of a safe and successful escape from your grasp, were powerfully confronted at this last hour by dark clouds of doubt and fear, making my person shake and my bosom to heave with the heavy contest between hope and fear. I have no words to describe to you the deep agony of soul which I experienced on that never to be forgotten morning—(for I left by daylight). I was making a leap in the dark. The probabilities, so far as I could by reason determine them, were stoutly against the undertaking. The preliminaries and precautions I had adopted previously, all worked badly. I was like one going to war without weapons—ten chances of defeat to one of victory. One in whom I had confided, and one who had promised me assistance, appalled by fear at the trial hour, deserted me, thus leaving the responsibility of success or failure solely with myself. You, sir, can never know my feelings. As I look back to them, I can scarcely realize that I have passed through a scene so trying. Trying however as they were, and gloomy as was the prospect, thanks be to the Most High, who is ever the God of the oppressed, at the moment which was to determine my whole earthly career. His grace was sufficient, my mind was made up. I embraced the golden opportunity, took the morning tide at the flood, and a free man, young, active and strong, is the result.

I have often thought I should like to explain to you the grounds upon which I have justified myself in running away from you. I am almost ashamed to do so now, for by this time you may have discovered them yourself. I will, however, glance at them. When yet but a child about six years old, I imbibed the determination to run away. The very first mental effort that I now remember on my part, was an attempt to solve the mystery, Why am I a slave? and with this question my youthful mind was troubled for many days, pressing upon me more heavily at times than others. When I saw the slave-driver whip a slave woman, cut the blood out of her neck, and heard her piteous cries, I went away into the corner of the fence, wept and pondered over the mystery. I had, through some medium, I know not what, got some idea of God, the Creator of all mankind, the black and the white, and that he had made the blacks to serve the whites as slaves. How he could do this and be good, I could not tell. I was not satisfied with this theory, which made God responsible for slavery, for it pained me greatly, and I have wept over it long and often. At one time, your first wife, Mrs. Lucretia, heard me singing and saw me shedding tears, and asked of me the matter, but I was afraid to tell her. I was puzzled with this question, till one night, while sitting in the kitchen, I heard some of the old slaves talking of their parents having been stolen from Africa by white men, and were sold here as slaves. The whole mystery was solved at once. Very soon after this my aunt Jinny and uncle Noah ran away, and the great noise made about it by your father-in-law, made me for the first time acquainted with the fact, that there were free States as well as slave States. From that time, I resolved that I would some day run away. The morality of the act, I dispose as follows: I am myself; you are yourself; we are two distinct persons, equal persons. What you are, I am. You are a man, and so am I. God created both, and made us separate beings. I am not by nature bound to you, or you to me. Nature does not make your existence depend upon me, or mine to depend upon yours. I cannot walk upon your legs, or you upon mine. I cannot breathe for you, or you for me; I must breathe for myself, and you for yourself. We are distinct persons, and are each equally provided with faculties necessary to our individual existence. In leaving you, I took nothing but what belonged to me, and in no way lessened your means for obtaining an honest living. Your faculties remained yours, and mine became useful to their rightful owner. I therefore see no wrong in any part of the transaction. It is true, I went off secretly, but that was more your fault than mine. Had I let you into the secret, you would have defeated the enterprise entirely; but for this, I should have been really glad to have made you acquainted with my intentions to leave.

You may perhaps want to know how I like my present condition. I am free to say, I greatly prefer it to that which I occupied in Maryland. I am, however, by no means prejudiced against the State as such. Its geography, climate, fertility and products, are such as to make it a very desirable abode for any man; and but for the existence of slavery there, it is not impossible that I might again take up my abode in that State. It is not that I love Maryland less, but freedom more. You will be surprised to learn that people at the North labor under the strange delusion that if the slaves were emancipated at the South, they would flock to the North. So far from this being the case, in that event, you would see many old and familiar faces back again to the South. The fact is, there are few here who would not return to the South in the event of emancipation. We want to live in the land of our birth, and to lay our bones by the side of our fathers'; and nothing short of an intense love of personal freedom keeps us from the South. For the sake of this, most of us would live on a crust of bread and a cup of cold water.

Since I left you, I have had a rich experience. I have occupied stations which I never dreamed of when a slave. Three out of the ten years since I left you, I spent as a common laborer on the wharves of New Bedford, Massachusetts. It was there I earned my first free dollar. It was mine. I could spend it as I pleased. I could buy hams or herring with it, without asking any odds of any body. That was a precious dollar to me. You remember when I used to make seven or eight, or even nine dollars a week in Baltimore, you would take every cent of it from me every Saturday night, saying that I belonged to you, and my earnings also. I never liked this conduct on your part—to say the best, I thought it a little mean. I would not have served you so. But let that pass. I was a little awkward about counting money in New England fashion when I first landed in New Bedford. I like to have betrayed myself several times. I caught myself saying phip, for fourpence; and at one time a man actually charged me with being a runaway, whereupon I was silly enough to become one by running away from him, for I was greatly afraid he might adopt measures to get me again into slavery, a condition I then dreaded more than death.

I soon, however, learned to count money, as well as to make it, and got on swimmingly. I married soon after leaving you: in fact, I was engaged to be married before I left you; and instead of finding my companion a burden, she was truly a helpmeet. She went to live at service, and I to work on the wharf, and though we toiled hard the first winter, we never lived more happily. After remaining in New Bedford for three years, I met with Wm. Lloyd Garrison, a person of whom you have possibly heard, as he is pretty generally known among slaveholders.* He put it into my head that I might make myself serviceable to the cause of the slave by devoting a portion of my time to telling my own sorrows, and those of other slaves which had come under my observation. This was the commencement of a higher state of existence than any to which I had ever aspired. I was thrown into society the most pure, enlightened and benevolent that the country affords. Among these I have never forgotten you, but have invariably made you the topic of conversation—thus giving you all the notoriety I could do. I need not tell you that the opinion formed of you in these circles, is far from being favorable. They have little respect for your honesty, and less for your religion.

But I was going on to relate to you something of my interesting experience. I had not long enjoyed the excellent society to which I have referred, before the light of its excellence exerted a beneficial influ-

*William Lloyd Garrison (1805–1879) was a journalist and abolitionist made famous for *The Liberator*, an abolitionist newspaper he published weekly in Boston from 1831 until 1866, when ratification of the 13th Amendment abolished slavery. Garrison, born in Newburyport, Massachusetts, also helped organize the Anti-Slavery Society.

ence on my mind and heart. Much of my early dislike of white persons was removed, and their manners, habits and customs, so entirely unlike what I had been used to in the kitchen-quarters on the plantations of the South, fairly charmed me, and gave me a strong disrelish for the coarse and degrading customs of my former condition. I therefore made an effort so to improve my mind and deportment, as to be somewhat fitted to the station to which I seemed almost providentially called. The transition from degradation to respectability was indeed great, and to get from one to the other without carrying some marks of one's former condition, is truly a difficult matter. I would not have you think that I am now entirely clear of all plantation peculiarities, but my friends here, while they entertain the strongest dislike to them, regard me with that charity to which my past life somewhat entitles me, so that my condition in this respect is exceedingly pleasant. So far as my domestic affairs are concerned, I can boast of as comfortable a dwelling as your own. I have an industrious and neat companion, and four dear children—the oldest a girl of nine years, and three fine boys, the oldest eight, the next six, and the youngest four years old. The three oldest are now going regularly to school—two can read and write, and the other can spell with tolerable correctness words of two syllables: Dear fellows! they are all in comfortable beds, and are sound asleep, perfectly secure under my own roof. There are no slaveholders here to rend my heart by snatching them from my arms, or blast a mother's dearest hopes by tearing them from her bosom. These dear children are ours—not to work up into rice, sugar and tobacco, but to watch over, regard, and protect, and to rear them up in the nurture and admonition of the gospel—to train them up in the paths of wisdom and virtue, and, as far as we can to make them useful to the world and to themselves. Oh! sir, a slaveholder never appears to me so completely an agent of hell, as when I think of and look upon my dear children. It is then that my feelings rise above my control. I meant to have said more with respect to my own prosperity and happiness, but thoughts and feelings which this recital has quickened unfits me to proceed further in that direction. The grim horrors of slavery rise in all their ghastly terror before me, the wails of millions pierce my heart, and chill my blood. I remember the chain, the gag, the bloody whip, the deathlike gloom overshadowing the broken spirit of the fettered bondman, the appalling liability of his being torn away from wife and children, and sold like a beast in the market. Say not that this is a picture of fancy. You well know that I wear stripes on my back inflicted by your direction; and that you, while we were brothers in the same church, caused this right hand, with which I am now penning this letter, to be closely tied to my left, and my person dragged at the pistol's mouth, fifteen miles, from the Bay side to Easton to be sold like a beast in the market, for the alleged crime of intending to escape from your possession. All this and more you remember, and know to be perfectly true, not only of yourself, but of nearly all of the slaveholders around you.

At this moment, you are probably the guilty holder of at least three of my own dear sisters, and my only brother in bondage. These you regard as your property. They are recorded on your ledger, or perhaps have been sold to human flesh mongers, with a view to filling your own ever-hungry purse. Sir, I desire to know how and where these dear sisters are. Have you sold them? or are they still in your possession? What has become of them? are they living or dead? And my dear old grandmother, whom you turned out like an old horse, to die in the woods—is she still alive?* Write and let me know all about them. If my grandmother be still alive, she is of no service to you, for by this time she must be nearly eighty years old—too old to be cared for by one to whom she has ceased to be of service, send her to me at Rochester, or bring her to Philadelphia, and it shall be the crowning happiness of my life to take care of her in her old age. Oh! she was to me a mother, and a father, so far as hard toil for my comfort could make her such. Send me my grandmother! that I may watch over and take care of her in her old age. And my sisters, let me know all about them. I would write to them, and learn all I want to know of them, without disturbing you in any way, but that, through your unrighteous conduct, they have been entirely deprived of the power to read and write. You have kept them in utter ignorance, and have therefore robbed them of the sweet enjoyments of writing or receiving letters from absent friends and relatives. Your wickedness and cruelty committed in this respect on your fellow-creatures, are greater than all the stripes you have laid upon my back, or theirs. It is an outrage upon the soul—a war upon the immortal spirit, and one for which you must give account at the bar of our common Father and Creator.

The responsibility which you have assumed in this regard is truly

*In a letter to Auld written a year later, Douglass corrects the record and acknowledges that he learned that Auld had not abandoned his grandmother but had kept her until her death.

awful—and how you could stagger under it these many years is marvel-lous. Your mind must have become darkened, your heart hardened, your conscience seared and petrified, or you would have long since thrown off the accursed load and sought relief at the hands of a sin-forgiving God. How, let me ask, would you look upon me, were I some dark night in company with a band of hardened villains, to enter the precincts of your elegant dwelling and seize the person of your own lovely daughter Amanda, and carry her off from your family, friends and all the loved ones of her youth—make her my slave—compel her to work, and I take her wages—place her name on my ledger as prop-erty—disregard her personal rights—fetter the powers of her immortal soul by denying her the right and privilege of learning to read and write—feed her coarsely—clothe her scantily, and whip her on the naked back occasionally; more and still more horrible, leave her unpro-tected—a degraded victim to the brutal lust of fiendish overseers, who would pollute, blight, and blast her fair soul—rob her of all dignity— destroy her virtue, and annihilate all in her person the graces that adorn the character of virtuous womanhood? I ask how would you regard me, if such were my conduct? Oh! the vocabulary of the damned would not afford a word sufficiently infernal, to express your idea of my God-provoking wickedness. Yet sir, your treatment of my beloved sisters is in all essential points, precisely like the case I have now supposed. Damning as would be such a deed on my part, it would be no more so than that which you have committed against me and my sisters.

I will now bring this letter to a close, you shall hear from me again unless you let me hear from you. I intend to make use of you as a weapon with which to assail the system of slavery—as a means of con-centrating public attention on the system, and deepening their horror of trafficking in the souls and bodies of men. I shall make use of you as a means of exposing the character of the American church and clergy—and as a means of bringing this guilty nation with yourself to repentance. In doing this I entertain no malice towards you personally. There is no roof under which you would be more safe than mine, and there is nothing in my house which you might need for your comfort, which I would not readily grant. Indeed, I should esteem it a privilege, to set you an example as to how mankind ought to treat each other. I am your fellow man, but not your slave,
     Frederick Douglass

Fugitive Slaves to Enslaved Brethren

This letter, published in the North Star *on November 5, 1850, reprinted in several other papers, and read in Congress, was adopted at a gathering known as the Fugitive Slave Convention in Cazenovia, New York, on August 21–22, 1850. More than two thousand people—among them Frederick Douglass and some fifty fugitive slaves—attended the meeting to galvanize opposition to the Fugitive Slave Act, proposed federal legislation that mandated the capture and return of fugitive slaves, even those found in the North, where slavery was illegal. It also imposed stiff penalties for harboring a fugitive slave. The controversial measure was passed by Congress on September 18, 1850, and helped energize the abolitionist movement and the Underground Railroad.*

Afflicted and Beloved Brothers:

The meeting which sends you this letter, is a meeting of runaway slaves. We thought it well, that they, who had once suffered, as you still suffer, that they, who had once drunk of that bitterest of all bitter cups, which you are still compelled to drink of, should come together for the purpose of making a communication to you.

The chief object of this meeting is, to tell you what circumstances we find ourselves in—that, so you may be able to judge for yourselves, whether the prize we have obtained is worth the peril of the attempt to obtain it.

The heartless pirates, who compelled us to call them "master," sought to persuade us, as such pirates seek to persuade you, that the condition of those, who escape from their clutches, is thereby made worse, instead of better. We confess, that we had our fears, that this might be so. Indeed, so great was our ignorance that we could not be sure that the abolitionists were not the friends, which our masters represented them to be. When they told us, that the abolitionists, could they lay hands upon us would buy and sell us, we could not certainly know, that they spoke falsely; and when they told us, that abolitionists are in the habit of skinning the black man for leather, and of regaling their cannibalism on his flesh, even such enormities seemed to us to be possible. But owing to the happy change in our circumstances, we are not as ignorant and credulous now, as we once were; and if we did not know it before, we know it now, that slaveholders are as great liars, as they are great tyrants.

The abolitionists act the part of friends and brothers to us; and our

only complaint against them is, that there are so few of them. The abolitionists, on whom it is safe to rely, are, almost all of them, members
of the American Anti-Slavery Society, or of the Liberty Party. There are
other abolitionists: but most of them are grossly inconsistent; and,
hence, not entirely trustworthy abolitionists. So inconsistent are they,
as to vote for anti-abolitionists for civil rulers, and to acknowledge the
obligation of laws, which they themselves interpret to be pro-slavery.

We get wages for our labor. We have schools for our children. We
have opportunities to hear and to learn to read the Bible—that blessed
book, which is all for freedom, notwithstanding the lying slaveholders
who say it is all for slavery. Some of us take part in the election of civil
rulers. Indeed, but for the priests and politicians, the influence of most
of whom is against us, our condition would be every way eligible. The
priests and churches of the North, are, with comparatively few exceptions, in league with the priests and churches of the South; and this, of
itself, is sufficient to account for the fact, that a caste-religion and a
Negro-pew are found at the North, as well as at the South. The politicians and political parties of the North are connected with the politicians and political parties of the South; and hence, the political
arrangements and interests of the North, as well as the ecclesiastical
arrangements and interests, are adverse to the colored population. But,
we rejoice to know, that all this political and ecclesiastical power is on
the wane. The callousness of American religion and American democracy has become glaring: and, every year, multitudes, once deluded by
them, come to repudiate them. The credit of this repudiation is due, in
a great measure, to the American Anti-Slavery Society, to the Liberty
Party, and to antisectarian meetings, and conventions. The purest sect
on earth is the rival of, instead of one with, Christianity. It deserves not
to be trusted with a deep and honest and earnest reform. The tempta-
tions which beset the pathway of such a reform, are too mighty for it to
resist. Instead of going forward for God, it will slant off for itself. Heaven
grant, that, soon, not a shred of sectarianism, not a shred of the current
religion, not a shred of the current politics of this land, may remain.
Then will follow, aye, that will itself be, the triumph of Christianity:
and, then, white men will love black men and gladly acknowledge that
all men have equal rights. Come, blessed day—come quickly.

Including our children, we number in Canada, at least, twenty
thousand. The total of our population in the free States far exceeds
this. Nevertheless, we are poor, we can do little more to promote your

deliverance than pray for it to the God of the oppressed. We will do what we can to supply you with pocket compasses. In dark nights, when his good guiding star is hidden from the flying slave, a pocket compass greatly facilitates his exodus. Candor requires the admission, that some of us would not furnish them, if we could; for some of us have become nonresistants, and have discarded the use of these weapons: and would say to you: "love your enemies; do good to them, which hate you; bless them that curse you; and pray for them, which despitefully use you." Such of us would be glad to be able to say, that all the colored men of the North are nonresistants. But, in point of fact, it is only a handful of them, who are. When the insurrection of the Southern slaves shall take place, as take place it will unless speedily prevented by voluntary emancipation, the great majority of the colored men of the North, however much to the grief of any of us, will be found by your side, with deep-stored and long-accumulated revenge in their hearts, and with death-dealing weapons in their hands. It is not to be disguised, that a colored man is as much disposed, as a white man, to resist, even unto death, those who oppress him. The colored American, for the sake of relieving his colored brethren, would no more hesitate to shoot an American slaveholder, than would a white American, for the sake of delivering his white brother, hesitate to shoot an Algerine slaveholder. The State motto of Virginia: "Death to Tyrants"; is as well the black man's, as the white man's motto. We tell you these things not to encourage, or justify, your resort to physical force; but, simply, that you may know, be it to your joy or sorrow to know it, what your Northern colored brethren are, in these important respects. This truth you are entitled to know, however the knowledge of it may affect you, and however you may act, in view of it.

We have said, that some of us are nonresistants. But, while such would dissuade you from all violence toward the slaveholder, let it not be supposed, that they regard it as guiltier than those strifes, which even good men are wont to justify. If the American revolutionists had excuse for shedding but one drop of blood, then have the American slaves excuse for making blood to flow "even unto the horse-bridles."*

Numerous as are the escapes from slavery, they would be far more so, were you not embarrassed by your misinterpretations of the rights of property. You hesitate to take even the dullest of your master's

---

*This is a reference to a passage in Revelation 14:20 in the King James Bible.

horses—whereas it is your duty to take the fleetest. Your consciences suggest doubts, whether in quitting your bondage, you are at liberty to put in your packs what you need of food and clothing. But were you better informed, you would not scruple to break your master's locks, and take all their money. You are taught to respect the rights of property. But, no such right belongs to the slaveholder. His right to property is but the robber-right. In every slaveholding community, the rights of property all center in them, whose coerced and unrequited toil has created the wealth in which their oppressors riot. Moreover, if your oppressors have rights of property, you, at least, are exempt from all obligations to respect them. For you are prisoners of war, in an enemy's country—of a war, too, that is unrivalled for its injustice, cruelty, meanness—and therefore, by all the rules of war, you have the fullest liberty to plunder, burn, and kill, as you may have occasion to do to promote your escape.

We regret to be obliged to say to you, that it is not everyone of the Free States, which offers you an asylum. Even within the last year, fugitive slaves have been arrested in some of the Free States, and re-plunged into slavery. But, make your way to New York or New England, and you will be safe. It is true, that even in New York and New England, there are individuals, who would rejoice to see the poor flying slave cast back into the horrors of slavery. But, even these are restrained by public sentiment. It is questionable whether even Daniel Webster, or Moses Stuart, would give chase to a fugitive slave; and if they would not, who would?—for the one is chief-politician and the other chief-priest.

We do not forget the industrious efforts, which are now in making to get new facilities at the hands of Congress for re-enslaving those, who have escaped from slavery. But we can assure you, that as to the State of New York and the New England States, such efforts must prove fruitless. Against all such devilism—against all kidnappers—the colored people of these States will "stand for their life," and, what is more, the white people of these States will not stand against them. A regenerated public sentiment has, forever, removed these States beyond the limits of the slaveholders' hunting ground. Defeat—disgrace—and, it may be, death—will be their only reward for pursuing their prey into this abolitionized portion of our country.

A special reason why you should not stop in that part of the Nation which comes within the bounds of John McLean's judicial district, is, that he is a great man in one of the religious sects, and an aspirant for the Presidency.* Fugitive slaves and their friends fare hard in the hands of this judge. He not only puts a pro-slavery construction on the Federal Constitution, and holds, that law can make property of man— a marketable commodity of the image of God, but, in various other ways, he shows that his sympathies are with the oppressor. Shun Judge McLean, then, even as you would the Reverend Moses Stuart. The law of the one is as deadly an enemy to you, as is the religion of the other.

There are three points in your conduct, when you shall have become inhabitants of the North, on which we cannot refrain from admonishing you.

1st. If you will join a sectarian church, let it not be one which approves of the Negro-pew, and which refuses to treat slaveholding as a high crime against God and man. It were better, that you sacrifice your lives than that by going into the Negro-pew, you invade your self-respect—debase your souls—play the traitor to your race—and crucify afresh Him who died for the one brotherhood of man.

2d. Join no political party, which refuses to commit itself fully, openly, and heartfully, in its newspapers, meetings, and nominations, to the doctrine, that slavery is the grossest of all absurdities, as well as the guiltiest of all abominations, and that there can no more be a law for the enslavement of man, made in the image of God, than for the enslavement of God himself. Vote for no man for civil office, who makes your complexion a bar to political, ecclesiastic or social equality. Better die than insult yourself and insult our social equality. Better die than insult yourself and insult every person of African blood, and insult your Maker, by contributing to elevate to civil office he who refuses to eat with you, to sit by your side in the House of Worship, or to let his children sit in the school by the side of your children.

3d. Send not your children to the school which the malignant and murderous prejudice of white people has gotten up exclusively for colored people. Valuable as learning is, it is too costly, if it is acquired at the expense of such self-degradation.

*John McLean (1785–1861) was born in Morris County, New Jersey, and eventually relocated to Ohio, where in 1812 he was elected to the U.S. Congress. He served in Congress until 1816 when he was elected to the Supreme Court of Ohio. He served until 1822 and in 1829 was appointed associate justice of the U.S. Supreme Court by President Jackson. In 1836 McLean was endorsed by the Ohio legislature as a candidate for president. In 1848 he unsuccessfully sought the 1848 Whig Party nomination.

The self-sacrificing, and heroic, and martyr-spirit, which would impel the colored men of the North to turn their backs on pro-slavery churches and pro-slavery politics, and pro-slavery schools, would exert a far mightier influence against slavery, than could all their learning, however great, if purchased by concessions of their manhood, and surrenders of their rights, and coupled, as it then would be, by characteristic meanness and servility.

And now, brethren, we close this letter with assuring you, that we do not, cannot, forget you. You are ever in our minds, our hearts, our prayers. Perhaps, you are fearing, that the free colored people of the United States will suffer themselves to be carried away from you by the American Colonization Society. Fear it not. In vain is it, that this greatest and most malignant enemy of the African race is now busy in devising new plans, and in seeking the aid of Government, to perpetuate your enslavement. It wants us away from your side, that you may be kept in ignorance. But we will remain by your side to enlighten you. It wants us away from your side, that you may be contented. But we will remain by your side, to keep you, and make you more, discontented. It wants us away from your side to the end, that your unsuccored and conscious helplessness may make you the easier and surer prey of your oppressors. But we will remain by your side to sympathize with you, and cheer you, and give you the help of our rapidly swelling membership. The land of our enslaved brethren is our land, and death alone shall part us.

We cannot forget you, brethren, for we know your sufferings and we know your sufferings because we know from experience, what it is to be an American slave. So galling was our bondage, that, to escape from it, we suffered the loss of all things, and braved every peril, and endured every hardship. Some of us left parents, some wives, some children. Some of us were wounded with guns and dogs, as we fled. Some of us, to make good our escape, suffered ourselves to be nailed up in boxes, and to pass for merchandise. Some of us secreted ourselves in the suffocating holds of ships. Nothing was so dreadful to us, as slavery; and hence, it is almost literally true, that we dreaded nothing, which could befall us, in our attempt to get clear of it. Our condition could be made no worse, for we were already in the lowest depths of earthly woe. Even should we be overtaken, and resubjected to slavery, this would be but to return to our old sufferings and sorrows and should death itself prove to be the price of our endeavor after freedom, what would that be but a welcome release to men, who had, all their lifetime, been killed every day, and "killed all the day long."

We have referred to our perils and hardships in escaping from slavery. We are happy to be able to say, that every year is multiplying the facilities for leaving the Southern prison house. The Liberty Party, the Vigilance Committee of New York,* individuals, and companies of individuals in various parts of the country, are doing all they can, and it is much to afford you a safe and a cheap passage from slavery to liberty. They do this however, not only at great expense of property, but at great peril of liberty and life. Thousands of you have heard, ere this, that, within the last fortnight, the precious name of William L. Chaplin has been added to the list of those, who, in helping you gain your liberty, have lost their own.† Here is a man, whose wisdom, cultivation, moral worth, bring him into the highest and best class of men—and, yet, he becomes a willing martyr for the poor, despised, forgotten slave's sake. Your remembrance of one such fact is enough to shed light and hope upon your darkest and most desponding moments.

Brethren, our last word to you is to bid you be of good cheer, and not to despair of your deliverance. Do not abandon yourselves, as have many thousands of American slaves, to the crime of suicide. Live! live to escape from slavery, live to serve God! Live till He shall Himself call you into eternity! Be prayerful—be brave—be hopeful. "Lift up your heads, for your redemption draweth nigh."

Annie Davis to President Abraham Lincoln

An enslaved woman who hoped to reunite with her family wrote this letter to President Lincoln to ask if African Americans had in fact been emancipated a year after he issued the Emancipation Proclamation. The historic presidential proclamation freed all enslaved African Americans except those

*The New York City Committee of Vigilance was formed to protect blacks from kidnappers who sought to return them to Southern slavery. David Ruggles (1810–1849) was its secretary.
†In August 1850, William L. Chaplin was among those arrested by Washington police for conspiring in the escape of two Maryland slaves. Chaplin was kept in jail in Rockville, Maryland, until December and was indicted in the District of Columbia on a charge of assault with intent to kill, and in Maryland on three counts of assault with intent to murder, two counts of assisting slaves to escape, and two counts of larceny of slaves. Bail was set at $6,000 in the District and $19,000 in Maryland. During the meeting of the fugitive slaves, it was recommended that Chaplin be nominated for President of the United States. Supporters raised the money to free Chaplin from jail.

in states that were in rebellion and in four Southern states captured by the Union. It was not until 1865 that the Thirteenth Amendment officially abolished slavery in the United States.

Belair, Maryland

August 25, 1864

Mr. president   It is my Desire to be free to go to see my people on the eastern shore my mistress wont let me   you will please let me know if we are free   and what I can do   I write to you for advice. Please send me word this week   or as soon as possible and oblidge.

    Annie Davis

Sojourner Truth to Rowland Johnson

Sojourner Truth (c. 1797–1883), the abolitionist, women's activist, and Pentecostal preacher, was born into slavery in Swartekill, New York, as Isabella Bomefree. She escaped to New York City and changed her name to Sojourner Truth when slavery was outlawed there in 1827. Truth, who dictated letters because she never learned to read or write, was a commanding orator who lectured widely. In this letter to Rowland Johnson (1816–1886), an early supporter of abolition who had led the antislavery party in New York, she provides a detailed account of her meeting with President Lincoln. At the time Truth worked in Washington, D.C., for the National Freedmen's Relief Association.

Freedman's Village, Va.

Nov. 17, 1864

Dear Friend:—

    I am at Freedman's Village. After visiting the President, I spent three weeks at Mrs. Swisshelm's, and held two meetings in Washington, at Rev. Mr. Garnet's Presbyterian Church, for the benefit of the Colored Soldiers' Aid Society. These meetings were successful in raising funds. One week after that I went to mason's Island, and saw the Freedman there, and held several meetings, remained a week and was present at the celebration of the Emancipation of the slaves at Maryland, and spoke on that occasion.

    It was 8 o'clock a.m., when I called on the President. Upon entering his reception room we found about a dozen persons in waiting, among them two colored women. I had quite a pleasant time waiting until he was disengaged, and enjoyed his conversation with others; he showed as much kindness and consideration to the colored persons as to the whites—if there was any difference, more. One case was that of a colored woman, who was sick and likely to be turned out of her house on account of her inability to pay her rent. The President listened to her with much attention, and spoke to her with kindness and tenderness. He said he had given so much he could give no more, but told her where to go and get the money, and asked Mrs. C——n to assist her, which she did.

The President was seated at his desk. Mrs. C. said to him, "This is Sojourner Truth, who has come all the way from Michigan to see you." He then arose, gave me his hand, made a bow, and said, "I am pleased to see you."

I said to him, "Mr. President, when you first took your seat I feared you would be torn to pieces, for I likened you unto Daniel, who was thrown in the lions' den; and if the lions did not tear you into pieces, I knew that it would be God that had saved you; and I said if He spared me I would see you before the four years expired, and he has done so, and now I am here to see you for myself."

He then congratulated me on my having been spared. Then I said: "I appreciate you, for you are the best President who has ever taken the seat." He replied thus: "I expect you have reference to my having emancipated the slaves in my proclamation. But," said he, mentioning the names of several of his predecessors (and among them emphatically that of Washington), "they were all just as good, and would have done just as I have done if the time had come. If the people over the river (pointing across the Potamac) had behaved themselves, I could not have done what I have; but they did not, which gave me the opportunity to do these things." I then said: "I thank God that you were the instrument selected by him and the people to do it." I told him that I had never heard of him before he was talked of for President. He smilingly replied, "I had heard of you many times before that."

He then showed me the Bible presented to him by the colored people of Baltimore, of which you have no doubt seen a description. I have seen it for myself, and it is beautiful beyond description. After I had looked it over, I said to him: "This is beautiful indeed; the colored people have given this to the Head of the government, and that government once sanctioned laws that would not permit its people to learn enough to enable them to read this Book. And for what? Let them answer who can."

I must say, and I am proud to say, that I never was treated by any one with more kindness and cordiality than were shown to me by that great and good man, Abraham Lincoln, by the grace of God President of the United States for four years more. He took my little book, and with the same hand that signed the death warrant of slavery, he wrote as follows:

"For Aunty Sojourner Truth,
Oct. 29, 1864.
A. Lincoln."

As I was taking my leave, he arose and took my hand, and said he would be pleased to have me call again. I felt that I was in the presence of a friend, and I now thank God from the bottom of my heart that I always have advocated his cause, and have done it openly and boldly. I shall feel still more in duty bound to do so in time to come. May God assist me.

Now I must tell you something of this place. I found things quite as well as I expected. I think I can be useful and will stay. The Captain in command of the guard has given me his assistance, and by his aid I have obtained a little house, and will move into it to-morrow. Will you please ask Mrs. P., or any of my friends, to send me a couple of sheets and a pillow? I find many of the women very ignorant in relation to house-keeping, as most of them were instructed in field labor, but not in household duties. They all seem to think a great deal of me, and want to learn the way we live in the North. I am listened to with attention and respect, and from all things I judge it is the will of both God and the people that I should remain.

Now when you come to Washington, don't forget to call and see me. You may publish my whereabouts, and anything in this letter you think would interest the friends of Freedom, Justice and Truth, in the *Standard* and *Anglo-African*, and any other paper you may see fit.

Enclosed please find four shadows (carte de visites).* The two dollars came safely. Anything in the way of nourishment you may feel like

*Commonly abbreviated as CDV, the photographs mounted on cards were popular in the mid-1800s.

sending, send it along. The captain sends to Washington every day. Give my love to all who inquire for me, and tell my friends to direct all things for me to the care of Capt. George B. Carse, Freedman's Village, Va. Ask Mr. Oliver Johnson to please send me the *Standard* while I am here, as many of the colored people like to hear what is going on, and to know what is being done for them. Sammy, my grandson, reads for them. We are both well, and happy, and feel that we are in good employment. I find plenty of friends

    Your friend,

      Sojourner Truth

Frederick Douglass to Readers

This letter, published in the New National Era *on June 13, 1872, was written after the abolitionist's Rochester, New York, home was burned to the ground by arsonists. A year before the fire, the Ku Klux Klan Act, passed by Congress to protect freedmen from terrorism, expired. After the fire, Douglass moved his wife and family to Washington, D.C., where he remained until his death in 1895 at the age of seventy-seven.*

LETTER FROM THE EDITOR

[Rochester, New York]

June 13, 1872

Dear Readers:

    I am here among the ashes of my old home in Rochester, New York. As soon as I learned of the fire I hurried here from Washington, and have been here ever since. A summons home to find one's house in ashes is almost like going home to a funeral, and though only sadness greets one at the end of the journey no speed is too great to bring him there. The house destroyed had been my home during more than twenty years; and twenty years of industry and economy had there brought together many things valuable in themselves, and rendered more valuable by association. Several questions are naturally suggested by every fire; First, How did it happen? How was it extinguished? What was saved? What was lost? What was damaged? I do not mean to answer these questions in detail, nor to indulge in sentimental description. The fire was doubtless the work of an incendiary. It began in a barn well filled with hay on the south side of the house, and was first seen at midnight, when the family of my son-in-law (who occupied the dwelling) had been in bed two hours. No fire or light had been carried into the barn by any of the family for months. What could be the motive? Was it for plunder, or was it for spite, or was it mere wanton wickedness on the part of persons of the baser sort, who wander on the outskirts of cities by starlight at late hours? I do not know and I cannot guess. One thing I do know and that is, while Rochester is among the most liberal of Northern cities, and its people are among the most humane and highly civilized, it nevertheless has its full share of that Ku Klux spirit which makes anything owned by a colored man a little less respected and secure than when owned by a white citizen. I arrived in Rochester at one o'clock in the night in the thick darkness and drenching rain, and not knowing where my family might be, I applied for shelter at two of the nearest hotels and was at first refused by both, with the convenient excuse that "We are full," till it was known that my name was Frederick Douglass, when a room was readily offered me. Though the house was full! I did not accept, but made my way to the police headquarters to learn if possible where I might find the scattered members of my family. Such treatment as this does not tend to make a man secure either in his person or property. The spirit which would deny a man shelter in a public house, needs but little change to deny him shelter even in his own house. It is the spirit of hate, the spirit of murder, the spirit which would burn a family in their beds. I may be wrong, but I fear that that the sentiment which repelled me at Congress Hall burnt my house.

The fire did its work quick and with marked thoroughness and success. Scarcely a trace of the building, except brick walls and stone foundations, is left, and the trees surrounding the building, planted by my own hands and of more than twenty years' growth were not spared, but were scorched and charred beyond recovery. Much was saved in the way of furniture and much was lost, and much was damaged. Eleven thousand dollars worth of government securities (of which I have fortunately the numbers), were destroyed. Sixteen volumes of my old papers the *North Star* and *Frederick Douglass Paper*, were destroyed; a piano worth five hundred dollars was saved, but much damaged, the same with three sofas, and many mahogany chairs, and other furniture. My loss, not covered with insurance, will reach from four to five thousand dollars. Every effort possible was made by the police and fire department to save property, and the neighbors (all white) did everything in their power to afford relief to the shelterless family. Assured of the sympathy of my readers in this calamity, I have felt at liberty to make this brief statement, as an apology for absence from my post of public duty, which after all will not be long.

Frederick Douglass

Whitefield McKinlay to Booker T. Washington

Whitefield McKinlay (1857–1941), a prosperous real estate broker in Washington, D.C., was a confidant of Booker T. Washington, who, following the death of Frederick Douglass, became the nation's most prominent African American and a major dispenser of political patronage as an adviser to Presidents William McKinley and Theodore Roosevelt. The latter triggered the outrage of Southern whites when he invited Washington to the White House for dinner in October 1901. Washington regularly consulted McKinlay regarding the political appointments of African Americans to positions in state and federal government.*

Washington, D.C.
November 1, 1901

My Dear Mr. Washington:—

Since your last kind favor I have thought not a little, and seriously too, in regard to the appointments we discussed, and since our interview with the Attorney General, I firmly believe that the best possible course to pursue would be for you to make this matter a personal one with the President. I am afraid without such action on your part the Attorney General might allow political considerations to influence him in appointing someone whose character and standing would defeat the object we hold most dear. I am thoroughly convinced that if the President in this matter could be reached and made to understand the very great importance of appointing only men qualified morally as well as intellectually, he would all the more appreciate our unselfish advice. You must throw off all reserve and go into this matter with the determination to win, and the only way we can accomplish this is to be aggressive from the beginning. The very mention of that unsavory character (Jones) by the Attorney General makes me tremble at the thought that

---

*On October 16, 1901, the *Memphis Scimitar* called the visit "the most damnable outrage which has ever been perpetrated by any citizen of the United States." Senator Benjamin R. Tillman of South Carolina declared that, as a result of the episode, "a thousand niggers in the South would have to be killed to teach them 'their place again.'"

he might make the mistake of appointing such a man. We have suffered already too much in the past to take any chances in the future on such appointments. I am selfish to the extent only as you are in accomplishing such results as will reflect our last credit upon the race.

I have talked quietly with several prominent business men here, among whom is the President of the Washington Title Company who stated that with his knowledge of all the colored attorneys he would unhesitantly urge the appointment of Prof. Robert H. Terrell as one of the justices, and offered to write a strong letter to the appointing power.* I have had a conference with Prof. Terrell who stated that he can satisfy the Attorney General that he is eligible, and while he will in no sense be a candidate yet if the position were tended to him he would consider it a great honor and would gladly accept.

Viewing this matter in all of its bearings, and after mature thought and thorough investigation, I have reached the conclusion that we will make no mistake in selecting Professor Terrell and Mr. Joseph Stewart.†

Very truly,

W. McKinlay

Booker T. Washington to Whitefield McKinlay

Booker T. Washington (1856–1915) was born into slavery near Hale's Ford, Virginia, and spent his childhood on a plantation working as a so-called houseboy. Upon their emancipation in 1865, he and his family moved to West Virginia, where Washington was hired by a wealthy family who taught him to read and sent him to a school for African Americans. He then enrolled in Hampton Institute in Hampton, Virginia, where he was mentored by its founder, General Samuel Chapman Armstrong, a white missionary and leading advocate of industrial education for blacks‡. In 1881 Washington was selected by Armstrong to become the first principal of Tuskegee Institute (now Tuskegee University) in Tuskegee, Alabama, which was based on the Hampton model. Washington gained a national reputation following his speech in 1895, known as the Atlanta Compromise, in which he advocated

---

*On November 12, 1901, President Theodore Roosevelt appointed Robert Terrell to serve as justice of the peace.

†Joseph Stewart practiced law in Washington, D.C.

‡Armstrong considered the kind of classical education taught at schools like Lincoln and Fisk universities too bookish for African Americans, who he insisted should instead be taught to work with their hands.

industry, thrift, and accommodation of blacks to racial segregation and in-
equality. His fame was secured by the publication in 1901 of his autobiog-
raphy, Up from Slavery.

Tuskegee, Alabama
November 6, 1901

My dear Mr. McKinlay:—

Referring to your letter again of November 1st I would say that I have a letter this morning from the Attorney General acknowledging receipt of mine in which I recommend the two lawyers agreed upon by yourself and myself. I also stated in the letter that I should put first Mr. Robert H. Terrell provided he was eligible and asked him to give Mr. Terrell an opportunity to prove his eligibility. The Attorney General expressed his desire to see Mr. Terrell and consequently I telegraphed him today to call to see him.

I cannot agree with you, however, as to the wisdom of my going in any wholesale manner into securing such appointments; to do so in one case would mean that I meant to do so in a number of other cases.

I am sure that we put before the Attorney General the very best persons for this position and I have faith to believe that he and the President will do the proper thing by them. If Mr. Terrell proves his eligibility, the recommendations will then stand Mr. Terrell and Mr. Stewart. I hardly believe that the President would go outside of these three names at least without consulting me.

I am writing a letter to the President today in which I am cautioning him about giving too much attention to what white men say when recommending colored people. I am reminding him that in many cases white men do not know the character of colored men whom they recommend. I am doing this while answering a letter from him asking direct information about an individual whom you and I both feel is unworthy.

If you think of anything else I can do please write or telegraph me as the matter will be settled within a few days.

The president was immensely pleased with the visit of R. L. Smith.* Smith made a fine impression on him.

---

*Robert Lloyd Smith (1861–1942), a supporter of Booker T. Washington, was a graduate of Atlanta University who served in the Texas state legislature from 1895 to 1899. In 1902 President Roosevelt appointed him deputy U.S. marshal for the Eastern District of Texas.

I read your friend Leupp's article in the *New York Evening Post* with a great deal of interest.* I certainly want to meet him when I am next in Washington.

I do believe that the President will appoint Ferguson over Smith.†

I am also under the impression that Crum, in case Koester is not appointed in South Carolina, is going to stand a very good chance.‡ In case Koester is not appointed, it will give an opportunity for me to call attention again to both Dr. Crum and Col. Kauffman.** My understanding is that you know Kauffman well and can recommend him; is this so?

Yours very truly,

Booker T. Washington

Booker T. Washington to Whitefield McKinlay

Tuskegee, Alabama
February 18, 1902

My dear Mr. McKinlay:—

I think your idea of calling on the President with a few gentlemen is an excellent one, and I hope that you will prepare yourself to talk frankly and fully with the President; he is a man who does not fall out with one who differs from him, and I feel that he is honestly seeking information and I hope you will let him know exactly what the feeling

*Francis Ellington Leupp (1849–1918) was a correspondent for the *New York Evening Post* and from 1889 to 1904 headed the Washington bureau of *The Nation*.

†Charles M. Ferguson (c. 1860–1906) was born in Houston, Texas, and graduated from Fisk University in Nashville, Tennessee. He served as clerk of the federal district court in Fort Bend County and as delegate to several national Republican Party conventions. In 1900 President McKinley appointed him deputy collector of customs in San Antonio County, Texas, a position he held until he died.

‡William D. Crum (1859–1912) of South Carolina was a physician who attended the University of South Carolina and Howard University Medical School. In 1902 President Roosevelt, encouraged by Washington, appointed Crum as customs collector of South Carolina, sparking white protests throughout the South. Crum failed to win confirmation until 1905. George R. Koester (1871–1939) was a newspaper editor who founded the *Columbia Record* in South Carolina in 1890. In 1901 President Roosevelt appointed Koester, a Democrat, collector of internal revenue for South Carolina, triggering a storm of protest by Republicans, some of whom accused Koester of participating in a lynching. Koester denied the charge and said he was only a witness, but he was not confirmed.

**Abraham Charles Kaufman (1839–unknown), a philanthropist, financier, and racial moderate, served as commissioner of Charleston public schools from 1895 to 1903 and as a trustee of Avery Normal Institute, a black school, in South Carolina. In 1900 President McKinley appointed him to the board of visitors of the U.S. Military Academy.

of the colored people is. I have written him this morning as you suggest and I feel sure that if you call to see him after he has had time to receive my letter that he will give you a cordial reception. He may be very much engaged during the next few days in connection with the reception of Prince Henry, as it might be wiser to omit calling on him until after this reception is over.*

The only thing I would suggest in connection with the composition of your committee is that you might add another gentleman who might give a little more "color" to the delegation.

I have taken the liberty to tell the President that you are not to call for the sake of urging any individual for office or asking for office but to talk with him frankly concerning the general attitude of the race.

Yours truly,
Booker T. Washington

Ida B. Wells-Barnett to Anti-Lynching Bureau

Ida B. Wells-Barnett (1862–1931) was a journalist, teacher, suffragist, and lecturer who led an international crusade against the widespread lynching of African Americans at the turn of the twentieth century. Born to enslaved parents in Holly Springs, Mississippi, in 1880 she moved to Memphis, where she became editor and, eventually, co-owner of Free Speech, *a local black newspaper. Following the lynching of three of her friends, Wells wrote an editorial that condemned the attack and urged blacks to leave the city. The editorial sparked calls for violent revenge in local white newspapers, and her newspaper office was destroyed while she was in New York. In 1892, Wells published* Southern Horrors: Lynch Law in All Its Phases, *which documented in detail cases of lynching throughout the country. That pamphlet brought her international fame and was followed in 1895 by* A Red Record: Tabulated Statistics and Alleged Causes of Lynchings in the United States, 1892–1894. *In both texts she undermined the mythology surrounding lynching, purportedly the result of black men raping white women, concluding that lynching was instead typically motivated by economics. Many of the victims were successful businessmen. Her autobiography,* Crusade for Justice *(1928), was published posthumously nearly four decades after she died of kidney disease.*

*Prince Henry of Prussia (1862–1929), the brother of Germany's emperor, King Frederick II, visited the White House in 1902.

Office of Anti-Lynching Bureau
2939 Princeton Avenue
Chicago
Jan. 1st, 1902

To the Members of the Anti-Lynching Bureau:

The year of 1901 with its lynching record is a thing of the past. There were 135 human beings that met death at the hands of mobs during this year. Not only is the list larger than for four years past, but the barbarism of this lawlessness is on the increase. Six human beings were burned alive between January 1st 1901 and Jan. 1st 1902. More persons met death in this horrible manner the past twelve months than in three years before and in proportion as the number roasted alive increases, in the same proportion has there been an indifference manifested by the public.

Time was when the country resounded with denunciation and the horror of burning a human being by so called christian and civilized people. The newspapers were full of it. The last time a human being was made fuel for flames it was scarcely noticed in the papers editorially. And the chairman of your bureau finds it harder every year to get such matter printed. In other words, the need for agitation and publication of facts is greater than ever, while the avenues through which to make such publications have decreased. Nowhere does this apathetic condition prevail to a greater extent than within the membership of the Anti-Lynching Bureau. When the bureau was first organized three years ago, it was thought that every man, woman, and child who had a drop of Negro blood in his veins and every person else who wanted to see mob law put down would gladly contribute 25 cents per year to this end. There were upward of 300 responses to the first appeal and less than 50 per cent renewed at the end of that year. The third year of the bureau's existence is half over and although the chairman has determined to issue a periodical, there are absolutely no funds in the treasury to pay postage much less the printer. Nevertheless my faith in the justice of our cause and the absolute need of this agitation leads me to again address those who have shown 25 cents worth of interest in the matter heretofore. I send with this circular a pamphlet which friends have helped to pay for. It was thought best to begin with what to us was the beginning of history for our race in the United States the Reconstruction period. In view of the recent agitation in Congress and out anent the disfranchisement of the Negro and the causes alleged therefore it was thought best to throw some light on those times and give some unwritten history. This history is written by one who can say with Julius Caesar of the history he wrote: "All of which I saw and part of which I was."

He has given his time and money to aid the publication. Will not the members of the bureau bestir themselves to circulate this number and aid in the publication of others. We can only change public sentiment and enforce laws by educating the people, giving them facts. This you can do by 1st, Renewing your membership in the Anti-Lynching Bureau and securing others. 2nd, By paying for the copy sent you and purchasing others to distribute. 3rd, By paying for the copy of the Reconstruction "Review" to your Congressman together with a letter urging the cutting down of the representation in Congress of the states which have nullified the Constitution. It rests with you to say whether the Anti-Lynching Bureau shall be strengthened to do its work for the future.

Ida B. Wells-Barnett, Chairman

Robert Smalls to Whitefield McKinlay

Robert Smalls (1839–1915) was born into slavery in Beaufort, South Carolina, and became a military hero in 1862 after he made a daring escape aboard a Confederate ship that he piloted out of Charleston harbor and then delivered to the Union fleet. Smalls served in the South Carolina House of Representatives from 1868 to 1870 and in the South Carolina Senate from 1870 to 1874. He then was elected to the U.S. Congress, and served from 1875 to 1879 and from 1881 to 1887. He won his last election against Benjamin Tillman, an avowed racist mentioned in the following letter.* Smalls later served as the U.S. collector of customs in Beaufort.

United States Customs Service
Port of Beaufort, S.C.
November 10, 1909

My Dear Whittie,

Your letter at hand and its contents are duly noted. In reply to same I beg to state that I regret much that I am unable to give you the infor-

---

*A *New York Press* article on February 27, 1900, quoted Tillman bragging about the violent intimidation of black voters. "The people of South Carolina, in their Constitution, have done their level best to prevent the niggers from voting . . . We are charged with fraud and corruption and ballot-box stuffing. After the bayonets had come to us again in 1876, we rose in righteousness and might. We took the Government. We stuffed ballot boxes, we bull-dozed the niggers and shot 'em. And we are not ashamed of it."

mation asked for. The debate on the suffrage question during which Ben Tillman stated that no one who has one drop of negro blood in his veins should be considered white, brought forth the statement from his brother, George Tillman, that he had better let that alone, for if it becomes a law, it would raise hell in South Carolina, at the same time naming a few counties, especially. The convention had no stenographer, hence there were no official records kept, to my recollection. I think the *News and Courier* did make some comment on it. I know there was a little sketch of it in the journal next day, the date of which I am unable to give you. I have looked over everything I have touching the convention, since your letter reached me, but cannot find anything, and it is not mentioned in the journal of the convention. I have not given up the search and if I should find anything to help you, sooner or later, I will send same to you.

I am glad to see that you are still on the alert for those things that will be for the good of the Race, when properly mentioned.

I see by the *News and Courier* of Monday quite a statement coming from Sen. Cullom in regards to the elimination of the Negro from politics in the South and relegating him to the rear [. . .]* Those articles speak for themselves, and I would like very much to hear from you regarding your views as to them, as soon as you have read and digested them.

In your letter before the last, you stated that you thought yourself that all Negroes in office, except myself, are more than apt to be dropped, especially when their term expires. Now, my dear friend, I am Negro and nothing could make me otherwise and when the time comes, I have no doubt that I will still be a Negro. Any little thing that a white man does makes him a big man, but no matter what a Negro does he is still nothing. He, in the white man's estimation, can do nothing that will make him a great man. I believe that the prejudice against the Negro today in this country is because he is improving, for in every instance where he is put alongside the white man in a test of any kind, he either comes out ahead or stands his equal. For this reason he is feared. This is the reason why every white man, especially in the South, seems now willing to see him relegated to the rear before he becomes too powerful and strong. But notwithstanding all this, the same God still lives, in whom we place our hope.

*Shelby Moore Cullom (1829–1914), Republican of Illinois, served in the U.S. Senate from 1883 to 1913.

With the hope that you and yours are well, and with best wishes for your continued success.

I am as ever yours truly,
Robert Smalls

Robert Smalls to Whitefield McKinlay

This letter was written in the midst of the presidential campaigns of Woodrow Wilson, Democrat from Virginia; William Howard Taft, a Republican; and the former president Theodore Roosevelt, running on the Progressive Party line. Wilson won the election and served for two terms.

Beaufort, South Carolina
September 12, 1912

Dear Whitefield,

Enclosed you will find a marked copy of the *News and Courier* which speaks for itself. I think the colored voters of Ohio and New York and of the entire North should see it. I send it to you because I know that you can give it the proper publicity, in order that they may see the necessity of sticking to the regular republican party.

No man had a higher regard for Theo. Roosevelt than I, but his course in trying to split the party of Lincoln and [Ulysses S.] Grant and other illustrious men, that party which unshackled the necks of four million human beings, and by whose acts might elect a democratic president,—a man like Wilson, who is said to be a southerner by birth and who will be under the entire domination of the south, where more than 2/3 of the Negro voters have been robbed of their franchise,—I have lost all the respect for such a man. He will be under the domination of such men as the Governor of our state who is said to be reelected, a man who is so bitter against the Negro, that he has refused to commission a single Negro as even a notary public in the State.*

I ask that every colored man in the North who has a vote to cast, would cast that vote for the regular republican party and thus bury the democratic party so deep that there will not be seen even a bubble

---

*Coleman Livington Blease (1868–1942), a populist Democrat, avowed racist, and protégé of Benjamin Tillman, was governor of South Carolina from 1911 to 1915. He openly supported lynching and was opposed to the education of African Americans.

coming up from the spot where the burial took place. Best love to all.
As ever, yours,

    Robert Smalls

W.E.B. Du Bois to President Woodrow Wilson

When Woodrow Wilson ran for president in 1912, he vowed to advance the cause of African Americans, who were primarily loyal to the Republican Party. Wilson's promises won him the endorsement of W.E.B. Du Bois (1868–1963), among others. However, by the time Wilson sought a second term, many African Americans were wary of his conservative racial policies, including his administration's imposition of complete racial segregation in Washington, D.C., and in government offices. In an open letter published in The Crisis, *the NAACP's journal, Du Bois asks Wilson to address publicly the epidemic lynching of African Americans. In 1916 there were fifty-four recorded lynchings of African Americans.*

New York
October 10, 1916

To the President of the United States
Sir:

As an organization representing the Negro race and thousands of their friends we are deeply interested in the presidential election.

During the last campaign, believing firmly that the Republican Party and its leaders had systematically betrayed the interests of colored people, many of our members did what they could to turn the colored vote toward you. We received from you a promise of justice and sincere endeavor to forward their interests. We need scarcely to say that you have grievously disappointed us. We find ourselves again facing a presidential campaign with but indifferent choice. We have waited for some time to gather from your writings and speeches something of your present attitude toward the colored people. We have thought that perhaps you had some statement or explanation which would account for the dismissal of colored public officials, segregation in the civil service, and other things which have taken place during your administration. You must surely realize that if Negroes were Americans—if they had a reasonable degree of rights and privileges, they need ask for no especial statement from a candidate for the high office of President; but being as they are, members of a segregated class and struggling against tremendous prejudices, disabilities and odds, we must for their own salvation and the salvation of our country ask for more than such treatment as is today fair for other races. We must continually demand such positive action as will do away with their disabilities. Lynching is a national evil of which Negroes are the chief victims. It is perhaps the greatest disgrace from which this country suffers, and yet we find you and other men of influence silent in the matter. A republic must be based upon universal suffrage or it is not a republic; and yet, while you seem anxious to do justice toward women, we hear scarcely a word concerning those disenfranchised masses of the South whose stolen votes are used to make Rotten Boroughs of a third of the nation and thus distort and ruin the just distribution of political power. Caste restrictions, fatal to Christian civilization and modern conceptions of decency, are slowly but forcibly entering this land and making black folk the chief victims. There should be outspoken protest against segregation by race in the civil service, caste in public travel and in other public accommodations.

As Negroes and as their friends; as Americans; as persons whose fathers have striven for the good of this land and who ourselves have tried unselfishly to make America the land of just ideals, we write to ask if you do not think it possible to make to the colored and white people of America some further statement of your attitude toward this grievous problem such as will allow us at least to vote with intelligence.

We trust, Sir, that you will not regard this statement and request as beyond the courtesy due you or as adding too much to the burdens of a public man.

We beg to remain, Sir,

Very respectfully yours,

National Association for the Advancement of Colored People

W. E. Burghardt Du Bois

Director of Publications and Research

James Weldon Johnson to President Warren G. Harding

WESTERN UNION TELEGRAM

President Warren G. Harding
White House
Washington, D.C.
September 19, 1921

The National Association for the Advancement of Colored People on behalf of 12,000,000 colored Americans desires to add its voice to those already asking your endorsement of a thorough federal investigation followed if necessary by Congressional action on the menace of commercialized race hatred as represented by the Ku Klux Klan. The National Association for the Advancement of Colored People bases this request upon its own information about the Ku Klux Klan which has been placed in the hands of public officials. The Association was one of the first to volunteer its information about the Ku Klux Klan to the Department of Justice and again takes this occasion to assure you of its desire to assist the government in every way possible.

James Weldon Johnson,
Secretary to the National Association for the Advancement
of Colored People

Arthur A. Schomburg to Wendell Dabney

Arthur Schomburg (1874–1938), born in San Juan, Puerto Rico, was a noted bibliophile who collected the works of people of African descent across the African Diaspora. He served as curator of the Arthur A. Schomburg Collection of Negro Literature and Art from 1932 until his death in 1938. In 1926 the New York Public Library, with a grant from the Carnegie Foundation, purchased his extensive collection of rare books, artwork, prints, and manuscripts from across the African Diaspora, which form the foundation for the institution that now bears his name. Wendell Dabney (1865–1935) was a crusading journalist who edited, owned, and managed The Cincinnati Union, *an African American weekly, from 1905 until shortly before this letter was written.*

December 12, 1933

My dear Nestor:

I have just finished reading the last issue of the *Union* and a feeling of sadness came over me, when I read you intended folding your tent known as 412 McAlliser street, the street of many quaint reminiscences during the days that called for great courage and stamina. I refer to Coffin's Underground railway ramifications that led the poor slave to breathe sunshine and liberty. Few people know much of the historic background of the street where the editor with the night-cap and the knowledge of culinary matters, who knows how to prepare the most edible oysters with butter and lemon juice, skin a magician with his wand. Presto! The pen of combat would rest peacefully, the frying pan become triumphant and soon thereafter George who was the editor's shadow, would have a table prepared fit for the Knights of the Quills to partake. Music would flow by the unerring fingers of the only Editor who can play a guitar with the touch of a master, the banjo will come for playing in the old and the new methods of approach, and should these instruments be not at hand there was the piano just waiting for the touch of the master. No wonder all friends would drop a nickel upon getting off the train, to touch the phoning bells to chat with the inspiring editor of the *Cincinnati Union*.

What I always admired in Wendell P. Dabney, was the sterling manifestation of courage at all times. I consider him one of the most fearless of men who sat behind an editor's chair, and was always willing and ready to tell any one who crossed his path, what he told the KKK when they burned a flaming cross in his back yard, that he was there to stay and he stayed until when tired he will walk with his usual gait, like the sage of antiquity without much ado. He has been courageous to a fault, in defense of his race he brooked noninterference. It was the Holy Grail so to speak, beyond a certain imaginary line there could be no compromise. The white press of his city will lament the music master hanging his instrument behind the door peg. I would like to be the beneficiary of that old penholder that carried the nib that brought us such lovely morsels of pristine philosophy. The page of "Gossip and Reflections" will no longer animate our thoughts, for the double edged meanings of a few words put together by the only Dabney, we will ever have in our lifetime. But before we part from the company of our inspirational brother let us cheer him for the many hours of joy and sunshine that came from the soul of his witticisms.

The former Paymaster of the city of Cincinnati was in days gone and days to come the son of a Virginian, a host of hosts, charming and loving, the booklover and the collector of beauty and joy, to my mind there is only one other loose and that is Henry P. Slaughter of Kentucky.* Yes sir, both are unique in their ways. May God bless them, the old fashioned editors.

A. Schomburg

Roy Wilkins to Eleanor Roosevelt

Roy Wilkins (1901–1981) was raised in St. Paul, Minnesota. He worked at the Kansas City Call, *an African American paper, before becoming assistant executive secretary for the NAACP in 1931. Wilkins succeeded W.E.B. Du Bois as editor of* The Crisis, *the organization's publication, in 1934. He was appointed executive director of the NAACP in 1955 and led the organization through the turbulent Civil Rights Movement.*

Wilkins wrote this letter to First Lady Eleanor Roosevelt, a close friend of NAACP President Walter White and a civil rights supporter who failed to convince her husband, President Franklin Roosevelt, to support the Costigan-Wagner Anti-Lynching bill, introduced in 1934.† That year she arranged a meeting between White and her husband to discuss the legislation. In 1945 she joined the NAACP Board of Directors.

Mrs. Franklin D. Roosevelt
White House
Washington, D.C.
[Undated, 1934]

My dear Mrs. Roosevelt:

We do not believe that anyone in America can doubt your deep interest in the welfare of all the people of the United States, and certainly this Association does not doubt it. For in addition to our general knowledge, we have the testimony of Mr. Walter White, our Secretary, who has had several personal conferences with you.

We know you are an extremely busy woman with engagements in all parts of the country, but we wish to invite you to do this Association and the colored citizens of America the great honor of speaking this

*Henry P. Slaughter (1875–1958) was editor of the *Lexington Standard*. A graduate of Howard University Law School, he collected papers on black history and culture. More than ten thousand volumes from his collection were sold to Clark Atlanta University.
†The legislation, introduced by Senators Robert F. Wagner (Democrat, New York) and Edward Costigan (Democrat, Colorado), proposed federal trials for law enforcement officers who failed to uphold the law when a lynching occurred. It did not win passage.

year at the 25th Annual Conference of this Association in Oklahoma City, Oklahoma, Sunday afternoon, July 1, 1934.

This Association, which began in 1909 with a small committee of white and colored persons in New York City, has grown in twenty-five years to have 375 branches in forty states and the District of Columbia. It has both white and colored members, and the Board of Directors, as you can see from the letterhead, is composed of distinguished white and colored citizens. The Association is recognized as the foremost organization of and for colored people in the country.

We appreciate fully that your time is taken with many matters and that Oklahoma City is far in the Southwest. It is only because we are certain that the appearance of no other single person, excepting our distinguished President, could so hearten and inspire colored Americans in this period of rehabilitation than that of yourself, that we presume to request this favor of you. We hope very much, and we know we are joined in our hopes by millions of fellow citizens, that you will find will it possible to accept our invitation.

Very sincerely yours,
Roy Wilkins
Assistant Secretary

Walter White to Thurgood Marshall

Walter White (1893–1955), a light-skinned, blue-eyed African American who could and sometimes did pass for white to investigate the lynching of blacks, joined the NAACP in 1918 as an assistant to the then executive secretary, James Weldon Johnson, whom he succeeded in 1931. He served as executive secretary of the organization until 1955 and played a major role in efforts to desegregate the armed forces and to secure antilynching legislation. He also hired Charles Houston (1895–1950), the organization's first chief counsel, resulting in a series of important legal challenges, culminating in the landmark Brown v. Board of Education of Topeka *decision, which desegregated public schools.*

Thurgood Marshall (1908–1993) became the first African American to serve on the U.S. Supreme Court when President Lyndon Johnson appointed him in 1967 and held the position until his retirement in 1991. Marshall had served as chief counsel for the NAACP and successfully argued the Brown v. Board *case. As chief counsel, Marshall won twenty-nine of the thirty-two cases he argued before the Supreme Court, including Browder v. Gayle, which ended the Montgomery Bus Boycott in Alabama. In 1935 the NAACP openly criticized President Franklin Roosevelt for failing to support civil rights legislation. When this letter was written, Marshall was working for Charles Houston.*

69 Fifth Avenue
New York
March 1, 1935

Dear Thurgood:

I am delayed in answering your letter of February 20th due to having been out of town a good bit and also to a great mass of work here which had me almost swamped.

Thank you for letting me see Tydings' letter.* It is a thoroughly mistaken one in many respects. It is either ignorance or viciousness to say that lynchings occur because of the failure of the courts to function properly. If you will read my testimony before the Senate Judiciary Committee last year you will see that I tried to deal with this argument. I pointed out that the majority of the victims of lynchings occurred in isolated, remote areas of the deep South where no persons would dare assert that when a Negro was accused of a serious crime against a white person that there would be the slightest delay in bringing him to trial; and that the persons who attempted to use this as an argument against effective anti-lynching legislation were either ignorant or vicious, or both. I hope you will answer this thoroughly and vigorously and that you will give copies of your reply to the *Afro-American* and to other papers which may be interested to carry the story.

As for Tydings' contention that the bill punishes the innocent as well as the guilty through the imposition of a fine, such a contention is just about as vicious as the previous one. This is an old established principle of law. Many states, about eleven in number, if I remember correctly, (you will find this in Chadbourn's *Lynching and the Law*) have provisions for the fining of counties which permit lynchings to take place and the right to impose such financial penalty has been repeat-

---

*Millard Tydings (1890–1961), a Democrat from Maryland, served in the U.S. Senate from 1927 to 1951.

edly upheld by the court.* I enclose a copy of a memorandum which I prepared when this argument was used last year by other senators against the Costigan-Wagner Bill.

Furthermore, such a provision will stir to action the hitherto quiescent property-owning, tax-paying, "respectable" elements of communities in which lynchings occur. It will impel them to action if only to escape the financial penalty. They will get busy and get behind sheriffs and other law enforcement officers to break up the mobs at their very inception. Few, if any, mobs would ever be able to consummate lynching if the officers of the law and the decent people got busy soon enough.

Thus this financial penalty clause, which is perhaps the most important phase of the bill, will act as all law should act—namely, as a preventive rather than a punitive measure. I venture to predict that passage of the bill with this clause in it will do more to stop lynching than any other thing.

And, finally, I wish you would challenge Tydings to propose some other method of stopping lynching if he does not come out for the Costigan-Wagner Bill. He may be honest in his contentions but I frankly doubt it. You and every other thoughtful Marylander should put the screws on him and put them on hard and not let them up until he declares himself definitely on one side of the fence or the other—either for or against lynching.

Do your utmost.
Cordially,
    Walter

Claude McKay to James Weldon Johnson

Claude McKay (1889–1948), a Jamaican-born writer whose bestselling Home to Harlem *(1928) was one of the major works published during the Harlem Renaissance, had flirted with Communism and wrote for a socialist paper in London. In this letter to James Weldon Johnson, he seeks to distance himself from Communism, with which he had become disillusioned before turning to Roman Catholicism.*

Lynching and the Law (1933), by James Harmon Chadbourn, a University of North Carolina Law School professor, was the culmination of a two-year investigation of the legal aspects of lynching sponsored by the Southern Commission on the Study of Lynching. The book argued that lynching was a cultural problem that required stronger legal sanctions and recommended model antilynching statutes.

Dear JWJ,

I am enclosing a copy of Mr. Embree's letter, which, as you will see, is not so very favorable, although it does not definitely close the door.* I wonder if you would mind writing an urgent word to him about me, as that might help. I so much want to get right down to the writing of that book.† There is a false idea current among the left intellectuals, that I went to Russia as a Communist and later went back on my principles, and I'd like to devote a chapter to show that I worked my way across to Europe in 1922 and went to Russia voluntarily, through the help of an English friend who was a go-between and interpreter for the Russian Communists in Berlin. In Russia the American Communists did everything in their power to prevent my making contacts and attending conferences (for I was not a party member) and it was only through Sen Katayama‡ (who knew me on the *Liberator*) going over their heads to the big shots, that I did get on the inside. The fact is that my color intrigued for me, the colored American delegate was light-skinned and the Moscow propagandists wanted a real Negro type to put over. The people were excited about me in the streets long before the Bolshevist leaders became aware, it was the popular interest that irresistibly pushed me forward. But in the Soviet records I am listed as a non-partisan. I went into Russia as a writer and a free spirit and left the same, because I was always convinced that however far I was advanced in social ideas, if I could do something significantly creative as a Negro, it would mean more to my group and the world than being merely a social agitator.

I wanted to show that my traveling in Europe and thru Spain and over to Africa were logical steps in my pilgrimage. I am ready to admit that I had profound experiences in Europe and in Africa that made me less cocksure about radical theories, especially as related to propaganda among Negroes. But there is nothing in that to be ashamed of.

---

*This is likely a reference to Edwin R. Embree, who served as president of the Julius Rosenwald Fund, which awarded millions of dollars to African American educational initiatives, including fellowships to black writers. Among the fellowship recipients were James Weldon Johnson, W.E.B. Du Bois, and Langston Hughes.

†McKay's autobiography, *A Long Way from Home*, was published in 1937, followed by *Harlem: Negro Metropolis* in 1940.

‡Born Yabuki Sugataro, Sen Katayama (1859–1933) was an early member of the American Communist Party and cofounder of the Japan Communist Party.

A couple up at Harmon on the Hudson has offered me a barn and some lumber to fix it up, so I could stay up there for a few months and write. But I am in such a tight fix, I can't even take advantage of the offer. And so, anything you can do by way of exerting your influence to help will be much appreciated. I owe so much to you considering all you did to bring me back again, that I do hate the idea of giving you further trouble. But I know you don't consider it that.

Yours sincerely,

Claude McKay

Congressman Adam Clayton Powell, Jr., to Eleanor Roosevelt

In 1956 Adam Clayton Powell, Jr. (1908–1972), broke with the Democratic Party to support Dwight D. Eisenhower, a Republican, over Adlai Stevenson, who ran unsuccessfully in 1952 and 1956. Eisenhower was reelected with 40 percent of the black vote and went on to propose the Civil Rights Act of 1957, which allowed the Justice Department to sue on behalf of blacks denied the right to vote. Eisenhower signed the Civil Rights Acts of 1957 and 1960 into law. In 1960 Powell vigorously supported the presidential candidacy of Sen. John F. Kennedy.

Democratic National Headquarters
Washington, D.C.
November 5, 1956

I am extremely flattered that you have been taking cognizance of my stand on civil rights. No matter what you may ever say about me, I shall always consider you as a very great American and I have been saying so in cities throughout the country. I cannot, however, understand how Mr. Stevenson can continue to hide behind your petticoats and is unwilling to publicly take a stand on the question that is the most important to America today. I am certain that you agree with me that America is being judged not on rigid price supports, Tidelands oil, natural gas nor private versus public power but on human decency, freedom and the right to vote.

I noted in today's press that you stated that the Democratic Party has its Eastlands but the Republicans have their Jenners.* I respect-

---

*James Oliver Eastland (1904–1986, Democrat, Mississippi) served in the U.S. Senate from 1943 to 1978, during which time he was an ardent segregationist and opponent of the Civil Rights Movement. William Ezra Jenner served in the U.S. Senate for Indiana from 1947 to 1959.

fully call your attention to the fact that Dwight David Eisenhower has publicly stated that he expects no support from [U.S. Senator Joseph] McCarthy, Jenner nor Malone. I have repeatedly tried to reach Mr. Stevenson and perhaps you can do it for me. Will he now, before the votes are cast on Tuesday, stand up and publicly repudiate his support of not one but all of the Eastlands—particularly Eastland, Talmadge and [Huey P. Long]?*

Will he publicly himself state his position on school integration in the south and just what he would advocate doing when school officials defy Federal Court orders and all due process has been exhausted at the state level?

[. . .] Does Mr. Stevenson favor the immediate introduction and passage of a right to vote bill which will give every American his own precious heritage?

And, finally, does he agree with Senator [Robert] Byrd that we must have a Democrat for the chairman of the Rules Committee so that civil rights legislation can be bottled up in Committee and never permitted to reach the Floor of the House?†

These are the issues in my opinion which are the most important in America today. And yet, Mr. Stevenson will not speak out. If he does not speak out, I must assume that it is because he cannot.

You have been a great champion and a great fighter for civil rights and I hope that you will always continue to be. All that I have been asking and continue to ask is that Mr. Stevenson stand up and repudiate the elements of his Party and the concepts which are completely opposed to everything you stand for before the world.

ADAM CLAYTON POWELL, JR.

* George Wilson Malone (1890–1961), a conservative Republican, represented Nevada in the U.S. Senate from 1947 to 1959. Herman Eugene Talmadge (1913–2002) was an ardent segregationist who served as governor of Georgia from 1948 to 1955, and in the U.S. Senate from 1957 to 1981. Huey P. Long (1893–1935) served as governor of Louisiana from 1928 to 1931 and as a U.S. senator from 1932 to 1935. He was a populist who championed segregation and the common (white) man.

†Robert Byrd (b. 1917) was elected to the House of Representatives from West Virginia in 1952 and served until 1959, when he began his tenure as a U.S. senator. In 2006 he was reelected to an unprecedented ninth term. A former member of the Ku Klux Klan, Byrd opposed integration and voted against the Civil Rights Act of 1964, which outlawed segregation in U.S. schools and in public places, a position he later renounced.

Congressman Adam Clayton Powell, Jr.,
to U.S. Senator John F. Kennedy

Washington, D.C.
November 5, 1957

Dear Jack:

Sorry to delay so long in replying to your letter of September 31st. I have been on the move and have had a great deal of personal trouble.*

1. In reference to your statement endorsing the President's action, I have checked with all my newspaper reporters in Washington and none of them have heard of such a statement. Therefore I surmise it was either buried or not played up correctly.
2. The June 12th issue of the *Daily Constitution* reported, following a two day tour of the State of Georgia by Senator Kennedy. J. S. Bell, Democratic State Chairman stated, "it is highly probable that the Georgia delegation to the Democratic National Convention will support Kennedy for the next Presidential nomination.["]
3. As regards your vote to refer the civil rights bill to Senator Eastland's Committee, I completely disagree with your reasoning. At this particular time of history after eighty-two years of failure on the part of the United States to pass any civil rights legislation, any method that is taken to achieve it that is legal, is justifiable and you know better than I do that it would never have come before the Senate had your vote prevailed.

I read the account of your visit to Mississippi and I think you did well with a very difficult situation.

I look forward to see you while you are in my town. I can always be reached thru Audubon 6-2026 my appointment secretary, William Hampton.

With every good wish.
Sincerely yours,
Adam

---

*This could be a reference to his divorce from Hazel Scott that year.

Dr. Martin Luther King, Jr., to President John F. Kennedy

In 1962 Martin Luther King, Jr. (1929–1968), and other civil rights lead-ers were arrested after they held a massive sit-in and marching campaign in Albany, Georgia, to protest segregation and discrimination. That year nearly a dozen black churches were burned down in Georgia, and President Kennedy signed an executive order outlawing racial discrimination in fed-erally financed housing. King sent the following telegram to Kennedy in the midst of the racial chaos.

September 11, 1962

I HAVE LEARNED FROM AUTHENTIC SOURCES THAT NEGROES ARE ARMING THEMSELVES IN MANY QUARTERS WHERE THIS REIGN OF TERROR IS ALIVE. I WILL CONTINUE TO URGE MY PEOPLE TO BE NONVIOLENT IN THE FACE OF BITTEREST OPPOSITION, BUT I FEAR THAT MY COUNSEL WILL FALL ON DEAF EARS IF THE FEDERAL GOV-ERNMENT DOES NOT TAKE DECISIVE ACTION. IF NEGROES ARE TEMPTED TO TURN TO RETALIATORY VIOLENCE, WE SHALL SEE A DARK NIGHT OF RIOTING ALL OVER THE SOUTH.

Dr. Martin Luther King, Jr., to White Clergymen

This letter, one of the most famous in American history, was written while King was incarcerated for leading a protest against segregation in Birming-ham, Alabama. The letter, written during King's solitary confinement, ad-dressed an ad placed by eight Alabama clergymen who criticized the demonstrations and labeled King a lawbreaker. Without writing paper, King began the letter in the margins of a newspaper and continued on scraps of paper. Four months later, some 260,000 people gathered for the March on Washington, where King made the "I Have a Dream" speech.

[Birmingham, Alabama]
April 16, 1963

My Dear Fellow Clergymen:

While confined here in the Birmingham city jail, I came across your recent statement calling my present activities "unwise and untimely." Seldom do I pause to answer criticism of my work and ideas. If I sought to answer all the criticisms that cross my desk, my secretaries would have little time for anything other than such correspondence in the course of the day, and I would have no time for constructive work.

But since I feel that you are men of genuine good will and that your criticisms are sincerely set forth, I want to try to answer your statements in what I hope will be patient and reasonable terms.

I think I should indicate why I am here in Birmingham, since you have been influenced by the view which argues against "outsiders coming in." I have the honor of serving as president of the Southern Christian Leadership Conference, an organization operating in every southern state, with headquarters in Atlanta, Georgia. We have some eighty-five affiliated organizations across the South, and one of them is the Alabama Christian Movement for Human Rights. Frequently we share staff, educational and financial resources with our affiliates. Several months ago the affiliate here in Birmingham asked us to be on call to engage in a nonviolent direct-action program if such were deemed necessary. We readily consented, and when the hour came we lived up to our promise. So I, along with several members of my staff, am here because I was invited here. I am here because I have organizational ties here.

But more basically, I am in Birmingham because injustice is here. Just as the prophets of the eighth century B.C. left their villages and carried their "thus saith the Lord" far beyond the boundaries of their home towns, and just as the Apostle Paul left his village of Tarsus and carried the gospel of Jesus Christ to the far corners of the Greco-Roman world, so am I compelled to carry the gospel of freedom beyond my own home town. Like Paul, I must constantly respond to the Macedonian call for aid.

Moreover, I am cognizant of the interrelatedness of all communities and states. I cannot sit idly by in Atlanta and not be concerned about what happens in Birmingham. Injustice anywhere is a threat to justice everywhere. We are caught in an inescapable network of mutuality, tied in a single garment of destiny. Whatever affects one directly, affects all indirectly. Never again can we afford to live with the narrow, provincial "outside agitator" idea. Anyone who lives inside the United States can never be considered an outsider anywhere within its bounds.

You deplore the demonstrations taking place in Birmingham. But your statement, I am sorry to say, fails to express a similar concern for the conditions that brought about the demonstrations. I am sure that none of you would want to rest content with the superficial kind of social analysis that deals merely with effects and does not grapple with underlying causes. It is unfortunate that demonstrations are taking place in Birmingham, but it is even more unfortunate that the city's white power structure left the Negro community with no alternative.

In any nonviolent campaign there are four basic steps: collection of the facts to determine whether injustices exist; negotiation; self-purification; and direct action. We have gone through all these steps in Birmingham. There can be no gainsaying the fact that racial injustice engulfs this community. Birmingham is probably the most thoroughly segregated city in the United States. Its ugly record of brutality is widely known. Negroes have experienced grossly unjust treatment in the courts. There have been more unsolved bombings of Negro homes and churches in Birmingham than in any other city in the nation. These are the hard, brutal facts of the case. On the basis of these conditions, Negro leaders sought to negotiate with the city fathers. But the latter consistently refused to engage in good-faith negotiation.

Then, last September, came the opportunity to talk with leaders of Birmingham's economic community. In the course of the negotiations, certain promises were made by the merchants—for example, to remove the stores' humiliating racial signs. On the basis of these promises, the Reverend Fred Shuttlesworth and the leaders of the Alabama Christian Movement for Human Rights agreed to a moratorium on all demonstrations. As the weeks and months went by, we realized that we were the victims of a broken promise. A few signs, briefly removed, returned; the others remained.

As in so many past experiences, our hopes had been blasted, and the shadow of deep disappointment settled upon us. We had no alternative except to prepare for direct action, whereby we would present our very bodies as a means of laying our case before the conscience of the local and the national community. Mindful of the difficulties involved, we decided to undertake a process of self-purification. We began a series of workshops on nonviolence, and we repeatedly asked ourselves: "Are you able to accept blows without retaliating?" "Are you able to endure the ordeal of jail?" We decided to schedule our direct-action program for the Easter season, realizing that except for Christmas, this is the main shopping period of the year. Knowing that a strong economic-withdrawal program would be the by-product of direct action, we felt that this would be the best time to bring pressure to bear on the merchants for the needed change.

Then it occurred to us that Birmingham's mayoralty election was coming up in March, and we speedily decided to postpone action until after election day. When we discovered that the Commissioner of Public Safety, Eugene "Bull" Connor, had piled up enough votes to be in the run-off we decided again to postpone action until the day after the run-off so that the demonstrations could not be used to cloud the issues. Like many others, we waited to see Mr. Connor defeated, and to this end we endured postponement after postponement. Having aided in this community need, we felt that our direct-action program could be delayed no longer.

You may well ask: "Why direct action? Why sit-ins, marches and so forth? Isn't negotiation a better path?" You are quite right in calling for negotiation. Indeed, this is the very purpose of direct action. Nonviolent direct action seeks to create such a crisis and foster such a tension that a community which has constantly refused to negotiate is forced to confront the issue. It seeks so to dramatize the issue that it can no longer be ignored. My citing the creation of tension as part of the work of the nonviolent-resister may sound rather shocking. But I must confess that I am not afraid of the word "tension." I have earnestly opposed violent tension, but there is a type of constructive, nonviolent tension which is necessary for growth. Just as Socrates felt that it was necessary to create a tension in the mind so that individuals could rise from the bondage of myths and half-truths to the unfettered realm of creative analysis and objective appraisal, so must we see the need for nonviolent gadflies to create the kind of tension in society that will help men rise from the dark depths of prejudice and racism to the majestic heights of understanding and brotherhood.

The purpose of our direct-action program is to create a situation so crisis-packed that it will inevitably open the door to negotiation. I therefore concur with you in your call for negotiation. Too long has our beloved South land been bogged down in a tragic effort to live in monologue rather than dialogue.

One of the basic points in your statement is that the action that I and my associates have taken in Birmingham is untimely. Some have asked: "Why didn't you give the new city administration time to act?" The only answer that I can give to this query is that the new Birmingham administration must be prodded about as much as the outgoing one, before it will act. We are sadly mistaken if we feel that the election of Albert Boutwell as mayor will bring the millennium to Birmingham. While Mr. Boutwell is a much more gentle person than

Mr. Connor, they are both segregationists, dedicated to maintenance of the status quo. I have hope that Mr. Boutwell will be reasonable enough to see the futility of massive resistance to desegregation. But he will not see this without pressure from devotees of civil rights. My friends, I must say to you that we have not made a single gain in civil rights without determined legal and nonviolent pressure. Lamentably, it is an historical fact that privileged groups seldom give up their privileges voluntarily. Individuals may see the moral light and voluntarily give up their unjust posture; but, as Reinhold Niebuhr has reminded us, groups tend to be more immoral than individuals.*

We know through painful experience that freedom is never voluntarily given by the oppressor; it must be demanded by the oppressed. Frankly, I have yet to engage in a direct-action campaign that was "well timed" in the view of those who have not suffered unduly from the disease of segregation. For years now I have heard the word "Wait!" It rings in the ear of every Negro with piercing familiarity. This "Wait" has almost always meant "Never." We must come to see, with one of our distinguished jurists, that "justice too long delayed is justice denied."

We have waited for more than 340 years for our constitutional and God-given rights. The nations of Asia and Africa are moving with jetlike speed toward gaining political independence, but we still creep at horse-and-buggy pace toward gaining a cup of coffee at a lunch counter. Perhaps it is easy for those who have never felt the stinging dark of segregation to say, "Wait." But when you have seen vicious mobs lynch your mothers and fathers at will and drown your sisters and brothers at whim; when you have seen hate-filled policemen curse, kick and even kill your black brothers and sisters; when you see the vast majority of your twenty million Negro brothers smothering in an airtight cage of poverty in the midst of an affluent society; when you suddenly find your tongue twisted and your speech stammering as you seek to explain to your six-year-old daughter why she can't go to the public amusement park that has just been advertised on television, and see tears welling up in her eyes when she is told that Funtown is closed to colored children, and see omi-

*Karl Paul Reinhold Niebuhr (1892–1971), the son of German immigrants, was a prominent theologian and social activist who, in *Moral Man and Immoral Society* (1932), argued that individuals had a greater capacity than do groups to unselfishly care for others. Niebuhr recieved his BDiv and MA degrees from Yale University in 1914 and 1915, respectively, and was named Honorary Doctor of Divinity by Yale, Oxford, and Harvard universities. He taught theology at the Union Theological Seminary in New York from 1928 to 1960.

nous clouds of inferiority beginning to form in her little mental sky, and see her beginning to distort her personality by developing an unconscious bitterness toward white people; when you have to concoct an answer for a five-year-old son who is asking: "Daddy, why do white people treat colored people so mean?"; when you take a cross-county drive and find it necessary to sleep night after night in the uncomfortable corners of your automobile because no motel will accept you; when you are humiliated day in and day out by nagging signs reading "white" and "colored"; when your first name becomes "nigger," your middle name becomes "boy" (however old you are) and your last name becomes "John," and your wife and mother are never given the respected title "Mrs."; when you are harried by day and haunted by night by the fact that you are a Negro, living constantly at tiptoe stance, never quite knowing what to expect next, and are plagued with inner fears and outer resentments; when you are forever fighting a degenerating sense of "nobodiness"—then you will understand why we find it difficult to wait. There comes a time when the cup of endurance runs over, and men are no longer willing to be plunged into the abyss of despair. I hope, sirs, you can understand our legitimate and unavoidable impatience.

You express a great deal of anxiety over our willingness to break laws. This is certainly a legitimate concern. Since we so diligently urge people to obey the Supreme Court's decision of 1954 outlawing segregation in the public schools, at first glance it may seem rather paradoxical for us consciously to break laws. One may well ask: "How can you advocate breaking some laws and obeying others?" The answer lies in the fact that there are two types of laws: just and unjust. I would be the first to advocate obeying just laws. One has not only a legal but a moral responsibility to obey just laws. Conversely, one has a moral responsibility to disobey unjust laws. I would agree with St. Augustine that "an unjust law is no law at all."

Now, what is the difference between the two? How does one determine whether a law is just or unjust? A just law is a man-made code that squares with the moral law or the law of God. An unjust law is a code that is out of harmony with the moral law. To put it in the terms of St. Thomas Aquinas: An unjust law is a human law that is not rooted in eternal law and natural law. Any law that uplifts human personality is just. Any law that degrades human personality is unjust. All segregation statutes are unjust because segregation distorts the soul and damages the personality. It gives the segregator a false sense of superiority and the segregated a false sense of inferiority. Segregation, to use the terminology of the Jewish philosopher Martin Buber, substitutes an "I it" relationship for an "I thou" relationship and ends up relegating persons to the status of things.* Hence segregation is not only politically, economically and sociologically unsound, it is morally wrong and awful. Paul Tillich said that sin is separation.† Is not segregation an existential expression of man's tragic separation, his awful estrangement, his terrible sinfulness? Thus it is that I can urge men to obey the 1954 decision of the Supreme Court, for it is morally right; and I can urge them to disobey segregation ordinances, for they are morally wrong.

Let us consider a more concrete example of just and unjust laws. An unjust law is a code that a numerical or power majority group compels a minority group to obey but does not make binding on itself. This is difference made legal. By the same token, a just law is a code that a majority compels a minority to follow and that it is willing to follow itself. This is sameness made legal.

Let me give another explanation. A law is unjust if it is inflicted on a minority that, as a result of being denied the right to vote, had no part in enacting or devising the law. Who can say that the legislature of Alabama which set up that state's segregation laws was democratically elected? Throughout Alabama all sorts of devious methods are used to prevent Negroes from becoming registered voters, and there are some counties in which, even though Negroes constitute a majority of the population, not a single Negro is registered. Can any law enacted under such circumstances be considered democratically structured?

Sometimes a law is just on its face and unjust in its application. For instance, I have been arrested on a charge of parading without a permit. Now, there is nothing wrong in having an ordinance which requires a permit for a parade. But such an ordinance becomes unjust when it is used to maintain segregation and to deny citizens the First Amendment privilege of peaceful assembly and protest.

I hope you are able to see the distinction I am trying to point out. In no sense do I advocate evading or defying the law, as would the rabid segregationist. That would lead to anarchy. One who breaks an unjust law must do so openly, lovingly, and with a willingness to accept

---

*Martin Buber (1878–1965), Austrian philosopher and author of *I and Thou* (1923).
†Paul Tillich (1886–1965), German American theologian and existentialist philosopher, author of *The Courage to Be* (1952).

the penalty. I submit that an individual who breaks a law that conscience tells him is unjust and who willingly accepts the penalty of imprisonment in order to arouse the conscience of the community over
its injustice, is in reality expressing the highest respect for law.

Of course, there is nothing new about this kind of civil disobedience. It was evidenced sublimely in the refusal of Shadrach, Meshach
and Abednego to obey the laws of Nebuchadnezzar, on the ground that
a higher moral law was at stake. It was practiced superbly by the early
Christians, who were willing to face hungry lions and the excruciating
pain of chopping blocks rather than submit to certain unjust laws of
the Roman Empire. To a degree, academic freedom is a reality today
because Socrates practiced civil disobedience. In our own nation, the
Boston Tea Party represented a massive act of civil disobedience.

We should never forget that everything Adolf Hitler did in Germany
was "legal" and everything the Hungarian freedom fighters did in Hun-
gary was "illegal." It was "illegal" to aid and comfort a Jew in Hitler's
Germany. Even so, I am sure that, had I lived in Germany at the time,
I would have aided and comforted my Jewish brothers. If today I lived
in a Communist country where certain principles dear to the Christian
faith are suppressed, I would openly advocate disobeying that country's
antireligious laws.

I must make two honest confessions to you, my Christian and Jewish brothers. First, I must confess that over the past few years I have
been gravely disappointed with the white moderate. I have almost
reached the regrettable conclusion that the Negro's great stumbling
block in his stride toward freedom is not the White Citizen's Councilor
or the Ku Klux Klanner, but the white moderate, who is more devoted
to "order" than to justice; who prefers a negative peace which is the absence of tension to a positive peace which is the presence of justice;
who constantly says: "I agree with you in the goal you seek, but I cannot agree with your methods of direct action"; who paternalistically believes he can set the timetable for another man's freedom; who lives
by a mythical concept of time and who constantly advises the Negro
to wait for a "more convenient season." Shallow understanding from
people of good will is more frustrating than absolute misunderstanding
from people of ill will. Lukewarm acceptance is much more bewilder-
ing than outright rejection.

I had hoped that the white moderate would understand that law
and order exist for the purpose of establishing justice and that when

they fail in this purpose they become the dangerously structured dams that block the flow of social progress. I had hoped that the white moderate would understand that the present tension in the South is a necessary phase of the transition from an obnoxious negative peace, in which the Negro passively accepted his unjust plight, to a substantive and positive peace, in which all men will respect the dignity and worth of human personality. Actually, we who engage in nonviolent direct action are not the creators of tension. We merely bring to the surface the hidden tension that is already alive. We bring it out in the open, where it can be seen and dealt with. Like a boil that can never be cured so long as it is covered up but must be opened with all its ugliness to the natural medicines of air and light, injustice must be exposed, with all the tension its exposure creates, to the light of human conscience and the air of national opinion before it can be cured.

In your statement you assert that our actions, even though peaceful, must be condemned because they precipitate violence. But is this a logical assertion? Isn't this like condemning a robbed man because his possession of money precipitated the evil act of robbery? Isn't this like condemning Socrates because his unswerving commitment to truth and his philosophical inquiries precipitated the act by the misguided populace in which they made him drink hemlock? Isn't this like condemning Jesus because his unique God-consciousness and never-ceasing devotion to God's will precipitated the evil act of crucifixion? We must come to see that, as the federal courts have consistently affirmed, it is wrong to urge an individual to cease his efforts to gain his basic constitutional rights because the quest may precipitate violence. Society must protect the robbed and punish the robber.

I had also hoped that the white moderate would reject the myth concerning time in relation to the struggle for freedom. I have just received a letter from a white brother in Texas. He writes: "All Christians know that the colored people will receive equal rights eventually, but it is possible that you are in too great a religious hurry. It has taken Christianity almost two thousand years to accomplish what it has. The teachings of Christ take time to come to earth." Such an attitude stems from a tragic misconception of time, from the strangely rational notion that there is something in the very flow of time that will inevitably cure all ills. Actually, time itself is neutral; it can be used either destructively or constructively. More and more I feel that the people of ill will have used time much more effectively than have the people of good will. We will have to repent in this generation not merely for the hateful words and actions of the bad people but for the appalling silence of the good people. Human progress never rolls in on wheels of inevitability; it comes through the tireless efforts of men willing to be co-workers with God, and without this hard work, time itself becomes an ally of the forces of social stagnation. We must use time creatively, in the knowledge that the time is always ripe to do right. Now is the time to make real the promise of democracy and transform our pending national elegy into a creative psalm of brotherhood. Now is the time to lift our national policy from the quicksand of racial injustice to the solid rock of human dignity.

You speak of our activity in Birmingham as extreme. At first I was rather disappointed that fellow clergymen would see my nonviolent efforts as those of an extremist. I began thinking about the fact that I stand in the middle of two opposing forces in the Negro community. One is a force of complacency, made up in part of Negroes who, as a result of long years of oppression, are so drained of self-respect and a sense of "somebodiness" that they have adjusted to segregation; and in part of a few middle class Negroes who, because of a degree of academic and economic security and because in some ways they profit by segregation, have become insensitive to the problems of the masses. The other force is one of bitterness and hatred, and it comes perilously close to advocating violence. It is expressed in the various black nationalist groups that are springing up across the nation, the largest and best-known being Elijah Muhammad's Muslim movement.* Nourished by the Negro's frustration over the continued existence of racial discrimination, this movement is made up of people who have lost faith in America, who have absolutely repudiated Christianity, and who have concluded that the white man is an incorrigible "devil."

I have tried to stand between these two forces, saying that we need emulate neither the "do-nothingism" of the complacent nor the hatred and despair of the black nationalist. For there is the more excellent way of love and nonviolent protest. I am grateful to God that, through the

---

*Elijah Muhammad, born Elijah Poole (1897–1975), was born to sharecropper parents in Sandersville, Georgia. In 1934, Muhammad succeeded Wallace Fard Muhammad as leader of the Nation of Islam, which promoted black economic self-reliance, separatism, and a rejection of notions of white supremacy. Under Muhammad, the group opened schools, restaurants, and mosques around the country, published a national newspaper, *Muhammad Speaks*, and formed its own security force. Before leaving the group, Malcolm X had served as the spokesman.

influence of the Negro church, the way of nonviolence became an integral part of our struggle.

If this philosophy had not emerged, by now many streets of the South would, I am convinced, be flowing with blood. And I am further convinced that if our white brothers dismiss as "rabble-rousers" and "outside agitators" those of us who employ nonviolent direct action, and if they refuse to support our nonviolent efforts, millions of Negroes will, out of frustration and despair, seek solace and security in black nationalist ideologies—a development that would inevitably lead to a frightening racial nightmare.

Oppressed people cannot remain oppressed forever. The yearning for freedom eventually manifests itself, and that is what has happened to the American Negro. Something within has reminded him of his birthright of freedom, and something without has reminded him that it can be gained. Consciously or unconsciously, he has been caught up by the Zeitgeist, and with his black brothers of Africa and his brown and yellow brothers of Asia, South America and the Caribbean, the United States Negro is moving with a sense of great urgency toward the promised land of racial justice. If one recognizes this vital urge that has engulfed the Negro community, one should readily understand why public demonstrations are taking place. The Negro has many pent-up resentments and latent frustrations, and he must release them. So let him march; let him make prayer pilgrimages to the city hall; let him go on freedom rides—and try to understand why he must do so. If his repressed emotions are not released in nonviolent ways, they will seek expression through violence; this is not a threat but a fact of history. So I have not said to my people: "Get rid of your discontent." Rather, I have tried to say that this normal and healthy discontent can be channeled into the creative outlet of nonviolent direct action. And now this approach is being termed extremist.

But though I was initially disappointed at being categorized as an extremist, as I continued to think about the matter I gradually gained a measure of satisfaction from the label. Was not Jesus an extremist for love: "Love your enemies, bless them that curse you, do good to them that hate you, and pray for them which despitefully use you, and persecute you." Was not Amos an extremist for justice: "Let justice roll down like waters and righteousness like an ever-flowing stream." Was not Paul an extremist for the Christian gospel: "I bear in my body the marks of the Lord Jesus." Was not Martin Luther an extremist: "Here

I stand; I cannot do otherwise, so help me God." And John Bunyan: "I will stay in jail to the end of my days before I make a butchery of my conscience." And Abraham Lincoln: "This nation cannot survive half slave and half free." And Thomas Jefferson: "We hold these truths to be self-evident, that all men are created equal . . ." So the question is not whether we will be extremists, but what kind of extremists we will be. Will we be extremists for hate or for love? Will we be extremists for the preservation of injustice or for the extension of justice? In that dramatic scene on Calvary's hill three men were crucified. We must never forget that all three were crucified for the same crime—the crime of extremism. Two were extremists for immorality, and thus fell below their environment. The other, Jesus Christ, was an extremist for love, truth and goodness, and thereby rose above his environment. Perhaps the South, the nation and the world are in dire need of creative extremists.

I had hoped that the white moderate would see this need. Perhaps I was too optimistic; perhaps I expected too much. I suppose I should have realized that few members of the oppressor race can understand the deep groans and passionate yearnings of the oppressed race, and still fewer have the vision to see that injustice must be rooted out by strong, persistent and determined action. I am thankful, however, that some of our white brothers in the South have grasped the meaning of this social revolution and committed themselves to it. They are still too few in quantity, but they are big in quality. Some—such as Ralph McGill, Lillian Smith, Harry Golden, James McBride Dabbs, Ann Braden and Sarah Patton Boyle—have written about our struggle in eloquent and prophetic terms.* Others have marched with us down nameless streets of the South. They have languished in filthy, roach-infested jails, suffering the abuse and brutality of policemen who view them as "dirty nigger lovers." Unlike so many of their moderate broth-

---

*As editor in chief and publisher of The Atlanta Constitution, Ralph McGill (1898–1969) was an outspoken critic of racial intolerance in the South. Lillian Smith (1897–1966) similarly attacked racism in a series of books, including Now Is the Time (1955), which promoted Southern compliance with the Brown v. Board decision. Harry Golden (1902–1981) published the anti–Jim Crow newspaper The Carolina Israelite from 1942 to 1968. His books include Only in America (1958). James McBride Dabbs (1896–1970), of Sumter County, South Carolina, became a leading white spokesman for social justice in the South. He was the author of four major books, including The Southern Heritage (1958), The Road Home (1960), and Who Speaks for the South? (1964). Ann Braden (1924–2006), a native of Louisville, Kentucky, wrote The Wall Between (1958), which explored the psychology of white Southern racism. Sarah Patton Boyle (1906–1994), a native of Virginia, was the author of The Desegregated Heart (1962), which maps her road to racial tolerance as a Southerner.

ers and sisters, they have recognized the urgency of the moment and sensed the need for powerful "action" antidotes to combat the disease of segregation.

Let me take note of my other major disappointment. I have been so greatly disappointed with the white church and its leadership. Of course, there are some notable exceptions. I am not unmindful of the fact that each of you has taken some significant stands on this issue. I commend you, Reverend Stallings, for your Christian stand on this past Sunday, in welcoming Negroes to your worship service on a non-segregated basis. I commend the Catholic leaders of this state for integrating Spring Hill College several years ago.

But despite these notable exceptions, I must honestly reiterate that I have been disappointed with the church. I do not say this as one of those negative critics who can always find something wrong with the church. I say this as a minister of the gospel, who loves the church; who was nurtured in its bosom; who has been sustained by its spiritual blessings and who will remain true to it as long as the cord of life shall lengthen.

When I was suddenly catapulted into the leadership of the bus protest in Montgomery, Alabama, a few years ago, I felt we would be supported by the white church. I felt that the white ministers, priests and rabbis of the South would be among our strongest allies. Instead, some have been outright opponents, refusing to understand the freedom movement and misrepresenting its leaders; all too many others have been more cautious than courageous and have remained silent behind the anesthetizing security of stained glass windows.

In spite of my shattered dreams, I came to Birmingham with the hope that the white religious leadership of this community would see the justice of our cause and, with deep moral concern, would serve as the channel through which our just grievances could reach the power structure. I had hoped that each of you would understand. But again I have been disappointed.

I have heard numerous southern religious leaders admonish their worshipers to comply with a desegregation decision because it is the law, but I have longed to hear white ministers declare: "Follow this decree because integration is morally right and because the Negro is your brother." In the midst of blatant injustices inflicted upon the Negro, I have watched white churchmen stand on the sideline and mouth pious irrelevancies and sanctimonious trivialities. In the midst of a mighty struggle to rid our nation of racial and economic injustice, I have heard many ministers say: "Those are social issues, with which the gospel has no real concern." And I have watched many churches commit themselves to a completely other worldly religion which makes a strange, un-Biblical distinction between body and soul, between the sacred and the secular.

I have traveled the length and breadth of Alabama, Mississippi and all the other southern states. On sweltering summer days and crisp autumn mornings I have looked at the South's beautiful churches with their lofty spires pointing heavenward. I have beheld the impressive outlines of her massive religious-education buildings. Over and over I have found myself asking: "What kind of people worship here? Who is their God? Where were their voices when the lips of Governor Barnett dripped with words of interposition and nullification? Where were they when Governor Wallace gave a clarion call for defiance and hatred? Where were their voices of support when bruised and weary Negro men and women decided to rise from the dark dungeons of complacency to the bright hills of creative protest?"

Yes, these questions are still in my mind. In deep disappointment I have wept over the laxity of the church. But be assured that my tears have been tears of love. There can be no deep disappointment where there is not deep love. Yes, I love the church. How could I do otherwise? I am in the rather unique position of being the son, the grandson and the great-grandson of preachers. Yes, I see the church as the body of Christ. But, oh! How we have blemished and scarred that body through social neglect and through fear of being nonconformists.

There was a time when the church was very powerful—in the time when the early Christians rejoiced at being deemed worthy to suffer for what they believed. In those days the church was not merely a thermometer that recorded the ideas and principles of popular opinion; it was a thermostat that transformed the mores of society. Whenever the early Christians entered a town, the people in power became disturbed and immediately sought to convict the Christians for being "disturbers of the peace" and "outside agitators." But the Christians pressed on, in the conviction that they were "a colony of heaven," called to obey God rather than man. Small in number, they were big in commitment. They were too God intoxicated to be "astronomically intimidated." By their effort and example they brought an end to such ancient evils as infanticide and gladiatorial contests.

Things are different now. So often the contemporary church is a weak, ineffectual voice with an uncertain sound. So often it is an arch defender of the status quo. Far from being disturbed by the presence of the church, the power structure of the average community is consoled by the church's silent and often even vocal sanction of things as they are.

But the judgment of God is upon the church as never before. If today's church does not recapture the sacrificial spirit of the early church, it will lose its authenticity, forfeit the loyalty of millions, and be dismissed as an irrelevant social club with no meaning for the twentieth century. Every day I meet young people whose disappointment with the church has turned into outright disgust.

Perhaps I have once again been too optimistic. Is organized religion too inextricably bound to the status quo to save our nation and the world? Perhaps I must turn my faith to the inner spiritual church, the church within the church, as the true ekklesia and the hope of the world. But again I am thankful to God that some noble souls from the ranks of organized religion have broken loose from the paralyzing chains of conformity and joined us as active partners in the struggle for freedom. They have left their secure congregations and walked the streets of Albany, Georgia, with us. They have gone down the highways of the South on tortuous rides for freedom. Yes, they have gone to jail with us. Some have been dismissed from their churches, have lost the support of their bishops and fellow ministers. But they have acted in the faith that right defeated is stronger than evil triumphant. Their witness has been the spiritual salt that has preserved the true meaning of the gospel in these troubled times. They have carved a tunnel of hope through the dark mountain of disappointment.

I hope the church as a whole will meet the challenge of this decisive hour. But even if the church does not come to the aid of justice, I have no despair about the future. I have no fear about the outcome of our struggle in Birmingham, even if our motives are at present misunderstood. We will reach the goal of freedom in Birmingham and all over the nation, because the goal of America is freedom. Abused and scorned though we may be, our destiny is tied up with America's destiny. Before the pilgrims landed at Plymouth, we were here. Before the pen of Jefferson etched the majestic words of the Declaration of Independence across the pages of history, we were here. For more than two centuries our forebears labored in this country without wages; they made cotton king; they built the homes of their masters while suffering gross injustice and shameful humiliation—and yet out of a bottomless vitality they continued to thrive and develop. If the inexpressible cruelties of slavery could not stop us, the opposition we now face will surely fail. We will win our freedom because the sacred heritage of our nation and the eternal will of God are embodied in our echoing demands.

Before closing I feel impelled to mention one other point in your statement that has troubled me profoundly. You warmly commended the Birmingham police force for keeping "order" and "preventing violence." I doubt that you would have so warmly commended the police force if you had seen its dogs sinking their teeth into unarmed, nonviolent Negroes. I doubt that you would so quickly commend the policemen if you were to observe their ugly and inhumane treatment of Negroes here in the city jail; if you were to watch them push and curse old Negro women and young Negro girls; if you were to see them slap and kick old Negro men and young boys; if you were to observe them, as they did on two occasions, refuse to give us food because we wanted to sing our grace together. I cannot join you in your praise of the Birmingham police department.

It is true that the police have exercised a degree of discipline in handing the demonstrators. In this sense they have conducted themselves rather "nonviolently" in public. But for what purpose? To preserve the evil system of segregation. Over the past few years I have consistently preached that nonviolence demands that the means we use must be as pure as the ends we seek. I have tried to make clear that it is wrong to use immoral means to attain moral ends. But now I must affirm that it is just as wrong, or perhaps even more so, to use moral means to preserve immoral ends. Perhaps Mr. Connor and his policemen have been rather nonviolent in public, as was Chief Pritchett in Albany, Georgia, but they have used the moral means of nonviolence to maintain the immoral end of racial injustice. As T. S. Eliot has said: "The last temptation is the greatest treason: To do the right deed for the wrong reason."

I wish you had commended the Negro sit-inners and demonstrators of Birmingham for their sublime courage, their willingness to suffer and their amazing discipline in the midst of great provocation. One day the South will recognize its real heroes. They will be the James Merediths, with the noble sense of purpose that enables them to face jeering, and hostile mobs, and with the agonizing loneliness that characterizes the life of the pioneer.* They will be old, oppressed, battered Negro women, symbolized in a seventy-two-year-old woman in Montgomery, Alabama, who rose up with a sense of dignity and with her people decided not to ride segregated buses, and who responded with ungrammatical profundity to one who inquired about her weariness: "My feets is tired, but my soul is at rest." They will be the young high school and college students, the young ministers of the gospel and a host of their elders, courageously and nonviolently sitting in at lunch counters and willingly going to jail for conscience' sake. One day the South will know that when these disinherited children of God sat down at lunch counters, they were in reality standing up for what is best in the American dream and for the most sacred values in our Judaeo-Christian heritage, thereby bringing our nation back to those great wells of democracy which were dug deep by the founding fathers in their formulation of the Constitution and the Declaration of Independence.

Never before have I written so long a letter. I'm afraid it is much too long to take your precious time. I can assure you that it would have been much shorter if I had been writing from a comfortable desk, but what else can one do when he is alone in a narrow jail cell, other than write long letters, think long thoughts and pray long prayers?

If I have said anything in this letter that overstates the truth and indicates an unreasonable impatience, I beg you to forgive me. If I have said anything that understates the truth and indicates my having a patience that allows me to settle for anything less than brotherhood, I beg God to forgive me.

I hope this letter finds you strong in the faith. I also hope that circumstances will soon make it possible for me to meet each of you, not as an integrationist or a civil rights leader but as a fellow clergyman and a Christian brother. Let us all hope that the dark clouds of racial prejudice will soon pass away and the deep fog of misunderstanding will be lifted from our fear-drenched communities, and in some not too distant tomorrow the radiant stars of love and brotherhood will shine over our great nation with all their scintillating beauty.

Yours for the cause of Peace and Brotherhood,

Martin Luther King, Jr.

*James Meredith (b. 1933) was twice denied admission to the University of Mississippi before being admitted by court order in 1962. Attorney General Robert Kennedy dispatched federal marshals to protect Meredith against threats of violence. The decision sparked riots during which 160 marshals were wounded. Meredith persevered, graduating from the university in 1964.

James Baldwin to His Nephew James

James Baldwin (1924–1987), who emerged as one of the most important writers and social critics of the twentieth century, was born in Harlem and raised, with his seven step-siblings, by his mother and a strict stepfather who was a factory worker and Pentecostal minister. Baldwin's first book, Go Tell It on the Mountain *(1953), was largely autobiographical and chronicled his troubled relationship with his stepfather. Baldwin, who was openly gay, tackled the struggle for acceptance and identity in his next two works of fiction,* Giovanni's Room *(1956) and* Another Country *(1962). Those books were accompanied by three nonfiction works,* Notes of a Native Son *(1955);* Nobody Knows My Name *(1961); and* The Fire Next Time *(1963). Baldwin moved to Paris in 1948 and spent the rest of his life as an expatriate, although he frequently traveled to the United States to lend his voice to the Civil Rights Movement. He wrote his letter on the one hundredth anniversary of the Emancipation Proclamation.*

1963

Dear James:

I have begun this letter five times and torn it up five times. I keep seeing your face, which is also the face of your father and my brother. Like him, you are tough, dark, vulnerable, mood—with a very definite tendency to sound truculent because you want no one to think you are soft. You may be like your grandfather in this, I don't know, but certainly both you and your father resemble him very much physically. Well, he is dead, he never saw you, and he had a terrible life; he was defeated long before he died because, at the bottom of his heart, he really believed what white people said about him. This is one of the reasons that he became so holy. I am sure that your father has told you something about all that. Neither you nor your father exhibit any tendency towards holiness: you really are of another era, part of what happened when the late E. Franklin Frazier called "the cities of destruction."* You can only be destroyed by believing that you really are what the white world calls a nigger. I tell you this because I love you, and please don't forget it.

I have known both of you all your lives, have carried your Daddy in my arms and on my shoulders, kissed and spanked him and watched

---

*Born Edward Franklin Frazier (1894–1962) in Baltimore, Maryland, Frazier was a sociologist whose landmark work exploring black family life included *The Negro Family in the United States* (1939).

him learn to walk. I don't know if you've known anybody from that far back; if you've loved anybody that long, first as an infant, then as a child, then as a man, you gain a strange perspective on time and human pain and effort. Other people cannot see what I see whenever I look into your father's face as it is today are all those other faces which were his. Let him laugh and I see a cellar your father does not remember and a house he does not remember and I hear in his present laughter his laughter as a child. Let him curse and I remember him falling down the cellar steps, and howling, and I remember, with pain, his tears, which my hand or your grandmother's so easily wiped away. But no one's hand can wipe away those tears he sheds invisibly today, which one hears in his laughter and in his speech and in his songs. I know what the world has done to my brother and how narrowly he has survived it. And I know, which is much worse, and this is the crime of which I accuse my country and my countrymen, and for which neither I nor time nor history will ever forgive them, that they have destroyed and are destroying hundreds of thousands of lives and do not know it and do not want to know it. One can be, indeed one must strive to become, tough and philosophical concerning destruction and death, for this is what most of mankind has been best at since we have heard of man. (But remember: most of mankind is not all of mankind.) But it is not permissible that the authors of devastation should also be innocent. It is the innocence which constitutes the crime.

Now, my dear namesake, these innocent and well-meaning people, your countrymen, have caused you to be born under conditions not very far removed from those described for us by Charles Dickens in the London of more than a hundred years ago. (I hear the chorus of the innocents screaming, "No! This is not true! How bitter you are!"—but I am writing this letter to you, to try to tell you something about how to handle them, for most of them do not yet really know that you exist. I know the conditions, under which you were born, for I was there. Your countrymen were not there, and haven't made it yet. Your grandmother was also there, and no one has ever accused her of being bitter. I suggest that the innocents check with her. She isn't hard to find. Your countrymen don't know that she exists, either, though she has been working for them all their lives.)

Well, you were born, here you came, something like fourteen years ago: and though your father and mother and grandmother, looking about the streets through which they were carrying you, staring at the walls into which they brought you, had every reason to be heavy-hearted, yet they were not. For here you were, Big James, named for me—you were a big baby, I was not—here you were: to be loved. To be loved, baby, hard, at once, and forever, to strengthen you against the loveless world. Remember that: I know how black it looks today, for you. It looked bad that day, too, yes, we were trembling. We have not stopped trembling yet, but if we had not loved each other none of us would have survived. And now you must survive because we love you, and for the sake of your children and your children's children.

This innocent country set you down in a ghetto in which, in fact, it intended that you should perish. Let me spell out precisely what I mean by that, for the heart of the matter is here, and the root of my dispute with my country. You were born where you were born, and faced the future that you faced because you were black and for no other reason. The limits of your ambition were, thus, expected to be set forever. You were born into a society which spelled out with brutal clarity, and in as many ways as possible, that you were a worthless human being. You were not expected to aspire to excellence: you were expected to make peace with mediocrity. Wherever you have turned, James, in your short time on this earth, you have been told where you could go and what you could do (and how you could do it) and where you could do it and whom you could marry. I know that your countrymen do not agree with me about this, and I hear them saying "You exaggerate." They do not know Harlem, and I do. So do you. Take no one's word for anything, including mine—but trust your experience. Know whence you came. If you know whence you came, there is really no limit to where you can go. The details and symbols of your life have been deliberately constructed to make you believe what white people say about you. Please try to remember that what they believe, as well as what they do and cause you to endure, does not testify to your inferiority but to their inhumanity and fear. Please try to be clear, dear James, through the storm which rages about your youthful head today, about the reality which lies behind the words acceptance and integration. There is no reason for you to try to become like white people and there is no basis whatever for their impertinent assumption that they must accept you. The really terrible thing, old buddy, is that you must accept them. And I mean that very seriously. You must accept them and accept them with love. For these innocent people have no other hope. They are, in effect, still trapped in a history which they do not understand; and until they understand it, they cannot be released from it. They have had to believe for so many years, and for innumerable reasons, that black men are inferior to white men. Many of them, indeed, know better, but, as you will discover, people find it very difficult to act on what they know. To act is to be committed, and to be committed is to be in danger. In this case, the danger, in the minds of most white Americans, is the loss of identity. Try to imagine how you would feel if you woke up one morning to find the sun shining and all the stars aflame. You would be frightened because it is out of the order of nature. Any upheaval in the universe is terrifying because it so profoundly attacks one's sense of one's own reality. Well, the black man has functioned in the white man's world as a fixed star, as an immovable pillar: and as he moves out of his place, heaven and earth are shaken to their foundations. You, don't be afraid. I said that it was intended that you should perish in the ghetto, perish by never being allowed to go behind the white man's definitions, by never being allowed to spell your proper name. You have, and many of us have, defeated this intention; and, by a terrible law, a terrible paradox, those innocents who believed that your imprisonment made them safe are losing their grasp of reality. But these men are your brothers—your lost, younger brothers. And if the word integration means anything, this is what it means: that we, with love, shall force our brothers to see themselves as they are, to cease fleeing from reality and begin to change it. For this is your home, my friend, do not be driven from it; great men have done great things here, and will again, and we can make America what America must become. It will be hard, James, but you come from sturdy, peasant stock, men who picked cotton and dammed rivers and built railroads, and in the teeth of the most terrifying odds, achieved an unassailable and monumental dignity. You come from a long line of poets, some of the greatest poets since Homer. One of them said, The very time I thought I was lost, My dungeon shook and my chains fell off.

You know, and I know, that the country is celebrating one hundred years of freedom one hundred years too soon. We cannot be free until they are free. God bless you, James, and Godspeed.

Your uncle

James

Rev. Adam Clayton Powell, Jr., to Dr. Martin Luther King, Jr.

New York
January 27, 1964

My dear Dr. King:

Enclosed is a check in the sum of $625.00. This check represents a contribution from the Sunday School Children of Abyssinian Baptist Church. The children decided themselves to give up the usual gifts the church purchases for them each year so that the money could go toward your work. This check represents the childrens' pennies they took in an offering and part of the Christmas Offering of the Church.

Please be assured of the continued prayers of the children, the youth and adults of this, the Abyssinian Baptist Church. May God give you strength and courage.

Sincerely,
Adam C. Powell, Minister

Shirley Du Bois to Langston Hughes

Born Lola Bell Graham in Evansville, Indiana, Shirley Du Bois (1896–1977) was a playwright and director who in the 1940s wrote a number of biographies of African American luminaries, including Frederick Douglass, Phillis Wheatley, and Booker T. Washington. In 1943 she became the New York field secretary for the NAACP and worked with W.E.B. Du Bois, whom she married in 1951. In 1961 the couple moved to Ghana, where W.E.B. Du Bois died in 1963. Langston Hughes (1902–1967) was a prolific writer of poetry, novels, essays, and plays who emerged as a seminal figure of the Harlem Renaissance. Born James Mercer Langston Hughes in Joplin, Missouri, to Carrie Langston Hughes, a teacher, and James Nathaniel Hughes, who abandoned his young family to relocate to Mexico, Hughes made Harlem home and inspiration and infused racial pride and a celebration of African American culture and history in his work. His most famous poem, "The Negro Speaks of Rivers," was first published in The Crisis *in 1921. Hughes received a B.A. from Lincoln University, which in 1943 awarded him an honorary doctorate.*

Accra, Ghana
March 7, 1965

Dear Langston,

Thank you for sending me your column following Malcolm's assassination. I am glad you used W.E.B.'s lines. It is well that people in the United States acknowledge the justice and rightness of his oft-repeated pleas, denunciations and appeals to reason. You are mistaken, however, in your final comment. If Du Bois were living today, he would not be asking once more, "What meaneth this?" HE WOULD KNOW THE MEANING. Anyone who looks around the United States, Africa and Asia with clear, unbias [sic] eyes can know the full meaning of all that you described.

I am sending you an article written by William Gardner Smith.* I brought him from Paris to Ghana last year to train our television news unit. He went about his job with such professional finish, understanding and political awareness that this month he has been appointed Director of Ghana's School of Journalism. His analysis of Malcolm's death gives you the answers. Unlike the majority of Afro-Americans who make the "tour of Africa," Malcolm came and <u>learned</u>. He did not take his "briefings" from foreign embassies. He sought out and listened to <u>Africans</u>—those in high places and on all levels. And we learned to respect and understand his strivings. As time passed we learned to honor and love him as we did no Afro-American who has crossed this continent: Today, we mourn his murder and we feel more sorry than ever for our brothers and sisters in America.

We in Ghana will carry on and finally achieve that African Unity which will make us strong.

Sincerely,

Shirley Du Bois.

Jean Fairfax to Minnie and A. J. Lewis

Jean Fairfax, a civil rights activist and philanthropist, served as director of the Southern Civil Rights Program for the American Friends Service Committee from 1957 to 1965, and for twenty years was on the staff of the NAACP Legal Defense and Educational Fund, where she was intimately

---

*William Gardner Smith (1929–1974) was a novelist whose works addressed racial tension. They include *Last of the Conquerors* (1948), *Anger at Innocence* (1950), and *The Stone Face* (1963).

involved in the struggle to desegregate schools. She wrote this letter to an African American couple who sought her help identifying architects and contractors who would work with them to build a home.

July 23, 1965

Dear Minnie and A.J.:

We must have been thinking of each other at the same time. I received your letter this morning; you probably got one from me today, too.

I am sorry to hear that you have had trouble finding someone to prepare your blueprints and to construct your home. This certainly is an effort to freeze you out, especially since the contractor had promised not long ago to build your home and did not seem to be prejudiced at all.

I have telephoned a man in New York who is the attorney for an organization which helps Negroes buy homes. They are only interested in certain kinds of cases and they are limited to working with builders who are part of their organization. This man is going to check to see whether they have a builder in Mississippi. If they have a Mississippi builder, this would be a good solution. It would be a well-built house, the man would take a personal interest in your total situation and the financing would be arranged through this national group. He will be in touch with me in about ten days. Meanwhile, continue to make your own investigations. Since everything takes time and since most things don't work out, it is good to have lots of irons in the fire! So much depends on your finding a builder because he will play a key role in your financing of the house. By the time you have talked with the contractor whom Mrs. MacDonald's son-in-law recommends, I hope I will have some information for you from this New York contact.

Keep your spirits up! We'll work out something.

Sincerely,

Jean Fairfax
National Representative for Southern Programs

U.S. Senator Edward W. Brooke III to
President Richard M. Nixon

March 27, 1969

My dear Mr. President:

I am writing you to express my deep and growing concern over the absence of black Americans in policy-making positions in the area of foreign affairs.

At the present time there is only one Negro in the State Department with the rank of Assistant Secretary. There are no black assistant Secretaries in any of the geographic bureaus, and black Americans are noticeably absent in the functional areas such as Policy Planning Council, Congressional Relations, Bureau of Public Affairs, Bureau of Economic Affairs, Bureau of Intelligence and Research, and many others. Four black Americans are now serving their country in the rank of Ambassador, but all of them are in Class IV posts.

The numerical ratio of black to white Americans serving in the Department of the State is roughly equivalent to the actual representation of blacks in American society: of 14,565 employees, 1,364 are black. But it is a matter of deep distress to me that so few of these black employees have apparently been deemed worthy of appointment to high-ranking or policy-making positions.

I know that many members of the black community feel very strongly that the next Assistant Secretary of State for African Affairs and/or the next AID administrator for Africa be a black American. Persons who might be qualified for these positions include Clyde Ferguson, Franklin Williams, George Carter, Ted Harris, Clinton Knox, C. Fred Marrow, and Sam Westerfield.

In addition, I am most hopeful that the present serious gaps in black representation in the higher echelons of the Department be corrected as soon as possible. For this reason, I am taking the liberty of including a list of particularly qualified individuals and their areas of expertise which are known to me, whom you and the Secretary of State might wish to consider for these positions: [A list was attached.]

I know that your concerns in this area parallel my own, and I am most appreciative of the attention which you and the members of your Cabinet have already shown in this important and sensitive area.

With kind personal regards, I am,
Sincerely yours,
    Edward W. Brooke

U.S. Senator Edward W. Brooke III to
Secretary of State William P. Rogers

Senator Brooke remained an ardent critic of the system of racial apartheid in South Africa, as indicated by this letter to Secretary of State William P. Rogers. In 1976, in the midst of violent uprisings by blacks throughout southern Africa, he continued to criticize the inadequate attention to the situation by the United States and other countries.

Washington, D.C.
May 27, 1969

Dear Mr. Secretary

It is my understanding that the Department of State is presently conducting a thorough review of United States policy toward Southern Africa.

This is a matter which is of deepest concern to the nations of Black Africa, and indeed to all people who place high value on the principles of human freedom and equality of opportunity. As I pointed out in a speech to the Senate over a year ago, trouble is brewing in this area where 32 million people are denied, solely on the basis of race, the right to participate in making the laws by which they are governed.

It has long been my view that our country cannot condone, and should not support, repressive racist regimes. There is little we can do as a free nation to prohibit private investment or private travel in these areas, though we can and should continue our policy of offering no incentives for these transactions. But there is much we can do in the public sphere to publicize our disapproval and to press for substantial change.

We can continue our support for the international policy of economic sanctions against Southern Rhodesia, whose trade has never been vital to our interests, and whose domestic policies are inimical to both our interests and our principles.

We can begin to discontinue any official support for the government of the Republic of South Africa, including the sugar quota and our military and scientific investments.

We can continue to make clear our disapproval of the policies of the white majority regimes, through public statements and private diplomacy.

We can continue our embargo against the sale of arms to all the Southern African governments.

We can continue to support the efforts of the United Nations to moderate developments in the region.

In all of these matters, I have been encouraged by the positions taken by the new Administration thus far. In December of 1968, in response to a letter to Henry Kissinger I received assurance that no change was contemplated in our policy toward Southern Rhodesia, despite some rather widely voiced expectations to the contrary on the part of Rhodesian Prime Minister Ian Smith.

I was also heartened to read the text of the message delivered by United States Representative Waldemar Nielsen to the 10th Anniversary Meeting of the UN Economic Commission for Africa. At that time he stated that our refusal to "condone abroad what we oppose at home" was "an enduring part of our government's policy toward these African problems."

And I was pleased to see that in your recent testimony before the Senate Foreign Relations Committee and the remarks before the American Society of Newspaper Editors convention in Washington, indicated continuing support for the principles of self-determination in Southern Africa.

Personally, I would advocate even stronger measures to indicate United States' concern regarding Southern Africa. But I recognize that our power and our interests [in] this area of the world are somewhat limited at the present time. We should keep in mind our national priorities and confine our efforts to the realm of the possible; even with these limits, however, we have a good share of influence, which should be exercised in such a way as to encourage the evolution of a system of government which will be in the best interests of all the people of Southern Africa, and with which we can live and work. Stated briefly, I do not believe that our interests or those of the people of South Africa will be served either by a continuation for the present form of government, or by a reaction which brings to power a regime supported by and dependent upon the forces of world communism. I believe we have many interests in common with the liberation movements, and that our posture should not be such as to cut us off from constructive contact with these groups.

I anticipate a lengthy and increasingly bloody struggle in this region of the world, until and unless the minority governments adopt a more open political policy. And I believe very strongly that America must be prepared to maintain its support for the principle of self-determination and to refrain from aiding those forces which oppose them, if we are to enjoy any credibility and respect with the vast majority of the world's population which lives in the developing world.

With appreciation for your attention to these views, and with kind personal regards, I am,

Sincerely yours,

Edward W. Brooke

Bayard Rustin to Eldridge Cleaver

Bayard Rustin (1912–1987) was born in West Chester, Pennsylvania, and raised by his maternal grandmother, a Quaker. In 1937 Rustin moved to Harlem, where he became a civil rights activist and, later in life, an outspoken proponent of gay rights. Rustin was one of the principal organizers of the 1963 March on Washington and a key adviser to Dr. Martin Luther King, Jr., on the strategy of nonviolent resistance, which he learned in India from leaders of the Gandhian movement. He was also one of the founders of the Congress of Racial Equality and with King organized the Southern Christian Leadership Conference.

Eldridge Cleaver (1935–1998) rose to prominence as spokesman of the Black Panther Party and as author of Soul on Ice *(1968), an influential book of essays written while he was in prison. In 1968 he fled to Algeria after he was charged with attempted murder following a confrontation between the Panthers and Oakland police. He renounced the Panthers when he returned to the United States in 1975 and was sentenced to probation for assault. By 1980 Cleaver had become a conservative Republican and endorsed Ronald Reagan for President.*

New York City
January 24, 1977

Dear Eldridge:

We've been out of touch with each other, far too out of touch, which is one of the reasons that impels me to write you at this time.

After your return to this country I offered to help you in any way I could. I knew that many of your old friends would probably have little to do with you, given your new and more positive attitude toward the United States; and that few new people would be coming to your aid because of your past activities and statements. I was not sure how effective my help would be, but as in many other cases during my career, I did what I thought was right, not what was expedient.

I set up the Eldridge Cleaver Defense Committee with three main purposes in mind. The first was to get the parole hold lifted so that you could put up bail. The second was to try to raise money both for the bail and for legal expenses, since it was our view that without such money you could not be assured of the proper legal representation. Finally, I thought it was necessary to provide a platform for you, since I felt you had an important message which the American people has to hear. I am of course referring to your views on democracy and on the possibilities which exist within the democratic American system to achieve the goals of human freedom and social equality.

The first purpose has been achieved, but I am afraid we could not achieve the second since there was simply not a constituency that I could reach from which we could raise the large amounts of money needed. In any event, it appears that you have found other benefactors. As to the third purpose, it would also appear from what I have read that you now have other intellectual and spiritual interests which take precedence in your own mind over the issues of democracy which previously had been your chief concern. I write "from what I have read" since we have not been in communication and I have no alternative but to draw conclusions from the available evidence.

Therefore, and after much thought, I have decided that except for trying to raise some limited funds to pay back bills the time has come to dissolve the Defense Committee. Judging from your lack of communication it would seem that you don't think you need its services anymore, particularly in light of the alternative sources of support you have been able to develop.

Personally, I wish you nothing but the best in the future, and should you feel any need or desire to reach me for whatever reason, you know that my door is always open.

With warmest regards,

Sincerely,

Bayard

Bayard Rustin to Mayor Edward I. Koch

New York City
February 25, 1985

Dear Ed,

I understand from meeting with representatives of the Coalition for Lesbian and Gay Rights that you are in the midst of a lobbying effort to pass the long overdue lesbian and gay rights bill in the City Council this Spring. I'd like to help in any way that I can and have several proposals.

Since the Black members of the Council are 4–2 against the legislation at present, I am sending them each personal letters, thanking the supporters and urging the opponents to reconsider. If you plan to call any of them in for a meeting on this matter, I would be happy to attend if you feel my presence would be of help and my schedule permits.

The Coalition is working on having the bill called up for a "discharge" motion vote in May if efforts to dislodge the bill from committee are unsuccessful. First, if the bill does come up for a hearing I would like to testify. If all we are left with is the discharge motion, I feel we should call attention to the fact that the legislation is being filibustered (much the way civil rights bills were held up by Southerners in the past) and that it deserves a fair vote. We could call together a group of prominent citizens in support of the bill and hold a press conference the day before the vote. Is there a room we could use at City Hall for this purpose? Perhaps the Council chamber itself?

Please let me know how I can aid your efforts.

Thanks for your work on this issue.

Sincerely,

Bayard Rustin

Rev. Jeremiah A. Wright, Jr., to Jodi Kantor

Jeremiah A. Wright, Jr. (b. 1941), was the senior pastor of Trinity United Church of Christ in Chicago, where Senator Barack Obama attended church. Wright commanded national headlines during the 2008 Democratic presidential primary when one of his videotaped sermons criticizing America was broadcast on television. The controversy prompted Obama to deliver a widely hailed speech on race. He would later sever his ties with the controversial pastor. In this letter, posted on his website and widely circulated on the Internet, Wright criticized a March 6, 2007, New York Times article that examined his relationship with Obama, whose bestselling book The Audacity of Hope *(2006) was titled after a Wright sermon.* Jodi Kantor (b. 1975) was an editor at* Slate *before joining* The New York Times, *for which she covered the 2008 presidential campaign.*

Dear Jodi:

Thank you for engaging in one of the biggest misrepresentations of the truth that I have ever seen in sixty-five years. You sat and shared with me for two hours. You told me you were doing a "Spiritual Biography" of Senator Barack Obama. For two hours, I shared with you how I thought he was the most principled individual in public service that I have ever met.

For two hours, I talked with you about how idealistic he was. For two hours I shared with you what a genuine human being he was. I told you how incredible he was as a man who was an African American in public service, and as a man who refused to announce his candidacy for President until Carol Moseley Braun indicated one way or the other whether or not she was going to run.

I told you what a dreamer he was. I told you how idealistic he was. We talked about how refreshing it would be for someone who knew about Islam to be in the Oval Office. Your own question to me was, Didn't I think it would be incredible to have somebody in the Oval Office who not only knew about Muslims, but had living and breathing Muslims in his own family? I told you how important it would be to have a man who not only knew the difference between Shiites and Sunnis prior to 9/11/01 in the Oval Office, but also how important it

---

*The article, "Disinvitation by Obama Is Criticized," discloses that Wright was not invited to Obama's announcement of his presidential candidacy. Another article, "A Candidate, His Minister and the Search for Faith," was published by *The New York Times* on April 30, 2007.

would be to have a man who knew what Sufism was; a man who understood that there were different branches of Judaism; a man who knew the difference between Hasidic Jews, Orthodox Jews, Conservative Jews and Reformed Jews; and a man who was a devout Christian, but who did not prejudge others because they believed something other than what he believed.

I talked about how rare it was to meet a man whose Christianity was not just "in word only." I talked about Barack being a person who lived his faith and did not argue his faith. I talked about Barack as a person who did not draw doctrinal lines in the sand nor consign other people to hell if they did not believe what he believed.

Out of a two-hour conversation with you about Barack's spiritual journey and my protesting to you that I had not shaped him nor formed him, that I had not mentored him or made him the man he was, even though I would love to take that credit, you did not print any of that. When I told you, using one of your own Jewish stories from the Hebrew Bible as to how God asked Moses, "What is that in your hand?," that Barack was like that when I met him. Barack had it "in his hand." Barack had in his grasp a uniqueness in terms of his spiritual development that one is hard put to find in the 21st century, and you did not print that.

As I was just starting to say a moment ago, Jodi, out of two hours of conversation I spent approximately five to seven minutes on Barack's taking advice from one of his trusted campaign people and deeming it unwise to make me the media spotlight on the day of his announcing his candidacy for the Presidency and what do you print? You and your editor proceeded to present to the general public a snippet, a printed "sound byte" and a titillating and tantalizing article about his disinviting me to the Invocation on the day of his announcing his candidacy.

I have never been exposed to that kind of duplicitous behavior before, and I want to write you publicly to let you know that I do not approve of it and will not be party to any further smearing of the name, the reputation, the integrity or the character of perhaps this nation's first (and maybe even only) honest candidate offering himself for public service as the person to occupy the Oval Office.

Your editor is a sensationalist. For you to even mention that makes me doubt your credibility, and I am looking forward to see how you are going to butcher what else I had to say concerning Senator Obama's "Spiritual Biography." Our Conference Minister, the Reverend Jane

Fisler Hoffman, a white woman who belongs to a Black church that Hannity of "Hannity and Colmes" is trying to trash, set the record straight for you in terms of who I am and in terms of who we are as the church to which Barack has belonged for over twenty years.

The president of our denomination, the Reverend John Thomas, has offered to try to help you clarify in your confused head what Trinity Church is even though you spent the entire weekend with us setting me up to interview me for what turned out to be a smear of the Senator; and yet *The New York Times* continues to roll on making the truth what it wants to be the truth. I do not remember reading in your article that Barack had apologized for listening to that bad information and bad advice. Did I miss it? Or did your editor cut it out? Either way, you do not have to worry about hearing anything else from me for you to edit or "spin" because you are more interested in journalism than in truth.

Forgive me for having a momentary lapse. I forgot that *The New York Times* was leading the bandwagon in trumpeting why it is we should have gone into an illegal war. *The New York Times* became George Bush and the Republican Party's national "blog." *The New York Times* played a role in the outing of Valerie Plame.* I do not know why I thought *The New York Times* had actually repented and was going to exhibit a different kind of behavior.

Maybe it was my faith in the Jewish Holy Day of Roshashana. Maybe it was my being caught up in the euphoria of the Season of Lent; but whatever it is or was, I was sadly mistaken. There is no repentance on the part of *The New York Times*. There is no integrity when it comes to *The Times*. You should do well with that paper, Jodi. You looked me straight in my face and told me a lie!

Sincerely and respectfully yours,

Reverend Jeremiah A. Wright, Jr.,

Senior Pastor

Trinity United Church of Christ

---

*Valerie Plame (b. 1963) is a former U.S. CIA Operations Officer whose covert and classified identity was disclosed in Robert Novak's syndicated column, prompting her retirement and a grand jury investigation. I. Lewis "Scooter" Libby, Assistant to the President, was convicted for perjury, obstruction of justice, and making false statements to federal investigators.

Toni Morrison to U.S. Senator Barack Obama

Toni Morrison (b. 1931), was born Chloe Anthony Wofford in Lorain, Ohio, to George Wofford, who was a welder, and Ramah Willis Wofford. Morrison received a B.A. in English from Howard University, and a Master of Arts degree from Cornell University. Her first novel was* The Bluest Eye *(1970), followed by* Sula *(1973), which was nominated for the National Book Award. Her third novel,* Song of Solomon *(1977), won the National Book Critics Circle Award, and* Beloved *(1987) won the Pulitzer Prize for fiction and was adapted into a film starring Oprah Winfrey and Danny Glover. In 1993 Morrison became the first African American woman awarded the Nobel Prize in Literature. She was awarded an honorary Doctor of Letters degree from Oxford University in 2005. A year later she retired from Princeton University, where since 1989 she had held the Robert F. Goheen Chair in the Humanities.*

She wrote the following letter to Senator Obama in support of his presidential bid. The letter was released by the Obama campaign, and published by The New York Observer.

January 28, 2008

Dear Senator Obama,

This letter represents a first for me—a public endorsement of a Presidential candidate. I feel driven to let you know why I am writing it. One reason is it may help gather other supporters; another is that this is one of those singular moments that nations ignore at their peril. I will not rehearse the multiple crises facing us, but of one thing I am certain: this opportunity for a national evolution (even resolution) will not come again soon, and I am convinced you are the person to capture it.

May I describe to you my thoughts?

I have admired Senator Clinton for years. Her knowledge always seemed to me exhaustive; her negotiation of politics expert. However, I am more compelled by the quality of mind (as far as I can measure it) of a candidate. I cared little for her gender as a source of my admiration, and the little I did care was based on the fact that no liberal woman has ever ruled in America. Only conservative or "new-centrist" ones are allowed into that realm. Nor do I care very much for your

---

*Morrison took the name of her husband, Harold Morrison, to whom she was married from 1958 to 1964. They had two sons.

race[s]. I would not support you if that was all you had to offer or because it might make me "proud."

In thinking carefully about the strengths of the candidates, I stunned myself when I came to the following conclusion: that in addition to keen intelligence, integrity and a rare authenticity, you exhibit something that has nothing to do with age, experience, race or gender and something I don't see in other candidates. That something is a creative imagination which coupled with brilliance equals wisdom. It is too bad if we associate it only with gray hair and old age. Or if we call searing vision naiveté. Or if we believe cunning is insight. Or if we settle for finessing cures tailored for each ravaged tree in the forest while ignoring the poisonous landscape that feeds and surrounds it. Wisdom is a gift; you can't train for it, inherit it, learn it in a class or earn it in the workplace—that access can foster the acquisition of knowledge, but not wisdom.

When, I wondered, was the last time the country was guided by such a leader? Someone whose moral center was un-embargoed? Someone with courage instead of mere ambition? Someone who truly thinks of his country's citizens as "we," not "they"? Someone who understands what it will take to help America realize the virtues it fancies about itself, what it desperately needs to become in the world?

Our future is ripe, outrageously rich in its possibilities. Yet unleashing the glory of that future will require a difficult labor, and some may be so frightened of its birth, they will refuse to abandon their nostalgia for the womb.

There have been a few prescient leaders in our past, but you are the man for this time.

Good luck to you and to us.

Toni Morrison

Alice Walker to President-Elect Barack Obama
The Pulitzer Prize–winning author penned this letter to Obama the day after he was elected president.

November 5, 2008

Dear Brother President (Elect),

You have no idea, really, of how profound this moment is for us. Us being the black people of the Southern United States. You think you know, because you are thoughtful, and you have studied our history. But seeing you deliver the torch so many others carried, year after year, decade after decade, century after century, only to be brought down before igniting the flame of justice and of law, is almost more than the heart can bear. And yet, this observation is not intended to burden you, for you are of a different time, and, indeed, because of all the relay runners before you, North America is a different place. It is really only to say: *Well done*. We knew, through all the generations, that you were with us, *in* us, the best of the spirit of Africa and of the Americas. Knowing this, that you would actually appear, someday, was part of our strength. Seeing you take your rightful place, based solely on your wisdom, stamina, and character, is a balm for the weary warriors of hope, previously only sung about.

I would advise you to remember that you did not create the disaster that the world is experiencing, and you alone are not responsible for bringing the world back to balance. A primary responsibility that you do have, however, is to cultivate happiness in your own life. To make a schedule that permits sufficient time of rest and play with your gorgeous wife and lovely daughters. And so on. One gathers that your family is large. We are used to seeing men in the White House soon become juiceless and as white-haired as the building; we notice their wives and children looking strained and stressed. They soon have smiles so lacking in joy that they remind us of scissors. This is no way to lead. Nor does your family deserve this fate. One way of thinking about all of this is: It is so bad now that there is no excuse not to relax. From your happy, relaxed state, you can model real success, which is only what so many people in the world really want. They may buy endless cars and houses and furs and gobble up all the attention and space they can manage, or barely manage, but this is because it is not clear to them yet that success is truly an inside job. That it is within the reach of almost everyone.

I would further advise you not to take on other people's enemies. Most damage that others do to us is out of fear, humiliation, and pain. Those feelings occur in all of us, not just in those of us who profess a certain religious or racial devotion. We must all of us learn actually not to have enemies, but only confused adversaries who are ourselves in disguise. It is understood by all that you are Commander in Chief of the United States and are sworn to protect our beloved country; this we understand, completely. However, as my mother used to say, quoting a Bible with which I often fought, "Hate the sin, but love the sinner." There must be no more crushing of whole communitites, no more torture, no more dehumanizing as a means of ruling a people's spirit. This has already happened to people of color, poor people, women, children. We see where this leads, where it has led.

A good model of how to "work with the enemy" internally is presented by the Dalai Lama, in his endless caretaking of his soul as he confronts the Chinese government that invaded Tibet. Because, finally, it is the soul that must be preserved, if one is to remain a credible leader. All else might be lost; but when the soul dies, the connection to Earth, to Peoples, to Animals, to Rivers, to Mountain Ranges, purple and majestic, also dies. And your smile, with which we watch you do gracious battle with unjust characterizations, distortions, and lies, is that expression of healthy self-worth, spirit, and soul, that, kept happy and free and relaxed, can find an answering smile in all of us, lighting our way, and brightening the world.

We are the ones we have been waiting for.

In Peace and Joy,

Alice Walker

PART IV

Education and the Art of Scholarship

For African Americans, the pursuit of education has always been inextricably linked to the struggle for equality and social justice. State prohibitions against the education of slaves, beginning in the 1600s, ensured widespread illiteracy until the Emancipation Proclamation opened the legal gateway to reading and writing. Around the country, education became a common quest of the newly freed who pooled their meager resources to build schools and gain the literacy they had long been denied.

For decades the education of African Americans remained largely the task of segregated and underfunded schools, a disparity that was challenged in the historic Supreme Court case *Brown v. Board of Education of Topeka*. While many believed the Court had dealt a death knell to racial segregation and inequality, it would take two decades of resistance, progress, and setbacks before integration became a reality. Still, true integration continued to elude many African Americans who failed to achieve parity in education with whites.

Booker T. Washington to Emily Howland

Emily Howland (1827–1929) was a wealthy white philanthropist who had long supported the Tuskegee Institute. Born in Sherwood, New York, to abolitionist, Quaker parents, she made her home a stop on the Underground Railroad and taught former slaves to read and write during the Civil War. From 1857 to 1859, she taught at the Normal School for Colored Girls in Washington, D.C.

[Undated]

My dear Miss Howland:

I am very glad to receive yours written on the day of the election. It is a great relief to have the struggle over, and I feel that it has ended in the right way. I am very glad that Mr. Livingston has communicated with you and I hope that a quietness will be put on Mr. Smallwood in the West.

Last Saturday I drove 36 miles into the country to visit a school that is being built up by the colored people, and I have seldom seen any work that has given me more encouragement than this. They have in process of erection a large two-story school house and it is almost wholly the result of the efforts of the colored people themselves. They are now to the point where they have spent almost all the money they can spare for this year, and I feel that if you wish to put a few dollars where you are sure that every cent will tell for good you would be safe in helping this school a little if you feel so disposed. The address of the Principal is Mr. Clinton J. Calloway, Elmore Co., Alabama. I am glad to say that Mrs. Washington is at home and much improved in health.

We are very glad to hear that you feel that you may be able to help us some this year.

Yours truly,

    Booker T. Washington

W.E.B. Du Bois to Harvard University

At the time of this letter, W.E.B. Du Bois (1868–1963) was a student at Fisk University in Nashville, Tennessee. He would graduate with a B.A. the following year and attend Harvard, where he received a second bachelor's degree in 1890 and a master's degree in 1891. He then attended the University of Berlin before returning to Harvard, where he received a Ph.D. in 1895.

[Nashville, Tennessee]
29 October, 1887

Dear Sir:

I am a Negro, a student of Fisk University. I shall receive the degree of A.B. from this institution next June at the age of 20. I wish to pursue at Harvard a course of study for the degree of Ph.D. in Political Science after graduation. I am poor and if I should enter your college next year would probably not be able to raise more [than] $100 or $150. If I should teach a year and then enter I could earn enough to pay my expenses for a year. I wish your advice as to what I had better do. You can see by the catalogue I shall send herewith what our course of instruction is here. I can furnish satisfactory certificates of character and scholarship from the President and Professors of Fisk, and from Western Massachusetts where I was born, and graduated from the public schools. I am also Editor of the *Fisk Herald*, a copy of which I send. As I said I wish your advice as to whether I had better teach a year or two or come immediately after graduation. I expect to take the special field of Political Economy.

I am, Sir,

Yours truly,

    W.E.B. Du Bois

W.E.B. Du Bois to the John F. Slater Fund

In this letter to the John F. Slater Fund, created in 1882 by the textile man-ufacturer John Slater to support the education of African Americans, Du Bois outlined his academic endeavors while a student at the University of Berlin. From 1882 to 1891, the philanthropic fund was directed by Atticus Green Haygood, the president of Emory College, who maintained that blacks and whites are intellectual equals. However, by the time this letter was written, the fund's general agent was Jabez L. M. Curry, a former Con-federate congressman who was far less supportive of academic education for African Americans, favoring instead the kind of industrial training publicly advocated by Booker T. Washington. The appeal by Du Bois for more fund-ing was denied, and he returned to Harvard.

Berlin
10 March, '93

Gentlemen:

I have the honor to make hereby my second report concerning my study in Europe as a scholar of the honorable Trustees.

During the winter semester, October 16 to March 15, 1892–3, I have been a resident student at the University of Berlin, following the plan of study outlined in my first report. Most of my time was spent in the sem-inary [sic] of Economics under Professor Gustav Schmoller. For this seminary [sic] I prepared a thesis on *"Der Gross- und Klein Betrieb des Ackerbaus, in der Südstaaten der Vereinigten Staaten, 1840–90."* This was prepared from material already in my possession, from the United States census report, Agriculture and labor reports, etc. Professor Schmoller ex-pressed himself as much pleased with the work, and wishes me to con-tinue it and either publish it as a doctor's thesis or let it appear in his *"Jahrbuch für Gesetzgebung, &c."*

I have attended two sets of lectures by Professor Wagner. He has expressed himself as interested in my work and will admit me to mem-bership in his seminary next semester. I have also found the lectures of Treitschke and Gneist of especial interest.

Besides my regular work, I have been following the present inter-esting and important political and social movements in Germany; as e.g., socialism, agrarianism, and anti-Semitism. I have attended meet-ings, conversed with the students and people, etc. I have lately joined the "Verein für Sozial Politik" which meets here soon, and includes in its membership many well-known economists. I have also put myself to considerable pains to ascertain just the sort of reception a Negro receives in Germany socially, both in public and in private, with curious and instructive results. My chief relaxation has been attending concerts, etc., where I have heard the masterpieces of music for a nominal sum.

My Christmas vacation I spent in making a trip through South Germany, visiting Weimar, Frankfort, Heidelberg, Strassburg, Stuttgart, Ulm, Augsburg, Nuremberg, Munich, Prague, and Dresden. In the Pfalz region we stopped for a week in a small country village where I had the opportunity of studying peasant life and comparing it with the country life in the United States, north and south. We visited perhaps twenty different families, talked and ate with them, went to their assemblies, etc. In the other places we gave our attention to sightseeing, to the art galleries and to the museums. The whole trip cost $80.

My expenses from July until April 18, are as follows:

Received			Paid		
1892 Cash on hand	$50	July, 1892	Outfit, clothes, &c	$50.
July Slater Fund Scholarship	$750	18	Passage to Rotterdam	50.
		Aug. 1–15	Travel in Holland & Rhine	75.
		"15 to Oct. 1892	Pension in Eisenach	125
		Oct. 16–Apr 16	Expense 1st semester	270.
		Dec '92	Christmas Journey	80
		April 18	Cash on Hand	150
Total	$800			$800

My plans for the future are these:

I shall spend the month of vacation at Cassel where it will be cheap and pleasant. I shall then return to the University of Berlin and commence this course of study, which the professors here have recommended:

Seminary in Economics: Prof. Adolf Wagner
Seminary in Modern History; Prof. Lenz.
General Political Economy, Prof. Schmoller.
History of Philosophy, Prof. Dilthey,
Labor question, Prof. Schmoller,
History of 18th Century, Prof. Lenz

and a few other minor lectures in economics. My money on hand will I calculate enable me to stay until July 10th or 15th, when, if I do not receive a reappointment to my scholarship, I shall return to America.

In case the accompanying petition is favorably acted upon, I shall spend the next two semesters, i.e., until March '94, at this University in the study of Economics and History. I have been assured by Professor Dr. Hirschfeld, Dean of the Philosophical Faculty, and by Prof. Dr. Schmoller, that I have a fair possibility of being allowed to take my examination here for the degree of PH.D., at the end of three semesters. This is an unusually short time—the Berlin degree being the most difficult of German degrees for foreigners to obtain—and indeed for Germans. I am very anxious therefore on my own account but especially for the sake of my race, to try to obtain this degree.

After these three semesters, I shall go to the School of Economics at Paris where I shall stay as long as my money purse allows, and then return, *via* London, to America. I estimate my expenses as follows:

Semester at Univ of Berlin, Apr 18–Aug 18, '93	$175
Vacation, Aug & Sept '93	75
Semester, Oct. 18 '93 to Mch 18 '94,	200
Cost of doctors examination	100
"at Paris, Journey &c., Mch 18–Aug. (?), '94	275
Journey to U. S. *via* London,"	75
	———
Total	$900
Apr 18, '93 Cash on hand	150
	———
Scholarship petitioned for =	$750

Just how I shall commence my work after I return to America I cannot of course now say. My plan is something like this: to get a position in one of the Negro universities, and to seek to build up there a department of history and social science, with two subjects in view: (a) to study scientifically the Negro question past and present with a view to its best solution. (b) to collect capable young Negro students, and to see how far they are capable of furthering, by independent study and research, the best scientific work of the day.

Such a work to be successful must enlist the services not only of devotion and long patient strife, but also of the ripest and best scholarship—in no other way would it be a fair experiment. I therefore desire, so far as in me lies, to obtain the best results of European scholarship and culture, and to this end, I regard another year here, occupied as I have indicated, absolutely necessary.

I therefore wish humbly to petition for a renewal of my scholarship for the coming year on the same terms as last year. I would even be willing to accept less favorable terms than to lose this which I must needs regard as the opportunity of my life. I have made bold to make this petition (which I address to the trustees and send enclosed) because in my appointment the committee while making "no promise either expressed or implied" nevertheless expressed a willingness to consider the question of a second year.

I send also enclosed a letter from Professor Schmoller, with translation, etc. Professor Hart of Harvard will communicate with you later.

Allow me to express to the Committee my heartfelt thanks for their interest and pains.

I remain, gentlemen,
Respectfully yours
W.E.B. Du Bois

Booker T. Washington to W.E.B. Du Bois

Booker T. Washington and W.E.B. Du Bois fiercely debated the role of education in the life of African Americans, with Washington promoting industrial education, industry, and patience in attaining social parity with whites, and Du Bois advocating classical liberal arts education for a "Talented Tenth" and full social and political equality. In this letter, however, Washington commends Du Bois for his investigation of public schools in the South, just as Du Bois had congratulated Washington for his 1895 speech known as the Atlanta Compromise. By the time this letter was written, it is likely that Du Bois had already singled out Washington's strategy for racial uplift for criticism in his book The Souls of Black Folk, *which was published the following year.*

My dear Dr. Du Bois:—

I have just read the editorial in the last number of *The Outlook* based upon your investigation of the condition of the public schools in the South, and I want to thank you most heartily and earnestly for the investigation of the subject referred to and also for the work which you are doing, through your conference and through your writings. This editorial shows the value of such investigation. I know it is hard work and you may feel often that you are not very much encouraged in your efforts, but such an editorial ought to prove of great comfort to you. Constantly putting such facts before the public cannot but help our cause greatly in the long run.

Yours truly,
Booker T. Washington

W.E.B. Du Bois to Vernealia Fereira

Sometime in December 1904, W.E.B. Du Bois received a letter from Margaretta Atkinson, a high school teacher from a Philadelphia suburb who asked how she might motivate a bright but underachieving African American student who felt hopeless about her prospects. Du Bois replied to her questions and enclosed this letter for the girl.

December 14, 1904

I wonder if you will let a stranger say a word to you about yourself? I have heard that you are a young woman of some ability but that you are neglecting your school work because you have become hopeless of trying to do anything in the world. I am very sorry for this. How any human being whose wonderful fortune it is to live in the 20th century should under ordinarily fair advantages despair of life is almost unbelievable. And if in addition to this that person is, as I am, of Negro lineage with all the hopes and yearnings of hundreds of millions of human souls dependent in some degree on her striving, then her bitterness amounts to crime.

There are in the U. S. today tens of thousands of colored girls who would be happy beyond measure to have the chance of educating themselves that you are neglecting. If you train yourself as you easily can, there are wonderful chances of usefulness before you: you can join in the ranks of 15,000 Negro women teachers, of hundreds of nurses and physicians, of the growing number of clerks and stenographers, and above all of the host of homemakers. Ignorance is a cure for nothing. Get the very best training possible & the doors of opportunity will fly open before you as they are flying before thousands of your fellows. On the other hand every time a colored person neglects an opportunity, it makes it more difficult for others of the race to get such an opportunity. Do you want to cut off the chances of the boys and girls of tomorrow?

    W.E.B. Du Bois

John Hope to W.E.B. Du Bois

John Hope (1868–1936) was one of W.E.B. Du Bois's closest friends. Hope was born in Augusta, Georgia, one of five children of Fanny Butts, an African American, and James Hope, a native Scotsman who died when John was eight years old. He attended Worcester Academy in Massachusetts and then Brown University, where he studied philosophy and graduated with honors in 1894. He later became the first African American president of a Baptist college, Atlanta Baptist College (now Morehouse College). Hope was also, along with Du Bois, one of the founders of the Niagara Movement, a precursor to the National Association for the Advancement of Colored People. In this letter he alludes to the legendary ideological clash between Du Bois and Booker T. Washington.

                                    Providence, R.I.
                                    January 17, 1910

My dear Du Bois:

    I must ask you to pardon this use of pencil, though it must be confessed I am half as glad that I cannot find a pen as I can write better with pencil. Since I left you last Tuesday this is the first leisure that I have had to write. I have been very tediously busy and much on the go. Now that I have an hour, will you listen patiently while I talk about one thing that I want you to hear from me.

    I frankly confess that you people at Matthews' home some nights ago let me down much more easily than I could have expected, much more easily than I probably would have let another down, if I had had quite so good a joke with so much fact behind the joke as you folks had on me. I have often taken and given "roasts" and felt, therefore, as I say, quite cheerful that it was so light for me—not a scorching, just a comfortable warm brown.

However, as I thought afterwards of what had been said, as I knew the attitudes of many, if not all, there, it occurred to me wherein the ideas of any might be erroneous it would still not be worth my while to clear up anything. Moreover, I have been misunderstood, seriously misinterpreted, even in public print several times in my life and have never made an explanation. Nor should I now depart from my course. And yet I did know that their ideas about me were erroneous, and there was one to whom I possibly owed an explanation, though I regretted even to imagine that he might believe some things that his perfectly pleasant joking implied. Du Bois was the one man to whom I thought I might owe an explanation. Why Du Bois? Because I have followed him; believed in him; tried even, where he was not understood, to interpret him and show that he is right; because I have been loyal to him and his propaganda—not blatantly so, but, I think, really loyal; and because, in spite of appearances, I am just as truly as ever a disciple of the teachings of Du Bois regarding Negro freedom.

It is also true that through the kindness of Mr. Booker Washington I was enabled to secure a conditional offer of ten thousand dollars from Mr. Andrew Carnegie. I may here say that I have credit for more good scheming than I deserve. Without any effort on my part a friend of the school first approached Mr. Washington and pointed a way to me which seemed, and still seems, to me perfectly honorable and so generous as to have called for selfishness on my part not to accept on behalf of a school that needed the assistance and ought to be helped rather than hampered by its president. All of this I carefully thought over and—naïve as it may appear to you—prayed over. Then without any persuasion or pressure from any one I went frankly to Mr. Washington; told of what I heard; told him my purpose for the school and that larger facilities would mean better opportunity for carrying on the work of this school as it now is without any change of its educational policy and ideals. After hearing this, he was quite as willing to help and did so.

Now Du Bois, I expect to be criticized, perhaps publicly; would be surprised if so great a flop, flop as it seems, should go unnoticed and unknocked. I should not wonder that from your position you would have to knock quite savagely. All this and more I expect, would be surprised if I did not get, but would not lift my finger to avert.

Then why write you all this? My impression is that friendship—not acquaintanceship or perfunctory intercourse but real friendship—is based not so much on agreement in opinion and policies and methods but upon downright confidence, upon simple faith, no matter what the view or appearances. You and I for nearly ten years have been friends, at least I have fancied so. I write to ask, no matter whether you doubt the wisdom of or resent my action, are we friends?

You may remember that in the early and bitterly misunderstood efforts of the Niagara Movement, I was the only college president that ventured to attend the Harper's Ferry meeting to take part in its deliberations. You may remember too, that while some may have answered the call to that seemingly radical meeting in New York last May, I was the only president, colored or white, of our colleges that took part in the deliberations of that meeting. I cite this to show that I have dared to live up to my views even when they threw me in the midst of the most radical. Furthermore, every man on our faculty does the same and will as long as I am head of the institution. But, Du Bois, may there not be a tyranny of views? Have we not required such severe alignments that it has been sometimes as much a lack of courage as a mark of courage to stand either with Du Bois or Washington to the absolute exclusion of one or the other in any sort of intercourse? I confess it is unpleasant to be charged with apostasy even in joke when one is not truly apostate. But the unpleasant feature in my case finds full compensation in the certainty of my courage to do what I regard as right. There is a feeling of emancipation that a man of genius cannot quite know or appreciate. You go unfalteringly, almost unthinkingly, to a conclusion that has much concerned you in your thinking because you have hardly needed them in your equation. That is genius. I am a plodder. My even petty thinking calls for great travail of mind and spirit; and, in the process, I carry along most hospitably all opposing views with which I am acquainted. I am plodding, canny—you go on the wings, and are daring. Yet we can both follow truth and be loyal to it and to each other.

Now, I have not known Washington long, but what I know of him in my personal relations is perfectly pleasant and generous. If I should find out later otherwise, I suppose I would express it as simply and with as little vehemence as I am now writing. I am glad that as a man interested in education I can associate properly with another man who is interested in education yet from a different angle as Washington is. I am primarily interested in education. Quite as heartily as ever I shall disagree with Washington's views where they do not accord with mine, and I would not yield a principle for the benefit of myself or my school, obviously for such could not really benefit.

I write to ask you whether you have me in your heart—not on your calling list or your mailing list but in your heart—on your list of friends. I am asking this question fearlessly as a strong man would ask his chieftain. I will receive the answer just as fearlessly. And however it may be, I shall be loyal to my chieftain still. This letter is absolutely personal and I should feel hurt ever to have it mentioned or quoted except between you and me. It comes too much out of my heart. It is no apology to anybody. It is an explanation carrying a question to you. It is a letter from a man to a man between whom a friendship has developed based on mutual interests in a race that we love and are working for. I want that friendship to last. If it does, we shall do even more than we have ever done. Why should it not last?

Your very dear friend,

John Hope

W.E.B. Du Bois to John Hope

Atlanta, GA.
January 22, 1910

My dear Hope:

You must not think that I have not known and appreciated your friendship for me or that I ever have doubted or doubt now your loyalty to the principles which we both so sincerely believe. If I thought even that you were going back on those principles, my friendship is not of so slight a texture that I would easily give you up. Of course I am sorry to see you or anyone in Washington's net. It's a dangerous place, old man, and you must keep your eyes open. At the same time under the circumstances I must say frankly I do not see any other course of action before you but the one you took. In your position of responsibility your institution must stand foremost in your thought. One thing alone you must not, however, forget: Washington stands for Negro submission and slavery. Representing that, with unlimited funds, he can afford to be broad and generous and most of us must accept the generosity or starve. Having accepted it we are peculiarly placed and in a sense tongue-tied and bound. I may have to place myself in that position, yet, but, by God, I'll fight hard before I do it.

I know, however, that you, my friend, are going to do the right as you see it, and I'm too sensible of my own short comings and mistakes to undertake to guide you. As I have said, so far, you have done what you had to do under the circumstances. I only trust that the pound of flesh demanded in return will not be vital.

I thank you with greater feeling than I dare express for your kind letter.

Your,

W.E.B. Du Bois

Alice Dunbar to John Edward Bruce

After her separation from the poet Paul Laurence Dunbar, Alice Dunbar (1875–1935) worked as a teacher and administrator at Howard High School in Wilmington, Delaware, a position she held until 1920. In 1916 she married George Nelson, a journalist and activist with whom she coedited The Wilmington Advocate *from 1920 to 1922. In this note to the journalist and amateur historian John Edward Bruce, Dunbar sought his help as she prepared materials to teach black history.*

[Wilmington, Delaware]
March 23, 1914

My dear Mr. Bruce:

If you have very many English and African correspondents I should think you'd suffer from paralysis of the vocabulary in trying to express your feelings about their penmanship to yourself. Dear me, don't they write awfully! I'd always use a typewriter if I wrote like that. It's like translating a foreign language.

I am planning a little reader, a supplementary thing to be used in the 6th, 7th, and 8th grades in Negro schools. May I call upon you for help again—I mean this time in finding just the kind of extracts I need, and the biographies to go with them. You know you promised to let me know the price of your book of biographies, and did not, and I need the book. False and fickle man!*

I suppose the library of the [Negro Society for Historical Research] plus Mr. [Arthur] Schomburg's private collection would be just what I

---

*Bruce's *Eminent Negro Men and Women in Europe and the United States*, a collection of biographical sketches, was published in 1910.

would want to dig into.* If I can I'll try to come to New York during the week of our spring vacation, which occurs the third week of April (I think). Should I get my plans a-working and spend the week in New York or its vicinity, and you want me to spout before the [Negro] Society [for Historical Research] that week, may as well get it done and over with. What say you?

Many, many thanks for your great kindness in translating Miss Marples' letter. The Recording Angel blotted out all your sins for that act of charity, and Gabriel added another star to your crown.

Sincerely yours,
Alice Dunbar

James Emman Kwegyir Aggrey to Sadie Peterson Delaney

James E. K. Aggrey (1875–1927) was an American-educated teacher and minister from Ghana who, along with the Gold Coast governor Gordon Guggisberg, was cofounder of Achimota College, modeled after Hampton and Tuskegee institutes. Aggrey was the only nonwhite member of two Phelps-Stokes Commissions on Education in Africa, in 1920 and 1924. The commissions traveled throughout the continent surveying schools for two influential reports.† In 1924 Aggrey gave speeches across East Africa promoting black and white racial cooperation and industrial education for Africans. Sara "Sadie" Peterson Delaney (1889–1958), born Sara Marie Johnson in Rochester, New York, was a librarian who was internationally renowned for her pioneering work in bibliotherapy. She was the chief librarian at the U.S. Veterans Administration Hospital in Tuskegee, Alabama.

Kampula, Uganda
March 14, 1924

My dear Mrs. Peterson:

Your very welcome letter reached me here last week. I was so glad to hear from you and to know that you are doing so well at Tuskegee.

*In 1926 Arthur Schomburg's private collection of books, manuscripts, paintings, and letters related to the African Diaspora was purchased by the New York Public Library with a $10,000 grant from the Carnegie Foundation. The collection forms the foundation of the Schomburg Center for Research in Black Culture in Harlem.
†*Education in Africa: A Study of West, South and Equatorial Africa* (1922) and *Education in East Africa: Report of the Second Phelps-Stokes Fund African Education Commission* (1925).

You are now your own boss as far as making good is concerned. All you have to do is to keep up with your fine reputation. I have no doubt but that you will succeed. I know the greatness you did in New York City. Anybody who had anything to do with the 135th Street Library in New York City knows Mrs. Peterson. I was so well impressed with you and your very efficient service that had I accepted the presidency [I was] asked to consider I should immediately have offered you a position at our school and would have felt ourselves fortunate if you accepted the offer. You deserve the best, the very best and you are going to come to your own as I keep telling you every time I saw you.

[Aggrey began writing again on the same page nearly two weeks later, on March 27, 1924.]

I was hurriedly called away while writing the above, and I have just come back to it. I have been kept very very busy. In Kenya Colony besides inspecting the schools, hospitals, reformatory, homes, etc., I spoke thirty times on many occasions in two weeks time. One day I spoke seven times. In Uganda I beat my own record. There was such a demand that in two weeks time I spoke forty-one times and last time I was asked by the captain of the ship that is carrying me back on Victoria Nyanga to address the crew, and we had a fine time, making 42 times, or 81 times in a month!

Last Sunday when I preached at the Cathedral in Mongo there were present Protestants, Roman Catholics [. . .] White ministers came seventeen miles, bankers and other European merchants were present, and natives came from as far as 12, 40, 50, and a hundred and over miles. The Cathedral was overcrowded, some three to five thousand present, people outdoors. That was the 8:30 a.m. service. At 11 o'clock I spoke to the Roman Catholic College . . . At 2:30 I received the Prince. At 5:15 I preached at the European Episcopal Church. At 7 spoke to a select audience of whites of all denominations, judges etc. at the Provincial Commissioner's House. At 8:30 I spoke to the students and to the Mango High School. That was a day's job, a Sabbath "busyness," Monday I was entertained by the King and his Cabinet from 4:30 to 7:30. When leaving to Mingo Central School students walked two miles with brass band to the station. The High School walked nine miles to the pier with bananas and brass band to see me off the boat. They want me to return . . . Wish I could divide myself a thousand fold.

Keep me informed of your success and purpose. I know you will succeed. I am praying for you. Write to my London address.

Always your friend,

J. E. Kwegyir Aggrey.

John Hope to W.E.B. Du Bois

Atlanta, GA.

November 15, 1924

Dear Du Bois:

I have come across your letter of July 21st which I did not answer. Any answer now is quite out of the question. [President Calvin] Coolidge is elected. I myself intended to vote for him and did do so. On the other hand, I had no complaint to make about colored people who saw and voted differently. I furthermore think it hardly worthwhile to talk as much as we used to about the Negroes' vote being divided, because the Negroes' vote is already divided. We are not by any means voting solidly Republican. Some Negroes even in the South voted for [U.S. Senator Robert] La Follette.* But this letter is not written for publication or anything else except as an acknowledgment.

Now, to something else. I read in the *American Mercury* some weeks ago your kind words about Morehouse College and me. I have gone along here for many years about the best I could. Here and there I might have done better. Here and there I might have done worse. But on the whole with all the agencies, circumstances, conveniences and inconveniences, I suppose I have done about the best I could. During these years I have often wondered what some of my dearest friends were thinking about my work, and how they were valuing it. But I suppose I would allow myself to burst wide open before asking them what they thought about it. That is the way with many of us. Few of us tell our closest friends those things which lie deepest in us, which distress us most, or which thrill us most with joy. Those things are ever beneath the surface. They are with us. Now you come to me at the beginning of my 19th year as President of this school, at the beginning of my 31st year as a teacher of colored boys and men, and tell me that

*Robert La Follette (1855–1925) led the progressive faction of the Republican Party and ran for president with a populist message supporting labor unions and civil liberties that appealed to many groups, including African Americans. He was governor of Wisconsin from 1900 to 1906 and served in the Senate from 1906 until his death.

I have not made altogether a miserable failure, but on the contrary have done something worthwhile. I am grateful to you for this quite beyond words.

Two nights ago I was at Tuskegee and talked with Dr. Moton about several matters.* One of these was the Fisk situation.† Moton told me that he was coming to New York sometime next week to talk with you and [Matthew Virgile] Boutté.‡ It is my impression that not only is he in a position to render valuable assistance, but he wishes to do this— he is ready to take very strong ground if what he regards as the facts warrant it. I am sure that you and Boutté will let him help you in every way that he can. I would suggest that you sort of mark time until after this conference. The chances are, you men can work things out much more easily than it may now appear. As you work on this question of Fisk University, bear in mind that I along with many other people desire the best things for Fisk, and it is my wish that these best things will come to pass, with the least commotion possible and with as little embarrassment as possible to Fisk University, because an institution of learning is such a delicate organism, it is almost human. It is human. The slightest touch sometimes disturbs its healthy function. If I can be of any service, you know well from our conversation last summer that I am willing.

When I come to New York again I believe I will look you up and ask you to spend the evening with me. I come to New York frequently, but we get together less frequently than we used to. Years ago it was one of the thrills that I got out of a trip to New York, to spend an evening with you, but you are so busy now with so many demands upon your time that I rather hesitate to take you for a whole night. After all, the most and the best that I have got out of life has been beautiful comradeships, and the memories of these will probably cling with me out of this difficult, unsatisfactory world into some abode where I may feast and think with fewer interruptions and no clangor of alarm. Courage,

*Robert Moton (1867–1940) succeeded Booker T. Washington as principal of Tuskegee Institute following Washington's death in 1915.
†Between 1924 and 1925, students at Fisk protested many administrative policies, culminating in a strike.
‡A Louisiana Creole, Matthew Virgile Boutté was a graduate of Fisk University and the University of Illinois and served in the 92nd Division of the American Expeditionary Force in France during World War I. During the 1920s he owned a successful drugstore in New York City.

the necessity of the enterprise, and a certain amount of pugnacity, along with a modicum of self-respect, make me continue rather cease-lessly in the fight; but I am bound to tell you, my dear friend, that blowing one's brains out is a great sight easier than some of the things we have to do and stand.

This is a much longer letter than I expected to write.

Affectionately yours,

    John Hope

W.E.B. Du Bois to John Hope

March 25, 1925

My dear Mr. Hope:

I want to bring to your attention the claims of Carter G. Woodson as Spingarn Medalist for the year 1925.*

Several times his name has been mentioned and always with appre-ciation, but it seems to me that on the 10th anniversary of the found-ing of *The Journal of Negro History* that Woodson becomes the one outstanding figure for honor at our hands. Woodson is not a popular man. He is, to put it mildly, cantankerous. But he has done the most striking piece of scientific work for the Negro race in the last ten years of any man that I know. He has kept an historical journal going almost singled-handed, founded a publishing association, and published a se-ries of books with but limited popular appeal. At the same time he has maintained his integrity, his absolute independence of thought and ac-tion, and has been absolutely oblivious to either popular applause or bread and butter. It is a marvelous accomplishment. He ought to have a Spingarn medal.

Very Sincerely yours,

    W.E.B. Du Bois

---

*Created by NAACP President Joel Spingarn in 1914, the medal is awarded annually to an African American for distinguished achievement. James Weldon Johnson received the award in 1925, followed by Carter G. Woodson, founder of the Association for the Study of Negro Life and History, in 1926.

W.E.B. Du Bois to Bureau of Education
Commissioner William John Cooper

In a November 19, 1929, letter to Secretary of the Interior Roy O. West, W.E.B. Du Bois protested the exclusion of African Americans from a conference the Education Bureau was hosting on illiteracy. He received a response from William John Cooper, a commissioner of the bureau, to which the following is Du Bois's reply.

December 18, 1929

My dear Sir:

Referring to your letter of December 4, you say "the Conference called by the Secretary of the Interior on Saturday next consists very largely of individuals who have been engaged in illiteracy crusades more or less as a private venture." Will you permit me to say by the way of commentary that if there are any people in the United States who have been more consistently and continuously, both as individuals and as a group, engaged in "illiteracy crusades" than American Negroes, I should be very much interested to know their names and race. It seems to me little less than outrageous that a Conference on illiteracy will omit representatives of the most illiterate group in the United States; the group for whom illiteracy was for two centuries compulsory, and a group which by its own efforts, as well as the efforts of friends, has done more to reduce its illiteracy than any similar group in the world in the same length of time.

I trust you will permit me to say that this seems to me [a] most inauspicious beginning of your leadership of the Bureau of Education.

Very sincerely yours,
W.E.B. Du Bois

Carter G. Woodson to John Hope

Carter G. Woodson (1875–1950) launched an extensive letter-writing campaign against The Encyclopedia of the Negro, *which was to be edited by W.E.B. Du Bois and underwritten by the Phelps-Stokes Fund. In a letter to the educator Benjamin Brawley, he accused the fund of trying "to destroy the work of the Association for the Study of Negro Life and History." He alleged that the fund convinced donors to withdraw support from his association. While Du Bois worked until his death to make his dream of an encyclopedia of the African Diaspora a reality, it did not materialize during his lifetime. However, his efforts helped inspire the creation of* Africana: Encyclopedia of the African and African American Experience, *which, under the direction of the Harvard professors Henry Louis Gates, Jr., and Kwame Anthony Appiah, was published in 1999.*

Atlanta, Ga.
December 24, 1931

My dear Sir:

Inasmuch as you have taken up with me the matter of attending the next conference which will devise plans for duplicating our efforts to produce an Encyclopedia of the Negro, I must address you further to state exactly what I think about the matter. This letter, too, is not confidential.

I am disinclined to take any part in a procedure which originates as this undertaking has among men who have already done us much harm, but I would offer no objection to the production of an additional Encyclopedia of the Negro if the work is to be done by Negro scholars. I welcome competition, for it is the spice of life.

If this enterprise is to be dominated by men like Thomas Jesse Jones and Thomas Jackson Woofter, however, I desire to register against it a militant protest.* These men have already demonstrated their narrowness and bias in works which they have produced. They do not live among Negroes, they do not work in their institutions. Consequently they have no conception of the thought, feeling, or aspiration of Negroes and, therefore, cannot properly evaluate their achievements or interpret their philosophy of life.

Instead of encouraging men of this type to write further on the Negro we who have some regard for the future of the race should do all we can to prevent them from producing any more treatises in this field. If these men have twenty-five or fifty hundred thousand dollars or can raise such an amount, let them go off somewhere with it and study the Eskimos, investigate the evils of the boll-weevil or devise some means for the prevention of the pellagra. By all means, however, deliver the Negroes from their hands.

---

*Thomas Jesse Jones was an influential educator who chaired several Phelps-Stokes Fund commissions on education for Africans and African Americans, for whom he advocated industrial training. Thomas Jackson Woofter was a professor of philosophy and education at the University of Georgia who studied rural life in the South. Among his books are *Landlord and Tenant on the Cotton Plantation* (1936).

The harm already done the Negro race by these men should not be overlooked. Thomas Jesse Jones's report on Negro Education speaks for itself.* This work gave a false picture of Negro education and contributed to the rise of a man who has done the Negro almost as much harm as Thomas Dixon did with the "Klansman."† Woofter in his basis of "Race Adjustment" justified segregation and in his recent report on agricultural conditions he makes by his silence a good case for peonage and slavery enforced on the cotton and sugar plantations. These works are prejudicial to the interests of the Negro in that, although they contain much truth they contain also much misrepresentation which is the worst sort of falsification.

You will say that the board of editors of the encyclopedia will determine what will go into it. It will, therefore, be impossible for any man of this type to publish therein any thing which will not be perfectly scientific. The history of such a cooperative effort, however, runs to the contrary. Negroes engaged in the work of the Y.M.C.A. had a conference with J. D. Weatherford and others who produced a volume which eventually appeared as *Present Forces in the Progress of the Negro* [(1912)]. One or two conferences were held, the opinions and attitudes of the Negroes were clearly stated, and Weatherford was appointed as the chief editor to embody them and produce the book. This was the last the Negroes heard of it until the book was published. The work presented only those facts and opinions which Weatherford desired to be incorporated therein.

Other men have tried this same sort of thing of working through others to get the truth about the Negro published in the *Dictionary of American Biography*. In the beginning I was asked to cooperate, and I drew up a list of about two hundred Negroes whom I believed should be mentioned in such a monumental work. Some of these Negroes, of course, were not considered worthy. The judgment of certain white

Negro Education: A Study of the Private and Higher Schools for Colored People in the United States, a two-volume report released in 1917, underwritten by the Phelps-Stokes Fund. The report recommended that the majority of African American schools offering college courses should be discontinued and replaced by schools giving manual education, arguing that manual and industrial education was especially critical for African Americans because of the comparable poverty of the race and "the Negro's highly emotional nature." The study catapulted Jones to national prominence as an expert on Negro education. He served as education director of the Phelps-Stokes Fund from 1913 to 1946.

†Thomas Dixon, Jr. (1864–1946), wrote a trilogy about the Reconstruction era that included *The Clansman: An Historical Romance of the Ku Klux Klan* (New York: Doubleday, Page & Co., 1905), which glorified the Ku Klux Klan and defended the lynching of African Americans, who were grossly caricatured.

men was considered better than mine, although these same persons say that I am the best informed investigator in this particular field.

The chief editor, moreover, assigned the writing of the sketches of outstanding Negroes to white persons and called on me and one or two other Negroes to write on those who were colorless figures in history, restricted, as a rule, to a space of about six hundred words each; and the interesting turn in the matter was that the white men to whom these subjects were assigned came to me for the facts with which to produce the sketches required.

Later I learned, moreover, that Benjamin Banneker, who was one of the outstanding men of his time, and had been weighed in the balance and found wanting and would not be mentioned at all in the *Dictionary of American Biography*. I was therefore forced to resign from the staff in protest. Science seems to be proceeding very much in the same way as the staff of the *Dictionary of American Biography* has dealt with Negroes.

Because of my attitude with respect to white man's writing on the Negro I have been charged with opposing interracial cooperation. However, I am very much in favor of interracial cooperation but I seriously object to racial domination even in writing books on the Negro. I am willing to grant white men the same consideration producing an Encyclopedia of the Negro as they grant Negroes in producing the *Dictionary of American Biography* or the *Encyclopedia of the Social Sciences*. Negroes called upon to cooperate in these productions are restricted altogether to Negro subjects and even then to such topics about the Negro as they think white men may not be able to develop.

I would say, then, that in this proposed production, in case you want to write, for example, about L. H. Hammond, a white man who was President of Paine College, Augusta, Georgia, some white man who may know certain things about him that a Negro has not the opportunity to learn should develop such a sketch with respect to his contribution to the uplift of the Negro. If I wanted to write about a thing of greater significance than Hammond's contribution, however, say for example, the work of Dr. J. H. Dillard, although he is a white man, I should want the evaluation of his efforts by a Negro scholar, for this work is too vitally connected with the life of the Negro in various ramifications to permit some one outside of the race to write scientifically on it.* This is pre-

* James H. Dillard (1856–1940) helped create and directed the Jeanes Fund and the Slater Fund, which supported the education of African Americans. Dillard University in New Orleans is named in his honor.

cisely what white men do with respect to the Negro scholars today and I am willing to grant them in writing on the Negro the same consideration that they grant me.

This is a matter of great importance, and you who have been chosen to cooperate in this enterprise naturally assume a great responsibility. I must urge you, therefore, to proceed cautiously, for a blunder in this matter may mean that the Negro race may be further afflicted with misrepresentation. One Encyclopedia of the Negro will be produced anyway. Why, then, should you stimulate the further perversion of the writing on Negro life and history to increase the burdens of agencies like the Association for the Study of Negro Life and History to the extent that they have to sweat blood in struggling against handicaps to uproot the well financed propaganda of men like Weatherford, Woofter, and Jones?

Respectfully yours,
C. G. Woodson
Director

Alain Locke to James Weldon Johnson

Alain Locke (1886–1954) was a writer, literary critic, and philosopher who was called "Father of the Harlem Renaissance" for his role in articulating and promoting the movement in The New Negro, *an anthology that he edited. Born in Philadelphia, he received his Ph.D. in philosophy from Harvard University and in 1907 became the first African American Rhodes scholar. He taught at and chaired the Philosophy Department at Howard University for thirty years, until his retirement in 1953.*

March 7, 1934

Dear Mr. Johnson,

Heartiest thanks for your recent letter. I value your approbation and appreciation highly, and in these days when we are mentally as well as economically depressed, a psychic boost means a lot, and is mighty welcome.

Your suggestion about a critical study of the Negro in American Literature clinches a much postponed intention. I have been waiting all along for a year or half year on sabbatical to get it done, but something always seems to happen to postpone it. The first real set-back was when the stenographic notes to eight lectures that I gave at Fisk in the spring of 1928 were lost. A white "lady stenographer," employed after several local transcribers had fallen down on my vocabulary, just suddenly got "too busy" to transcribe her notes, despite the pleadings of President Jones. Really I think it was her Confederate ancestors, who kicked her in the shins of memory. However, I am much more mature now and the perspective is better, so may I solemnly promise you and myself to get right down to the travails of pregnancy. I'll welcome and look forward to the earliest possible chance of talking the matter through with you, and can then thank you warmly and personally for the thoughtful and generous encouragement.

Best remembrance and best regards to you and Mrs. Johnson,

Cordially,

Locke

Countee Cullen to James Weldon Johnson

June 7, 1934

Dear Mr. Johnson,

I feel that the notification which I have just received that I am to have a place on the faculty of Dillard when it opens next year is due in no small measure to the good word which you must have put forward for me. Do be assured of my gratitude and of my hope that I shall not disappoint your recommendation.

With all good wishes to you and Mrs. Johnson, I am

Yours sincerely,

Countee Cullen

Shirley Graham to W.E.B. Du Bois

W.E.B. Du Bois's future wife, Shirley Graham, born Lola Bell Graham (1896–1977), wrote this letter of admiration while she was a student at Oberlin College.

Kokomo, Indiana
June 23, 1934

My dear Dr. Du Bois:

To you, who have lived a thousand years of thinking, of study, of working and striving, to you, whose face has turned ever towards a far distant horizon, I, whose foot is barely lifted to begin that endless climb up a path which some folks call Achievement, but others know is Calvary, I dare to hail and bring greetings.

All great men have lived years ahead of their time—Socrates, Plato, Galileo, John Locke, Descartes. They have all lived surrounded by that consuming fire of loneliness. They have been born with the curse of work upon them, "born to work and to love it." Critics may not consider Michelangelo's last works his best, but for me certainly one of the most powerful and truly the most poignant work of the renaissance is the group in which beneath the monk's cowl he has carved his own face—that face which has looked upon life for nearly ninety years. Pain, disappointment, disillusion show in this face, fatigue, such as fell upon it during those years he spent upon his back painting the Sistine ceiling, heartbreak over thwarted hopes and broken dreams. But his head is bowed over the burden which he bears in his arms—the dying Christ—and in his eyes and over his face transfiguring age and pain glows his belief in the importance of his Mission.

Who has ever understood you—the youth in school, sure of the manhood which lifted his head, certain that Right makes Might, leaping over bars with careless indifference, developing every faculty, laughing at boundaries; the young teacher, anxious to impart knowledge, bewildered by the stupidity, the bigotry and shortsightedness of his "superiors"; the man, heart torn with grief, raising his hands to high heaven and calling down the wrath of God upon the hordes of a maddened city?

You have gone on.

The years have passed and you have seen the things "you gave your life for broken, twisted by knaves to make a trap for fools." Discrimination, hate, segregation, misunderstanding would seem to be increasing rather than decreasing. Our churches have fallen into disrepute, our best schools air their grievances through the newspapers, our "leaders" are either ignorantly quarrelsome or wrapped in gloomy silence.

Monroe Trotter is dead.*

We build monuments for our great men when they are dead. I like the German word better—*denkmal*. It is well that we should set up a

---

*William Monroe Trotter (1872–1934) was editor and publisher of Boston's uncompromising *Guardian*, which staunchly advocated black equality and often criticized the conservative politics of Booker T. Washington. A graduate of Harvard University, Trotter was, with W.E.B. Du Bois, one of the founding membes of the Niagara Movement, a precursor to the National Association for the Advancement of Colored People.

thinking mark for them. After all, only in so far as any man has made us think is he great. It is therefore only fitting that at this time, when the outward appearance of things is so discouraging, you should know that there is a group in America in whose hearts has been set up for you a "denkmal." I bring you this word from the students who are today going forth from every college and university of the land. You have said that education would bring solutions and we, white and black students, believe that it is true. You know how in the leading colleges of the country the Negro and his contribution is being studied as never before. Dr. Herbert A. Miller will again this summer conduct classes at Swarthmore. No doubt you also will speak there. You know the attitude of the men who gather there, but even more important is the attitude of the college youth who will in a few years control the affairs of the country.

The increasing number of Negro students in the colleges, universities, conservatories and art schools, the honors which they are receiving are having their effect upon the increasing numbers of white students. There is the incident of the conservatory in which a black violinist was not only the acknowledged best musician but was also socially the most popular student. A girl from Georgia in begging him to assist her on her senior recital and share honors with her at the reception emphasized her request by saying that her father and mother "might as well learn." At Western Reserve this spring the college magazine printed a bitter editorial of indictment against the national debating fraternity, which would not admit John Cobb simply because "he is a Negro." At another university a marriage between the two races has been carefully concealed from the authorities. The groom, who is white, is one of the most brilliant graduate students in the country. His student friends seem to heartily approve of his marriage. You know of the reaction of the students in several southern colleges when asked whether or not Negroes should be admitted.

We firmly believe that the discrimination which seems to be increasing in America represents the last stand of the "old guard" who see the end of the day of racial hatred fast approaching. Many parents are being "shown" by their children. They are appalled and they are doing everything in their power to hold the Negro back. It is too late. You and Monroe Trotter have led us too far. And with us are thousands of other young folks who see no reason why we should be held back. It is true that some will weaken when they come in contact with certain issues, but we ourselves are gaining strength and enough of us will hold on to make real that progress.

I think we have fewer illusions than our parents had. We do not expect miracles, we have no faith in the white man's religion. We know that "social equality" and "amalgamation" are but by-products of a natural process. We are not particularly interested in either. We do not expect the white man to give us anything. We are preparing ourselves to take our places in the sun as other men have taken theirs.

For all that you have done for us, we thank you.

We, who are about to live, salute you, our Chief.

Sincerely yours,

Shirley Graham

Sterling A. Brown to W.E.B. Du Bois

Sterling A. Brown (1901–1989) was a poet and literary critic who taught English at Howard University for forty years. His first collection of poetry, Southern Road, *was published in 1932. In this letter, Brown offers his impression of the manuscript for* Black Reconstruction in America, *which Du Bois sent him to read before its publication later that year.*

Washington, D.C.
January 29, 1935

My dear Dr. Du Bois,

I have just got through an examination siege. I wanted to get this letter written earlier, but the pressure of a speed-up and stretch-out to complete the semester, and the racking worry incidental to college dramatics and avalanches of freshman themes would not permit it.

When the manuscript got to me (much later than your note predicted) I was myself in the act of getting a rather tardy manuscript in shape. I could steal time only now and again for the type of proofreading that I knew was expected, and was due a work so important. I went over the manuscript twice. I ran down many errors, some of punctuation, but more of spelling (I am afraid I attended Webster more closely than Woolley in my elementary schooling). I wrote these in the margins, with other corrections or queries. Your letter states that there was no word of criticism, and asks if I found anything wrong. I did find many things wrong in the proof; I hope that the penciled corrections were not overlooked.

I should have been better able to give criticism of the book if I had not considered myself primarily proof-reader. I do think, however, from the two readings I gave it, that *Black Reconstruction* is a first rate piece of work that has for a long time needed doing. I have read quite a few of the histories of Reconstruction: Dunning, Fleming, Bowers, the revisionists on Johnson—Stryker, Winston—and popularized things of Thompson and Don Seitz—I am therefore glad that you wrote the last chapter as you did, although condemnation of the lost cause school of historians is implicit throughout your book—in the point of view, and in the evidence you advance which they consider inadmissible—or never went to the pains to hunt up. The book seemed original in the best sense. The tying-up with American labor history will stand it in good stead, I believe. I think it important to point out as you have done here—and in some essays in *Souls of Black Folk*—the true tragedies of Reconstruction—and the real lost cause—which wasn't that of planters but of the people, poor people whether black or white—Walter Hines Page's two "forgotten men." I am glad that you point out—if my memory serves me right—that it wasn't the "radicalism" of Stevens, et al. that was to blame for the prostrate South—but the fact that "radicalism" in its best and contemporary sense was not given a chance.

I think your book will be attacked by the vested Southern—and perhaps Northern—interests, but that is a mark of its distinction. It is certainly no piece of bloody-shirt waving—though some fire-eater may call it so. I thought it tempered, and restrained—although it has its own pungency. I could see the large amount of work necessary for its documentation. In some cases I could not see that you had given the reader fullest points of reference for checking. I did not always think that the poetry quoted was fortunate as some of the prose it followed, but that is a matter of taste.

I think you have done a much needed job, excellently. I realize my limitations as a student of history, and that partly accounts for my not writing this commentary earlier. As I promised this summer, I was more than ready to help with the proof. But as for rushing as critic into this field—I was hesitant.

If I had the book before me my comments could be more specific. But the general impressions, after a period of many interventions, are as I have told you. I think *Black Reconstruction* belongs with the best historical interpretations I have read. I think it belongs with the best of your writings; I surely do not need to tell you that I believe that best to be very high.

Sincerely yours,

Sterling A. Brown

Horace Mann Bond to Arthur A. Schomburg

Horace Mann Bond (1904–1972) was the first African American president of Lincoln University, from which he graduated with honors at age nineteen. He went on to become the dean of the Atlanta University School of Education and later director of the Atlanta University Bureau for Educational and Social Research. His son is Julian Bond (b. 1940), the civil rights activist and past president of the NAACP. This letter was written while the elder Bond was a dean at Dillard University.

[New Orleans, Louisiana]
September 19, 1936

Dear Mr. Schomburg:

I was glad to learn that the African exhibit was on its way here.

You referred to Mr. Heartman* who was driven from the city because of his praise for Phillis Wheatley. You imply that since I have been able to stay here for two years I am a diplomat. Let me remind you that Mississippi is a curious place to flee to from New Orleans.

In Heartman's latest catalog he lists the New Orleans Blue Book, which was a directory of the red light district published without date and without printer in the early nineteen hundreds. I have just bought a copy of it for a dollar less than the six dollars charged by Mr. Heartman, and found it one of the most interesting documents I have ever seen.

I am still looking forward to have you in our neighborhood during this coming year.

With best wishes, I am,

Sincerely,

Horace M. Bond

Arthur A. Schomburg to Jacob Drachler

In a letter written five months before his death, Arthur Schomburg responded to the inquiry of a teacher who wished to introduce his students to African American literature.

---

*Charles Frederick Heartman (1883–1953) was a well-known antiquarian book dealer who amassed an important collection of rare African American books, letters, and manuscripts. During his lifetime he created two Heartman collections, one at Xavier University in New Orleans and the other at Texas Southern University. Heartman moved to New Orleans in 1935 and in 1936 purchased a four-hundred-acre estate in Hattiesburg, Mississippi, where he lived until 1943.

New York, New York
January 10, 1938

My dear Mr. Drachler:

I am very glad to know that you are interested in bringing to the knowledge of the students of your high school knowledge of Negro life and customs. You have mentioned Booker T. Washington's "Up from Slavery," as well as an article written by me which appears in Calverton's anthology, "The Negro Digs Up His Past."

We have in this branch of the library a number of books that will give you a selection that can be used in your school rooms. Frederick Douglas's "Life and Times," forty years ago was adapted as one of the reading volumes for the public schools of New York City. I think the life of this man sets a beautiful example to be brought to the minds of young students of today. The fact that he was born in slavery and after indefatigable struggles he rose to the distinction of holding many important positions. We note the fact he was United States Minister to Haiti and his integrity in developing this small nation against the North American colossus. You have mentioned Benjamin Brawley's work and while his books are dedicated specially to the classroom, I believe there are others that will fit better in the scheme of your work.

May I take the liberty of inviting you to call at this branch of the library by appointment. I will be glad to show you the collection.

Very truly yours,
Arthur A. Schomburg

Kenneth B. Clark to Mr. Swift

Kenneth B. Clark (1914–2005) in 1940 became the first African American to receive a Ph.D. in psychology from Columbia University. He met his future bride, Katherine (Mamie) Phipps (1917–1983), while she was an undergraduate student at Howard University, where he was earning his master's degree in psychology. In 1943 Mamie Clark became the first African American woman and the second African American to earn a Ph.D. in psychology from Columbia University. Together the couple received a Rosenwald Fellowship to conduct their groundbreaking experiment with dolls, which concluded that black children preferred dolls with white or lighter skin due to internalized racism. The study was cited in the landmark Supreme Court Brown v. Board of Education decision, which outlawed segregated schools. Together, in 1946, the couple founded the Northside Center for Child Development in Harlem. They also had two children, Kate and Hilton.

Clark wrote the following letter to an official at the W.P.A. Nursing School in Springfield, Massachusetts.

New York, N.Y.
Sept. 17, 1940

Dear Mr. Swift

Miss Agnes Hardie, a former schoolmate and student of mine, spoke to you concerning my projected research on an aspect of the personality development of the Negro child. My wife and I were granted a Rosenwald fellowship to conduct this research during the present school year. Our specific problem is to attempt to chart the course and determine the nature of the development of racial awareness in Negro pre-school children. We have already obtained some data and have published three articles in the psychological journals presenting them. Our fellowship permits us to continue this work on a more extensive scale.

It was in connection with this widening of the scope of the problem that I asked Miss Hardie to speak with you concerning the possibility of obtaining some subjects in the nursery schools over which you have jurisdiction.

The procedure used in our investigation is similar to that of the usual intelligence testing. But we are not directly interested in the intelligence of a given child. Our materials consist of the drawings and dolls which, from our past experiences, elicit and hold the child's spontaneous interests. We have planned our procedure in such a way as to appeal to the child in terms of "playing a sort of game." The duration of work with each child is determined by his individual rate, but usually is no longer than twenty minutes.

If the above program meets with your approval I should like to begin work in your area in about two weeks from now. I shall gladly answer any questions concerning specific aspects of the study, at your request.

Sincerely,

Kenneth B. Clark

Congressman Adam Clayton Powell, Jr., to Rev. Hugh Burr

In 1961, the Baptist pastor and congressman Adam Clayton Powell, Jr., became chair of the influential House Education and Labor Committee, where he passed the record number of bills in a single session. Rev. Hugh

Burr of the Federation of Churches of Rochester, New York, chaired the State Commission Against Discrimination and was a proponent of integrated schools and housing.

March 16, 1956

Dear Rev. Burr:

I cannot understand how a group of religious people and loyal Americans can sanction the use of federal funds to build jim-crow segregated schools in Mississippi, Alabama, etc which is immoral, illegal and to use your own phrase, "contrary to the spirit of the Supreme Court decision."

"PRAYER CHANGES THINGS,"

Adam Clayton Powell, Jr.

Jean Fairfax to U.S. Education Commissioner Francis Keppel

For twenty years Jean Fairfax worked on the staff of the NAACP Legal Defense and Educational Fund, and from 1957 to 1965 she directed the Southern Civil Rights Program of the American Friends Service Committee. As this letter illustrates, the mass dismissal of African American teachers and principals was one of the unintended consequences of school desegregation. Francis Keppel (1916–1990) served as U.S. Commissioner of Education from 1962 to 1965.*

March 6, 1967

Dear Friend:

When I was in North Carolina recently, I heard about the school desegregation plan of Asheboro (Randolph County), N.C. I do not know how the plan provides for the desegregation of elementary schools, but I understand that the Negro high school will be closed and their Negro students will be integrated into the formerly all-white high schools.

According to very reliable sources, the Negro high school teachers have been told to look for jobs elsewhere. None of them has been given a contract for next year. If these facts are correct, you will be faced

*Francis Keppel, a Harvard graduate, served as dean of the School of Education at Harvard from 1948 to 1962. He later served as vice chair of the New York City Board of Education (1967–1971).

with an important precedent-making decision as you review this plan to determine whether it represents good faith compliance with the requirement of nondiscrimination. Your approval of a school desegregation plan which in this implementation clearly discriminates against Negro teachers as a group would not only set an unfortunate precedent. You would lose the confidence of good Negro teachers in the South who are concerned about their job security and who have a right to be considered on their individual merits as school boards abolish their dual systems.

We have heard conflicting statements from Federal officials about what school desegregation plans should indicate so far as the eventual desegregation of teaching and administrative staffs is concerned. A clear statement from you at this time about your expectations regarding the desegregation of public school teachers within the framework of Title VI regulations would be very helpful. However, whatever plans promise eventually, if school desegregation in its initial period completely eliminates Negro teachers, commitments to nondiscrimination at a later date will be meaningless.

Sincerely yours,

Jean Fairfax

Derrick Bell, Jr., to Office for Civil Rights Staff

Derrick Bell, Jr. (b. 1930), the writer, legal scholar, activist, and director of the U.S. Department of Health, Education, and Welfare's Office for Civil Rights, wrote the following memorandum to his staff and attached a letter he received from a student who attended one of the schools Bell and others fought to desegregate.

August 15, 1967

As I have probably indicated to all of you <u>ad nauseum</u>, there are joys and satisfactions to be found in the private civil rights area which are extremely difficult to match in government. An example is contained in the attached letter from Miss Elnora Fondren who was one of the few pupils I succeeded in having enrolled in an all-white school in the very difficult and largely unsuccessful Clarksdale school desegregation effort.

Miss Fondren left a Negro school in the 11th grade and survived unbelievable harassment and other problems, including economic, to graduate with honor. I am sure it was a thrilling moment for her and vicariously for me. I want to share it with you.

P.S. Pete suggests that some of you may wish to join me in sending Elnora a small check. If so, I shall be happy to receive your contributions and forward them without the substantial deductions for fundraising fees and costs usually associated with worthwhile causes.

U.S. Senator Edward W. Brooke III to President Richard M. Nixon

Fifteen years after the Supreme Court decision in Brown v. Board of Education *outlawed school segregation, efforts to desegregate public schools continued to face stiff resistance. Senator Edward W. Brooke sent the following telegram to President Nixon urging him to uphold the Johnson Administration's desegregation guidelines, which were challenged by Southern officials.* The telegram also urged Nixon to extend the Voting Rights Act of 1965, which bolstered the Fifteenth Amendment and prohibited the denial or abridgment of the right to vote based on literacy tests and the like. The measure also provided for federal enforcement by designating, when needed, federal examiners to monitor polling places.*

[June 25, 1969]

MY DEAR MR. PRESIDENT:

I AM DEEPLY DISTURBED AT RUMORS THAT MAJOR CHANGES ARE BEING CONTEMPLATED IN SCHOOL DESEGREGATION GUIDELINES. THIS QUESTION AND THE EXTENSION OF THE VOTING RIGHTS ACT OF 1965 ARE OF PARAMOUNT IMPORTANCE TO MILLIONS OF AMERICANS DEDICATED TO THE CAUSE OF EQUAL OPPORTUNITY. HASTY OR ILL-CONSIDERED ACTION ON EITHER OF THESE ISSUES WOULD DESTROY CONFIDENCE IN THE ADMINISTRATION AND WOULD BADLY

---

*Under the guidelines, five segregated Southern schools would lose federal funds if they did not desegregate by the fall of 1969. A month after Brooke's telegram, the Nixon administration retreated from the deadline noting that "in some districts there may be sound reasons for some limited delay." NAACP Executive Director Roy Wilkins accused the administration of breaking the law. See "The Politics of Principle: Richard Nixon and School Desegregation," by Lawrence J. McAndrews, *The Journal of Negro History,* Vol. 83, No. 3 (Summer 1998), pp. 187–200.

DIVIDE THE COUNTRY. I RESPECTFULLY URGE YOU TO APPROVE NO CHANGES UNTIL WE HAVE HAD AN OPPORTUNITY TO CONSULT IN DETAIL ON THE EFFECTS AND IMPLICATIONS OF ANY PROPOSED REVISIONS.

SINCERELY,

EDWARD W. BROOKE

UNITED STATES SENATOR

Derrick Bell, Jr., to Justice Thurgood Marshall

Shortly after joining the Harvard University Law School faculty, Derrick Bell, Jr., wrote this letter to Thurgood Marshall (1908–1993), the former chief counsel at the NAACP Legal Defense and Educational Fund who by then was on the Supreme Court. Bell had worked for Marshall as an assistant counsel at the NAACP Legal Defense and Educational Fund. Thurgood Marshall was born Thoroughgood Marshall in Baltimore, Maryland, where he attended segregated schools. He graduated from Lincoln University in Pennsylvania and then Howard University Law School in Washington, D.C. As chief counsel for the NAACP Legal Defense and Educational Fund, he successfully argued before the Supreme Court in Brown v. Board of Education, *resulting in the landmark decision that declared separate-but-equal in education unconstitutional. President Lyndon B. Johnson appointed Marshall to the Supreme Court in 1967, making him the first African American to serve on the nation's highest court.*

Cambridge, Massachusetts
October 2, 1969

Dear Boss:

Just a note to indicate officially (I assume Gloria Branker has already given you the word) that one of your former employees is now occupying a desk in these hallowed halls.

I have been here only a month and find it all quite interesting. I am particularly enjoying working with the more than 100 black law students presently enrolled here. I have no teaching responsibilities during this semester but in the spring will be teaching a course I designed on the West coast entitled "Race, Racism and American Law."

As one of the side benefits of my present position, I shall be able to recommend to you and any other black members of the Judiciary around the country the names of outstanding black law graduates for consideration as law clerks. I would be interested in learning your needs as to this.

Ed Rutledge's son, John, who will graduate from the Golden Gate Law School in San Francisco this year, called to request that I permit my name to be used in his application for a clerkship with you. I gave approval, but frankly indicated to him that one of the disadvantages of graduation from a law school of lesser prestige is the difficulty of obtaining a really top clerkship appointment. Beyond this, John impresses me as a young man of substantial commitment and maturity.

This should prove a most exciting and demanding year on the Court. There are many fears in academic circles and elsewhere that the forces of conservatism and reaction will not only bar further progress in the area of social reform but will create a climate leading toward retrogression that could prove of critical danger to the society in general and black people in particular. In this regard, I cannot help but add my view that the Court has placed on your shoulders the burden of issuing more than your share of orders which are technically correct but disappointing, at least to the socially sensitive segments of the populace. I refer specifically to the Eldridge Cleaver, Aspen H Bomb Test and Chicago demonstration trial matters.*

I am certain there are aspects to each of these cases about which I am ignorant, but I would repeat the hope that decisions in this area might be spread about just a bit more.

My regards to the family and my best wishes to you.

Sincerely,

Derrick A. Bell, Jr.

Justice Thurgood Marshall to Derrick Bell, Jr.

Supreme Court of the United States
Washington, D.C. 20543
[October 1969]

Dear Derrick:

It was good to get your letter of October 2. For once, Gloria Branker did not let me know a good news item. Needless to say, you have all my good wishes for making a success of a good challenge.

*A reference to the trial of Eldridge Cleaver (1935–1998), author of *Soul on Ice* (1968) and cofounder of the Black Panther Party, who was wounded in a 1968 shootout with Oakland police. He eventually fled the country and returned to the United States in 1975.

The point you raise in your note can be answered to you, although I have made a flat rule of not discussing my actions with anyone. You single out for criticism the Eldridge Cleaver case, the Aspen H Bomb Test and Chicago demonstration trial matters. The Cleaver case came to me in routine fashion when it was discovered that Mr. Justice Douglas was not in town. The Aspen case came to me routinely when it was discovered that Mr. Justice White was in Europe. Believe it or not, the Chicago demonstration case came to me because I happen to be the Circuit Justice for the Seventh Circuit. This, I believe, will allay any fears you might have.

With all best wishes,

Sincerely,

Thurgood

Kenneth B. Clark *to* The New York Times

The Editor
The New York Times
New York, New York 10036
August 7, 1979

Dear Sir:

On July 24, 1979, the New York Times uncritically endorsed the "Truth In Testing" legislation, which was signed by Governor Carey.* Your editorial stated that this amendment to the education law would take "the mystery out of college testing," and that "students deserve to know how they are being rated and judged."

In spite of the good intentions of The Times editorial, it was misleading. So was Ralph Nader's assertion, in a letter published by The Times on August 3, 1979, that the legislation will require test companies "to explain to students what the scores mean and how they will be reported to schools." And Nader's claim that the objections to this legislation reflect only the "corporate style lobbying efforts of testing services" is inaccurate. The Board of Regents and The Commissioner of Education of the State of New York have independently advised the Govenor against signing this legislation. It is my contention that this so-called "Truth In Testing" law is a placebo. However laudable its in-

*The "Truth In Testing" law, which went into effect January 1, 1980, gives students the right to obtain a copy of the questions and answers sheet from testing companies after their scores are tabulated.

tentions, this law cannot force test companies to explain the meaning of test scores to students; and certainly this law cannot deal with the complex issues of test validity and the role of cultural factors in influencing test results. The construction, evaluation and interpretation of tests are highly technical matters which must be dealt with by on-going research by those who are trained in this speciality. The important problem of the use and abuse of standardized tests cannot be resolved by a simplistic law which confuses this issue with consumer protection problems.

Admission tests measure the abilities developed by individuals over a long period of time, both in and out of school. The value of test results is directly related to the equality of opportunity afforded to the candidates taking a particular test. The assumption that a candidate's examination of a test already taken will somehow improve scores or reduce the chances of abuse is highly questionable. One can further assume that only the more privileged students will avail themselves of the opportunity to examine the test materials. These students will seek private tutoring on the assumption that this will increase their future test scores. Those individuals who cannot afford this privilege will cretainly not improve their test scores by merely examining the test questions and scores. This is a deceptive and meaningless exercise.

The New York State version of the "Testing In Truth" law is misleading and confuses the public. It will not benefit minority and poor students. It could, in fact, be detrimental to already-disadvantaged individuals. Appropriate legislation in the general area of the abuse and the premature exclusionary use of standardized tests might be desirable, but such legislation should be the culmination of serious inquiry, rather than a political gesture. It is my firm belief that this is such an important matter that the New York State Legislature should hold a series of hearings with concerned professionals for the purpose of amending this law, which promises much more than it can possibly deliver.

Sincerely,

Kenneth B. Clark

Derrick Bell, Jr., to Dean Robert Clark

Bell wrote this letter to the dean of Harvard Law School to request an indefinite leave to protest the school's failure to offer a tenured position to a woman of color. Bell never returned to Harvard and became a visiting professor at New York University Law School.

Cambridge, Massachusetts
April 9, 1990

Dear Bob,

I regret that I must give you this inadequate but quite firm notice of my intention to request a leave without pay effective with the end of the current school year and continuing until a woman of color is offered and accepts a tenured position on this faculty. While addressed to you as dean, I consider this a matter of community concern and will share this letter with all regular faculty members. I hope you and they will honor my request not to share this letter with either students or the media.

During this, my 20th year of law school teaching, I have been trying to assess whether my teaching and writing have done justice to the student petitions and persistent requests for black faculty that preceded my appointment. In fairness, I think there have been successes and failures, but until now, I genuinely believed that I was keeping the faith with those students and their successors who took substantial risks so that I might be hired.

Although I have never forgotten my representational function on this faculty, I was slow to recognize that as a black man, I am not able to understand, interpret, and articulate the unique conditions and challenges black women face. While I urged the hiring of black women, I thought that as a black man, I could both comprehend and represent the needs and interests of black women. A modicum of exposure to feminist writings, particularly those by black women, and [our current visitor's] presence and effectiveness have disabused me of this unintended but no less inexcusable presumptuousness. The large role our black women students are playing in the recent diversity protests here confirms what should have been obvious to me years ago.

I wish the push for women of color on the faculty was simply a matter of seeking conformity with a currently popular social goal. It is not. As each day's newspapers reveal and a flood of studies confirm, black and Hispanic men are faring quite poorly in contemporary society. It is not fortuitous that—despite the best efforts of our admissions office—there are many more women than men of color in our student body. The disparity is larger at the college level and is most obvious at black colleges where the ratio of black women to black men is often five and six to one. We simply must do justice by our black and Hispanic women for it appears they will have to handle an ever-increasing share of the leadership role in the 1990s and beyond.

Unfortunately, I have never been able to convince this faculty to act on those racial matters of the most basic concern to me. Thus, I was not pleased but hardly surprised that not one member of the Appointments Committee responded substantively to my February 4th memorandum (copy enclosed) urging a permanent appointment for [our current visitor]. When I raised the issue during a meeting on another matter, you indicated that because of the faculty policy deferring tenure votes on visitors during the year of their residence, it would be prudent to delay consideration of [our current visitor] until next year. I understand the factors that likely motivated faculty adoption of this policy, but after giving the matter more thought, have concluded that it is both unfair and unwise to apply this policy to visitors who are members of groups not now represented or seriously under-represented on the faculty.

It is unfair because, at the very least, the policy poses the potential for lengthy delays in correcting our current non-representation of black women, Hispanics, Asians, Native Americans, gays and lesbians, and the handicapped, to cite those groups represented in the Coalition for Civil Rights. I confess that I have been as insensitive to these special diversity concerns of other groups as I have regarding those of black women.

It is unwise because visitors who are members of unrepresented groups with credentials and performance records sufficient to earn them a visit here will also be seriously sought after by other schools. Indeed, their presence here as visitors will likely help generate permanent offers from other schools. This was the case with [two other visitors] and now [our current visitor] who has a tenured offer from Michigan and a visiting offer from Stanford. It is likely that Penn, [her] home school, will not allow her to depart without offering her a strong inducement to return. Given this demand, we have a far better chance of keeping her than we have of getting her to return after visits at Michigan and Stanford, assuming she does not accept the Michigan tenure offer outright. I imagine that if by some combination of unexpected factors, none of the six black men now on the faculty was able to teach for the next several years, all would deem our loss a crisis. It would not be difficult for you to generate a consensus that minority replacements—women as well as men—must be found and pressed into service by next September. But in terms of our students' present needs, that is precisely the position we are in with no tenured black women or other unrepresented minorities on the premises and—under the present policy—no possibility of tenure for anyone until at least the 1991–92 school year.

I realize that in hiring and promoting faculty, perhaps you and certainly a number of faculty members resist appointments based on any consideration other than academic potential as traditionally measured. The experience of the last two decades though teaches that persons of color, by utilizing their non-traditional credentials, can make valuable contributions to the school and to legal scholarship. Moreover, their presence in representative numbers enhances the school's ability to attract minority candidates with qualifications that all agree are outstanding.

Despite the progress we have made in hiring and promoting black men, I must agree with our students who are telling us that the faculty is as seriously unrepresentative now as it was before I joined it in 1969. I very much want to teach here next year and, quite frankly—despite my support for a faculty salary freeze—simply cannot afford not to teach. I do hope that this explains why I cannot in good conscience continue in a role that limits rather than expands the faculty diversity I think we all want and need.

Sincerely,
Derrick Bell

Walter J. Leonard to Angela M. Leonard

The former Fisk University president Walter J. Leonard (b. 1929) wrote this letter to his daughter, Angela (b. 1954), a Hedgebrook Fellow in the Department of History at Loyola University in Maryland. At the time Walter Leonard was a visiting law professor at Oxford University.

Oxford, England
July 28, 1997

Dear Angela,

My, how time has flown! I am deeply into my fourth month of what has been a joy-filled, hardworking and richly rewarding experience. It would now seem appropriate for me to share some observations about this rare opportunity.

First, just a word about Oxford—both the University and the City. It is not always easy to determine where one ends and where the other begins. So it is likely that attempts at descriptions look suspiciously as though they are an indistinguishable whole. What is clear is that Oxford is a place of colleges and other schools, cloisters, chapels, bicycles, The Congregation, The Hebdomadal Council (the University's governing body), Saints, Sirs, seasons, rivers, spires, students, scholars and traditions—and I do mean <u>TRADITIONS</u>. After four months, I find the collection of cloisters, quadrangles and streets—with multiple names—a little less mystical and considerably less confusing. But I continue to make new discoveries, for, after all, the city began near the end of the seventh century about four hundred years before students and "schollers" came to the "Towne."

Oxford, the University, offers a virtual cornucopia of lectures, seminars, symposia and other learning activities, all open to members of the University. For the student with sufficient discipline and the necessary pertinacity, a festival of instructional experience awaits.

During my stay, I have prepared and given one talk, one lecture, and one seminar. The talk was on and about the *Dred Scott* decision; the lecture was on Martin Luther King, Jr.; and the seminar was on the *Emancipation Proclamation*. Each one was well attended. In fact, I am informed that the lecture on Martin Luther King, Jr., established a record for attendance at Wolfson College. It was a very good evening.

The seminar on the Emancipation Proclamation involved a group of about 60 law and pre-law students from the United States. They are here in an Oxford Summer Program. This one is a collaborative effort with an American university. The group is composed of a nearly equal number of men and women. Three of the women (two African American and one Asian American) are the only non-Caucasian representation. When I asked, "Where are the black men?," one student replied, without hesitation, "In jail." Those calmly-said words were disturbing, shocking and sobering—made all the more wrenching in such a setting. It was not at all amusing.

To my amazement and very pleasant surprise, following the seminar five of the students formally requested that I serve as their Tutor as they prepared for the program's required papers and presentations. I am convinced that the operative motivation for their request was that they had never had an earlier reason to <u>really examine</u> the Declaration of Independence, the American Constitution, and the Emancipation Proclamation, along with relevant cases and documents.

As you are very much aware, this Institution welcomes and promotes a competition of ideas and information—a fact which should urge us to be mindful of the tenacity with which the thoughts and words of America's neo-conservatives and racists are promoted in this part of the world. Further, we should not lose sight of the fact that negative and exploitive movies and news stories about African American life receive a goodly amount of coverage and exposure in the various media. Seldom is the whole of the American experience tendered in an informative and sensitive fashion.

There is much work to be done.

As I prepare to return to the United States, and home, I do so with a very deep appreciation for the significance of this joyful, illuminating, learning and spiritual experience. And, I am even more aware that there is a Power and a Spirit without which we simply cannot reach and actualize that hope which lives and waits beyond despair.

With every good wish and warmest personal regards, I am,

Faithfully yours,

Dad

Walter J. Leonard to Angela M. Leonard

Walter Leonard refers to his daughter's scholarship on monuments, sacred sites, and the collective memory of African descendants.

Chevy Chase, Maryland
November 6, 2002

Dear Angela,

Week after week, as I note a nation struggling to recapture its equilibrium following the evil and murderous attacks on the World Trade Center and the Pentagon, I am struck by the timeliness and the importance of your research and scholarship. Few studies could be more important than to measure a people's memory of history—as a nation, as a community, and as a society.

A loss, or a denial, or a deprival of memory would be a tragedy, particularly as we attempt the weaving of a single fabric capable of containing—or covering—the diasporic experiences of the many threads of the cultural, economic, educational, political and social contributions of nearly 400,000,000 people (U.S. population now living) and the many millions more, now gone.

Since families, communities and nations are built on and around a collective memory, through a direct or indirect sharing of experiences, I very much hope—and I urge—that you consider the significance of your efforts.

I would not be surprised if the NEH [National Endowment for the Humanities], the Knight Foundation, or one of the other scholarly foundations (Schlesinger, Bunting, or Radcliffe) found a goodly measure of interest in your ideas.

Wishing you all the best, always,
Dad

Rev. Bernard Chris Dorsey to Walter Broadnax

Bernard Chris Dorsey (b. 1968), the university chaplain and director of Religious Life at Clark-Atlanta University, e-mailed these words of comfort to the university president, Walter Broadnax (b. 1944), during student and faculty protests as Broadnax revamped programs in an effort to balance the budget at the historically black college. Broadnax resigned in 2008 and Carlton E. Brown became the interim president.

Tuesday, April 17, 2007
11:13 PM

Walter,

I just wanted to check in with you to see how you are doing. I called the office today and Eunice told me you are doing okay and you are continuing to do what you need to do. I'm glad to hear that you are not letting the mess that people are stirring up stop you from moving forward. I want you to know that I think about you daily. You and Angel [Broadnax's wife] are constantly in my prayers. I think I've told you this before, but I am inspired by you and your ability to stand firm with integrity in the face of treachery and vindictiveness. The small amount of it that I face is tolerable in light of everything that you have to endure. I know from experience that it is difficult to lead people forward when all they want to do is remain stagnant. I've often thought that institutions can be like water at times. If water remains stagnant too long it becomes a breeding ground for bacteria and parasites. Unfortunately the bacteria and parasites had been accumulating at CAU long before you got here. You have been tasked with the job of getting the fresh water flowing again. Of course this doesn't sit well with the bacteria and the parasites, but I appreciate the work you have done and what you are doing to strengthen CAU.

I'm sure you are familiar with the experiences of Moses as he was trying to lead the people of Israel out of Egypt and into the promised land. When the people became uncomfortable wandering in the desert, they complained against Moses and they doubted his leadership. Some of them complained that [they] wished they could have remained in Egypt where they at least had meat to eat. Never mind the fact that they were slaves in Egypt, they just wanted to go back to what was familiar to them. I know that some people want CAU to go back to being in bondage to fiscal irresponsibility and uncertainty. They would rather let the institution die in Egypt than take a chance on securing a better future for future generations. I pray that God will continue to guide you and strengthen you as you do the work that he has brought you here to do.

Blessings,

Chris Dorsey

Dr. Frank L. Douglas to Claude Canizares, MIT Vice President for Research

Dr. Frank L. Douglas (b. 1943), was a professor at the Harvard–Massachusetts Institute of Technology Division of Health Sciences and Technology and executive director and founder of the MIT Center for Biomedical Innovation until his resignation in 2007. He e-mailed the following letters to his colleagues, including Claude Canizares, to explain his decision to resign from the faculty.

June 1, 2007
6:37 p.m.

Dear Claude,

It is with a deep sense of disappointment and a heavy heart that I have come to the decision to withdraw from MIT.

I have observed with consternation the inability of the institution to manage the James Sherley situation.* My dismay is even greater be-

---

*MIT professor James Sherley, a biological engineer, began a twelve-day fast on February 5, 2007, to protest the denial of tenure and the grievance process. Sherley received his Ph.D. and M.D. from Johns Hopkins University School of Medicine and was a postdoctoral fellow at Princeton University. He was one of twenty-three black professors.

cause the Institute, after having agreed to arbitration, which led to Prof Sherley ending his hunger strike, now, has negated that agreement and insists on his departure on June 30th, 2007. Frankly, I am so astonished that the Institute did not resolve this issue that it leaves me to believe that the *desire* to do this was and is lacking. Clearly, *where there is no will, there is no way!*

I would like to thank you, the Deans, Directors and Leaders of the Schools, Divisions and Departments of which I am a faculty member, for their support of my work in establishing the MIT Center for Biomedical Innovation. I would also like to thank my Co-Directors, Tony Sinskey, Ernie Berndt, and Steve Tannenbaum, as well as Dave Weber, for their help in giving form to the vision of MITCBI. Finally, I would like to thank Gigi Hirsch, Sherene Aram and Cheryl Mottley without whose dedication MITCBI would not have achieved its success and prominence.

I leave because I would neither be able to advise young Blacks about their prospects of flourishing in the current environment, nor about avenues available to effect change when agreements or promises are transgressed. I will leave on June 30th, 2007 and would recommend that I work with Tony Sinskey to ensure a smooth transition of leadership of the Center. I am gratified that I leave behind a Center that is well funded and that provides a Safe Haven where experts from academia, industry and government can collaborate to improve innovation and accessibility of novel therapeutics.

Sincerely,
Frank

Dr. Frank L. Douglas to His MIT Colleagues and Friends

June 1, 2007

Dear Colleagues and Friends,

Since you paid me the superb compliment of celebrating the Black History Maker Award with me, I wanted to give you a more detailed explanation for my resigning from MIT. I recognize that you might nonetheless still find it unfathomable.

I arrived in the USA in 1963 and almost from that first day have had to deal with the effects of racism on a personal basis. In 2005 I came to MIT and felt that my retirement from industry was also a retirement from having to deal with racism. I was accepted and judged, not 'by the color of my skin, but by the content of my character' and by what I contributed. You will never know how exhilarating this experience has been! Gradually, however, I felt an inner sense of unease as I witnessed both a lack of genuine commitment to something greater than oneself and a lack of a real focus on benefit to humanity.

Two events awoke me from my personal reverie. These were the James Sherley saga and a conference on Race that was held on campus by Dr. David Jones, the leader (?) of the Center on Race Relations. I will not comment further on the James Sherley issue as I addressed that in my second letter to Claude. I enclose that letter.

I was invited to present on BIDIL at the conference on Race Relations. I was amazed by the lack of interest in data, as well as the dogmatic and uninformed assertion that BIDIL was a "race drug" and therefore should never have been approved by the FDA. There was no interest in the fact that BIDIL demonstrated a 43% decrease in mortality in the Afro American patients in which it was studied and the fact that this patient population dies at a rate 1.5 to 2 times greater than that of white patients with [a] similar degree of congestive heart failure. As I remarked to the conference participants, I cannot believe that had similar findings been discovered for a non-minority group that we would have called it a "race drug." One only needs to see the enormous sums of monies that are raised to try to find cures for some diseases that disproportionately affect some ethnic groups to appreciate this. I found it remarkable that this conference was led by an MIT Center whose leader (?) was clearly on a mission against this drug and had little interest in understanding the complexities of the regulatory process or drug development. These two events caused me to look at the MIT environment, where many "flowers bloom," more critically.

I also became troubled by the absence of a sense of business ethics among some of the students and faculty. Yes, I know, it is a large institution of individuals. However, every institution has a character, a soul. That character defines its graduates and I sense that MIT is in danger of losing the humanity side of its character.

As you know, following the release of my resignation letter, I spent some 10 days reconsidering my decision to resign. I had many discussions and was genuinely touched by the personal support and, I would even say, affection that was expressed in the many emails and discussions. So what was missing?

Why was I not persuaded to reverse my intention to leave? It is very simple. I recommended that the Deans and some of the department chairs should call for an external group to evaluate and make recommendations to improve the climate and conditions that appear to be unsupportive of minority faculty at MIT. Only one person, namely Tom Magnanti, discussed this with me.

None of you, my colleagues, offered to support me in this. Instead, people focused on the sanctity of the tenure process, which was not my issue. In any case, I do not believe in the sanctity of anything that is created by men. Others of you tried to overwhelm me with guilt for the adverse effect that my decision would immediately have on a number of colleagues. This lack of support for my recommendation was ultimately the deciding factor. It signaled to me that the environment at MIT is so insensitive to this issue, that even friends and close colleagues could not comprehend nor recognize the essence of my "dilemma."

I often tell young people: Institutions survive, Individuals do not. (Incidentally, I did share this with James Sherley.) MIT will survive and I hope my legacy of launching and implementing MIT CBI will also survive. But I have no illusions: I will soon fade in your active memories. Such is the rhythm of life.

As I say to friends: Enjoy the mystery of the journey of your life. I try to do that also for my own sanity.

Frank.

PART V

War

From the Revolutionary War to the War in Iraq, African American troops have valiantly fought to defend a nation that for centuries denied them equality and respect. An estimated 10,000 blacks enlisted in the Revolutionary War despite General George Washington's initial support of a Continental Congress measure to ban their military service. During the War of 1812, one-sixth of the Navy seamen were African American and more than 2,500 African Americans defended Philadelphia against attack in 1814; another 1,000 engaged in the 1815 Battle of New Orleans against the British.

In 1863 the federal government sanctioned African American regiments as part of the Union Army and established the Bureau of Colored Troops. In the aftermath of the Civil War, African Americans continued to enlist in large numbers, believing that their patriotism and sacrifice would be rewarded with racial equality and respect. Thousands of African American troops, nicknamed Buffalo Soldiers, were dispatched in the Indian Wars on the western frontier between 1866 and 1890. The Buffalo Soldiers were the first professional African American soldiers during peacetime and later served with distinction in the Spanish-American War, Philippine-American War, and World Wars I and II.

More than 200,000 African Americans served in segregated units during World War I, but the inductees were initially restricted to non-combat posts. In 1917, under pressure from civil rights leaders, the War Department finally created the 92nd and 93rd Divisions' all-black combat units, and by the end of the war African Americans had served in cavalry, infantry, medical, engineer, and artillery units, and also as intelligence officers, surveyors, and chaplains.

However, despite their demonstrated patriotism and acts of valor,

African Americans continued to face discrimination and segregation in and outside the military. Many soldiers returned home to antiblack violence that reached a peak in 1919, in what was called Red Summer. During the summer and fall, riots instigated by whites erupted in twenty-six cities, resulting in hundreds of deaths and injuries, mostly sustained by blacks. Incidents of lynching spiked from fifty-eight in 1918 to seventy-seven in 1919, and at least ten of the victims were veterans, some still in uniform.

Nevertheless, more than 3 million African Americans registered under the Selective Service Act of 1940 even as civil rights leaders condemned their discriminatory treatment. In 1948 President Truman issued Executive Order 9981 to end segregation and discrimination in the armed forces and other areas of the federal government. However, as some of the letters in this part attest, it would take more than a presidential order to end segregation and discrimination in the military. After years of resistance and turmoil, the armed forces were finally fully desegregated in 1954.

John Boston to His Wife

John Boston was a runaway slave from Maryland who fled north and found refuge in a New York regiment of the Union army. He wrote this letter to his wife, Elizabeth, who remained in bondage.

Upton Hill [Va.]
January the 12 1862

My Dear Wife

it is with grate joy I take this time to let you know Whare I am   i am now in Safety in the 14the Regiment of Brooklyn   this Day I can Adress you thank god as a free man   I had a little truble in git- ing away But as the lord led the Children of Isrel to the land of Canon So he led me to a land Whare freedom Will rain in spite Of earth and hell   Dear you must make your Self content I am free from al the Slavers Lash   and as you have chose to Wise plan Of Serving the lord I hope you Will pray Much and I will try by the help of god To Serv him With all my hart   I am With a very nice man and have All that hart Can Wish But My Dear I Cant express my grate desire that I Have to See you   I trust the time Will Come When We Shal meet again And if We don't meet on earth We Will Meet in heven Whare Jesas ranes   Dear Elizabeth tell Mrs Own[ees] That I trust that She Will Continue Her Kindness to you and that god Will Bless her on earth and Save her In grate eternity   My Acomplements To Mrs Owens and her Children may They Prosper through life   I never Shall for- git her kindness to me   Dear Wife I must Close   rest yourself Contented I am free   I Want you to rite To me Soon as you Can Without Delay   Direct your letter to the 14th Regiment New York State militia Uptons Hill Virginea In Care of Mr Cranford Comary

Write my Dear Soon As you C   Your Affectionate Husban   Kiss
Daniel For me
        John Boston

Lewis Douglass to Amelia Loguen

Lewis Douglass (1840–1908), Frederick Douglass's eldest son, was one of the first recruits in the all-black volunteer 54th Massachusetts Infantry during the Civil War. He wrote the following letter to his fiancée two days after his regiment's ill-fated attack against Fort Wagner in the harbor of Charleston, South Carolina. When he wrote this letter, Douglass apparently did not know the full extent of his unit's casualties.

Morris Island, South Carolina
July 20, 1863

My dear Amelia:

I have been in two fights, and am unhurt. I am about to go in another I believe to-night. Our men fought well on both occasions. The last was desperate—we charged that terrible battery on Morris Island known as Fort Wagner, and were repulsed with a loss of 3 killed and wounded. I escaped unhurt from amidst that perfect hail of shot and shell. It was terrible. I need not particularize—the papers will give a better account than I have time to give. My thoughts are with you often, you are as dear as ever, be good enough to remember it as I [have] no doubt you will. As I said before we are on the eve of another fight and I am very busy and have just snatched a moment to write you. I must necessarily be brief. Should I fall in the next fight killed or wounded I hope to fall with my face to the foe.

If I survive I shall write you a long letter. DeForrest of your city is wounded, George Washington is missing, Jacob Carter is missing, Chas Reason is wounded, Chas Whiting, Chas Creamer all wounded. The above are in hospital.

This regiment has established its reputation as a fighting regiment, not a man flinched, though it was a trying time. Men fell all around me. A shell would explode and clear a space of twenty feet. Our men would close up again, but it was no use—we had to retreat, which was a very hazardous undertaking. How I got out of that fight alive I cannot tell, but I am here. My Dear girl I hope again to see you. I must bid you farewell should I be killed. Remember if I die I die in a good cause. I wish we had a hundred thousand colored troops—we would put an end to this war. Good Bye to all.

Your own loving Lewis

Write soon

James Henry Gooding to President Abraham Lincoln

James Henry Gooding (1837–1864) was a corporal in the 54th Massachusetts Infantry who died in a Confederate prison after his capture in the battle at Olustee in Florida. He wrote this letter to President Lincoln to protest the Militia Act of July 1862, which set a black soldier's pay at $7.00 a month plus $3.00 for clothing, compared with the $13.00 monthly pay and $3.50 clothing allowance for white soldiers.

Morris Island [S.C.].
Sept 28th 1863.

Your Excellency will pardon the presumption of an humble individual like myself, in addressing you. but the earnest Solicitation of my Comrades in Arms, besides the genuine interest felt by myself in the matter is my excuse, for placing before the Executive head of the Nation our Common Grievance: On the 6th of the last Month, the Paymaster of the department, informed us, that if we would decide to recieve the sum of $10 (ten dollars) per month, he would come and pay us that sum, but, that, on the sitting of Congress, the Regt would, in his opinion, be allowed the other 3 (three). He did not give us any guarantee that this would be, as he hoped, certainly he had no authority for making any such guarantee, and we can not supose him acting in any way interested. Now the main question is. Are we Soldiers, or are we LABOURERS. We are fully armed, and equipped, have done all the various Duties, pertaining to a Soldiers life, have conducted ourselves, to the complete satisfaction of General Officers, who, were if any, prejudiced against us, but who now accord us all the encouragement, and honour due us: have shared the perils, and Labour, of Reducing the first stronghold, that flaunted a Traitor Flag: and more, Mr President. Today, the Anglo Saxon Mother, Wife, or Sister, are not alone, in tears for departed Sons, Husbands, and Brothers. The patient Trusting Decendants of Africa's Clime, have dyed the ground with blood, in defense of the Union, and Democracy. Men too your Excellency, who know in a measure, the cruelties of the Iron heel of oppression, which in years gone by, the very Power, their blood is now being spilled to maintain, ever ground them to the dust. But When the war trumpet sounded o'er the land, when men knew not the Friend from the Traitor, the Black man laid his life at the Altar of the Nation,—and he was refused. When the arms of the Union, were beaten, in the first year of the War, And the Executive called more food. for its ravaging maw, again the black man begged, the privelege of Aiding his Country in her need, to be again refused. And now, he is in the War: and how has he conducted himself? Let their dusky forms, rise up, out the mires of James Island, and give the answer. Let the rich mould around Wagners parapets be upturned, and there will be found an Eloquent answer. Obedient and patient, and Solid as a wall are they. all we lack, is a paler hue, and a better acquaintance with the Alphabet. Now Your Excellency, We have done a Soldiers Duty. Why cant we have a Soldiers pay? You caution the Rebel Chieftain, that the United States, knows, no distinction, in her Soldiers: She insists on having all her Soldiers, of whatever, creed or Color, to be treated, according to the usages of War. Now if the United States exacts uniformity of treatment of her Soldiers, from the Insurgents, would it not be well, and consistent, to set the example herself, by paying all her Soldiers alike? We of this Regt. were not enlisted under any "contraband" act. But we do not wish to be understood, as rating our Service, of more Value to the Government, than the service of the ex-slave, Their Service is undoubtedly worth much to the Nation, but Congress made express, provision touching their case, as slaves freed by military necessity, and assuming the Government, to be their temporary Guardian:—Not so with us—Freemen by birth, and consequently, having the advantage of thinking, and acting for ourselves, so far as the Laws would allow us. We do not consider ourselves fit subjects for the Contraband act. We appeal to You, Sir: as the Executive of the Nation, to have us Justly Dealt with. The Regt, do pray, that they be assured their service will be fairly appreciated, by paying them as american SOLDIERS, not as menial hirelings. Black men You may well know, are poor, three dollars per month, for a year, will supply their needy Wives, and little ones, with fuel. If you, as chief Magistrate of the Nation, will assure us, of our whole pay. We are content, our Patriotism, our enthusiasm will have a new impetus, to exert our energy more and more to aid Our Country. Not that our hearts ever flagged, in Devotion, spite the evident apathy displayed in our behalf, but We feel as though, our Country spurned us, now we are sworn to serve her.

Please give this a moments attention

James Henry Gooding

Nancy Allcorn to Missouri Provost Marshall

Although a March 3, 1865, joint resolution of Congress emancipated the wives and children of enlisted African American soldiers, maintaining their freedom remained a challenge, particularly in the border states of Kentucky and Missouri, where slaveholders often tried to hold on to the families of African Americans enlisted in the Union Army.

Palmyra, Missouri

May 16, 1864

Richard Allcorn, a man of color, is my husband and is a soldier in the United States Army. Witnesses for the proof of enlistment of my husband: Dr. A. Jones, Palmyra. Jerry, a man of color and others.

William Frances Kerrick is my master. He hired me to William Jackson last Christmas. I am not getting one cent for my services. As my husband is in the U.S. Service, I understand that I am entitled to go free and get the wages of my own labor. You will oblige me very much by giving me relief.

Nancy Allcorn

George Rodgers et al. to President Abraham Lincoln

George Rodgers and his comrades appealed to President Abraham Lincoln on behalf of his family and fellow African American soldiers who had not been compensated for their service.

New Orleans, Louisiana

Camp Parpit

August 1864

My Dear and Worthy Friend MR President.

I thake this opportunity of introducing my self to you By Wrteing thes fiew Lines To let you know that you have Proven A friend to me and to all our Race   And now I stand in the Denfence of the Country myself Ready and Willing to oBay all orders & demands that has A tendency to put Down this Rebelion In military Life or Civel Life. I Enlisted at Almira state of N. York, shemoung County Under Mr C. W. Cawing Provose Marshall And [when] I Enlisted he told me I would get 13 Dollars Per. Mounth or more if White Soldiers got it   he expected the wages would Raise And I would get my pay every 2 Months   hear I am in the survice 7 months And have Not Received Eney Monthly Pay   I have a wife and 3 Children Neither one of them Able to thake Care of Themselves and my wife is sick   And she has sent to me for money   And I have No way of getting Eney money to send to her Because I cant Get my Pay. And it gos very hard with me to think my family should be At home A suffering have money earnt and cant not get it   And I Don't know when I will Be Able to Beleave my suffering Family   And another thing when I Enlisted I was promised A furlow and I have Not had it   Please MR Lincm Don't think I Am Blameing you for it   I Dident think you knew Eney thing About it   And I dident know eney Other Course to thake To obtain what I think is Right I invested my money in Percuring A house an home for my wife and Children   And she write to me she has to work and can not surport the Children with out my Aid . . . I Do not say the Government is using us so   I [do not] Believe the Government knows Eney thing About how we are treated   we came out to be true union soldiers the Grandsons of Mother Africa Never to Flinch from Duty . . . I wonce Before was a Slave 25 years   I made escape 1855 Came In to York state from Maryland   And I Enlisted in the survice got up By the union League Club   And we ware Promised All satisfaction Needful   But it seem to Be A failure   We Are not treated Like we are soldiers in coleague Atall   we are Deprived of the most importances things we Need in health and sickness Both That surficint Food And quality   As for The sick it is A shocking thing to Look into thire conditions   Death must Be thire Doom when once they have to go to the Hospital Never Return Again   such is the medical Assistance of the 20th Rig n y   your sarvent under Arms sincerely

George Rodgers
Thomas Sipple
Samuel Sampson
Wilmington, Delaware

Roanoke Island, North Carolina, Freedmen
to Secretary of War Edwin M. Stanton

Roanoke Island, North Carolina
March 9, 1865

We want to know from the Secretary of War has the Rev Chaplain James which is our Superinetendent of negros affairs has any wright to take our boy Children from us and from the School and Send them to newbern to work to pay for they ration without they parent Consint   if he has we thinks it very hard indeed   he essued a Proclamation that no boys Should have any rations at 14 years old   we thought was very hard that we had to find our boy Children to Goe to School hard as times are, but rather then they Should Goe without learning we thought we would try and doe it and say no more a bout it and the first thing we knowed Mr Streeter the Gentlemen that ration the Contrabands had Gone a round to all the White School-Teachers and told them to Give the boys orders to goe and get they ration on a Cirtain day   so the Negroes as we are Call are use to the Cesesh plots Suspicion the Game they was Going to play and a Greate many never Sent they Children. So Some twenty or twenty-five went and Mr. Streeter Give them they rations and the Guard march them down to the head quarters and put them on board the boat and carried them to newbern . . . Some of these little ones he sent off wasen oer 12 years olds. The mothers of Some went to Chaplain and Grieved and beg for the little boys but he would not let them have them   we want to know if the Prisident done essued any ration for School boys . . . we have men on the Island that Can Support the boys to Goe to School but here are Poor woman are not able to do it So the orphans must Goe without they learning   The next is Concerning of our White Soliders   they Come to our Church and we treat them with all the Politeness that we can and Some of them treats us though we were beast and we cant help our Selves   Some of them brings Pop Crackers and Christmas devils and throws a mong the woman and if we Say any thing to them they will talk about mobin us. we report them to the Capt   he will Say you must find out Which ones it was and that we cant do but we think very hard it   they put the pistols to our ministers breast because he Spoke to them about they behavour in the Church.   the next is Capt James told us When he got the mill built he would let us have plank to buil our houses   we negroes went to work and cut and hewd the timber and built the mill under the northern men derection and now he Charges us 3 and 4 dollars a hundred for plank and if we Carry 3 logs to the mill he takes 2 and Gives us one.   That is he has the logs haul and takes one for hauling and one for Sawing and we thinks that is too much Without he paid us better then he does.   and the next thing is he wont allow a man any ration While he is trying to buil him Self a house. To live in and how are negroes to live at that rate   we Cant see no way to live under Such laws, Without Some Altiration

M. W. Saddler *to* The Freeman *Newspaper*

M. W. Saddler, of the 25th Regiment, was one of the two thousand Buffalo Soldiers who fought in the Spanish-American War and the Philippine-American War. He wrote this letter while serving in the latter, which lasted from 1899 to 1901.

September 1899

Nothing of a historical nature has been experienced since my last letter. Everything is hustle and bustle, great preparations are being made, and everything indicated a hard campaign in the near future. Officers and enlisted men of my regiment are undergoing rigid training, mentally and physically. Our greatest aim is to maintain our standing among American soldiers and add another star to the already brilliant crown of the Afro American soldier. I am not a correspondent by profession but am willing to keep my people informed in regards to our arduous Orient duties. We are now arrayed to meet what we consider a common foe, men of our own hue and color. Where it is right to reduce these people to submission is not a question for a soldier to decide. Our oath of allegiance knows neither race, color nor nation, and if such a question should arise, it would be disposed of as one of a political nature by a soldier. There is one great desire among the colored soldiers now-a-days that did not exist probably a decade ago. That is to be represented in the file as well as that ranks. As the situation now stands, we moisten the soil with our precious blood, stain the colors with our oozing brains, only to make an already popular race more famous. Many of the intelligent heroes of the ranks would probably give their undivided attention to military training if there was an open avenue to a commission from the ranks and many inspired youths would cast their lot with us and display courage on the fields of battle. The

Afro Americans are represented in these islands by two thousand sable sons, as a Manila paper puts it "Greek against Greek" and in the usual old way we are here as an experiment. But experimenting with the colored soldiers has always added another laurel to support my assertion. I point with pride to the 54th Massachusetts, the regular army in the Indian campaigns, the 9th and 10th Cavalry and 24th Infantry at San Juan Hill, the 25th Infantry at El Caney and before Santiago.* The latter regiment in which the writer had the honor to exercise military skill and face cannon balls. The honors of the campaign in the Philippines are to come. Military maneuvering and fighting between civilized colored men is not recorded in history. The results of black regiments against black regiments are not known. The coming campaign is indeed one of an experimental nature. The Filipinos, in my estimation, are far superior to the Cubans in every degree, though Spanish rule has made them treacherous, but they are trying to carry on civilized warfare, and for an American to fall a captive to them does not mean present death as the case of the Spanish prisoners in the hands of the Cubans. I am thoroughly convinced that if these people are given home rule under American protection it will finally result in absolute independence.

M. W. Saddler
Serg't Co. K, 25th Inf.

Patrick Mason to Editor of The Gazette Newspaper

Patrick Mason, a soldier in the Philippine-American War, wrote this letter to express his outrage over the treatment by white American troops of the Filipinos fighting for independence from Spain.

November 19, 1899

Editor, Gazette.
Dear Sir:

I have not had any fighting to do since I have been here and don't care to do any. I feel sorry for these people and all that have come under the control of the United States. I don't believe they will be justly dealt by. The first thing in the morning is the "Nigger" and the last thing at night is the "Nigger." You have no idea the way these people

---

*The 9th and 10th Cavalries and the 24th and 25th Infantries were all-black regiments that were among the first four units dispatched to Cuba during the Spanish-American War.

are treated by the Americans here. I know their feeling toward them [Filipinos], as they speak their opinion in my presence thinking I am white. I love to hear them [white Americans] talk that I may know how they feel. The poor whites don't believe that anyone has a right to live but the white Americans, or to enjoy any rights or privileges that the white man enjoys. I must stop. You are right in your opinions. I must not say much as I am a soldier. The natives are a patient, burden baring people.

  Patrick Mason
  Sgt., Co. I, 24th Infantry

Unnamed Soldier to New York Age Editor

This unsigned letter from a soldier in the Philippine Islands was published in the Wisconsin Weekly Advocate *in Milwaukee on May 17, 1900.*

I have mingled freely with the natives and have had talks with American colored men here in business and who have lived here for years, in order to learn of them the cause of their dissatisfaction and the reason for this insurrection, and I must confess they have a just grievance. All this never would have occurred if the army of occupation would have treated them as people. The Spaniards, even if their laws were hard, were polite and treated them with some consideration; but the Americans, as soon as they saw that the native troops were desirous of sharing in the glories as well as the hardships of the hard-won battles with the Americans, began to apply home treatment for colored peoples: cursed them as damned niggers, steal [from] and ravish them, rob them on the street of their small change, take from the fruit vendors whatever suited their fancy, and kick the poor unfortunate if he complained, desecrate their church property, and after fighting began, looted everything in sight, burning, robbing the graves.

  This may seem a little tall—but I have seen with my own eyes carcasses lying bare in the boiling sun, the results of raids on receptacles for the dead in search of diamonds. The troops, thinking we would be proud to emulate their conduct, have made bold of telling their exploits to us. One fellow, member of the 13th Minnesota, told me how some fellows he knew had cut off a native woman's arm in order to get a fine inlaid bracelet. On upbraiding some fellows one morning, whom I met while out for a walk (I think they belong to a

Nebraska or Minnesota regiment, and they were stationed on the Malabon road) for the conduct of the American troops toward the natives and especially as to raiding, etc., the reply was: "Do you think we could stay over here and fight these damn niggers without making it pay all it's worth? The government only pays us $13 per month, that's starvation wages. White men can't stand it." Meaning they could not live on such small pay. In saying this they never dreamed that Negro soldiers would never countenance such conduct. They talked with impunity of "niggers" to our soldiers, never once thinking that they were talking to home "niggers" and should they be brought to remember that at home this is the same vile epithet they hurl at us, they beg pardon and make some effeminate excuse about what the Filipino is called.

I want to say right here that if it were not for the sake of the 10,000,000 black people in the United States, God alone knows on which side of the subject I would be. And for the sake of the black men who carry arms and pioneer for them as their representatives, ask them to not forget the present administration at the next election. Party be damned! We don't want these islands, not in the way we are to get them, and for Heaven's sake, put the party in power that pledged itself against this highway robbery. Expansion is too clean a name for it.

[Unsigned]

James A. Davis to Pecola Johnson Davis

James A. Davis, Sr. (1890–1967), and Pecola Johnson Davis (1897–1995) grew up in eastern North Carolina, where they raised ten children. Davis, who taught himself to read with biblical passages, wrote this letter to his wife during his service in World War I.

Oct. 1st [19]18

Dear Little Wife,

To Day is one Day that I have long to see. I have just recid a complment from you. To my very heart I am Happyer than I have bn for sometime. It found me well and getting along nicely. Very sorry to hear of the storm. But it could not be prevented. I am glad also that you and family are getting along so nicely. That makes me feel better, Oh, I am just crazy to see the kid and also the garden and all of our people. That will be a happy day when I get home. I will be glad to see the time roll around that we can meet again. There is nothing new that I can say. Only don't be disencurage. I am expecting to be home in a few weeks. I don't know for sure the exact time. I am glad that you had a successfully meeting. Also have learned that Bro. has bin call to camp. But I think he will have it lite. Understood that Floyd Davis and Manuel were on there way to France and there has bin a registration that taken the age from 18 to 40 and there have bin a good many of our boys called to camps. When I have the chance I will get a picture made and send it to you. Hope you and family will remain your potion of health as this leaves me extremely well. Desire of you the same. Give my regards to Mother and Dad. Tell them that I am as fat as a pig. Look in your other letters and you will find my Occupation. My best wishes to you and family.

Your dear Husband. Ans. Soon.

James A. Davis

Canute Frankson to a Dear Friend

Canute Frankson was a volunteer member of the Abraham Lincoln Brigade defending the Republic during the Spanish Civil War. He was among the first 550 Americans—10 of whom were African American—who formed the brigade to fight fascism. About eighty African Americans in all fought in the war.

Albacete, Spain
July 6, 1937

My Dear Friend:

I'm sure that by this time you are still waiting for a detailed explanation of what has this international struggle to do with my being here. Since this is a war between whites who for centuries have held us in slavery, and have heaped every kind of insult and abuse upon us, segregated and jim-crowed us; why I, a Negro who have fought through these years for the rights of my people, am here in Spain today? Because we are no longer an isolated minority group fighting hopelessly against an immense giant. Because, my dear, we have joined with, and become an active part of, a great progressive force, on whose shoulders rests the responsibility of saving human civilization from the planned destruction of a small group of degenerates gone mad in their lust for power. Because if we crush Fascism here we'll save our people in

America, and in other parts of the world from the vicious persecution, wholesale imprisonment, and slaughter which the Jewish people suffered and are suffering under Hitler's Fascist heels.

All we have to do is to think of the lynching of our people. We can but look back at the pages of American history stained with the blood of Negroes; stink with the burning bodies of our people hanging from trees; bitter with the groans of our tortured loved ones from whose living bodies ears, fingers, toes have been cut for souvenirs—living bodies into which red-hot pokers have been thrust. All because of a hate created in the minds of men and women by their masters who keep us all under their heels while they suck our blood, while they live in their bed of ease by exploiting us.

But these people who howl like hungry wolves for our blood, must we hate them? Must we keep the flame which these masters kindled constantly fed? Are these men and women responsible for the programs of their masters, and the conditions which force them to such degraded depths? I think not. They are tools in the hands of unscrupulous masters. These same people are as hungry as we are. They live in dives and wear rags the same as we do. They, too, are robbed by the masters, and their faces kept down in the filth of a decayed system. They are our fellowmen. Soon, and very soon, they and we will understand. Soon, many Angelo Herndons will rise from among them, and from among us, and will lead us both against those who live by the stench of our burnt flesh.* We will crush them. We will build us a new society—a society of peace and plenty. There will be no color line, no jim-crow trains, no lynching. That is why, my dear, I'm here in Spain.

Canute

Canute Frankson to "My Dear"

Taracon, Spain
July 23, 1937

My dear:

We stopped outside of this town to get a rest and something to eat. The commander of the convoy with one of the men is in town getting

---

*Angelo Herndon (1913–1997) was an African American labor organizer and coal miner who was convicted in 1932 for insurrection after communist literature was found in his home. His conviction sparked national protests and in 1937 was overturned by the U.S. Supreme Court. Herndon's autobiography, *Let Me Live* (1937), was written during his imprisonment.

food. The rest of them are all stretched out over the field sleeping. I've not received an answer to any of my letters. And according to the men who are here longer than I, it will be another month before I get one. That's not so hot.

I'm just about starved enough to eat a calf with its hair on. I'm also very tired. But if I go to sleep now, I'll only have to wake up when the food gets here. And then I wouldn't like that so well . . . How are you? Are you angry? Or, have you forgiven me?

I ought to tell you about my experience on the "Queen Mary" coming over. That ship is really a marvel of man's inventive mind. It's size and beauty is a credit to the genius of the human race. I sure appreciated the opportunity of being on that ship. But I'm still burning up. Because they segregated, or may I say, jim-crowed me. I cannot yet see how segregation, that despicable scourge of human society, could be alongside of such beauty. But it sure enough was. And with bells on. I spend hours in the salons looking at the pictures and carvings. It surely is an expression of the most modern art and culture. I wondered how the creators of such art could also be responsible for the jim-crow policy administered with such subtlety, as only the British know.

But on second thought I realize that creative genius is not the creator nor the instigator of racial segregation and discrimination. Such sordid products of human degeneracy can only be the work of a class which suppresses and exploits man's genius for its selfish gains. The men who built the "Queen Mary" are representatives of progress. Those who own it are our exploiters. They are representatives of Fascism, destruction, and war. The more I think of it the more justified I feel in having come here to help to stop the Fascist madmen. They would crush and enslave these lovely people under their iron heels. But we won't let them.

When I went into the salon to get my table number the chief steward was talking to a woman. After waiting for about five minutes he asked me if I wanted something. Suddenly I thought of a Georgia Cracker. I gave him the card with my name, and cabin and berth number. He was sitting in front of a table. The diagram of the dining room was inlaid on its surface. Each table was represented by small, rectangular blocks. Removable signs with numbers, in slots, represented the seats.

He looked down at the diagram, swirled around in the chair, looked up at me, then at the woman. He frowned, took off his cap, took a handkerchief from his pocket and wiped his face. The woman walked away uneasily. She kept her eyes shifting from one to the other of us. He shifted two slips from a table of two—one to a table of six, the other to a table of eight, then gave me a number corresponding to the table of two. He forced a sickening grin as he handed me the little card with the number. I thanked him coldly.

After chasing all over the vast dining room I found the table in one of the farthest corners, all by itself like a despised step-child. I was furious. But as everyone in the dining-room was staring at me I decided not to demonstrate. As I was about to sit down I noticed a picture on one of the walls representing an English hunting scene. For the moment I was distracted from my thought of some sort of revenge. Walking over toward the picture I discovered that each color and shade was not brought out by the painter's brush, but by the skillful inlaying of small pieces of hard-woods in their natural colors. I was so enchanted by the genius which created such a masterpiece that for the moment I actually forgot the injustice of the ship management. I had seen some Mosaic work, but never knew that it could be done in wood.

I felt awfully disgusted when I returned to the table, but after the waiter came, in spite of his disgustingly submissive attitude, I felt a little better. When he returned with the first course of the meal he found, to his utter surprise and dismay, someone sitting at the table with me. He informed us that it was quite against ship rules to change tables. You know, sir, he added with his nauseating grin and politeness, it is the management. So far as I'm concerned it is perfectly alright for you to sit with the gentleman. Finally he took Hutner's order and brought him silverware and napkin.

[Dan] Hutner [an American volunteer] came over to my table because the men and women at his table and the adjoining one decided that something should be done about my sitting alone in the dining room. They had sensed the segregation, had a discussion on the subject and decided that some action should be taken. They decided that one of them should sit through the trip with me and he had volunteered.

They elected a committee and contacted the chief steward and told him, in no uncertain terms, that they did not like the idea of segregation. The chief gave them his slimy grin and told them how sorry he was but he thought that the passengers would not care to sit at a table with me. When they asked him if my feelings were not considered, he said he hadn't thought of that. They demanded that I be removed. But that, he explained, was quite impossible, as everything was already entered in the ship's log. And, of course he was very, very sorry. We could see how sorry he was, the dirty liar. When they told him that one of the passengers had volunteered to sit with me, he turned as white as a sheet. Then, I wished he would croak, the snake. Some of the women proposed a demonstration. But we discouraged that. It would not have been the wisest thing to do at that time, and under the circumstances. From then on most of my time was spent explaining to sympathetic people our problems. They asked many questions about us. Many of them wanted to know more about us than they read in the Hearst Press.

Now, some of our so-called leaders would still have us believe that white people are our enemies. They go to all extremes to convince us that we must be loyal to our race leaders and especially our race businessmen. But such is Kelly Miller's, George Schuyler's and Du Bois' contribution to America's jim-crow system.* It's beginning to smell in our nostrils. We just simply can't breathe much more of it.

Those people on board the "Queen Mary," you may note, were all whites, and strangers to me. But they were all workers. Some were shop workers, office workers, others domestic servants. Most of them were on their way to England, Ireland, and Scotland to visit relatives. Others were on their way to other parts of Europe. They are the people who represent progress and democracy. They are the people who fight with us against a common enemy for their and our freedom. For them we must have our rights as men. There must be no more jim-crow system. There must be no more lynching of our people. And with this kind of spirit that will be some day in the very near future an accomplished fact. The sad thing about it all is that it is from such people like those our so-called leaders would separate us. But they won't. Their preachment of isolation— for that is what it amounts to—is a plan to continue the system of segregation by which they live in their beds of ease. They must satisfy their masters who live by such treachery, and whose puppets they are.

*While Frankson attributes the promotion of isolation and segregation to W.E.B. Du Bois and George Schuyler (1895–1977), both men were ardent integrationists and Schuyler married a white Texas heiress. Schuyler, a popular syndicated columnist based at *The Pittsburgh Courier*, also famously argued in his 1926 article "The Art Hokum" that there was no distinctively African American aesthetic and that the "Aframerican" is "merely a lampblacked Anglo-Saxon." Kelly Miller (1863–1939) was a sociologist, essayist, and journalist on the faculty at Howard University whose columns appeared in many newspapers in the 1920s and '30s. Miller struck a balance between the radicalism of Du Bois and the conservatism of Booker T. Washington by advocating higher education for blacks but also racial solidarity and institution building.

But fortunately, we are not, any more, an isolated group, but an integral part of the progressive forces of the world. Those of our race who lay the claim to leadership must inevitably be identified with the progressive forces or be trampled underfoot. We, the common people, are joining hands with our white brothers who are on the progressive side of the fence. And we're going places. So God help those who choose to try to stop us.

Those men and women on the luxurious "Queen Mary," who valiantly defied the powers and spiked their lies, are symbols of a movement, a force, an unconquerable will to save the human race from ultimate destruction. This period in world history calls for immediate and decisive action. There are two distinct camps. We, by heritage, cannot be identified with the camp of re-action. We must choose the side of progress.

We must unite all our forces. We must support, and help to put into action, the program of the National Negro Congress.* Its program of United Action must be our slogan. We must encourage and urge our men and women who toil to join their respective unions. We must rally our people to support all men and organizations which fight for Negro rights. We must teach our people. We must convince them that the howling mob which lynches our people are victims of a system which keeps both lyncher and lynched in poverty and degradation by preaching and fostering bitter hatred between the races.

It is your duty in your social clubs and church groups to tell the people of our contribution to the cause of human liberation here in Spain. Tell them that our real enemies are those who supply Italy and Germany with arms with which to mercilessly slaughter Spain's innocent women and children. They are our moneyed lords. Those same gentlemen who use their Father Coughlins, Huey Longs, Lemkes and Landons to deceive and betray us. And, unfortunately, those of our moneyed class who are victims of the same system. Their Liberty Leagues, Ku Klux Klans, Vigilante groups, and Black Legions have killed many of our people, particularly those who had proven to be our most honest and tried leaders.

We must not fall into the trap of racial isolation. That's just what the enemy wants us to do. We are a part of the American progressive

*The National Negro Congress was established in 1935 to build a national movement for labor and civil rights. The first meeting was held in Chicago in 1936.

movement. We have one common enemy, and can only win by uniting our forces. Anyone who opposes unity, consciously or unconsciously, is our enemy. Whether he is black or white does not matter. The Negro who opposes unity while he preaches race loyalty and race consciousness is by far the worst of the enemies.

We are doing our part here. You and especially our people must take some part in the struggle. Because if Fascism gains power in America we and the Jews will be the baits. They did it in Germany. We are a strong military force, but the final victory is dependent on the international aid we get. The harder the blow here against the Fascist beast, the easier it will be to extract his teeth at home.

Tell the children in your Sunday School of the homes we have here for the war orphans whose mothers and fathers have been murdered by Fascist bombs. Many of these homes are supported by contributions from the sympathetic countries. Others from donations from our small pay. Don't forget; every person who respects the rights of others and has the slightest trace of democracy left in him will help. The small donation may mean a meal or even a glass of milk for one of these orphans. And there are many.

The fight is hard. The enemy is strong and cruel, vicious. But no existing force can ever withstand the tremendous advance or crush the formidable resistance of a united people defending its freedom and its country. And above all we are fighting not only for Spain, but for the cause of humanity and peace. I'll write again as soon as conditions permit. Until then—

Salud,

Canute

Canute Frankson to "Dearest"

Badalona, Spain
April 13, 1938

Dearest:

This is my birthday. At all events I should be happy. Especially since I've survived eleven months of war. And particularly since a bomb fell where we are staying yesterday and did not get me. The horrid slaughter of human beings haunts me so much I can hardly sleep at nights. Then, there's always the airplanes overhead. Very few nights that the siren does not awaken us. Some of the men get up frightened and screaming in the dark when they hear the siren. It's quite creepy, but somehow I'm able to hold myself together. I don't seem to get frightened by the bombs.

. . . Last night I was with some children—about fifteen of them, ranging from six to about twelve years. We were playing some games. After it got too dark to play we sat down for a chat. They asked me about my people. The average child in one of these larger cities is very intelligent. They talk very seriously. They wanted to know what was taught in our schools; if we had artists and teachers. I told them of some of our artists and famous orchestras. I also told them of some of our great singers. But I did not forget to tell them that some of the things which they saw in the American pictures here were not true of us; that this was done to keep constant hate between the two races. I told them also of the jim-crow system and the lynch mob. It is very difficult to convince them that our people are really lynched in America.

[. . .] I'm sitting in the sand on the beach of this beautiful, blue Mediterranean. So much has been written about this great inland sea. So many crimes have been committed against the people on its waters and within its peaceful shores. And it is from under its blue surface that submarines come up to torpedo ships which bring food and medicine for the unfortunate victims of Fascist barbarism while its water extends to the horizon in such seeming innocence. Some day, however, these waters will not contain mines, warships nor submarines for destruction. The mission of the vessels which will pass this very shore will be as peaceful as the water is today. Give my love to the folks.

SALUD,
    Canute

Leigh Whipper to Benjamin O. Davis

Leigh Whipper (1876–1975), a leading stage and screen character actor whose career spanned sixty-five years, wrote this letter to his childhood friend Benjamin O. Davis (1877–1970*), who in 1940 became the first African American to hold the rank of army general. Davis also taught at Tuskegee and Wilberforce, and was a private in one of the original legendary Buffalo soldier regiments.

*Marvin Fletcher, the biographer of Benjamin O. Davis, uncovered evidence that Davis was actually born in 1880 but lied to avoid having to obtain his parents' consent to join the army. Still, his tombstone and other documents give his birthdate as 1877.

Los Angeles, California
January 28, 1941

Dear Ollie:—

Just found out where you were stationed and I'm sending you a Christmas card, even at this late date. No one is prouder of your success than I am. My only regret is that your father didn't live to see it that he might say, "From General Logan to General Davis."*

That picture in your mother's dining room—over the mantelpiece—must have been a great inspiration to you. I know she's proud and also Mrs. Davis. I'm confident that under your guidance, unhampered by state politics and college professors, that the Ninth and Tenth Cavalrys' will again be the pride of the United States Army.

Just got a letter from Jack and his mother is dying.

My kindest regards to you and Mrs. Davis.

Your pal,
   Leigh

Mr. and Mrs. James S. Watson to Private James L. Watson

James S. Watson (1882–1952) was born in Spanish Town, Jamaica, where his father, James Michael Watson, was a sergeant of the Jamaica Constabulary and a dispatcher for the Jamaica Railway Company. Watson immigrated to the United States in 1905, and in 1913 he graduated from New York Law School. In 1930 Watson and his running mate, Charles E. Toney, became the first two justices of African descent elected to judicial office in New York City.

New York
January 23, 1943

Our fond son, Skiz:

You are leaving home and your loved ones to render patriotic service to your country, with the possibility of covering yourself with glory in paving the way for future achievements.

At all times and into whatsoever paths destiny may lead you, the fervent prayers of mother and dad, as well as those of your devoted sisters and brother, will be offered for your protection and guidance and for your safe return.

*Louis Davis, Benjamin Davis's father, worked as a servant for Gen. John A. Logan.

"In all thy ways acknowledge Him and He shall direct thy paths."
Be true to your God, loyal to your country and a source of inspiration
to your fellow soldiers.

We salute you in the name of Him who watches over all of us.

With the tenderest affection and devotion, we leave you into His
hands.

Lovingly,

Dad and Mother

Lenwood Waller to Pauline Perry

*Lenwood Waller (1921–1984) was drafted not long after the attack at
Pearl Harbor. He married Pauline Perry in 1947.*

New York, NY
May 7 '45

Dear Pauline:

It has been quite some time since I heard from you and I haven't
wrote you for quite some time for the last couple of weeks I have been
wondering why I haven't heard from you I hope you are well.

It couldn't be that you was waiting to hear from me was it?

I have been trying to write you for weeks but then I would say well,
I'll hear from you tomorrow which haven't come (smile)

Well as usually this leave me a little on the lonely side, as days goes
by without hearing from you

Well Dear everything here seems favorable at the Present, I only
hope I will be able to come that way when we start to moving again, of
course I Know I am yet in the army and by Germany surrendering don't
finish the war, but I cant see where it would hold up the war by sending me home, this is what soldiers call crying. (smile)

Well I haven't saw any good Pictures lately, although I was to a
French show last week and from the look of it the Picture it should have
been Very good, I really think it was, the People all spoke french. (smile)

We also had a company dance it was really on the ball.

Since I last heard from you we have had Some Good news and bad
news. Losing the President was quite a shock,* but since Hitler and

---

*A reference to the fatal cerebral hemorrhage of President Franklin Delano Roosevelt
(1882–1945) on April 12. Roosevelt, elected to four terms, served from 1933 until his death
in 1945.

Mossilini is out the way things seems pretty fair again. Pauline what I promist to send you, I will bring it instead I hope (smile).

I will close

As Ever Your
    Len

Bayard Rustin to Local Board No. 63, New York City

Bayard Rustin (1912–1987) was sentenced to three years in federal prison for not obeying the Selective Service Act. Although he had registered as a conscientious objector, in 1943 he refused to report for his physical examination to prepare for his assignment to a conscientious objector camp. He wrote this letter to his local draft board explaining his decision not to serve.

874 St. Nicholas Avenue
New York, N.Y.
November 16, 1943

Gentlemen:

For eight years I have believed war to be impractical and a denial of our Hebrew-Christian tradition. The social teachings of Jesus are: (1) Respect for personality; (2) Service the "summum bonum"; (3) Overcoming evil with good; and (4) The brotherhood of man. Those principles as I see it are violated by participation in war.

Believing this, and having before me Jesus' continued resistance to that which he considered evil, I was compelled to resist war by registering as a Conscientious Objector in October, 1940.

However, a year later, September 1941, I became convinced that conscription as well as war equally is inconsistent with the teachings of Jesus. I must resist conscription also.

On Saturday, November 13, 1943 I received from you an order to report for a physical examination to be taken Tuesday, November 16 at eight o'clock in the evening. I wish to inform you that I cannot voluntarily submit to an order springing from the Selective Service and Training Act for War.

There are several reasons for this decision, all stemming from the basic spirit of truth that men are brothers in the sight of God:

1) War is wrong. Conscription is a concomitant of modern war. Thus conscription for so vast an evil as war is wrong.

2) Conscription for war is inconsistent with freedom of conscience, which is not merely the right to believe, but to act on the degree of truth that one receives, to follow a vocation which is God-inspired and God directed.

Today I feel that God motivates me to use my whole being to combat by nonviolent means the over-growing racial tension in the United States; at the same time the State directs that I shall do its will; which of these dictates can I follow—that of God or that of the State? Surely I must at all times attempt to obey the law of the State. But when the will of God and the will of the State conflict, I am compelled to follow the will of God. If I cannot continue in my present vocation, I must resist.

3) The Conscription Act denies brotherhood—the most basic New Testament teaching. Its design and purpose is to set men apart—German against American, American against Japanese. Its aim springs from a moral impossibility—that ends justify means, that from unfriendly acts a new and friendly world can emerge.

In practice further, it separates black from white—those supposedly struggling for a common freedom. Such a separation also is based on the moral error that racism can overcome racism, that evil can produce good, that men virtually in slavery can struggle for a freedom they are denied. This means that I must protest racial discrimination in the armed forces, which is not only morally indefensible but also in clear violation of the Act. This does not, however, imply that I could have a part in conforming to the Act if discrimination were eliminated.

Segregation, separation, according to Jesus, is the basis of continuous violence. It was such an observation which encouraged him to teach, "It has been said to you in olden times that thou shalt not kill, but I say unto you, do not call a man a fool"—and he might have added: "For if you call him such, you automatically separate yourself from him and violence begins." That which separates man from his brother is evil and must be resisted.

I admit my share of guilt for having participated in the institutions and ways of life which helped bring fascism and war, Nonetheless, guilty as I am, I now see as did the Prodigal Son that it is never too late to refuse longer to remain in a non-creative situation. It is always timely and virtuous to change—to take in all humility a new path.

Though joyfully following the will of God, I regret that I must break the law of the State. I am prepared for whatever may follow.

I herewith return the material you have sent me, for conscientiously I cannot hold a card in connection with an act I no longer feel able to accept and abide by.

Today I am notifying the Federal District Attorney of my decision and am forwarding to him a copy of this letter.

I appreciate now as in the past your advice and consideration, and trust that I shall cause you no anxiety in the future. I want you to know that I deeply respect you for executing your duty to God and country in these difficult times in the way you feel you must, I remain

Sincerely yours,
Bayard Rustin

A. Philip Randolph to Bayard Rustin

Asa Philip Randolph (1889–1979) was president and cofounder of the Brotherhood of Sleeping Car Porters, the first African American labor union to sign a collective bargaining agreement with a major U.S. company. As founder of the League for Non-Violent Civil Disobedience Against Military Segregation, he called on blacks to refuse to register for the draft.

April 17, 1944

My dear Bayard:

I have read with great interest and feeling your statement to the Local Draft Board 63. I want to applaud you for your profound conviction as well as consecration to the principles on non-violence and the brotherhood of man. Your action will give heart and spirit even to those who may disagree with your philosophy and enable them to stand firm on the ideals they profess to possess even when they are alone. I hope I may have the pleasure of keeping in touch with you and getting a word from you now and then.

Be assured that the fight for racial equality and social justice will be carried on to the extent that my frail powers and abilities will enable me to do so, so that this world may be a better place to live in as the days and years speed on.

Your sincere friend,
A. Phillip Randolph

A. Philip Randolph to Secretary of Defense George C. Marshall

October 30, 1950

Dear Secretary Marshall:

We have noted with pleasure the alertness of Congressman Jacob K. Javits in bringing to your attention reported segregation of Negro troops at Fort Dix, New Jersey.*

Mr. Javits is eminently correct in protesting this undemocratic army procedure particularly when it takes place in the State of New Jersey which has outlawed segregation in its National Guard and has taken other vigorous action in behalf of civil rights for all its citizens.

While we are glad to learn from your reply to Congressman Javits that the "Secretary of the Army is giving this matter attention," we trust that your new administration will see to it that more effective and conclusive action will be taken by the Army in behalf of Negro GIs than was the case under the previous Secretary of Defense.

Nearly two and a half years have elapsed since President Truman issued his armed services executive order directing the abolition of racial distinctions. During that time, his civilian committee has thoroughly studied the matter of integration and made forthright recommendations toward that end.

We are confident that under your administration, the Department of Defense does not wish in any way, through the retention of undemocratic practices, to hamper and hamstring the great "truth campaign" of the Department of State. Segregation is not only a skeleton in the Army's closet. It also represents a major beachhead for Communist propaganda at home and among darker peoples of the world.

I shall take the liberty of releasing this letter to the press after you have received it.

Very truly yours,
A. Philip Randolph

Lester B. Granger to Navy Secretary Dan A. Kimball

Lester B. Granger (1896–1976) wrote this letter while executive director of the National Urban League.

---

*Jacob K. Javits (1904–1986) served as U.S. Senator from New York from 1957 to 1981. He was elected to the House of Representatives in 1946, joining the freshman class that included John F. Kennedy and Richard M. Nixon. He served in the House from 1947 to 1954.

October 24, 1952

Dear Secretary Kimball:

Thank you for your answer to my letter of October 3rd in which I requested information regarding the proportion which members of the Steward's branch constitute of the total negro Naval personnel. However, frankness compels me to confess disappointment over your letter, which seems to me to be a rather cursory disposal of my request. I would have hoped that my past associations with the Navy and the previous confidential relationships which I have enjoyed with the Department's leaders would have warranted a much fuller and franker statement.

Of course I know that correspondence of this sort is prepared for the Secretary's signature by his assistants; otherwise I should have felt surprised that it was considered necessary to advise me of past policy directives issued by the Secretary's office in regard to the use of Negro personnel. As a member of the president's Committee On Equal Treatment and Opportunity in the Armed Forces, and as a special advisor to the late Secretary Forrestal from early in 1945 until his resignation, I played a part in the development of the policies set forth definitively in Secretary Matthews' circular letter of June 23, 1949.

I hope that you will accept in the same spirit in which it is offered my assurance that I desire, in both my personal and my official capacity, to be in position to give the most constructive and helpful public interpretation possible of the Navy's progress toward complete equality of treatment and opportunity. I am sure that you are aware of the skepticism which has persisted among a certain part of the Negro public regarding the actuality of such progress in various branches of the Armed forces—a skepticism which is readily understandable in light of the long history in inequality of opportunity suffered by Negroes in uniform. I am sure also that the department realizes that as long as a majority of Negroes in Navy service are concentrated in the Steward's branch, and as long as that branch is composed entirely of non-white personnel, the Navy is apt to be held by some to be violating its own stated policy.

It would be helpful in dispelling skepticism if progress reports were issued from time to time showing a steady increase in the number of non-steward ratings for Negroes and a corresponding decrease in the proportion of those assigned to the Steward's branch. Of course the major problem will not be solved until BuPers [Bureau of Naval Personnel] has found a way to introduce a sufficiently large number of whites into the Steward's branch to transform its racial composition.

In the meantime, since it might be considered inappropriate for the Department itself to single out one special racial group for public discussion, it would seem to me all the more important to put every helpful bit of interpretive information at the disposal of individuals and organizations in whom you have confidence and who ask for such information.

Since this was the purpose of my original letter to you I am certain that you will understand why your response disappointed me. If there is fuller information that you would care to make available I shall be happy to receive it.

Sincerely yours,

Lester B. Granger

U.S. Senator Edward W. Brooke III to President Richard M. Nixon

October 23, 1969

Dear Mr. President,

I am transmitting under separate cover a large number of postal cards recently submitted to me by a group of constituents who wish to express their concern about the continuing war in Vietnam.

As I indicated to them last week, I know that you fully share their deep concern and have undertaken a great variety of fresh initiatives to reduce the American role in the war and to bring an early peace.

I am enclosing a copy of my statement on the recent Vietnam Moratorium in case it may be of interest to you. As you will see, I tried to make clear my appreciation that you have already initiated a number of important steps to reduce the violence in Vietnam and to encourage a negotiated settlement.

With best personal regards, I am,

Sincerely yours,

Edward W. Brooke

U.S. Senator Edward W. Brooke III to President Richard M. Nixon

May 11, 1970

Dear Mr. President,

Recent developments in Southeast Asia and the repercussions in the United States persuade me that it is more imperative than ever to harmonize legislative and executive policies with regard to the war in South Vietnam and the situation in Cambodia. I believe you will agree that constructive initiatives toward this end should be welcomed. I wish to propose for your consideration two suggestions which would contribute significantly to mutual confidence between our branches of government, as well as to public support for national policy.

You have now indicated that U.S. troops will not be used again in Cambodia after July 1st. Since avoidance of American involvement in Cambodia is the basic objective of those supporting the Cooper-Church amendment to the Foreign Military Sales Act, it would be most helpful if you would lend your support to this clear declaration that American military personnel will not be sent into Cambodia again.* I have suggested clarifying language to focus the Cooper-Church amendment on this point, without attempting in anyway to impede collective security arrangements between South Vietnam and Cambodia. This suggested language is appended. In light of your remarks at last Friday's press conference, some such formulation should be acceptable to the Administration and your endorsement would be a helpful step toward a sensible accommodation of views.

A second and larger issue has been posed by the critical development of the last two weeks. That is the question of national confidence in the Administration's steady course toward disengagement from the war in South Vietnam. As you know, I strongly support your effort to withdraw American forces from South Vietnam on an orderly basis. Your commitment to remove 150,000 additional troops by next Spring has won wide support, and has confirmed the growing expectation that you will continue to reduce American involvement in this bitter conflict. I know you will appreciate that much of the criticism of the strikes against the sanctuaries in Cambodia stems from apprehension that you were modifying your established policy.

It is essential to confirm unequivocally that the United States remains dedicated to shifting the burden of self-defense to the Vietnamese themselves and to curtailing direct American involvement in the war.

---

*Senators John Cooper, a Republican of Kentucky, and Frank Church, a Democrat from Idaho, introduced a bipartisan amendment to prohibit the deployment of American forces in Cambodia after June 30, 1979. The amendment was in response to President Nixon's order issued in April for South Vietnamese and American troops to invade Cambodia.

The enclosed amendment, which I will propose to the Foreign Military Sales Act, could serve this important purpose. It would enable the Congress to offer statutory concurrence in the program of troop withdrawals you have begun and to indicate that the U.S. will continue to disengage at the reasonable pace which you have established. The proposed amendment would make military assistance to the South Vietnamese government conditional upon the continuation of American troop withdrawals. This would provide a clear signal to the South Vietnamese that they must carry an increasingly large responsibility for their own defense.

Examination of the language will show you that it affords considerable flexibility and ample time for the program of Vietnamization to be implemented.* Should circumstances require adjustment in this plan, you could certainly consult with the Congress with respect to necessary changes.

The extraordinary tension which the current situation has provoked in this country convinces me that we must find a means of coordinating Presidential and Congressional policies on this vital issue, taking full account of the prerogatives and responsibilities of both branches. Congressional enactment of the orderly program which you have defined seems to me the most promising approach to resolving the tension. It would be a pledge to the country that the Government is agreed on a prudent course of action and is determined to proceed with it.

I respectfully invite your attention to these suggestions. I hope that after considering the proposals you will lend your support to them.

With best personal regards,

Sincerely yours,

Edward W. Brooke

Gen. Colin L. Powell to the Students of East Pike Elementary School

Colin L. Powell (b. 1937) was born and raised in New York City, the son of Jamaican immigrants. Powell joined the Reserve Officers' Training Corps while a student at City College of New York, served in Vietnam, and rose

---

*Vietnamization was the policy President Nixon outlined in March 1969 that was intended to encourage the South Vietnamese to take responsibility for the war and thereby enable the United States to withdraw its troops.

through the ranks of the Army to become general in 1979. He was national security adviser under President Ronald Reagan from 1987 to 1989 and chairman of the Joint Chiefs of Staff from 1989 to 1993. In 2001 he became the sixty-fifth secretary of state—the first African American to hold that title—under President George W. Bush.

Washington, D.C. 20318
22 August 1991

To the Students

As all of you know, your Principal, Dr. Kealey, was called to active duty in the Armed Forces of the United States as a key participant in Operation Desert Storm. Earlier this summer, while in the deserts of Saudi Arabia, he wrote to me.

Major Kealey asked me if he could get a copy of the painting I have in my office in the Pentagon. It is a painting of the 10th U.S. Cavalry ("Buffalo Soldiers") of Lieutenant Henry O. Flipper, the first black graduate of West Point. The painting is by Mr. Don Strivers and it is called "Chasing Victorio." Your Principal wanted a copy of this painting to hang in your school. The brave soldiers in the painting are part of the history of America and Dr. Kealey wants you to understand that history and appreciate the courage and sacrifice that were essential to it.

Today, I want you to know that your Principal is a part of our history also, just as the Buffalo Soldiers were in the past. By participating in Operations Desert Shield and Desert Storm, Major Kealey upheld a great American tradition called the tradition of the citizen-soldier. In times of crisis and war, citizen-soldiers such as your Principal have made the difference in this country throughout its history. They are brave, determined, and concerned. They not only do their vital jobs as teachers, policemen, firemen, doctors and lawyers, they also do their jobs as soldiers, sailors, airmen and marines.

You should be very, very proud of Dr. Kealey. And when he returns to school, I hope you will all take time to thank him for his hard work and sacrifice. I also hope that you will ask your parents and loved ones to do the same. Most importantly—and the best way to thank your Principal—you should study very hard this year and make him proud of you as students.

When you and your Principal and teachers are back in school again, I hope you will take the time to learn about Lieutenant Flipper and the famous Buffalo Soldiers with whom he rode. I also hope that each of you has a great year in school!

Sincerely,

Colin L. Powell

Gen. Colin L. Powell to Friends of Sgt. Maj. William Harrington

March 26, 1994

Dear Friends,

By this letter, my wife Alma and I are honored to share in your celebration of the life of Sergeant Major William Harrington.

I first met SMAJ Harrington in the summer of 1988. He contacted my office and asked for an appointment to meet me. I was reluctant because at his advanced age he was traveling alone to Washington during a hot summer week. Nevertheless, Old Sarge persisted. He marched in and I could see that I need not have worried about the spryness of this young trooper.

I told him I wanted to take him down the hall to see a fellow Cavalryman. We went in to the Oval Office where President Reagan was waiting along with Vice President Bush. SMAJ Harrington took it all in stride and in a few minutes you might have thought that he owned the Oval Office and they were visiting. They talked about the old days and about horses. I wasn't sure I would ever get him out of there.

That's the way he was—confident, proud, second to no man. He was a Buffalo Soldier. He was anyone's equal.

I will also never forget him interrupting my speech at the ground breaking ceremony for the Buffalo Soldier monument. I had just gotten going when he came out of the audience and made a donation on the spot. Clearly, he thought I was talking too much and it was time to get on with business.

If he had come along at a later time there is no telling what he might have accomplished in the Army. But he couldn't have lived a better life. He was an inspiration to us all and I have stood on his shoulders, as have so many others. He loved his country. He loved his Army and he loved his family. We are all better off for having known him.

May he enjoy eternal rest with his fellow Troopers.

Gl. C. Powell

Capt. Eric Mitchell to Friends and Family

Eric Mitchell (b. 1973), whose parents both served in the military where they met, was born on a base in Delaware and moved to South Carolina, then to Alabama and then to Buffalo, New York. After graduating from high school, he attended the Air Force Academy Prep School; in 1992 he was admitted into the Air Force Academy in Colorado Springs and graduated in 1996. A year later he finished flight school at the top of his class. In October 2002 the U.S. Senate voted on a Joint Resolution to authorize the use of force against Iraq, and Mitchell was deployed to Iraq to participate in Operation Iraqi Freedom, which began on March 20, 2003. Baghdad fell April 9, 2003, ending the twenty-four-year rule of Saddam Hussein. Mitchell wrote the following e-mail to loved ones during his mission in Baghdad, for which he was cited for outstanding achievement.*

[2003]

I appreciate all the prayers and support, but I think we all need to focus on the Iraqi people and the immense terror they are experiencing. We need to focus on the families of those twenty-one individuals who have already passed on to a place where there is indeed eternal peace. We need to focus on that eighteen-year-old Marine who is on his way to downtown Baghdad, who only a year ago was enjoying his high school prom. We need to focus on that unborn child who will never get the opportunity to meet his father because he gave his life in a land so far away. We need to focus on the newlyweds who will never get the chance to enjoy their first wedding anniversary. We need to focus on the Iraqi soldier who will die because he was trying to find a way to feed his family. Pray 4 a quick ending to this.

Maj. David Scott Harris to Lois D. Cherry

David Scott Harris (b. 1969) joined the Air Force in 1993. Harris exchanged these e-mails with his sister-in-law Lois while stationed in Iraq. The first is a reply to Lois's playful suggestion that she would practice driving in his car.

---

*This excerpt was originally published in *We Were There: Voices of African American Veterans, from World War II to the War in Iraq* (2005) by Yvonne Latty.

March 23, 2003
8:37 a.m.

I am glad to hear Mama Tatum is doing better, but you guys need to definitely stay on top of her doctor concerning her well being. You guys can send what you want. I have not heard of any restrictions. Tell Tyell [Lois's son] I will take him on the boat as soon as I can. Yes, my baby girl is definitely growing up and I am missing it. Now that really hurts. My boys are without their main buddy and my wife is holding it down. Sharon [his wife] is strong and I guess we all knew one day I would have to go TDY [Temporary Duty assignment], but we were not expecting this kind of trip. You guys go and have a good time. Hopefully Sharon will be able to take you guys to Mississippi to eat at the casino. The TRUCK is not for practice. [M]y big girl is not doing so good now that her daddy is not behind the wheel. You know I'm missing Turkey season fooling around in this desert. The only wildlife I have seen is a rabbit! What the heck is that all about. Alright you guys be good and I will halla at you later. By the way CD's (fishing/hunting) are always a good choice after Cheese Steaks.

Love yall
Scott

Lois D. Cherry to Maj. David Scott Harris

March 23, 2003
9:32 p.m.

Aw, let a sister get a little practice in the big green truck. I'll try not to back over any trash cans, cars, people, etc. I don't have my permit yet, but what does that matter between family members? Alright, maybe I'll just sit in it for awhile & remember that time we rode to the old movie set from the Alamo. That was kind of strange & for some reason I think about that a lot. Maybe that's the day I started to think of you as a brother & not just an in-law. I know a lot more about life because of you & not to mention the positive influence you have on Tyell. You are probably the most interesting family member we have. I'm so glad my baby sister married someone that was so easy for me to like & love. I'm going to work on a care package. I heard on the news today that they are encouraging family members & friends to send you guys mail & packages. I'd send cheese steaks if I thought they would travel well, but don't count on it (ha-ha) . . .

    LUV YA!

      LOIS

Maj. David Scott Harris to Lois D. Cherry

April 3, 2003
9:07 a.m.

[. . .] This better be the last trip for at least two years and the next TDY I expect no more than 90 days. This is definitely tuff, but I will be stronger hopefully in the end. I really miss my wife—this is eggs. I'm gonna start taking her everywhere with me—fishing, hunting, ping-pong, trips. That will probably last a couple of weeks and then I will have to leave her at home—joke. I just feel like I'm losing precious time with my family and I don't like it. I really started thinking about my career. I love the Air Force, but I will not put it before my family . . . so I'm gonna have to do some serious talking to Sharon when I get home. My boys and girls need their daddy.

    Luv yall too, take it easy.

      Scott.

Commanding Officer Craig S. Prather, PE, MBA, to My Dalton Family

Craig S. Prather, a Navy officer and a 1985 graduate of the Dalton School, a New York City private school, wrote this letter on Christmas Day 2006 to his alma mater.

Dear Dalton Family,

    On behalf of all of the United States Navy "Can Do" Seabees of Naval Mobile Construction Battalion 74, I bring you greetings from Ar Ramadi, Iraq. I just received the Fall 2006 copy of the *Dalton Connections* magazine, and wanted to drop you a line of appreciation for keeping in touch and a short update.

    First, if you had told me 21 years ago when I was a senior at Dalton that on Christmas day in 2006 I would be serving my country in Ar Ramadi, Iraq, I would have told you, you are crazy. That being said, here I am, the Commanding Officer of over 650 U.S. Navy Seabees deployed to Iraq, Afghanistan and Guam in support of the Global War on Terrorism. Needless to say, the living and working conditions in Iraq and Afghanistan are extremely limited, intense and life threatening, daily. Every day, there are many different challenges that require creative solutions, intrusive leadership and unfailing compassion, whether it is working in the 134 degree heat, taking cover from small arms fire and mortar rounds, constructing a building in a high combat risk environment, coaching a Seabee through a combat injury or counseling one of my Seabees who recently found out that a family member died in a car accident at home. Clearly, the most daunting aspect of being in command is having to call one of my Seabees' family to tell them that their service member—my Seabee—either was wounded or killed in action while proudly serving their country. Obviously, this is a phone call or visit that no commanding officer wants to make.

Many people, including my family ask me often, why am I still doing this "Navy stuff"? Along with my professional engineering license, two Masters degrees (Civil Engineering and an MBA), years of acquisition of expertise and depth of leadership experience, I am sure my credentials are solid for much more lucrative, less stressful employment. Frankly though, the answer started while I attended Dalton, where I learned to "go forth unafraid."* Then, it carried over to my time at the US Naval Academy where I accepted my commitment to defend freedom and democracy around the world and protect the American way of life, and then later I realized that service to my fellow citizens is what makes America truly great!

If you are not familiar with the U.S. Navy Seabees, I encourage that you rent the classic John Wayne movie, "The Fighting Seabees." Although, it is a little outdated, it gives you the gist of what we do. In a nutshell, we are skilled construction tradesmen, engineers and logisticians who can build infrastructure in any environment and defend what we build. Currently, my Seabee Battalion, the Fearless 74 Seabees are spread across the globe from Guam to Southwest Asia performing a full range of contingency and peacetime construction, disaster recovering, general engineering support and tactical operations valued at over several million dollars. At these locations, we are providing Seabee operations in direct support of U.S. Marine Corps, U.S. Army and U.S. Navy operations, the government of Iraq and several undisclosed

*This is a reference to the school motto.

clients, who can't be discussed for security purposes. My Fearless 74 Seabees are focused on achieving mission accomplishment safely, while maintaining our command theme of "One Command—One Team—One Family, Period."

So, after 18 years as a commissioned Naval Officer, here I am in Ar Ramadi, Iraq on Christmas Day proudly serving my country with the Navy's Core Values of honor, courage and commitment. Of course I miss my family and loved ones, but I am proud to be here serving. So, from my Fearless 74 Seabee Family to my Dalton Family, I truly wish you a happy and safe holiday season.

    Craig S. Prather, PE, MBA

    Commanding Officer

PART VI

Art and Culture

T here is perhaps no area where African Americans have been able to flower as fully as in art and entertainment. Inspired by and imbued with the aesthetic, spirit, and music of Africa, and less restricted by racial barriers, African Americans have soared in the arts, distinguishing themselves in music, drama, literature, painting, sculpture, and film.

But as these letters reveal, even with fewer limitations on their aspirations, African American artists have encountered obstacles as they've attempted to define and express their humanity. In the early years of the twenty-first century, they remained underrepresented in the worlds of literature, art, film, and television. In 1999 and again in 2001, the NAACP threatened to boycott the nation's major television networks because of the dearth of African American and other non-white characters on prime-time television shows. In 2002 Halle Berry became the first African American woman in a lead role to win the Academy Award. In 2004 Phylicia Rashad followed suit by taking the Best Actress Tony Award. Meanwhile artists like Fred Wilson and Robert Colescott have in their work wrestled with the exclusion or stereotypical representation of African Americans in the canon of Western art. At the dawn of the twenty-first century, African Americans were still dismantling racial barriers as they strove to convey their unique American experience.

Phillis Wheatley to Gen. George Washington

Phillis Wheatley (c. 1753–1784), who had become famous after the 1773 publication of her book Poems on Various Subjects, Religious and Moral, *wrote this letter to George Washington upon his appointment as general of the Grand Continental Army. He responded several months later, and in 1776 she was invited to meet him and read her poetry.*

Providence
October 26, 1775

To His Excellency General Washington
Sir:

I have taken the freedom to address your excellency in the enclosed poem and entreat your acceptance. Though I am not insensible of its inaccuracies. Your being appointed by the Grand Continental Congress to be Generalissimo of the armies of North America, together with the fame of your virtues, excite sensations not easy to suppress. Your generosity, therefore, I presume will pardon the attempt. Wishing your excellency all possible success in the great cause you are so generously engaged in.

I am,

Your excellency's most obedient humble servant,

Phillis Wheatley

Paul Laurence Dunbar to Alice Ruth Moore

The poet Paul Laurence Dunbar (1872–1906) wrote this letter of introduction to his future wife, the writer Alice Ruth Moore (1875–1935), after seeing a sketch and poem of hers in the Boston Monthly Review.

Dayton, Ohio
April 17, 1895

Miss Alice Ruth Moore:

You will pardon my boldness in addressing you, I hope, and let my interest in your work be my excuse. I sometimes wonder if in the rare world of art, earthly conventions need always be heeded. I am drawn to write you because we are both working along the same lines and a sketch of yours in the "Monthly Review" so interested me that I was anxious to know more of you and your work.

I suppose I must present my credentials, with as little egotism as possible. In the first place I am a writer, one trying to struggle up the thorny path of literature, with the summit of Parnassus not yet in sight. My chief work has been done on the *Chicago Record and News*, some on the *Detroit Free Press*. Lately I have had three acceptances from the *Century*—little things for "The Lighter Vein" department, the first of which was published this month. The *New York Independent* has accepted a 5000 word story and Kate Fields Washington two serious poems. But my regular work is done on the *Chicago News* for whom I furnish three to four short stories a month. I am hopeful at present both for myself and the future of our race in literature.

I want to know whether or not you believe in preserving by Afro-American—I don't like the word—writers of those quaint old tales and songs of our fathers which have made the fame of Joel Chandler Harris, Thomas Nelson Page, Ruth McEnery Stuart and others or whether you like so many others think we should ignore the past and all its capital literary materials.*

I should like to exchange opinions and work with you if you will agree. The counsel and encouragement of one who is striving toward the same end that I am would, I know, greatly help.

I understand you have written for the "Ladies Home Journal." Will you tell me in what numbers I will find your work? I shall always look with interest for anything from your pen.

---

*Dunbar cited the major white writers of the time who employed African American plantation dialect in their work. Joel Chandler Harris (1848–1908) was a journalist who became famous for collecting black folklore in works such as *Uncle Remus: His Songs and His Sayings* (1880). Thomas Nelson Page (1853–1922) helped popularize the stereotype of the ignorant and happy slave in works including *In Ole Virginia* (1887). Ruth McEnery Stuart (1852–1917) was one of the most prominent fiction writers of her time and published in many of the leading magazines. She applied Southern regional dialect to black and white characters.

I enclose to you my verses on [Frederick] Douglass who was a very dear friend of mine, and also my latest lines.

Hoping that I have not bored you very much and that I may have an early answer.

I am sincerely yours,
　　Paul Laurence Dunbar

Alice Ruth Moore to Paul Laurence Dunbar

[Postmarked May 7, 1895]

Dear Sir:—

Your letter was handed to me at a singularly inopportune moment—the house was on fire. So I laid it down, not knowing what it was and I must confess not caring very much.

After the house was declared safe and the excitement had somewhat subsided I found it laid in my desk and read it somewhere about ten days later. Strange combination of circumstances though it was, I was not to blame. Being partially blind and suffering from a bad hand burned in the fire. But I enjoyed it nevertheless when I did read it. And those dainty little verses have been ringing in my head ever since I read them.

I must thank you ever so much and though I don't like to appear greedy, still if you have any more like them, please send them down this way. Your name is quite familiar to me from seeing your poems in different papers. I always enjoyed them very much. You do a great deal of work in different lines which is fortunate for you, since you have the entrée in so many of our best papers.

I am sorry to say I have done very little. It seems I cannot possibly find time to write when I want. My regular everyday duties are so voluminous, so to speak, that I have no moments at all left for that which I love above all. I have never done any work for the *Ladies Home Journal,* I am sorry to say. You ask my opinion about Negro dialect in literature. Well I frankly believe in everyone following his best. If it is so that one has a special aptitude for dialect work, why it is only right that dialect work should be made a specialty. But if one should be like me—absolutely devoid of the ability to manage dialect—I don't see the necessity of cramming and forcing oneself into that plane because one is a Negro or a Southerner. Don't you think so?* Now as to getting away from one's race—well, I haven't much liking for those writers that wedge the Negro problem and social equality and long dissertations on the Negro in general into their stories. It is too much like a quinine pill in jelly. I hope I'm not treading on your corns. Somehow when I start a story I always think of my folk characters as simple human beings, not as types or a race or an idea, and I seem to be on more friendly terms with them. I have a little collection of short stories— a small book—in press now. I suppose you'll take a copy. I must not write more as the night grows old and tomorrow's duties are to be faced.

I shall be pleased to hear from you soon and often.

Yours Very Truly,

Alice Ruth Moore

Paul Laurence Dunbar to Booker T. Washington

By 1902, Paul Laurence Dunbar was the most celebrated African American writer in the world. Booker T. Washington (1856–1915) commissioned Dunbar to write the school song for the Tuskegee Institute. In this letter, Dunbar replies to Washington's reaction to the lyrics.

Washington, D.C.

January 23, 1902

My dear Mr. Washington,

I have your letter and note your objection to the song. In the first place, your objection to the lines, "Swift growing South" is not well taken because a song is judged not by the hundred years that it lives but from this time at which it was written, and the "swift growing" only indicates what the South has been, and will contrast with what it may achieve or any failure it may make. The "Star Spangled Banner" was written for the time, and although we may not be watching the stars and stripes waving from ramparts amid shot and shell, the song seems to be going pretty fairly still.

As to emphasizing the industrial idea, I have done merely what the school has done, but I will make this concession of changing the fourth

---

*Dunbar wrote in standard and dialect verse but achieved fame based on the latter. In an important review of Dunbar's collection *Majors and Minors* (1896), which appeared in *Harper's Weekly*, William Dean Howells emphasized Dunbar's work in dialect and called him "the first man of his color to study his race objectively . . . and to represent it in art as he felt and found it to be."

line of the third stanza into "Worth of our minds and our hands," although it is not easy to sing.

The Bible I cannot bring in. The exigencies of verse will hardly allow a paraphrase of it, or an auctioneer's list, and so I am afraid that I shall have to disappoint Mr. [Edgar J.] Penney.* As to that I am afraid that I cannot write verse up to Mr. Penney's standard of it but I believe if you will look over "Fair Harvard" you will note that they have not given their curriculum in the song or a list of the geological formation of the country around the school.

Very truly yours,
Paul Laurence Dunbar

Claude A. Barnett to Jean Toomer

Claude A. Barnett (1889–1967) founded the Associated Negro Press, a news service geared to African American newspapers, in 1919. Jean Toomer (1894–1967), grandson of Louisiana Governor Pinckney B. S. Pinchback, was a writer who gained prominence during the Harlem Renaissance. His best-known work is the critically acclaimed Cane *(1923), a collection of poems and short narratives that explore African American life in the South and urban North.*

Chicago, Illinois
April 23, 1923

My dear Sir:

For sometime we, and by we I mean a group of three friends, the other two of whom are literary men, one colored and the other white, have wondered who and also what you are. There have been several arguments, the literary men contending that your style and finish indicated that you were not Negroid, while I, who am but the business manager of a news service, felt certain that you were—for how else could you interpret "us" as you do unless you had peeked behind the veil.

All of which is not what I started to write about at all. What I wish to know, now that I have your address, is "Can we not have something by you?" Perchance, you know that the Associated Negro Press is a

*Rev. Edgar J. Penney was on the Tuskegee faculty and dean of the Bible School. He resigned in 1907 amid a student's allegation of sexual misconduct. Penney was a trustee and alum of Atlanta University.

news service distributing news to colored papers. Perhaps you also know that probably because we are pioneers we are recognized as the standard organization of its kind.

We would welcome an opportunity to publish anything which you felt would be suitable for these weekly papers which we serve. Good fiction they have never had. The field is really ripe and I believe much worthwhile effort and literary interest would be stimulated by your appearance in these papers.

Of means we have none. Yet we ought to find some way to get together. I hope so. What can you suggest?

    Claude A. Barnett

Jean Toomer to Claude A. Barnett

Washington, D.C.
April 29, 1923

Dear Mr. Barnett,

The arguments you have had with your friends, the different points of view and the consequent contentions, are not at all peculiar to your group. The fact is that I have had inquiries of like nature come in from New Orleans, New York, Milwaukee, and Hollywood. The true and complete answer is one of some complexity, and for this reason perhaps it will not be seen and accepted until after I am dead. (This sounds quite solemn, but I assure you that I am capable of the saving smile.) The answer involves a realistic and accurate knowledge of racial mixture, of nationality as formed by the interaction of tradition, culture and environment, of the artistic nature in its relation to the racial or social group, etc. All of which of course is too heavy and thick to go into now. Let me state then, simply, that I am the grandson of the late P. B. S. Pinchback. From this fact it is clear that your contention is sustained. I have "peeked behind the veil." And my deepest impulse to literature (on the side of material) is the direct result of what I saw. In so far as the old folk-songs, syncopated rhythms, the rich sweet taste of dark skinned life, in so far as these are Negro, I am, body and soul, Negroid. My style, my esthetic, is nothing more nor less than my attempt to fashion my substance into works of art. For it, I am indebted to my inherent gifts, and to the entire body of contemporary literature. I see no reason why my style and finish could not have come from an American with Negro blood in his veins. The pure fact is that they have, and hence your friends' contentions are thrown out of court.

Your suggestion as to the possibility of my contributing something to your association, interests me. First let me say that I would like to write something for the weekly papers. Events etc. are continually coming to my attention, events that I would like to give publicity to, events that would be of no interest to the reviews I write for, but which are of particular interest to the colored race. I am thinking especially of things that would allow me reflections and opinion on the rational world, on the world of literature and art. For instance, a week or so ago, Raymond O'Neill with his colored Folk Players were in town. My own critical reactions are possibly of interest to the general reader, and they certainly hold some value for the players themselves. Well, to write an article for a local paper would not have paid me. And the *Crisis* has proved itself to be most stupid and petty in its later dealings with me. Hence, nothing written. Again, to-night I gave a talk before the College Women's Club. I shall speak on Washington, its possibilities as material for literary art. My aim, of course, is to direct the people's sensitivity and perception to the beauty that is at hand, and, if I am particularly fortunate, to stimulate some one to an expression of his immediate life. Such a talk, if shaped and cut a little, might make good general reading. New books are coming out. And so I might attempt a series of articles on some subject that I am qualified to write about. And then I might possibly give you a long short story or a short novel to be run serially in these directions my desires run. But, naturally and inevitably, I am by no means free. My living is dependent upon the money I make from my writings. At present I am reading [the] proof of my book *Cane* which Boni and Liveright will bring out sometime this summer. Next week I start a short story and complete a criticism of a Study of Waldo Frank. But there is no reason in the world why I can't manage to get some stuff to you, if, somehow or other, big or little, you can pay me. You, together with most of the magazines I send ms to, are in a comparatively lean and difficult field. I realize that, and hence don't expect much from you. But some small dribs must come in, else I close shop.

The first chance I get, if I haven't heard from you in the meanwhile, I'll run off a few lines and send them in by way of experiment.

Cordially,

Jean Toomer

Countee Cullen to Langston Hughes

In this letter, the eminent poet Countee Cullen praises the work of fellow writer Langston Hughes.

34 West 131 Street

New York City

May 14, 1924

Dear Langston,

As you must realize, I was very anxious to receive both your letters and the card you sent me—and especially the poem which I consider, while not the best you have written, especially good, and most naturally adapted to music. You have a pronounced gift of singing and painting in your work. I would really give anything to possess your sense of color. I am going to send the poems out immediately. I am also going to send you copies of *Opportunity* and the *Messenger* in which poems of yours appeared. There is no need to send you the *Crisis*; Suppose Miss [Jessie] Fauset does that.*

By the way, have you read Miss Fauset's novel? I haven't had money enough to buy it yet; but I have read Harold's copy, and I like it fairly well. It is certainly a landmark in establishing the intellectual Negro in American literature.

We were all saying that you were not here for the dinner which was a most brilliant gathering. My table companions were Mary Austin and Walter Hampden. I was impressed with Hampden who was intelligent and gently humorous. But Mary Austin was a frightful bore—a crabbed old hag. She disgraced herself beyond retribution in her speech by calling us a young race, and dating the origin of the spirituals from the Indians. There were printed programmes upon which I had a poem for the occasion, a poem intending more than it effected. I shall send you a copy.

So you are in love at last? I question its depths, however, when you tell me so resignedly that you are determined that nothing shall come of it, basing your decision upon chimeric demerits. You are born out of your time, my boy, for in this age sacrifice of self is so infrequent that it is freakish. Don't call it love. Read this little poem of mine called En

---

*Jessie Fauset (1882–1961) discovered many of the writers of the Harlem Renaissance and published their work in *The Crisis*, where she was literary editor. She was the author of several novels, including *There Is Confusion* (1924), *Plum Bun* (1929), and *The Chinaberry Tree* (1931).

Passant and you will understand. But really, I do hope that it proves to be love.

In the *Southern Workman* for April, Professor Kirlin wrote an appreciation for two Young <u>Negro Poets</u>, Langston Hughes and Countee Cullen. If I am able to secure copies of the magazine I shall send you one. I was quite proud to have him call us <u>friends and kindred spirits</u>.

If you have the money to spare and can find them, I wish you would send me Rene Marau's Poetic works. I want to translate them.

Harold is thinking of going to Europe this summer. I cherish the idea, but little hope. Please write to Donald Duff 194 New St. Newark, NJ.

Send me whatever work you do, but do send yourself soon.

Your friend,
Countee

Countee Cullen to Langston Hughes

New York City
Oct. 8, 1924

Dear Langston,

I have been trying to write to you for at least a week, but everything here at home is so upset that I am absolutely unable to concentrate on anything. You see, we have just moved into a new house, and I am not yet nearly enough adjusted to the situation.

Besides, this is the time of the year in which the world begins to disinterest me. The sad, autumnal days are upon me, and I find myself mumbling, "The sea is deep; a knife is sharp and poison acid burns"— Tis good I am the coward I am, else would I yield me to this mood, and test the efficacy of your lovely suicide song. These are the days in which I feel poetry most and express it least. Would I were where you are!

Dr. [Alain] Locke writes me that he has some lovely lyrics of yours to show me. I am consumed with eagerness and envy,—eagerness to see them, envy that you did not send me copies. When are you coming back to us? There is so great a need for you here. The group is beginning to disintegrate. Miss [Jessie] Fauset has left for Paris; Gwendolyn Bennett has gone to Howard to teach, and the rest of us seem suffused with a poppied apathy. The old things are too familiar now to give us pleasure—and, so the sweet Hebraic singer says, there is nothing new under the sun. Que faire, alas? But write, and come home.

    Yours,

        Countee

W.E.B. Du Bois to Roland Hayes

In 1924 Roland Hayes (1887–1976), a concert singer born to former slaves in Curryville, Georgia, was the first African American to give a recital at Carnegie Hall. In 1920 he performed in London, where he received a special request to sing for the king and queen. By the end of the 1920s, Hayes had performed throughout Europe and was the highest paid tenor in the world. As the following note attests, one of his admirers was Du Bois, the eminent scholar.

November 30, 1925

My dear Mr. Hayes:

    May I tell you what very deep and enduring pleasure I received from listening to you at Carnegie Hall last Friday night? I am under great obligations to you for the opportunity and I hope that your health and strength will enable you to carry your great message further and further for an indefinite time.

    Very sincerely yours,

        W.E.B. Du Bois

Roland Hayes to W.E.B. Du Bois

Nashville, Tenn.
December 16, 1925

My dear Dr. Du Bois:

    What deep chords of infinite inspiration do the commendatory words, contained in your most kind letter, strike within my breast. Such understanding as here shown, helps to afford building stones to one foundation of a bridge which, when completed, will enable all to pass over into a fuller knowledge of the various benefits that each individual in the race, and of the races, can derive from the other.

    Yours sincerely,

        Roland Hayes

Alain Locke to A'Lelia Walker

The writer and philosopher Alain Locke (1886–1954) wrote this letter to the Harlem socialite A'Lelia Walker (1885–1931) to note the closing of The Dark Tower, a literary salon she hosted at her Harlem brownstone.

Washington, D.C.
October 12, 1928

Dear Madam Walker:

Permit me this expression of deep regret on receipt of your announcement announcing the closing of "The Dark Tower." Let me assure you that some of us fully appreciate the effort of this contribution. I hope that you will not be altogether discouraged and that some channel will open through which you may with greater certainty make an active contribution to the really rapid advance of Negro art.

Indeed I would sometime appreciate the opportunity of talking over with you my particular hobby,—the collection of African Art. It might just be that it would interest you also. Once acquired it is no further expense, and even increases substantially in value. And two, I also feel that I could make an approach to certain wealthy art patrons interested for a considerable museum donation provided I could have as a nest egg a substantial contribution from some interested and generous Negro of means.

This is merely suggestive of course, my main purpose is merely to express my regret at the failure of "The Dark Tower" and my personal regard and best wishes.

Sincerely,
Alain Locke

Zora Neale Hurston to Langston Hughes

Zora Neale Hurston (1891–1960) was a writer and folklorist best known for her classic novel Their Eyes Were Watching God *(1937). Born in Notasulga, Alabama, and raised in Eatonville, Florida, Hurston attended Howard University and later received her B.A. in anthropology from Barnard College. At Barnard, Hurston worked with the eminent anthropologist Franz Boas and documented African American folklore throughout the South. The results were published in her acclaimed work* Mules and Men *(1935). In 1926, Hurston, along with Langston Hughes, Aaron Douglas,*

Gwendolyn Bennett, and Wallace Thurman, published the literary maga-zine Fire!!

December 10, 1929

Dear Langston,

Your wires and your letters have all come safely. All helped but your last letter comforted my soul like dreamless sleep.

Now I am getting much more conjure material here in New Orleans, and I shall get a great deal more in the Bahamas. I am hoping for enough material to make an entire volume of just that. The religion would not be out of place in the volume, but I do think the song would jar. I have enough of them for a separate volume anyway. About a hundred. That ought to be enough I think. But we can discuss that when I am there.

It is good to have the counsel of both you and Alain [Locke.]

So sorry about the packing, but I thought I had done a good job in each case. That gold thing had some bits falling off when I got it, I hope it was not further damaged.

Well, I tell you, Langston, I am nothing without you. That's no flat-tery either. We will talk a lot when I get there.

I shall try to get back to the Bahamas for Xmas so that I can get some more pictures. That is their carnival season, and besides I have a letter saying that my man is back again, but may leave before long for Haiti.* I shall sail from there for New York. That means I am running here with my tongue hanging out to get everything I see. I have come to the conclusion that the birth certificate of Marie Laveau is not so important.† It is pretty well established about her birth, life and death. I shall photograph her tomb. I am finding so much more on my return here than I thought. Shows that I am getting better as a collector. I may have to ask for more time, but I hope not. G. has said that I may have it if I wish.

Love and everything deep and fine, Honey

Lovingly,

Zora

---

*Hurston's research during these trips became the book *Tell My Horse: Voodoo and Life in Haiti and Jamaica* (1938).

†Marie LaVeau (1794–1881) was a famous practitioner of voodoo in New Orleans. Her daughter and namesake (1827–1895) also practiced voodoo.

Jean Toomer to James Weldon Johnson

In this exchange with James Weldon Johnson (1871–1938), Jean Toomer replies to a request for a contribution to Johnson's revised edition of The Book of American Negro Poetry *(1922). Johnson also coedited, with his brother Rosamond,* The Book of American Negro Spirituals *(1925) and created the sermons in* God's Trombones: Seven Negro Sermons in Verse *(1927).*

Chicago, Illinois
July 11, 1930

Dear Mr. Johnson,

My view of this country sees it composed of people who primarily are Americans, who secondarily are of various stocks or mixed stocks. The matter of descent, and of divisions presumably based on descents, has been given, in my opinion, due emphasis, indeed over-emphasis. I aim to stress the fact that we all are Americans. I do not see things in terms of Negro, Anglo-Saxon, Jewish, and so on. As for me personally, I see myself an American, simply an American.

As regards art I particularly hold this view. I see our art and literature as primarily American art and literature. I do not see it as Negro, Anglo-Saxon, and so on.

Accordingly, I must withdraw from all things which emphasize or tend to emphasize racial or cultural divisions. I must align myself with things which stress the experiences, forms, and spirit we have in common.

This does not mean that I am necessarily opposed to the various established racial or sociological groupings. Certainly it does not mean that I am opposed to the efforts and forces which are trying to make these groups creative. On the contrary, I affirm these efforts. I recognize, for example, that the Negro art movement has had some valuable results. It is, however, for those who have and who will benefit by it. It is not for me. My poems are not Negro poems, nor are they Anglo-Saxon or white or English poems. My prose, likewise. They are, first, mine. And, second, in so far as general race or stock is concerned, they spring from the result of racial blendings here in America which have produced a new race or stock. We may call this stock the American stock or race. My main energies are devoted and directed towards the building of a life which will include all creative people of corresponding type.

I take this opportunity of noting these things in order to clear up a misunderstanding of my position which has existed to some extent ever since the publishing of *Cane*. I am stating the same things whenever opportunity allows to everyone concerned. I feel that just now the time is ripe to give a definite expression of these views.

My best wishes for your anthology; and my warm regards to you and Mrs. Johnson.

Sincerely,

Jean Toomer

James Weldon Johnson to Jean Toomer

July 26, 1930

My dear Mr. Toomer:

I have your letter, and I regret very much your unwillingness to have your poetry represented in the revised edition of *The Book of American Negro Poetry*. I must admit that it is a bit difficult for me to reconcile this with the fact that your work is included in Caroling Dusk—An Anthology of Verse by Negro Poets. It appears to me that an "anthology of verse by Negro poets" is more restricted than a "book of American Negro poetry"; because it is wholly conceivable that a Chinese poet might write "Negro" poetry.

However, I think I understand, and I do appreciate your point of view; and your point of view is not far from one I myself have often expressed. In most of my writings I have stressed the truth that the work done by the colored creative artist is a part of our common, national culture, and that within the past decade it has begun to be so recognized. I think such difference as there may be lies mainly in definitions.

Certainly, all you have written is a part of American literature; yet I feel you must agree that anyone reading *Cane* would call the stories in the book "Negro" stories, if for no other reason than that their subject matter is concerned with the life of the group so designated. This designation does not, in my opinion, imply any limitations upon the work or the author. In fact, the stories in *Cane* might have been written by a Russian author—and well might they have been—and still called "Negro" stories or stories of "Negro" life.

The elements going into the making of the new American race or stock have not yet reached a state of fusion, and until they do these group designations if only as a matter of linguistic convenience will continue to be used. In this I am merely stating what appears to me as a fact.

With kind regards, in which Mrs. Johnson joins me, I am,

Sincerely,

James Weldon Johnson

Langston Hughes to James Weldon Johnson

New York City
August 14, 1931

Dear Mr. Johnson,

Just recently back from Haiti, and I found your note with the enclosure waiting for me the other day when I went after my mail. I have a lot to tell you about my impressions of the Black Republic. Would also like to talk over with you a reading tour of the South which I hope to do this fall and winter if dates and a Ford can be procured. In a Ford we came all the way from Miami for less than $20.00, so I know such a tour by car could be done cheaply. I want to help build up a public (I mean a Negro public) for Negro books, and, if I can, to carry to the young people of the South interest in, and aspirations toward, true artistic expression, and a fearless use of racial material. I am asking the Rosenwald Fund if it wishes to help me in that and in the writing of some of the many things I have in mind to do. I would appreciate it immensely if you would allow me to use your name should they ask me for recommendations, etc., as I suppose they will . . . I hope your summer has been an enjoyable one. I know I remember with delight the afternoon I spent at your lovely place last year with Amy Spingarn* . . . I send all good wishes and best regards to Mrs. Johnson.

Sincerely,

Langston

*Amy Spingarn was a poet and the wife of Joel Spingarn, a Columbia University professor and literary critic who served as chair of the NAACP from 1914 to 1919. Joel Spingarn also sponsored The Crisis magazine's literary contests during the Harlem Renaissance and the Spingarn Award, which is the organization's highest recognition of merit.

Zora Neale Hurston to James Weldon Johnson

Longwood, Florida
April 16, 1934

My dear Dr. Johnson,

I referred the lady to you. I think that there is enough misinformation out about the Negroes without my adding a thing. I know that you know what she needs.

Just a word about my novel before you read it.* I have tried to present a Negro preacher who is neither funny nor an imitation Puritan ram-rod in pants. Just this human being and poet that he must be to succeed in a Negro pulpit. I do not speak of those among us who have been tampered with and consequently have gone Presbyterian or Episcopal. I mean the common run of us who love magnificence, beauty, poetry and color so much that there can never be too much of it. Who do not feel that the ridiculous has been achieved when some one decorates a decoration. That is my viewpoint. I see a preacher as a man outside of the pulpit and so far as I am concerned he should be free to follow his bent as other men. He becomes the voice of the spirit when he ascends the rostrum.

I am reading *Along This Way*† now. It is <u>grand</u>! My sister and I used to go around the house claiming things like that—what you and your brother did at the what-not. By the way, Prof. France of Rollins College is having it read in his class. Prof. Spreul in English (His sister married Dorothy Peters brother) is using it in his class-room also.

If the sponsors get the rest of the money I will see you in St. Louis.

Sincerely,

Zora Hurston

Zora Neale Hurston to Dorothy West

Zora Neale Hurston and Dorothy West (1907–1998) were close friends who tied for second place in a writing contest sponsored by Opportunity *magazine. West, who was nicknamed "The Kid" by Harlem Renaissance writers, had already won a fiction contest in the* Boston Post, *her hometown paper, at the age of fourteen. Her first novel,* The Living Is Easy, *was published in 1948.*

---

*A reference to Hurston's first novel, *Jonah's Gourd Vine*, published in 1934, which tells the story of a young pastor, John Buddy Pearson.
†*Along This Way: The Autobiography of James Weldon Johnson* (1933).

[Undated]
Sat. Night

Dearest Dot,

I'll take you up on the proposition on two conditions. #1—Please don't expect me to keep a very tidy kitchen. I aint that kind of person. Sometimes I clean it up beautifully & often I walk out on it.

#2. That you just feel at home & don't expect to be company.

#2A—That you tell yo' pa to send a can of asparagus along.

Don't mind me at anytime—just spread your jenk in your own way. Don't feel any more obligations to the dish-pan than I do. It is only an incident in life—not life itself. The Wilises are gone & I expect to move into their apartment. Wish you would take the old place. I suppose I shall move on Monday or so.

Love to the whole works up there in Boston.

Devotedly,
Zora

Claude McKay to James Weldon Johnson

Claude McKay (1889–1948) was a Jamaican immigrant and writer whose poetry collection Harlem Shadows *(1922) was among the first major works published during the Harlem Renaissance. His bestselling novel* Home to Harlem *(1928) won the Harmon Gold Award for Literature while being criticized by W.E.B. Du Bois for its depiction of Harlem nightlife and sexuality, which Du Bois said "for the most part nauseates me." For a while, McKay embraced Communism, and wrote for a socialist paper published in London.*

New York City
May 31, 1935

Dear JWJ

Nearly everybody that I have spoken or written to thinks that you are the one man who could do something really effective to help me get the pecuniary assistance necessary to write the book I want to write.

I am enclosing a copy of a letter from the Harmon Foundation, in which you are also mentioned. Would you be kind enough to introduce me to Dr. Keppel and also to Dr. Jones, if you know him. I haven't heard from Mr. Embree again and possibly nothing practical will come from that source.

I have been trying all along to get a job, but without any success. Max Eastman thinks that my prose, from *Home To Harlem* on, put the liberals and radicals against me and that is why I am finding it so difficult to get any help. But creatively I never felt that I was writing particularly for liberals and radicals, nor Negroes only as such, because I have been always obsessed with the idea of the universality of life under the different patterns and colors and felt it was altogether too grand to be distorted creatively in the interest of any one group. And so I have always striven to obtain a certain objective balance in my creative work.

If I could only find a publisher that would be willing to give me an advance, I wouldn't worry at all about a special fund. And if only I had the necessary leisure to concentrate on five chapters and complete them, I am sure that I could land a publisher. But that is the rub from any angle—getting the chance.

I have your letter of the 27th. I agree with you that whatever happens to the United States it is certainly not going Soviet after the Russian plan. In fact I sometimes think that something so big on a social and industrial scale may happen in this country that might bring Russia to school here to copy its methods.

We disagree about Labor, however. I think that so long as the White unions remain selfish and chauvinist, colored workers should organize in separate unions to fight for greater economic advantages, even if they have to pass through the scabbing phase to obtain same. They will surely not win economic justice if they are waiting for white labor to hand it to them as a gift. In the Steel Industry Negroes won their unique position by scabbing. I have been hearing some amazing stories of colored workers who were actually in white unions and the means that were used to discriminate against them, even when they were in.

I agree with you too about the impossibility of Negroes by themselves duplicating the social machinery. But I think it requires careful elucidation. We don't want to play the game of those radicals who see black chauvinism in the efforts of Negroes to get the best they can under the existing system. Recently Stolberg had an article in the *Nation* in which he spoke of the plight of Negroes as artisans and professionals as if he felt it was a pity that we had such Negroes, because they don't hold the places to which their education entitles them! But from what I have been hearing a similar situation exists in the radical groups!

Well, I can't write any more excepting to say that I hope we do get a chance of getting together this summer.

Sincerely,

Claude McKay

Ralph Ellison to Langston Hughes

August 24, 1936

Dear Langston Hughes,

I had no idea that you possessed such an old fashioned virtue—you even answer letters. Quite surprising in this age of read 'em and leave 'em. I'm very glad the books arrived safely. I had feared perhaps they wouldn't . . . I have learned quite a lot from Barthé.* Who by the way says "hello." I've done two heads and started my first torso. After seeing the work of several of our so-called sculptors, I quite agree with you about Barthé. Not only does his work excel in anatomical truthfulness, but in artistic feeling as well; I think I have been objective in this matter because I wanted to study with the person who could give me the most, regardless of the opinion of the Negro press.

Last time I didn't tell you I was after a job. Well right after you left I worked extra at the Y.M.C.A. cafeteria, much to my displeasure but I needed the money. I then started studying with Barthé who in turn started asking about for a job for me. Thanks to him I now work for a big name in psychiatry, Dr. Harry Stack Sullivan whom no doubt you know. I work five hours five days a week and use the rest of my day at sculpture. The only dark spot on the whole picture is that I won't have money enough to return to school this year. I was too late getting started. However I can stay here and take two subjects at Julliard so as not to completely lose touch with music.

Say something funny happened about my mother and Cleveland. She was there two weeks and didn't like it. Then she visited Dayton and found thirteen female relatives she had no idea she had so she has been there since. I don't know what her plans are, I wouldn't be surprised if she went back to Oklahoma City though. By all means send

*Born James Richmond Barthé (1901–1989), he was an African American sculptor from Bay St. Louis, Mississippi, known for his public works in Harlem and his portrayals of celebrities and figures from black history.

the "Literature and Dialectical Materialism," and the "Man's Fate"!*
I haven't had time to do much reading lately, but I don't wish to be ignorant of the Leftist Literature any longer. I did, however, get around
to buying T. S. Eliot's *Complete Poems*, and a biography of Berliaz the
French Conqueror. I was already familiar with Eliot's work and I felt I
knew his best work before I bought his collection.

. . . I do hope all your undertakings are successful.

Sincerely,

Ralph Ellison

Claude McKay to James Weldon Johnson

New York City
April 2, 1937

Dear JWJ

I'm wondering if you did come into town Labor Day and how I can
get in touch with you. I should hate to miss you this time, because I do
want to talk about the contemplated Negro writers organization and
get the benefit of your advice.

I hope that if we can get together I can induce Countee Cullen
to join us. I feel very strongly about Negro writers coming closer together in cultural contact and think that Negro writers who have made
a reputation should do something to encourage the younger fellows
and if possible keep them out of the destructive clutch of the Communists.

So please let me know. If you are going to stay longer in Great Barrington, it might be possible for me to accept your invitation and come
up some weekend.

Yours Sincerely

Claude McKay

P.S. At a small meeting held before I went on my vacation we decided
to wait until after the holidays to call a meeting.

Literature and Dialectical Materialism (1934), by the economist John Strachey, an influential early Marxist critique of literature. *Man's Fate* (1933), a novel by André Malraux about
the failed 1927 communist revolution in Shanghai.

Ralph Ellison to Langston Hughes

April 27, 1937

Dear Lang,

I am now in the depths of what for you would be a creative mood. My tonsils are as large as hens eggs, and the blood spurts through my head with as deadly an effect as a million demons in hobnail boots would have. Even the carpet—which is usually of a not unpleasing design—has isolated one of its motif[s] into the shape of a horrible little bat's head with enormous ears and now grins at my futile efforts to wade through the detailed style of Thomas Mann. This has been the state of things for four days now. Eventually I'll have to tell the world about it. That's the formula isn't it?

Speaking of Mann, I received the books, every first edition of them, and much to my unsuppressed delight. However I must thank you for more than just the first editions, the story of Tonio Kruger has a value to me all its own. It made clear many of the things we talked about and despite myself I found it impossible not to identify myself with the character. All of which might be very assumptious on the part of the ole ego but was none the less satisfying. I'm sure this will be one of the things I'll return to again and again when seeking self-explanation. Peace friend. It's truly wonderful! I must add that it is only since I've been ill I've found Mann difficult reading. He reminds me of [Joseph] Conrad and is, I think, no less an artist in prose.

All things you desired are done and I'm sorry it was necessary to remind me again of the Negro Genius. It has been in Chicago some few days now, but I am at a loss as to where *Angels In Undress*, *Pro Patria* and *Prancing Nigger* should be mailed. Let me know won't you. Did you ever see a typewriter beat a sick man down? Well I did! But dam my right leg, and dam my left big toe and my right ear—Get my left hand!!

Aw guy you spoiled all my old vices, the Apollo, the waffles. They don't seem quite the same after you and your conversation. However I still go through the motions and things kinda righted themselves [on] one or two occasions when Lou went along with me. Lou is fine and thanks to her I have two apartments over which to scatter the evidence of my malady. Nel is still with husband, Baby brother with infancy and the whole damned house is still like something out of the Mad Hatters teacup. Peace!

You know you had me worried on your last departure. It was too unlike you to have time to burn on the day of leaving N.Y. Now I feel much better about it. You were at yourself after all. I wish you and Mr. [William Grant] Still* a rich harvest from which I believe to be a most fortunate collaboration; even though he states in an aria in *Blue Steel* that "<u>beauty</u> gives birth to beauty." In the nick of time: The address of the Park-Lincoln is 321 Edgecombe Ave. N.Y.C.

Sincerely,
Ralph

Arthur A. Schomburg to Langston Hughes

Arthur Alfonso Schomburg (1874–1938) was a bibliophile whose rare and extensive collection of the letters, books, manuscripts, and ephemera of people from across the African Diaspora laid the foundation for the collection housed at the New York Public Library's Schomburg Center for Research and Black Culture. This letter was written while Hughes was in Valencia, Spain, translating works of Spanish writers.

New York City
January 3, 1938

My dear Hughes:

I want to thank you for the many little items you have sent to me. These will be exhibited from time to time in our glass cases for the education of our colored brethren.

I received from [Nicolás] Guillén three magazines and a very interesting copy of the publication with the autographed signatures of Nancy Cunard, Guillén and yourself.† I am very glad to see the very cordial reception that is being given to you in Spain. I should like to have you translate to the English language that famous poem of Guil-

---

*William Grant Still (1896–1978) was an African American composer, oboist, and conductor well known for his "Afro-American Symphony," which was widely performed by major orchestras. He was the first African American to conduct a major symphony orchestra or to have his own symphony performed by major orchestras. In 1949 his opera *Troubled Island* was performed by the New York City Opera.

†Nicolás Guillén (1902–1989), an Afro-Cuban poet, journalist, and activist, was a close friend of Hughes, who translated his work. Nancy Cunard (1896–1965) was born into the British aristocracy (her father was an heir to the Cunard Line) and devoted herself to fighting racism and fascism, becoming friends with many writers and artists of her time, including Hughes, Ernest Hemingway, and James Joyce.

lén of the Uncle Tom Negro, "Shabas." I think it should be brought to the knowledge of the American people that the Spanish speaking countries also have Uncle Toms. I am carried away with the very ingenious manner that the poet has painted this character. I know of no other person who could render this poem in the English version other than you. I think we ought to make known Guillén to the American people since he is after a Guggenheim fellowship.

[. . .] I am enclosing this letter in Guillén's folder which will go first to Paris. I am also enclosing a note to Nancy Cunard. Should the letter miss her, I am enclosing my most cordial remembrance.

I wish you success in your undertaking on behalf of the Spanish nation. I read in yesterday's *Times* a review of "El Guarap," and I noticed that you have translated this to the English language. I am going to stop at the bookshop and see if I can pick up a copy in Spanish and English, and let you know how I like the work.

With best regards to the triumvirate.

Cordially yours,

Arthur A. Schomburg

Arthur A. Schomburg to Caterina Jarboro

Caterina Jarboro (1903–1986), a native of Wilmington, North Carolina, was the first African American woman to sing on an American opera stage, performing in Verdi's Aïda at the Hippodrome in 1933. She traveled to Europe to pursue her career in theater, cheered on by Schomburg, with whom she corresponded for several years. In 1921 Jarboro made her Broadway debut in the hit musical Shuffle Along.

New York City
March 21, 1938

My dear Rosebud:

I want to thank you from the bottom of my heart for your gracious letter which came to hand safely with photographs as Queen of Sheba as well as your smiling face. It seems to me you are growing prettier every day with the help of the French masseurs. It was very nice of you to remember me with the programs which will make a very nice exhibit here long before you return to America. I am very glad you have added to your repertoire two more operas, putting you above all other colored artists in the world. I am glad you have had success in executing the intricate and great masterpieces, and to think you have not only been able to portray Aida and received the most generous criticism of the American music critics but in France you have had [Charles] Gounod's masterpieces "The Queen of Sheba" and "Africaine." I know that when you go to South America, especially Brazil and the Argentine Republic, your reward will be the greatest that you have ever had.

I also received safely the package containing the watercolor sketch which I understand will be only a loan, and I will treasure it with care until such time you return to our city. Other things that may come within your hand, reviewing pictures, and other items, always keep an extra copy which may be added to the collection we have here in our city.

With best regards and loving remembrance, I am

Very faithfully yours,

Arthur A. Schomburg

Richard Wright to Antonio Frasconi

Richard Wright (1908–1960), the grandson of slaves, was born on a plantation in Roxie, Mississippi, where his father was a sharecropper. In 1937 Wright moved to New York, where he was the Harlem editor of the Communist paper The Daily Worker. *He won acclaim for his first book,* Uncle Tom's Children *(1938), a collection of novellas that examine racial hatred and class. His first novel,* Native Son *(1940), was the first Book-of-the-Month Club selection by an African American writer. Wright wrote the following letter to Antonio Frasconi (b. 1919), a graphic artist in Buenos Aires who had sought his advice on whether to address racial politics in his art. Frasconi immigrated to the United States in 1945 and gained renown for his woodblock printing. His books include* A Whitman Portrait *(1960) and* A Kaleidoscope in Woodcuts *(1968).*

Brooklyn, New York
November, 1944

DEAR SENOR FRASCONI:

I have just read your letter of November 1 with great concern, and I want to tell you that I sympathize with the perplexity which moved you to appeal to me for advice across such a vast geographical and psychological distance. The question you pose and the nature of your choice are not new, and the situation in which you find yourself is common among the artists of my own country today. To me, the fact that you did not make a quick, careless judgement; that you felt unwilling to accept the easy counsel of your friends; and that you tried to weigh all the values of the factors involved, seems to imply that you feel the Negro's situation in the world today very keenly. And, in my opinion, that is how an artist should feel it.

But I regret to say that I cannot tell you exactly what to do in terms of your concrete political situation. I'm ignorant of the language and culture of South America, of its economics, and of the currents of political pressure that may be influencing you and those around you. Hence, my presumptuous words of counsel cannot be too specific; and, in order to make my attitude clear, I must assume that we share a common sense of life, a sense of life out of which we both are trying to create.

You ask me if the "moment is propitious" for presenting the plight of the Negro in your art, and if the presentation of that plight will damage the "unity forced by the anti-fascist war," and you imply that some of your friends, motivated by political fears, urged you to abandon your project lest it comfort the enemy and render more difficult the task of the soldiers of the United Nations.

Is there not something very dubious in the way in which the question is posed? What is the basis for the assumption that artistic representation of the plight of the Negro would make our victory over the fascists more difficult? Is it assumed that the basis of our morale rests upon the conviction that there is no justice in North and South America? I do not believe that any such conviction honestly exists in a wide degree in the whole of the New World. Then, why are the people so anxious today to conceal the facts of Negro life? What has North and South America let happen to Negroes that has evoked such a wide belief that if the truth of Negro life were known it would hinder the march of our armies?

Are we not confronted here with the attitude of "moral slackers," "moral dodgers," who, wanting to conquer the fascist enemy do not want to rid their lives of the fascist-like practices of which they have grown so profitably fond? The whole question, when looked at from this point of view, is wrapped and lost in the subjective fears of politicians.

I do not believe that the truth of Negro life, when expressed either artistically or factually will harm the cause of the United Nations. On the contrary, I believe that the opposite is true. Might it not be that the expression of the truth of the Negro life might clarify the issues for which we are fighting this war? Of course, it is commonly said that the fascist propagandists make great use of our acts of injustice; and, if this is so, I propose that we forthwith divest such facts of any advantage they might contain for fascists by removing injustice from our midst. I propose that we deliberately exhibit all those social cancers whose removal would facilitate and strengthen our morale and conviction in this war.

But I must admit that my arguments are pure speculation; I allowed myself the indulgence of expressing them to show that the OPINIONS OF POLITICIANS CAN BE WRONG. There is however, beyond the boundaries of imperious politics, a common ground upon which we can stand and see the truth of this problem. And that ground can be ours if I rephrase your question in more general terms: Out of what vision must an artist create? The question seems vague, but when it is conceived in terms of political pressure from Left or Right, it has vital meaning. Must an artist's vision—that complex condition of perception that compels him to express himself—stem on the whole from the pronouncements of political leaders, or must the artist accept mainly the evidence of his sensibilities to lead him?

I hold that, in the last analysis, the artist must bow to the monitor of his own imagination; must be led by the sovereignty of his own impressions and perceptions; must be guided by the tyranny of what troubles and concerns him personally; and that he must learn to trust the impulse, vague and compulsive as it may be, which moves him in the first instance toward expression. There is no other true path, and the artist owes it to himself and to those who live and breathe with him to render unto reality that which is reality's.

Your question implies that some of your advisers feel that your artistic representations of the Negro will create disunity; if that is so, then I would question seriously the kind of human unity that some of your advisers are trying to build. I, of course, take it for granted that your art is seeking passionately to render an honest reaction to the problem of the Negro in North or South America, and other oppressed men, black or white, wherever they are found on earth, a sense of unity that will make men feel that they are brothers!

Paint, draw, engrave, and let all facts that impinge upon your sensibilities be your subject matter, and let your heart strike the hour as to when you should give what you have said to others! And I assure you that in answering your letter I have not looked at the clock in my room to see what hour of the day it is; I have not consulted the calendar to determine the day of the month; I have not examined a map to see where our armies are standing; in short, I have not tried to give you advice conditioned or limited by expediency or fear. Instead, I sat right down and wrote you what was in my heart; and my heart is full of this: There are 13,000,000 black people in the United States who practically have no voice in the government that governs them; who must fight in the United States Army under Jim Crow conditions of racial humiliation; who literally have the blood, which they so generously offer out of their veins to wounded soldiers, segregated in blood (plasma) banks of the American Red Cross, as though their blood were the blood of subhumans; who on the whole, live lives that are possessed of but a few rights which others respect; who, daily and hourly, are restricted in their behavior to an orbit branded as inferior; who must, for the most part, live their lives in artificially marked-off, ghetto-like areas of our cities and countryside; and whose manliness and self-assertion generally warrant instant reprisal!

Can you know this and hesitate to speak or act? What I have described above is not only a picture of the plight of Negroes in the United States; it is a picture of the majority of mankind in the world today, colored and white. And if your art can further a popular unity of feeling based upon the common experiences of these oppressed, would you withhold that art?

If you reject my plea, then, pray, tell me, how will you finally determine to express yourself? Will you wait until those who say your artistic expression must be guided by global political issues grant permission? And who is qualified to give you the signal to begin? It might happen that when you are in the very throes of creation the "line" will change! Or that an entirely new "line" will have come into being! Or that, when your work is done, you will be criticized for not having expressed yourself with enough militancy, for not having been soft enough, subtle or tender enough in the light of a "new" political situation. Who knows?

I really believe that it would be far wiser for you to willingly and honestly hire yourself out to the business firms of your native country as an advertising copy writer than to try to reduce your artistic expression to another kind of advertising under the mistaken illusion that you are helping mankind by doing so. But, really, must you hire yourself out to anybody? Must we artists have bosses, Left or Right? Cannot our art be our guide to all men of good-will who want to know the truth of our time? Cannot we artists speak in a tone of authority of our own? A tone of authority that will depict the tissue, the texture, the quality, and the value of experience?

It is imperative that we artists seek and find a simpler, a more elementary, and a more personal guide to the truth of experience and events than those contained in the mandates of frenzied politicians; and I say that we shall find it where artists have always found it: in the visions which our eyes create out of the insistent welter of reality, and out of the surging feelings which those visions evoke in our hearts.

Life is sufficient unto life if it is lived and felt directly and deeply enough; and I would warn that we must beware of those who seek, in words no matter how urgent or crisis-charged, to interpose an alien and dubious curtain of reality between our eyes and the crying claims of a world which it is our lot to see only too poignantly and too briefly.

Fraternally yours,
Richard Wright

Richard Wright to David L. Cohn, The Atlantic Monthly

In the following letter, Wright responds to a review of his book Native Son *that appeared in* The Atlantic Monthly.

May 1945

I want to reply to Mr. David L. Cohn, whose article criticized my novel, *Native Son,* in the May issue of the *Atlantic Monthly.* In the eyes of the average white American reader, his article made it more difficult for a Negro (child of slaves and savages!) to answer a cultured Jew (who had two thousand years of oppression to recommend him in giving advice to other unfortunates!) than an American white. Indeed, Mr. Cohn writes as though he were recommending his "two thousand years of oppression" to the Negroes of America! No, thank you, Mr. Cohn. I don't think that we Negroes are going to have to go through with it. We might perish in the attempt to avoid it; if so, then death as men is better than two thousand years of ghetto life and seven years of Herr Hitler.

The Negro problem in America is *not* beyond solution. (I write from a country—Mexico—where people of all races and colors live in harmony and without racial prejudices or theories of racial superiority. Whites and Indians live and work and die here, always resisting the attempts of Anglo-Saxon tourists and industrialists to introduce racial hate and discrimination.) Russia has solved the problem of the Jews and that of the fall of all her other racial and national minorities. Probably the Soviet solution is not to Mr. Cohn's liking, but I think it is to the liking of the Jews in Russia and Biro-Bidjan. I accept the Russian solution. I am a proletarian and Mr. Cohn is bourgeois; we live on different planes of social reality, and we see Russia differently.

"He [Wright] wants not only complete political rights for his people, but also social equality, and he wants them now." Certainly I want them now. And what's wrong with wanting them now? What guarantee have we Negroes, if we were "expedient" for five hundred years, that America would extend to us a certificate stating that we were civilized? I am proud to declaim—as proud as Mr. Cohn is of his two thousand years of oppression—that at no time in the history of American politics has a Negro stood for anything but the untrammeled rights of human personality, *his* and *others*.

Mr. Cohn implies that as a writer I should look at the state of the Negro through the lens of relativity, and not judge his plight in an absolute sense. That is precisely what, as an artist, I try *not* to do. My character, Bigger Thomas, lives and suffers in the real world. Feeling and perception, from moment to moment, are absolute, and if I dodged my responsibility as an artist and depicted them as otherwise I'd be a traitor, not to my race alone, but to *humanity*. An artist deals with aspects of reality different from those which a scientist sees. My task is not to abstract reality, but to enhance its value. In the process of objectifying emotional experience in words—paint, stone, or tone—an artist uses his feelings, in an immediate and absolute sense. To ask a writer to deny the validity of his sensual perceptions is to ask him to be "expedient" enough to commit spiritual suicide for the sake of politicians. And that I'll *never* consent to do. No motive of "expediency" can compel me to elect to justify the ways of white America to the Negro; rather, my task is to weigh the effects of our civilization upon the personality, as it affects it *here* and *now*. If, in my weighing of those effects, I reveal rot, pus, filth, hate, fear, guilt, and degenerate forms of life, must I be consigned to hell? (Yes, Bigger Thomas hated, but he hated because he *feared*. Carefully, Mr. Cohn avoided to mention that fact. Or does Mr. Cohn feel that the "exquisite, intuitive" treatment of the Negro in America does not inspire fear?) I wrote *Native Son* to show what manner of men and women our "society of the majority" breeds, and my aim was to depict a character in terms of the living tissue and texture of daily consciousness. And who is responsible for his feelings, anyway?

Mr. Cohn, my view of history tells me this: *Only the strong are free.* Might may not make right, but there is no "right" nation without might. That may sound cynical, but it is nevertheless true. If the Jew has suffered for two thousand years, then it is mainly because of his religion and his otherworldliness, and he has only himself to blame. The Jew had a choice, just as the Negro in America has one. We Negroes prefer to take the hint of that great Jewish revolutionist, Karl Marx, and look soberly upon the facts of history, and organize, ally ourselves, and fight it out. Having helped to build the "society of the majority," we Negroes are not so dazzled by its preciousness that we consider it something holy and beyond attack. We know our weakness and we know our strength, and we are not going to fight America *alone.* We are not so naïve as that. The Negro in America became politically mature the moment he realized that he could not fight the "society of the majority" alone and organized the National Negro Congress and threw its weight behind John L. Lewis and the CIO!*

I urge my race to become strong through *alliances,* by joining in the common cause with other oppressed groups (and there are a lot of them in America, Mr. Cohn!), workers, *sensible* Jews, farmers, declassed intellectuals, and so forth. I urge them to master the techniques of political, social, and economic struggle and cast their lot with the millions in the world today who are fighting for freedom, crossing national and racial boundaries if necessary.

The unconscious basis upon which most whites excuse Negro oppression is as follows: (1) the Negro did not have a culture when he was brought here; (2) the Negro was physically inferior and susceptible to diseases; (3) the Negro did not resist his enslavement. These three falsehoods have been woven into an ideological and moral principle to justify whatever America wants to do with the Negro, and, whether Mr. Cohn realizes it or not, they enable him to say "the Negro problem in America is actually insoluble."

But there is not one ounce of history or science to support oppression based upon these assumptions.

---

*A reference to John Llewellyn Lewis (1880–1969), the labor leader who through the Congress of Industrial Organization fought for higher living standards for American workers. Born in Cleveland, Iowa, he was the son of a Welsh coal miner.

The Negro (just as the Mexican Indian today) possessed a rich and complex culture when it was brought to these alien shores. He resisted oppression. And the Negro, instead of being physically weak, is tough and has withstood hardships that have cracked many another people. This, too, is history. Does it sound strange that American historians have distorted or omitted hundreds of records of slave revolts in America?

We Negroes have no religion that teaches us that we are "God's chosen people"; our sorrows cannot be soothed with such illusions. What culture we did have when we were torn from Africa was taken from us; we were separated when we were brought here and forbidden to speak our languages. We possess no remembered cushion of culture upon which we can lay our tired heads and dream of our superiority. We are driven by the nature of our position in this country into the thick of the struggle, whether we like it or not.

In *Native Son* I tried to show that a man, bereft of a culture and unanchored by property, can travel but one path if he reacts positively but unthinkingly to the prizes and goals of civilization; and that one path is emotionally blind rebellion. In *Native Son* I did not defend Bigger's actions; I explained them through depiction. And what alarms Mr. Cohn is not what I say Bigger *is,* but what I say *made* him what he is. Yes, white boys commit crimes, too. But would Mr. Cohn deny that the social pressure upon Negro boys is far greater than that upon white boys? And how does it materially alter the substance of my book if white boys do commit murder? Does not Mr. Cohn remember the Jewish boy who shot the Nazi diplomat in Paris a year or two ago? No Jewish revolutionist egged that boy to do that crime. Did not the Soviet officials, the moment they came into power, have to clean up the roaming bands of Jewish and Gentile youth who lived outside the society by crime, youth spawned by the Czar's holy belief that social, racial, and economic problems were "actually insoluble"?

Now, let me analyze more closely just how much and what kind of hate is in *Native Son.* Loath as I am to do this, I have no choice. Mr. Cohn's article, its tone and slant, convinced me more than anything else that I was *right* in the way I handled Negro life in *Native Son.* Mr. Cohn says that the burden of my book was a preachment of hate against the white races. It was not. No *advocacy* of hate is in that book. *None!* I wrote as objectively as I could of a Negro boy who hated and feared whites, hated them because he feared them. What Mr. Cohn mistook for my advocacy of hate in that novel was something entirely different. In every word of that book are *confidence, resolution,* and the *knowledge* that the Negro problem will and can be solved *beyond* the frame of reference of thought such as that found in Mr. Cohn's article.

Further in his article Mr. Cohn says that I do not understand that oppression has harmed whites as well as Negroes. Did I not have my character, Britten, exhibit through page after page the aberrations of whites who suffer from oppression? Or, God forbid, does Mr. Cohn *agree* with Britten? Did I not make the mob as hysterical as Bigger Thomas? Did I not ascribe the hysteria to the same origins? The entire long scene in the furnace room is but a depiction of how warped the whites have become through their oppression of Negroes. If there had been *one* person in the Dalton household who viewed Bigger Thomas as a human being, the crime would have been solved in half an hour. Did not Bigger Thomas himself know that it was the denial of his personality that enabled him to escape detection so long? The one piece of incriminating evidence which would have solved the "murder mystery" was Bigger's humanity, and the Daltons, Britten, and the newspaper men could not see or admit the living clue of Bigger's humanity under their very eyes! More than two thirds of *Native Son* is given over to depicting the very thing which Mr. Cohn claims "completely escapes" me. I wonder how much my book escaped *him.*

Mr. Cohn says that Bigger's age is not stated. It is. Bigger himself tells his age on page 42. On page 348 it is stated again in the official death sentence.

Mr. Cohn wonders why I selected a Negro *boy* as my protagonist. To any writer of fiction, or anyone acquainted with the creative process, the answer is simple. Youth is the turning point in life, the most sensitive and volatile period, the state that registers most vividly the impressions and experiences of life; and an artist likes to work with sensitive material.

Richard Wright

Langston Hughes to John Johnson

John Johnson (1918–2005), the grandson of slaves, was born in Arkansas City, Arkansas, and as a teenager moved to Chicago, where in 1945 he created Johnson Publishing, an international media empire anchored by Ebony *and* Jet *magazines. In 1982 Johnson was listed among the four hun-*

dred wealthiest Americans in Forbes magazine. Among his many awards is the Presidential Medal of Freedom, presented by President Bill Clinton in 1996. In this letter, Langston Hughes congratulates him on the publication of Ebony, which began with a print run of 25,000.

October 14, 1945

Dear Johnson,

Ebony is terrific! Thanks a lot for sending me a copy. I like it very much, and hope it goes places!

Not quite correct when it says Richard Wright is "only Negro novelist in America who makes a living, and a good one, from creative writing." Zora Hurston does, if I am not mistaken. And I haven't had a job for twenty years. The phrase, "and a good one" is probably correct, though.

Here's a tip for you: Mrs. Grace Nail Johnson, Hotel Theresa, New York, has just given several crates of material of her late husband, James Weldon Johnson, to Carl Van Vechten for the James Weldon Johnson Memorial Collection which he founded at Yale.* All his hand-written original manuscripts of <u>all</u> his books, dozens of files of his correspondence with most of the great Americans of our time, wonderful collection of theatrical photographs from Williams and Walker days up to now, piles of NAACP and other clippings covering Negro life for past fifty years, etc. etc. Might make a good photo story for you to photo Mrs. Johnson and Carl Van Vechten sorting it out, etc. His whole Central Park West apartment is full of it. (I asked him and he is willing to permit photos there.) If you want to write him: Carl Van Vechten, 101 Central Park West, New York. (You know he gave his entire music library and manuscripts to Fisk as the George Gershwin Memorial Collection.)

I don't think "Eight to Two" is a piece for *Ebony*, but of course you may use it there, if you think it is. Would give the returning colored soldier boys coming back to this white land something to feel good about!

I just signed to do the libretto for a musical version of Elmer Rice's *Street Scene*, with Kurt Weill's music—*Lady in the Dark* composer. So will be pretty busy for next few months what with lectures and all.

---

*Carl Van Vechten (1880–1964) was a white American writer, photographer, and patron of many Harlem Renaissance writers, including Hughes and Zora Neale Hurston. He was also author of the controversial novel *Nigger Heaven* (1926), which sought to capture Harlem nightlife.

I'll be in Chicago in early November. Would Thursday, Nov. 8, be a good day to have dinner with you-all? Or Friday, 9th? Let me know.

Sincerely,

Langston Hughes

Ralph Ellison to Langston Hughes

South Londonderry, Vt.
August 25, 1947

Dear Langston:

We're here in Vermont living in the mountain summer place of some friends—all four of us. It's quite nice, much larger than our apartment and a million times quieter. I haven't heard that Lutcher woman yelling "The Lady's in Love with You" since over two weeks ago when she awoke me about two A.M.

There are no cats—either colored or feline—to howl in the dubious ecstacies of fornication at midnight (is they ferking or is they fighting?); no sad voiced homeboys to stand outside the window at 4 A.M. and holler to someone above you: 'Hey Joe! Hey, Joe!' and then without pausing for breath to moo out, "Joe, getupandopenthedoorsoIcanget-mykeyoutofyourwalletandgohomeandgetmesomesleep, please, Joe," as though rendering a recitative from a sad, sad opera; with Joe either gone away or dead, or sleeping like a rock, or, like Richard, just too damn ornery to throw down the key so the sad-voiced son-of-a-bitch can leave and the evil, half-asleep neighbors can pull in their stocking-capped conks and stop their snide and loud-mouthed signifying. No, it's quiet here, and I've been getting more work done than in the city, and Fanny seems to enjoy every minute of the day.

I was so busy for a month before we left that I forgot to get in touch with you. For one thing, Fanny's parents were visiting us from Chicago; for another, I was negotiating to go over to Random House (which I did with an additional advance) and trying to go to Yaddo, but which, fortunately, I was able to cancel when this opportunity came along.

Hope the summer is going well with you; give our regards to Aunt Toy, Emerson and Nat and we'll see you when we return.

Yours sincerely,

Ralph

Ralph Ellison to Kenneth Burke

Kenneth Burke (1897–1993), a literary theorist, philosopher, and leading interpreter of Shakespeare, is believed to have greatly influenced the work of Ralph Ellison.* He was the author of many books, including A Grammar of Motives *(1945) and* A Rhetoric of Motives *(1950).*

August 25, 1947

Dear Kenneth:

I was very disappointed to arrive at Bennington on your day of departure last June, for I had hoped to see you there. Especially, since until quite recently I've found it impossible to write letters—which explains why you haven't heard from me. I did manage to use the telephone and was thus able to keep in touch with Stanley, but with you this wasn't possible; so I had to contend with my vain resolutions and bad conscience.

Since I've been here in the mountains I've written some seven letters in less than a week, so I suppose the psychological ice-jam has been broken. God knows it's been hot enough. But then, my novel has been going rather smoothly up here, and though the economic determinists would insist that it is because I've recently signed a new publisher's contract (having shifted from Reynal & Hitchcock to Random House) and am thus more serene in my gut life, I have a notion that the answer lies in the effect which the mountain has had upon my dream life. In Harlem I live out my horrors during the day; here I have my nightmares at night and by eight in the morning after watching the thick mist sweeping before the swift rising of the sun, I've achieved enough of a precarious tranquility to turn in a rather successful day of writing.

I suppose it's rather difficult when one lives in an apartment which one must enter through a long, narrow (and ofttimes smelly) hallway, into a small and low-ceilinged warm little room, to deal facilely with the cloacal and subterranean imagery with which I'm concerned in my book. For if art isn't life, neither is life art; and when your nose is bumped against your life too consistently and in too short an arch, there's no perspective in which the imagination can come to focus. I see no solution except to move. Or change my theme. Perhaps when

---

*See Beth Eddy, *The Rites of Identity: The Religious Naturalism and Cultural Criticism of Kenneth Burke and Ralph Ellison* (Princeton: Princeton University Press, 2003).

upon mountains one should only write about holes; when in holes, only about mountain life. Think of what that might do for the imaginative quality of our literature.

What have you published recently? Just before leaving the city I hastily read your piece on Ideology and Myth and had it set off a few bells in my head.* When I return I plan to give it a careful study, as it reawakens my interests in a piece I planned concerning the relations between our "science" of sociology and racial ideology. [Gunnar] Myrdal's *American Dilemma*, for instance, is full of rhetoric and ideological manipulations.

As for myself, I've just corrected the proofs of a section of my novel which is to appear in the American number of *Horizon* next October. It looks very strange in print, but it's too late to do anything about it. [*Horizon* editor Cyril] Connolly was enthusiastic enough in his letter however, saying that he threw out two pieces to make space for it, and asking to be my English publisher. I only wish the damn thing was completely finished, agonized over, learned from, and forgotten in the enthusiasm for my next.

As ever,
Ralph Ellison

Fredi Washington to Darr Smith

A year after the debut of her final film, One Mile from Heaven *(1937), the actress Fredi Washington (1903–1994) cofounded the Negro Actors Guild and actively participated in the boycott, organized by her brother-in-law, Rev. Adam Clayton Powell, Jr., of Harlem businesses that refused to hire blacks. In this letter to a newspaper columnist, Washington criticizes the 1949 film* Lost Boundaries, *which cast white actors to play black characters. Based on the true story of Dr. Albert Chandler Johnston, a black physician, and his wife, and produced by the Academy Award–winning producer Louis de Rochemont, the film won the 1949 Cannes Film Festival award for best screenplay.*

---

*Burke's article *entitled* "Ideology and Myth" was published in the Summer 1947 issue of *Accent* magazine.

August 2, 1949

Dear Darr Smith:

Excerpts from your column dated July 15, 1949, in which you quote from an interview with Alfred Werker, director of "Lost Boundaries," has just been brought to my attention.* I am appalled and not a little fighting mad to think that a so-called intelligent adult could be so viciously ignorant as to give as his reason for not casting Negroes in the above mentioned picture that "the majority of Negro actors are of the Uncle Tom, Minstrel show, shuffling dancer type of performer."

Well, I would like to say something for public print on the subject. In the first place, neither Alfred Werker nor Louis de Rochemont from the beginning of the production plans ever considered using Negro actors to portray the roles of the Johnson family. Therefore, Negroes having the physical appearance and ability needed for these roles were never interviewed. There are many Negro actors and actresses who are consistently turned down for plays and screen fare on the excuse that they are too fair, too intelligent, too modern looking, etc. I know, because I am one who falls into this category. It was I who played the role of "Peola" the neurotic, sensitive, fair, Negro girl in Universal's "Imitation of Life"—but did Alfred Werker give me an interview for either of the two female roles in *Boundaries*? He did not. He simply was not interested in learning what he evidently did not know; that there are many legitimate Negro actors and actresses who are far more intelligent than Werker proves himself to be.

No, Werker's excuse for denying to us our right to express ourselves through the medium of screen, is not good enough. Indeed, his excuse is a gross insult to us as American citizens, as Negroes, and as actors. I, for one, do not intend for Alfred Werker to cover up his stupid error by defiling us. He is a liar on several counts. He calls his picture documentary. Well, perhaps his New Hampshire scenes may be documentary, but his Harlem scenes are a gross exaggeration. I live in Harlem, and I think I am a better judge of that area than Werker. His Negro hospital scenes are crummy and unclean looking, when, as a matter of fact, southern Negro hospitals are well appointed, have clean buildings.

*Alfred Werker (1896–1975) directed numerous films, including *The House of Rothschild* (1934) and *The Adventures of Sherlock Holmes* (1939).

The nurses and doctors on the staffs of such hospitals are uniformly neat and trim. His crowning lie, of course, is merely an excuse for using white actors in Negro roles.

I would say that Alfred Werker has carved a unique niche for himself in the world of picture-making. He now can take the Oscar for being Hollywood's number one anti-Negro bigot.

Yours truly,
Fredi Washington

James Hubert "Eubie" Blake to Flournoy E. Miller

James Hubert "Eubie" Blake (1883–1983), born in Baltimore, Maryland, to former slaves, was a composer, pianist, and lyricist. With his partner, Noble Sissle, he wrote the music for Shuffle Along *(1921), the first major hit Broadway musical written by and starring African American performers.*

Los Angeles Calif.
Oct. 30, 1949

Hello F.E.

I rec'd the letter and told [Noble] Sissle by phone, rather I mean read the letter over the phone to him. He said he would write. I have been so tired. This is the first time I've had time to write. Well anyhow this is what we decided on. Both of us thought it a good idea, but thought to hold it for another month because "Shuffle Along" looks hot again and we can always go back to the idea of putting it on the road as a one-hour show. If you can hold this thing open a little while I think we can make things come out ok. Write me and let me know if you've heard from Sissle. We had an audition this Thursday a week ago and the money has started to come in again. I have not seen Sissle or [Irving] Gaumont this week because I have been busy in and out all this week.* Gaumont said one man pledged $1000 last Thursday night. Anyhow Sissle if he writes which he said he would will tell you all about it. My best regards to Mrs. Miller.

Your Partner
Eubie Blake

*Irving Gaumont produced the 1952 revival of *Shuffle Along*, which closed after four performances.

Bobby Short to Fredi Washington

The cabaret singer Bobby Short (1924–2005) is best known for his interpretation of the works of great twentieth-century composers, including Cole Porter, George and Ira Gershwin, Duke Ellington, Eubie Blake, Fats Waller, and Billy Strayhorn.

Paris, France
May 18, 1952

Dear Fredi:

Big fat greetings from Paris!

Yesterday marked my first week in this fabulous place and the difference already has been amazing. Prices are certainly as high as you predicted but I've begun to learn the shortcuts so necessary for living here.

Achieved the impossible yesterday by getting a tiny apartment just across from the Bois. I'm told that half the visiting "residents" have been trying for years without success. A hotel at first was quite difficult and arriving on Saturday evening was of no help. Things, however, are looking up and I expect to stay awhile.

The number of American Negroes living here is not really large or small, surprisingly enough, you'd be amazed at the various come-ons being used by some of them. Competition in show business is particularly keen which makes for miserable salaries; half the performers are living in garrets and eating whatever they can find. There are, however, several who are doing good things and naturally, [Lena] Horne and Daniels created great sensations. My own job is going at a fine rate with lots of rich American tourists to keep the little place packed. My agent already has his eye on a much better spot in Paris and there are plans for the Cote d'Azur later in the summer.

Really wrote this to thank you for seeing me off. That other apple was finally consumed somewhere in Labrador!

Much love,

BS

P.S. Tell Isabel that my own poodle arrives in two weeks from London. Black, natch.

Langston Hughes to Arna Bontemps

Though overshadowed by the celebrity of his close friend Langston Hughes and other Harlem Renaissance writers, Arna Bontemps (1902–1973) was an important contributor to the literary movement. His best-known work, God Sends Sunday, *a novel, was published in 1931, and his children's book* Story of the Negro *(1948) received a Newbery Honor. He also wrote, with the poet Countee Cullen, the play* St. Louis Woman, *based on* God Sends Sunday, *which opened on Broadway in 1946.* Bontemps was the Fisk University librarian for twenty-two years.*

[New York]
February 18, 1953

Dear Arna,

If you'll tell me what Dick Wright's book is like (since I haven't read it) I'll tell you about James Baldwin's *Go Tell It on the Mountain* which I've just finished: If it were written by Zora Hurston with her feeling for the folk idiom, it would probably be a quite wonderful book. Baldwin over-writes and over-poeticizes in images way over the heads of the folks supposedly thinking them—often beautiful writing in itself—but frequently out of character—although it might be as the people <u>would</u> think if they <u>could</u> think that way, which makes it seem like an "art" book about folks who aren't "art" folks. That and the too frequent use of flashbacks (a la Lillian Smith's "Strange Fruit") slows the book down to a pace each time the story seems to be about to start to go somewhere. And everyone is so fear-ridden and frustrated and "sorry" that they might as well have all died a-borning. Out of all that religion SOMEbody ought to triumph somewhere in it, but nary a soul does. If it is meant to show the futility of religion, then it should be sharper and clearer and not so muddy and pretty and poetic and exalted without being exalting. It's a low-down story in a velvet bag—and a Knopf binding. Willard Motley–like writing without his heart-breaking characters fitting the poetry Motley weaves around them. As Motley's does, but Baldwin's don't. Has a feeling of writing—for-writing's-sake—quality. I'd hope it would be (and wish it were) a

---

*The show was criticized by the NAACP and others for its stereotypical portrayal of African Americans, and Lena Horne refused to play a lead character. The protests contributed to the show's early closing, after 113 performances.

more cohesive whole with the words and the people belonging to each other. The words here belong more to the author. Although there are one or two VERY good sections, it is on the whole not unlike "John Brown's Body" (stage version, not the poem itself) which I saw last night and which nearly wore me down trying to bear up and look cultural in a hot crowded theatre 7th row orchestra with a party of folks who'd paid an ENORMOUS price for benefit tickets and had just ate an enormous dinner starting with whole lobsters as just the first course, and running on down in dead tasses and brandy. With that and Baldwin's book, I've had my culture for the YEAR. When folks are dealing with God and John Brown there ought to be fire and FIRE-WORKS too, and just endlessly stretching taffy that lops over and pulls out again and declamation and taffy colored lights and heads held noble and all of it's kind of sticky. If you've read it, tell me what you think. Also about Dick's book.

Got your check for the London transcriptions, so will now pay that little bill . . . Read and returned the "Simple" proofs . . . Saw the Blacks yesterday at a cocktail party (heads of Doubleday) and they're still remembering our FINE "POETRY OF THE NEGRO" party that you advised. Also saw Buck Moon at a PEN party (did I tell you) and he's with Collier's . . . And did I tell you some Reading Circle in Midwest is buying 1500 "First Book of Negroes"? . . . And waded through my first big snow of season at Brandeis the other day where there are 7 Negroes amidst all those of "the other persuasion." Had a pleasant half hour with Ludwig Lewisohn at his place there.* I have now uttered my last public word for the season—in fact, the whole YEAR. Folks will just have to go to buy my records the rest of 1953 . . . Jane White and Bill Marshall are getting ready to do "readings" of plays and things, too,—just like white folks—which delights [. . .]. "GO TELL IT ON THE MOUNTAIN" should go swell done that way. [. . .] But it ain't my meat. I wish he had collaborated with Zora.

Sincerely yours truly,

Langston

---

*Ludwig Lewisohn (1882–1955) was a literary critic, novelist, Zionist, and translator of German literature who in 1948 was one of the founding faculty members of Brandeis University.

Arna Bontemps to Langston Hughes

[Nashville, Tennessee]
March 4, 1953

Dear Lang,

We've had rain and clouds without sun for nearly a week, and the happenings hereabouts have been in harmony with the weather. If ever you have rain and clouds without sun, even for an hour, be informed the mess can be general sometimes. Perhaps a good bit of it is mood, but the cares of parenthood do impress with time, the insistence and finnickyness of editors certainly do, and the tea-pot tempests of campus life do grow more numerous when the weather is bad. So woe, woe, woe!

Your spirited reaction to Baldwin's novel was a pick-up, however. I have sent in my piece about Dick's [Richard Wright's] *The Outsider* to the *Saturday Review*, and I am sure you will not find it thin or tame or much-ado-about-nothing, as I gather is the case with *Go Tell It on the Mountain*. Dick's new book is rougher, louder, bad[d]er, and probably more controversial than *Native Son*. It's certainly not dull. The spirit and outlook seem to be Existentialist, and the theme is not racial, though the characters and settings are. You will have to read it.

You will have to read also—in order to oppose—the short articles by Baldwin and Gibson in the 2nd issue of *Perspectives, USA*. Off on the wrong feet, by this periodical for foreign distribution of American ideas, etc. should be an attack on Negro writers by two aspiring new Negro writers. (Under influence of the New Critics mainly, I gather.) I would like to do a piece that might serve as a corrective but can't afford to do one for nothing at this moment. Hence I shan't volunteer.

Meanwhile watch for my essay-review of the *Sat. Rev.* I've got to get back to revising the [George Washingon] Carver story now.*

Best ever,
Arna

P.S. Owen due from Pasadena tonight, passing through.

The Story of George Washington Carver, a young adult book about the African American scientist, was published in 1954.

Ralph Ellison to Mrs. Turner

In this letter, Ralph Ellison replies to a reader who complained about the way his landmark work, Invisible Man, *had been misinterpreted and viewed as autobiography.*

March 31, 1953

Dear Mrs. Turner:

Your letter came at a time when my book was under a very irritating attack in one of the local Negro newspapers and it was reassuring, to say the least. I must say, however, that when I told the *Saturday Review* interviewer that there was more to invisibility than I had been able to get into the book, I, by no means, meant to imply that I would return to that theme, only that like any valid metaphor for an aspect of the human condition, it was impossible for one man to exhaust it. As for myself, I doubt if I have really been invisible myself. Certainly not in the dramatic sense that I have conjured up in my book.

I find, however, that many people assume that I am writing about myself and, indeed, one or two reviewers treated the book explicitly as autobiography. For me, the writing of this particular book was an act of social responsibility as well as an attempt at an artistic projection. Ironically, however, although my natural pace is that of the "walk," *Invisible Man* has had me running all over the place. Indeed, I was lecturing in North Carolina when your letter arrived—which reminds me that some of the Negro leaders in Greensboro, like the man in Baltimore, are so timid that they are not accepting as fast the new responsibilities of freedom as they might, which of course they rationalize as the sole fault of white people. Fortunately, this is not true of all. Evidently your friend feels, as many Negroes do, that the novel should be an elaborate way of putting the "race's" best foot forward and if left to us the agony of creation would be quite simple. One simply would portray Negro experience and Negro personality as the exact opposite of any stereotype set up by prejudiced whites. My work in attempting to define this particular aspect of personality only makes them afraid because it tries to reveal the extent to which each of us is responsible for his own fate . . .

Sincerely,
Ralph Ellison

James Hubert "Eubie" Blake to Flournoy E. Miller

While Eubie Blake and Flournoy Miller continued to work in the entertainment industry, by the 1950s their fame of the 1920s was a faded memory. In 1952 the final revival of Shuffle Along *closed after just four performances. In the 1970s Blake's career was resurrected when he was celebrated as a surviving ragtime legend, and he made new recordings of many of his classic songs, including "Strange What Love Will Do," which, as this letter notes, he cowrote with Miller.*

Los Angeles City
Oct. 9th 1954

Dear F.E.

    I've just received the three verses of "Strange What Love Will Do." They are all three so to the point and good I don't know which one to set. Boy you're getting to be a real lyricist. Those are the kind of verses people want. Short and to the point. I shall set this this very day. My very best to your family.

    Your friend
       Eubie Blake

P.S. Something will break soon. E.B.

Josephine Baker to Langston Hughes

The singer and dancer Josephine Baker (1906–1975) was an international sensation, known as "La Bakair" in her adopted home of Paris. Born Freda Josephine McDonald in St. Louis, Missouri, to a washerwoman and a vaudeville drummer, Baker made her Broadway debut at the age of fifteen in Shuffle Along. *In 1937 she became a citizen of France and received military honors for her service during World War II performing for the troops and carrying secret messages on her sheet music. She was also a champion for civil rights in the United States, speaking at the 1963 March on Washington and refusing to perform in segregated theaters. Baker died days after opening a critically acclaimed revue that marked her fifty years in show business.*

[Paris, France]
December 23, 1964

Dear dear Langston.

    You were here in Paris. I sent you a telegram when I heard, to the American Embassy to find your address (no answer) but Langston why didn't you come to see me. You were so near to the [illegible] and I did so want to talk to you here about the book I want to write on my life story. I would love to collaborate with you and [James] Baldwin who lives in Paris. Three negroes writing about a Negro Woman's life— then we could get someone from here to write about my life here if not I can do that of course. I am not [a] writer but that may have an interest for the readers knowing I am doing it myself but with you two, he Baldwin the revolutionary side you, the real home side, and I here-side—what do you think—please write at once—your Jos and children.

Merry Xmas and a very very happy New Year—thanks for your Xmas card. I would have preferred you in person to come see us.

Love Jos

Alice Walker to Derrick Bell, Jr.

Alice Walker (b. 1944) is a renowned writer and feminist whose novel The Color Purple *(1982) was awarded the Pulitzer Prize. Born to a sharecropping family in Eatonton, Georgia, Walker attended Spelman College in Atlanta and graduated from Sarah Lawrence College. She worked in voter registration drives in the South during the Civil Rights Movement, and was an editor at* Ms. Magazine. *An article she published in* Ms. *in 1975, "In Search of Zora Neale Hurston," helped generate renewed interest in the life and work of the Harlem Renaissance writer.*

May 20, 1986

Dear Derrick,

I have now read the *Civil Rights Chronicles*.* It is brilliant. Never have I been so involved (or even able to haltingly follow) a legal/moral discussion based on the law and the courts. Truly it is inspired work and I thank you for your persistence in sending it to me.

There have been many days when I haven't warmed to anything in my mailbox. You've had those times, I'm sure. Also, all the world news seems so awful, etc.

We're fine. Robert has jury duty for a month. A too typical case of a shopkeeper (Arab) and innocent by-stander (woman) gunned down by

* A reference to the allegorical stories contained in Derrick Bell's book *And We Are Not Saved* (1987).

brothers who, caught, show little (at least outward) remorse. Depressing. Rebecca is wonderful—doing very progressive video pieces for a young people's program on Channel 4. Last month an anti-nuke piece (really good!) and now a piece on the homeless. She is driving now and has a boyfriend. Next year she'll be a senior.

Occasionally she runs into Douglass [Bell's son.].

I am somewhere close to Geneva's trance.* At least today I am. Writing, of course, but very much in The Silence. The Waiting Upon the Voice. Amazed to feel the pieces fall into place—so many answers. Is this understanding, which feels so much like what I imagined enlightenment to be like, merely a consequence of age—plus experience. Plus the ability to listen to one's self?

The past year has had its stresses. Yet to balance them I've had some really sustaining thoughts about the universe. The reasons of our being. Like Geneva I seem to have reached a different place of existence; so much that might once have had meaning is utterly meaningless to me now. I'd rather watch what the wind does to trees and grass or lie in the sun than listen to any speech, argument or play imaginable.

Derrick, I am already living in eternity.

It is because of the kinship I feel with the spirit of the *Chronicles* that I can tell you.

Meanwhile, I cheer you on. It is always hard for me to think of travel, especially back East, but perhaps our paths will cross. I hope so. Ever drive through Mendocino?

My love to Jewel [Bell's wife] and to you. You are a blessed person.

Alice

William T. Williams to David C. Driskell

William T. Williams (b. 1942), a renowned abstract painter and professor of art at Brooklyn College, was born in Cross Creek, North Carolina, but as a young child moved to New York City where he received his BFA from Pratt Institute and his MFA from Yale University. His work has appeared in museums around the world and is included in numerous collections including the Museum of Modern Art, the Library of Congress, the Whitney Museum of Art, and the Studio Museum in Harlem, which in 1996 awarded him its lifetime achievement award. Williams is the 2006 recipient of the North

* Geneva Crenshaw is Bell's alter ego and heroine in *And We Are Not Saved.*

Carolina Governor's Award. David C. Driskell (b. 1931), born in Eatonton,
Georgia, is an artist, collector, and curator, and is one of the world's leading
authorities on African American art. He is distinguished university profes-
sor emeritus of art at the University of Maryland, College Park, which in
2001 established the David C. Driskell Center for the Study of the Visual
Arts and Culture of African Americans and the African Diaspora. Driskell's
own collection of African American masters toured nationally and was cat-
aloged in Narratives of African American Art and Identity: The David C.
Driskell Collection. *In 2000 President Bill Clinton awarded him the Na-*
tional Humanities Medal. Williams wrote the following letter to Driskell,
who co-curated an exhibit at the California Afro-American Museum.

[New York City]
October 5, 1988

Dear David:

After many efforts here is the statement requested by the California Afro-American Museum.

These works are concerned with memory—memory of place.
I hope they evoke the magic that place holds in our lives. My
memory of place is informed by the specifics of my historic cultural experience as well as by myth and fiction; it is through the
specifics of my personal history that I try to evoke a shared
sense of human place.

The title "Tune for Nila" refers to the way music has been
and is used to transmit cultural information. Humming a tune
long learned in childhood was its beginning. "Double Dare" refers
to the distance I have traveled as an adult. The souvenirs of endless summer childhood pranks, dares and general mischief.

It occurred to me that my memory had become a place rather
than a past event. As such, it contains a rich deposit of materials
that could be used—not to linger—but to illuminate the future.

Speaking of "places," my warmest thanks to you, Thelma [Driskell's
wife] and your family for inviting me to the reception for the participants in the American Visions conference. I left as always with a sense
of family, tradition and excellence.

Sincerely,

William T. Williams

Howardena Pindell to Charles Reeve, editor of Art Papers

Howardena Pindell (b. 1943) was born in Philadelphia, Pennyslvania, and received a BFA from Boston University and an MFA from Yale University. After graduating in 1967 she worked as a curator at the Museum of Modern Art in New York until 1979 when she joined the faculty at the State University of New York at Stony Brook as a professor of drawing and painting. As an artist and academic she has tackled issues of race in society at large and in the art world. She wrote the following letter to the magazine Art Papers in response to an article on the artist Kara Walker (b. 1969). In 1997 Walker, who holds an MFA from the Rhode Island School of Design, received a prestigious MacArthur Fellowship. Since that time her room-size paper silhouettes exploring race, sexuality, and violence on the antebellum plantation have been exhibited in major museums around the world and have sparked controversy in some segments of the African American community. The letter was never published.

May 30, 2002

Dear Charles Reeve:

After reading "A Conversation with Robert Hobbs," in the March [2002] issue of <u>Art Papers</u> concerning Kara Walker's work in the São Paulo Biennale, I sent a letter directly to Hobbs with a copy of my paper concerning negative racial stereotypes. This paper, "Diaspora/Realities/Strategies," appears on the website of a British publication, <u>Paradoxa</u>, and is an expanded version of a paper I delivered at the conference held during the 2nd Johannesburg Biennale in Johannesburg, South Africa. I sent a brief letter to the editor of <u>Art Papers</u> giving the website address. In response, I was asked to write a 500-to-700-word letter because the editor felt my brief letter did not clearly indicate my position relative to the controversy about work exploiting negative racial stereotypes, and some people did not have access to the Web.

I feel that art and exhibitions do not occur in a vacuum. Unlike Hobbs's "detached perspective," I do not feel that the controversy has died down over the use of negative racial stereotypes. It seems that actions of those who are a part of a "power and money" monopoly (who seem to be behind thrusting work forward that uses negative stereotypes of African Americans) has led to more stockholming consciously or unconsciously of those intimidated. (The Stockholm syndrome is a state of mind where a person is overwhelmed with helplessness as in a hijacking or kidnapping—and begins to identify with the oppressor.) I also do not see it as a negative attribute to have lived during the civil rights movement in the 1960s. Older people as well as young people oppose the "power and money" forces behind the pro–negative stereotype movement and their supporters who trivialize any experience that does not look on them favorably. The corporate forces that have stepped in to fill the vacuum after the government/NEA had cut off funding to individual artists favor a view that victims of corporate greed, malfeasance, etc. are to be mocked, ignored and vilified, and their suffering should wither, be dismissed or turned into a subject for amusement. (I feel this is the basis of the sly, snide remark "politically correct," which is so frequently used.)

Hence, I feel that encouraging and rewarding of the use [of] negative racial stereotypes supports negative public policy towards the groups affected. It is also worth noting that this is the second time that an artist who uses negative stereotypes has been selected to represent the United States (Robert Colescott, in the 1997 Venice Biennale, and Kara Walker, in the 2002 São Paulo Biennale). Just as the projection of non-objective and abstract art as the pinnacle of American art was a form of foreign policy used to counteract the social realism of art in communist countries, the projection of negative images of non-white people reflects the indifference to global suffering that increases under corporate globalization. (Two thirds to three quarters of the world lives in abject poverty, and only 9 to 10 percent of the world is white. The United States is 5 percent of the world and consumes 40 percent of the world's resources.) There were several relevant articles in The New York Times shortly after Hobbs's interview was published in Art Papers. One was about the issue of slavery in Brazil. Slavery is rampant in Brazil because people of color are being exploited in Brazil to clear the rain forest in order to meet, for example, North American (specifically the U.S.) demands for mahogany, which is destroying the Amazon's ecosystem. Slavery is not something to be amused by although the supporters of the use of negative racial stereotypes find titillation and amusement in work that exploits negative racial stereotypes of people once or currently enslaved. (See "Brazil's Prized Exports Rely on Slaves and Scorched Land," by Larry Rohter, The New York Times, March 25, 2002, p. A1.) According to Anti-Slavery International, there are 27 million enslaved people worldwide (Guardian Weekly, London, May 30–June 5, 2002, p. 2.)

Hobbs states that Kara Walker unleashes stereotypes on the world, as if she was doing someone a favor or doing something noble. They are already unleashed on the world and many suffer in their wake. On BET TV News (May 13, 2002), a white doctor referred to a recent report on medical care in the U.S. that showed how whites and blacks with the same types of jobs, salaries, and medical insurance got vastly different treatment leading blacks to have more amputations, fewer heart surgeries, and more deaths than their white counterparts. The white physician stated that this is the place where negative stereotypes operate at their worst. An article concerning this also appeared in The New York Times ("Race Gap Seen in Health Care of Equally Insured Patients," by Sheryl Gay Stolberg, March 21, 2002, p. A1.)

I feel that the popularity with whites of negative stereotypes is a combination of restricted gaze and constricted empathy. Children are taught by their parents who to respect and who not to respect . . . who to gaze on favorably and who not to see. I feel that the negative stereotype work is welcomed because the negative image is a reflection of what the child was permitted to see or imagine. A person of color was not seen in a positive way, if seen at all. To have a black person give you those images, as if to say that they agree with your imprinted gaze, makes the work, for whites, hypnotically enticing. One is let off the hook. No need to worry about racism. This person of color appears to agree with the restricted gaze and total lack of empathy.

I feel that there will be more work that is negative because of the conservative times we live in and all the hopelessness both naturally and globally, that vast numbers of people of color face. Negative stereotype work sells very well to the white community. I also feel that there will be more negative assimilation by people of color as they are "stockholmed" and take on the negative traits of those with the power and money, who manipulate national and global economies so fatal to large numbers of people of color. If you want to read more about the global picture, I suggest that you read Noam Chomsky's 9/11, Seven Stories Press (140 Watts Street, New York, New York, www.sevenstories.com).

I encourage the readers to read my paper on the Web as it more thoroughly reveals my position concerning the use of negative racial stereotypes. The Web address is web.ukonline.co.uk/n.paradoxa/pindell.htm.

Howardena Pindell
New York

PART VII

Across the Diaspora

Descendants of Africa, for centuries dispersed by slavery and deliberate immigration, continue to forge bonds across the globe. The first Pan-African Congress, held in Westminister Town Hall in London in 1900, demonstrated the desire of African descendants to mobilize around their common plight in Africa and across the Atlantic.* Marcus Garvey's Universal Negro Improvement Association, established in 1914 in Jamaica, also promoted the idea of black unity the world over. The UNIA, which by 1919 had thirty branches and more than 2 million members, published *The Negro World* newspaper and owned steamships to facilitate the return of African descendants to Africa.† Even before these Pan-African movements, black leaders like John Brown Russwurm (1799–1851), editor and cofounder of *Freedom's Journal*, were involved with the American Colonization Society, established in 1816 to support the emigration of free blacks to Africa. Russwurm eventually emigrated to Liberia to work for the American Colonization Society.‡

In more contemporary times, African American leaders have forged close ties with their African counterparts. W.E.B. Du Bois, Congressman Adam Clayton Powell, Rev. Martin Luther King, Jr., and A. Philip Randolph were among the American leaders who in 1957 traveled to

*The first congress was presided over by Bishop Alexander Walters, head of the African Methodist Episcopal Zion Church in the United States and president of the Afro-American Council.
†Garvey raised $10 million from supporters but was sentenced to prison in 1925 after being convicted for fraud. He was eventually deported to Jamaica, and by 1930 the UNIA had ceased to exist.
‡Russwurm served as colonial secretary in Liberia from 1830 to 1834 and edited the *Liberia Herald*. In 1836 he became the colonial governor. Liberia became an independent nation in 1847.

Ghana to celebrate its independence from Great Britain. A few years later Du Bois would relocate to Ghana, where he spent the final years of his life. In 1990 Rev. Jesse Jackson traveled to South Africa and witnessed the release from prison of the African National Congress leader Nelson Mandela. As the final letters in this part illustrate, relationships across the Diaspora have been sustained by greater access to air travel and the Internet.

Mack Nichols et al. to Rev. Alexander Crummel

Alexander Crummel (1819–1898) was born in New York City and attended the African Free School of New York and Noyes Academy in New Hampshire. In 1839 he graduated from the Oneida Theological Institute and five years later was ordained an Episcopal priest. After spending time in England, Crummel went to the African American colony in Liberia to work as a missionary. He became a leading proponent for the emigration of blacks to Africa, where he spent nearly two decades. He returned to the United States in 1872 and created St. Luke's Episcopal Church in Washington, D.C. He also founded the American Negro Academy in 1897 to promote and publish the scholarship of African American artists and scholars. W.E.B. Du Bois, who was a member of the academy, paid homage to Crummel in his book The Souls of Black Folk. *Crummel received this letter from an organization of freedmen who wished to emigrate to Liberia.*

Lynchburg, Va.
October 4, 1865

Rev. Alexander Crummel:

We['re] the members of a society known as the African Emigration Society we organized in Lynchburg, Va. for the purpose of going to Liberia and we have heard that you['re] in the United States and we desire you to meet us at the City of Washington. We have heard of your fame as a scholar and minister of the gospel and we learnt from Mr. Coppinger the corresponding Secretary of the American Colonization Society that you would accompany us on our voyage to Liberia on the 1st of November next. Mack Nichols, the presiding officer of our society is to attend business preparatory to our departure and we would like you to see him there if you cannot see us he will be there for we will be happy of your company with us and hope you will not fail to do so.

Your unknown friends

Mack Nichols
John J. Garland
Isam Bourne
Charles Lewis
Charles R. Loving
Geo. U. Roll
Wm. Eubanks
Addison Banks

We with our families will be over one hundred and fifty in number 150 emigrants.

George T. Downing to Alexander Crummel

George T. Downing (1819–1903), an abolitionist, civil rights activist, and successful Rhode Island businessman, wrote this letter to Alexander Crummel (1819–1898), the scholar, Episcopalian minister, and missionary who spent twenty years in Liberia and Sierra Leone, and was also one of the founders of the American Negro Academy.

May 18, 1897

My old friend, I am somewhat concerned about your going abroad, may it be for the last, may your health be improved, may you return to us invigorated, may your wife be benefited. I know that you will necessarily be engaged, but drop me a line or two before you go, I send you— God bless you. God preserve you, and should we not meet on earth again may we meet in a future which we shall find that we are in closer communion with our Heavenly father.

Affectionately,

George T. Downing

Alexander Crummel to John W. Cromwell

John W. Cromwell (1846–1927) was born into slavery in Portsmouth, Virginia, and upon emancipation moved to Philadelphia. He graduated from

Howard University Law School and became the first African American to practice law for the Interstate Commerce Commission. As president of Bethel Library and Historical Association in Washington, D.C., Cromwell promoted an interest in African American history and inspired the founding by Carter G. Woodson of the Association for the Study of Negro Life and History, of which Cromwell was secretary. He received this letter from Alexander Crummel during an 1897 trip to England, when Crummel met with two law students, Henry Sylvester Williams of Trinidad and T. J. Campbell of Sierra Leone, who had recently formed the African Association, the forerunner of the 1900 Pan-African Congress.

Colville Gardens,
Bayswater England
June 15, 1897

Dear Mr. Cromwell,

I have been endeavoring several days to scratch the opportunity to write you a letter; but Mrs. Crummel's illness has prevented me. I am glad to say that after a somewhat severe trial, she is now rapidly recovering.

We had a very pleasant passage across the ocean liner . . . in the comforts and companionship of our fellow passengers [. . .]

We landed at Liverpool on the 20th May, and came up at once to London, where we have recd a right cordial welcome from old friends. We shall sojourn here but a brief period, as we purpose the acceptance of invitations of a few acquaintances in the provinces. Of course we shall abide long enough in London to see, if possible, the magnificent pageant of the Queens Jubilee, which takes place on the 23rd.

Not a few Americans [of the African contingent] are here. One of my first finds was Paul Dunbar who [. . .] is now domiciling in the boarding house with me. Another is Miss Hallie Q. Brown, but I have not seen her. Sidney Woodward, the great tenor, called and spent a night [. . .] and breakfasted with us. And still another is Mr. Braithwaite, who comes from the South.

One of the surprises in this line was G. T. Downing who has been living here the last four years married to a white girl of Massachusetts.* She recognized me at once for some years ago [. . .] I went to

*George T. Downing was a classmate of Crummel at the African Free School in New York City. Downing became a prominent Newport, Rhode Island, entrepreneur who owned and operated a luxury hotel and catering business. He was also a champion of civil rights.

Wheaton College and addressed the young ladies and she was then a girl student there.

Today I had a long interview with Prof. Joseph, former of St. Augustine's College, Raleigh, N.C. We talked much about the "Academy." The organization gives him great delight. He looks upon its organization as giving the promise of great things, not only for U.S.A. but for the West Indies likewise. He has promised us a contribution for the annual. His topic will be substantially this—I can't find the exact wording—"Grounds for self appreciation of the Negro."*

Paul Dunbar (an academy member) is as enthusiastic an academician as any of its members and he will contribute a poem.

Dunbar is anxious to devote himself to literature as his life work. We have had long conversations upon the subject and I find him much perplexed as to plans for working out his purpose.

I have made the following suggestion to him, and I want you to take it into consideration and to lend me your views.

I propose as follows:—

1. His residence in Washington, which by the way is his great desire.
2. The establishment of a monthly magazine [. . .] for purely Negro literature, i.e., essays, reviews, poems, sales, & c.
3. That a subscription be started among our literary men—professional men, doctors, lawyers, clergymen, school teachers & etc., at five or ten dollars each; to secure at least 100 subscribers for annual payments & thus raising annually $500 or $1000 for the support of the magazine.
4. The sending out an agent to secure at the least 100 subscribers in each of the large cities of Washington, Balt., Phila., New York, Wilmington, Del., Richmond, Chicago; Charleston, S.C., New Orleans. We have not a small class of men and women [. . .] devoted to letters—but they have no channel of utterance. So great is the talent among the whites that it leaves the smallest opportunity for the talent of coloured men and women. A monthly magazine, purely or entirely literary, would command very wide patronage from especially our own people, to no small degree for the whites.

*The American Negro Academy published twenty-two occasional papers between 1897 and 1928. Authors included W.E.B. Du Bois, Arthur Schomburg, Cromwell, and John Hope, but none were written by a Joseph.

5. Joined to this should be an agency in all the coloured colleges, or colleges to which coloured men resort, giving constant reports of the efforts and genius of our youth.

Please consult some 4 or 5 of your literary coadjutors in Washington & give me your conclusions. Dunbar is exceedingly anxious to enter Washington early in the autumn.*

I would suggest much quietness [. . .] Anything like firecrackers or pop guns ought be avoided. Publicity should be avoided likewise. If a few men conclude that a subscription to raise 500, 1,000 dollars is a wise and desirable thing, I am ready with my subscription for either five or ten dollars. The battle in America is to be carried on in the world of minds; & it will be a shameful thing if the educated & cultivated minds of our people lack the moral energy to enter upon that battle. My impression is that a movement of the kind will be hailed in large white circles in every part of the land with support & acclamation.

If you hear of any publication of coloured men . . . advise me of the same. [. . .] Mrs. Crummel's best regards,

I am very truly yrs.
Alex Crummel

John R. Archer to John Edward Bruce

John R. Archer (1863–1932) was born in Liverpool, England. His father, a ship steward, was from Barbados and his mother from Ireland. In the 1890s he became politically active in the poor and overcrowded Battersea section of London. He attended the 1900 Pan-African Conference. In November 1913, Archer made history when he was elected mayor of Battersea. In this letter, he responds to the journalist John Bruce's letter of congratulations.

London, SW.
Town Hall Battersea, S.W.
January 17, 1914

Dear Mr. Bruce,

I feel especially attracted to you as you were the first coloured man in America to notice my elevation and to send me congratulations thereon.

*Paul Laurence Dunbar indeed moved to Washington, D.C., that year and took a job in the reading room at the Library of Congress, where he worked for a year. The magazine Crummel proposed was never launched.

You must not think that I have forgotten my promise to forward you my photograph for your collection. I have had a strenuous and arduous time since my Election. Sorrow has come to me, as a Member of the Council, and in my own home. It was my painful duty to attend on Christmas Eve at the funeral of one of the Members of my Party—late President of the Engineers' Society of this Borough and also a Member of the Council. And I was specially grieved at this man's death because he was one of the men who I thought would be against me. This man came to the Party Meeting a sick man, and those who favoured me had put him down as being against me and in favour of the Secretary of our Party who had been nominated. But he voted for me, and was taken ill in the room. I can see him now as he was leaving the Committee Room—he walked over to me, took my hand in both of his and congratulated me upon being the Nominee to go to the Council. I was the last of the Councillors that he shook hands with and spoke to in that Chamber. He left us, alas, to return no more and on Christmas Eve, as I have said he was laid to rest, leaving a widow and nine children very poorly off. Little did I dream that I should so soon again attend at a funeral, and of one who was most dearer and nearer to me! You have no doubt heard, ere this, of the death of the Honourable Jane Rose Roberts, at the ripe old age of 95. She was as you are doubtless aware, the widow of the first President of Liberia, J. J. Roberts. She was the last of those original emigrants who formed the Liberian Republic. For many years she has been with us here and it was our pleasant duty to make her last days happy. She was very dear to us, and we feel her loss very acutely. She passed peacefully away on Friday last and was buried yesterday. Originally, it was her strong desire to be sent to Liberia and I was to escort her body there, but of late years, she wished to be buried in England. We acceded to her request and she has been laid away in a very beautiful spot in a Cemetery that is only a tram-ride from our residence. In due course, a stone will be erected and all those members of the Race who visit this capital, will be able to see the last resting place of one who did honour to her Race, beloved by all who came in contact with her. A noble spirit, a generous benefactor to all in distress—she has gone to that bourn from whence no traveler returns. You can, therefore, understand how troubled in mind I have been, and have had the heart to do only that which my official duties demand. May the peace that passeth all understanding be with her, is our earnest prayer.

I note in your letter of the 7th December, that you ask if you may offer my name as a member of your Historical Society. If this does not entail a very heavy subscription, I should be only too delighted. I am unfortunately not possessed of much of this world's goods, and my elevation to the office of Mayor is making heavy inroads upon my slender purse. There is no salary attached to the Office as I understand is the case in America. I have merely been given the sum of 150 pounds towards the expenses of my official year, and when I tell you that some of the Mayors in London spend that amount in one night on a Reception, you will at once see that I have to be very careful. I am not in a position to entertain as other Mayors do, and my Party were fully aware of this when they nominated me, and the death of dear old Granny will make a great difference to me.

I have to thank you very heartily for your kindness in sending me your latest book, which will be of great interest and source of education to me. I have also received from Dr. Martin, your Vice-President, the History of Williams' that I have for so many years longed for,* and my thanks are due to you and Dr. Martin. I am placed in a quandary by the action of Dr. Martin, as of course it was my wish to purchase the books. I can assure you that I had no notion that the Doctor would send the books without charge otherwise I would not have mentioned it to you at all. I am of an independent nature and would have preferred to have purchased the volumes. But the Doctor wrote me so kindly and put it in such a way that I could hardly refuse the offer. I am sending him in due course enlargements of myself and the Mayoress in return.

I am still receiving letters of congratulation, and among those I prize most, I may mention those I have received from you and Members of your Society, from Judge Terrell, R. S. Abbott, Editor of the "Chicago Defender"; Miss Hallie Q. Brown of Wilberforce University; J. P. Bennett, Newspaper Correspondent of Birmingham, Alabama; Joseph Garner, Y.M.C.A. Pittsburgh; Mrs. Edith M. Davis, of Columbus, Ohio; Caesar A.A.P. Taylor, Author of "The Conflict and Com-

---

*The Rev. Dr. Charles D. Martin (1873–1942) was born in St. Kitts, British West Indies, and served as pastor of Beth-Tphilah Moravian Church in Harlem, New York, for about three decades until his death. He was the first African American minister of the Moravian Church in the United States when he was ordained in 1912. Martin was an avid book collector who was vice president of the Negro Society for Historical Research, founded in 1911 by John E. Bruce and Arthur A. Schomburg.

mingling of the Races," who has kindly sent me his book; and J. W. Cromwell, Secretary of the American Negro Academy.

The reading of these letters and books which you and Mr. Taylor have sent me, inspire me with great hope and incentive to uphold the dignity of our Race, who I feel sure will ultimately survive the petty prejudices of a race who, for 250 years, have subordinated them and kept them out of their just rights. But, as a minister said, the other Sunday [. . .]:—"Your Race has survived the effects of slavery, and it is useless to attempt to keep them down." This is quite true, and although the coloured Race of America were only liberated in 1865, you have risen since then and are now taking part in the administration of your country, by holding the highest positions of trust in the land of your birth. It took England with all its boasted civilization, over a thousand years to produce a Shakespeare; Scotland, its Bobbie Burns; Ireland, its Daniel O'Connell, and Wales, its Lloyd George, and it is only logical to say that men like [U.S. Senator Benjamin] Tillman, [Mississippi Governor James] Vardaman, [Thomas] Dixon, [South Carolina Governor Coleman] Blease, and others of that kidney, should leave it to their descendants when they have seen a thousand years of Negro liberty and education, before they can criticize the Negro's ability to rise to the standard of the Caucasian.* If not, they place their mental capacity upon a very low level if they expect the Negro in 50 years to reach such a standard of morality, civilization and education that it has taken them more than a thousand years to attain.

I do not know whether you observed the significance of my appointment at this period. I confess that I had no knowledge of what has come to me from America. My keen desire to attain this position this year was owing partly to the fact of the Anglo-American Exhibition that is to be opened this year at "The White City" in London here. I knew that it would be food for thought for those of the American whites when they arrive here, to find that a Metropolitan Borough of London permitted a man of colour to be its Chief Magistrate, otherwise I do not think that I would have undertaken the Office. Now I have had sent to me a Calendar—"What Cheer Dedicated to our 50th Anniversary of Freedom. Factors in our Progress." It is a picture Calendar, with

*Archer lists the names of some of the era's most ardent racists and segregationists. All, with the exception of Thomas Dixon, whose books celebrated the Ku Klux Klan, were elected officials.

a coloured child in the centre—"Our Hope," and then shows magnificent buildings, Universities, Churches and Hospital, and also gives comparative information of the first 50 years of our freedom from American slavery. This Calendar hangs up in my private Office under photographs of Members of our Race—Americans and others. You can, therefore, imagine my pride that during the 50th anniversary I am the Mayor of Battersea. No other year would have been as suitable as this, and I am more than repaid, if my elevation will advance the cause of our People thorough the world.

With very kind regards to yourself and the welfare of your Society.
Believe me to be,
Yours very sincerely,
    J. R. Archer, Jr.
    Mayor of Battersea

James Emman Kwegyir Aggrey to Arthur A. Schomburg

In the following letter to the bibliophile and librarian Arthur A. Schomburg, James E. K. Aggrey (1875–1927) shares his effort to introduce the work of Schomburg and other New York scholar-activists to fellow citizens in the Gold Coast of Africa, which is present-day Ghana.

Salisbury, North Carolina
May 28, 1918

My dear Mr. Schomburg:

Mighty glad to hear from you.

This is a very peculiar country—full duplicity and sham. It is always so refreshing to think of people like you, Mr. [John] Bruce and Dr. Martin.

I am trying to give up most of my annoying part of work here—most exacting, expensive and least appreciated—so I can treat my friends decently by writing them more regularly. I will explain when I see you in New York in July or August.

Your letter was so refreshing. This is to inform you that already I have written two very comprehensive letters to West Africa since I heard from you and Mr. Bruce. I did write soon after I received Mr. Bruce's letter asking for information. I wrote to the [unclear] Shipping Commission Agency at Axim, and to Mr. J. P. Brown at Cape Coast quoting at length Mr. Bruce's letter.

Since the two letters came from you and Mr. Bruce I have written each of the above a fourteen-page letter, quoting in each Mr. Bruce's letter and your letter at length.

Should I hear any time soon from Africa I shall lose no time in forwarding the information to you. In my letter I have introduced you and Mr. Bruce to the folk at home—told them who you are, your loyalty to the race, your love for its advancement and your self-sacrificing endeavors to have it attain its place in the sun in such a [manner] as to be able to play its part in the frame of world civilization and universal progress. I told them you are Africans indeed in whom there is no guile etc. etc. etc.

Your letters are inspiring and I am pushing them for all they are worth. I am trying to assemble the business geniuses there so we can do some real large business and thus bring to our fatherland economic liberty.

Mrs. Aggrey joins me in kindest regards to you and yours.

Sincerely yours,

J. E. Kwegyir Aggrey

James Emman Kwegyir Aggrey to John Edward Bruce

James E.K. Aggrey, the American-trained African educator and cofounder of Achimota College in British colonial Ghana, wrote this letter to John Bruce, whom he held in high regard as a Pan-African leader.

Phelps Stokes Fund
New York
June 28, 1922

Dear Daddie Bruce:—

I was certainly glad to hear from you upon my arrival from Williams College, Williamstown, Mass. I can never forget you. Your loyalty to the race is genuine. I know it. I have known it all the while, and we who have associated with you for at least eight years hope to carry on the good work which lies so close to your heart.

I was kept very busy while in Canada. I spoke once in Montreal, six homes in Toronto, six homes in Brantford the birthplace of Bell's telephone invention, twice in Maxwell, and twice in [. . .] Canada in God's country. It is astir for Africa as never before and God is speeding the day. Everywhere I speak the Lord grants me utterance. Dad, this fusion on behalf of my country and people of African descent lies heavily upon my heart—I make it my daily prayer. I fast sometimes over it. And I never speak anywhere at anytime without previous earnest prayers asking God to give me the right utterance, as it is His own work.

You have always worked for cooperation. You have used your pen and brain to make many a Negro and many a white man, and you have proven that some of both—when of the best type can do wonders in a short while. While in Canada I had many occasions to thank God. One wealthy white minister who heard me went home and told his wife that my appeal went home direct to him. I can talk to you in confidence. His salary is way in the thousands but he told me a week afterwards he does not need that salary. He wants to give up pastoring in a year or two. He has pastored City Temple in London, has spoken in some of America's leading churches. He makes quite much as pastor in Canada. He wants to make a tour through Africa at his expense (he inherited largely) and check up some of the things I had been saying, and [. . .] he wants to show up Great Britain and the American continent including Canada for a united effort to bring about the speedy evangelization and civilization of Africa. A retired wealthy bachelor [. . .] also told me he intends going to Africa for the same purpose. And one man who gives $500 a year toward African missions told me after he heard me that he was going to do better. [. . .]

In Toronto I spoke besides to A.M.E. Church, the only colored church there, in four of the leading churches . . . Already they have sent three letters from the Canada Congregational Church asking that I may be permitted to return in October for fifteen days to go to Ottawa, Hamilton and other strategic points. The Congregational, Methodist and Presbyterian Churches are looking forward to a union in a few years. When I get a chance to tell you of the plans they have for Africa your eyes will sparkle. They spoke to Dr. [Thomas Jesse] Jones, Dr. [Anson] Stokes and Prof. [Franklin] Giddings.* They have in mind a college, which will form into a university to serve some ten million of my people in Angola and nearby territories. They are only going to send missionaries of the highest and best type. They have four there now—three white and one colored. All McGill University men:

---

*Franklin Henry Giddings (1855–1931) became the first full professor of sociology when he joined the faculty of Columbia University in 1894. Giddings applied Herbert Spencer's theories of evolution to race. He worked with Thomas Jesse Jones, the education director at the Phelps-Stokes Fund.

The three whites were each highly trained. O Dad, I just can't tell it in writing. Wait until you get back.

And this week I received invitations to speak at Toronto University in December when from six to eight hundred delegates from all the universities and colleges of Canada will assemble there in a World Student Movement. I am to speak for Africa and the Africans. I have had some very startling things, but I know you can not now say much about me, as your paper may not permit you. But I know your heart, Dad and I want you to pray for me that I may not fail my people. You may not have the permission to say much about me in your paper, but Dad, I want to report to you time and again, so as to cheer your heart, and to show you that God is more ready for us than we are ourselves, that Christiandom means to redeem Africa in a generation, and that your son Aggrey shall keep true to the ideal of helping his country through arousing Christians of all races to combine in a grand cooperative movement to raise Africa.* I wish I could convince my people that co-operation of all the best of all races were the best method of helping God's Kingdom.

I am praying that you will enjoy your vacation to the fullest extent that you may return fully benefited and that I will soon have time to talk long with you. Good luck.

Yours,

Aggrey

J. E. Casely Hayford to John Edward Bruce

J. E. Casely Hayford (1866–1930) was a Pan-Africanist journalist, lawyer, and educator. Born in the British Gold Coast colony of Cape Coast, now Ghana, he was educated in London and returned to West Africa to practice law. He was one of the cofounders of the Mfantsipim School and edited several newspapers, including the Gold Coast Leader. *John Bruce wrote his column for the* New York Age *under the pen name Bruce Grit.*

---

*By 1922 Bruce had written for many newspapers, including *The African Times & Orient Review* of London. In 1920 he became a regular writer for *The Negro World*, the publication of Marcus Garvey's Universal Negro Improvement Association. The weekly paper had a global circulation and was, for a time, the most popular black newspaper in the United States.

Gold Coast
November 24, 1923

My dear friend Bruce Grit,

I have two of your valuable letters to acknowledge, first that of September 20th and secondly that of October 13th, for both of which I thank you very much.

To begin with I am so pleased that you appear to be benefiting by the treatment you are receiving and lovers of our race and of your good self must pray that God in mercy may spare you for many a long day to complete the great task that you in common with others have taken up in the cause of race up-lift. Sometimes one's fear is that one's task may be left uncompleted; but, surely, if the work is the Master's, He will see to it right enough. So, we can only work and wait.

I can well recall the tremendous progress the race has made all round since I first had the honour and the pleasure of making your friendship through our mutual friend, the late lamented Dr. Blyden.* Already our race from the four corners of the earth has joined hands and the signal is clear as also the demand. Again, therefore, I say we can only work and wait.

I am writing to the several persons you have kindly introduced me, and as soon as we start the new series of the "Leader" I shall send you 50 copies regularly to see what you can do with them.

I do not get the "Negro World" regularly. When I see it it is much too late and I like to keep abreast of what is going on. Can you kindly make sure and send me a copy each week well wrapped up to my Seccondee address?

I am putting on our exchange the publications recommended.

With every good wish,

Yours sincerely,

Casely Hayford

W.E.B. Du Bois to Liberian President Honorable Charles Dunbar Burgess King

The scholar and activist W.E.B. Du Bois wrote the following letter to Liberian president C.D.B. King (1875–1961). Born in Monrovia, King was president

---

*Edward Wilmont Blyden (1832–1912) was born in St. Thomas in the Virgin Islands but in 1851 emigrated to Liberia, where he was an educator, statesman, journalist, and Pan-African activist.

of Liberia from 1920 to 1930. His 1927 reelection was marked by charges of flagrant voter fraud by his party, and his opponent, Thomas Faulkner, who accused members of his party of engaging in slavery. The allegations were supported by a League of Nations report that implicated Vice President Allen Yancy, who, with King, resigned in 1930.

Monrovia, Liberia
January 21, 1924

Your Excellency:

On leaving Liberia I want to lay before you certain considerations of mine, as to the economic development of Liberia.

First: I believe that Liberia must have immediately at least fifty and preferably one hundred miles of railway from Monrovia up the St. Paul as far as the plateau. Eventually, a branch should run southwest to Cape Palmas.

Secondly: I believe Liberia should have a sound Bank and that this must be under Negro control.

Thirdly: I believe Liberia needs the aid of American Negro capital and of colored technical experts to help Liberians in the development of agriculture, industry and commerce.

To attain these things, I suggest, first, that Liberia approach New York Bankers with a definite proposition of railroad building, and that the suggestion be made that these Bankers finance the building of the railroad, on condition that the revenues of such a road, over and above the necessary expenses of economical upkeep, be used to repay the expense of building and the necessary interest.

Secondly: Liberia should approach the soundest of the various colored Bankers of America, with a proposal that they form under the strict laws of the New York State, and in the city of New York, a strong financial institution, to act as a National Banking and Trust Company. That this institution establish in Liberia under such conditions as seem equitable a branch which should become the fiscal agent of the Government and the depository of its funds.

Thirdly: That there should be formed in Liberia and in America an International Corporation of colored men for handling Liberian products, and for furnishing Liberia a regular stream of technically trained colored farmers, mechanics and merchants of high character and efficiency, covering a period of twenty-five years or more, with periodic recruiting, sanitary aids, industrial surveys and systematic study of resources and markets.

I would be glad to have from you Sir, either before or after I leave Liberia, your own opinion and the opinion of your advisers on these matters, and any official communication with which you would care to entrust me. I am now expecting to leave Monrovia, Tuesday, January 22, and shall do myself the honor of calling upon you before embarkation.

I am, Very sincerely Yours,
W.E.B. Du Bois

Marcus Garvey to Negroes of the World

Marcus Garvey (1887–1940) was born in Jamaica, West Indies, to Marcus Garvey, Sr., a mason, and Sarah Jane Richards, a domestic worker and farmer. In 1914, while still in Jamaica, he founded the Universal Negro Improvement Association to unite people of African descent the world over. He opened a chapter in Harlem in 1917, and the next year he began publishing The Negro World, *which became the most widely circulated black newspaper in the country. By 1919 his organization had more than 2 million members across the African Diaspora. Garvey also launched the Black Star Line to return people of African descent to Africa. In 1925 he was sentenced to five years in prison for mail fraud. President Calvin Coolidge commuted his sentence in 1927, and Garvey was deported to Jamaica. He spent the last five years of his life in London. This letter, which was published in his newspaper, was the first message he wrote from prison to his supporters.*

Atlanta Prison
February 10, 1925

Fellow Men of the Negro Race, Greeting:

I am delighted to inform you, that your humble servant is as happy in suffering for you and our cause as is possible under the circumstances of being viciously outraged by a group of plotters who have connived to do their worst to humiliate you through me, in the fight for real emancipation and African Redemption.

I do trust that you have given no credence to the vicious lies of white and enemy newspapers and those who have spoken in reference to my surrender. The liars plotted in every way to make it appear that I was not willing to surrender to the court. My attorney advised me that no mandate would have been handed down for ten or fourteen days, and is the custom of the courts, and that would have given me time to keep speaking engagements I had in Detroit, Cincinnati and Cleveland. I hadn't left the city for ten hours when the liars flashed the news that I was a fugitive. That was good news to circulate all over the world to demoralize the millions of Negroes in America, Africa, Asia, the West Indies and Central America, but the idiots ought to know by now that they can't fool all the Negroes at the same time.

I do not want at this time to write anything that would make it difficult for you to meet the opposition of the enemy without my assistance. Suffice to it say that the history of the outrage shall form a splendid chapter in the history of Africa redeemed, when black men will no longer be under the heels of others, but have a civilization and country of their own.

The whole affair is a disgrace, and the whole black world knows it. We shall not forget. Our day may be fifty, a hundred or two hundred years ahead, but let us watch, work and pray, for the civilization of injustice is bound to crumble and bring destruction down upon the heads of the unjust.

The idiots thought that they could humiliate me personally, but in that they are mistaken. The minutes of suffering are counted, and when God and Africa come back and measure out retribution these minutes may multiply by thousands for the sinners. Our Arab and Riffian* friends will be ever vigilant, as the rest of Africa and ourselves shall be. Be assured that I planted well the seed of Negro or black nationalism which cannot be destroyed even by the foul play that has been meted out to me.

Continue to pray for me and I shall ever be true to my trust. I want you, the black peoples of the world, to know that <u>W.E.B. Du Bois</u> and that vicious Negro-hating organization known as the Association for the Advancement of "Colored" People are the greatest enemies the black people have in the world. I have so much to do in the few minutes at my disposal that I cannot write exhaustively on this or any other matter, but be warned against these two enemies. Don't allow them to fool you with fine sounding press releases, speeches and books; they are the vipers who have planned with others the extinction of the "black"

*A Berber tribe in Morocco.

race. My work is just begun, and when the history of my suffering is complete, then future generations of Negroes will have in their hands the guide by which they shall know the "sins" of the twentieth century. I, and I know you, too, believe in time, and we shall wait patiently for two hundred years, if need be, to face our enemies through our posterity.

You will cheer me much if you will now do even more for the organization than when I was among you. Hold up the hands of those who are carrying on. Help them to make good, so that the work may continue to spread from pole to pole.

I am also making a last minute appeal for support to the Black Cross Navigation and Trading Company. Please send in and make your loans so as to enable the directors to successfully carry on the work.

All I have I have given to you. I have sacrificed my home and my loving wife for you. I entrust her to your charge, to protect and defend her in my absence. She is the bravest little woman I know. She has suffered and sacrificed with me for you; therefore, please do not desert her at this dismal hour, when she stands alone. I have left her penniless and helpless to face the world, because I gave you all, but her courage is great, and I know she will hold up for you and me.

After my enemies are satisfied, in life or death I shall come back to you to serve even as I have served before. In life I shall be the same; in death I shall be a terror to the foes of Negro liberty. If death has power, then count on me in death to be the real Marcus Garvey I would like to be. If I may come in an earthquake, or a cyclone, or plague, or pestilence, or as God would have me, then be assured that I shall never desert you and make your enemies triumph over you. Would I not go to hell a million times for you? Would I not like Macbeth's ghost, walk the earth forever for you? Would I not lose the whole world and eternity for you? Would I not cry forever before the footstool of the Lord Omnipotent for you? Would I not die a million deaths for you? Then, why be sad? Cheer up, and be assured that if it takes a million years the sins of our enemies shall visit the millionth generation of these that hinder and oppress us.

Remember that I have sworn by you and my God to serve to the end of all time, the wreck of matter and the crash of worlds. The enemies think that I am defeated. Did the Germans defeat the French in 1870? Did Napoleon really conquer Europe? If so, then I am defeated, but I tell you the world shall hear from my principles even two thousand years hence. I am willing to wait on time for my satisfaction and the retribution of my enemies. Observe my enemies and their children and posterity, and one day you shall see retribution settling around them.

If I die in Atlanta my work shall then only begin, but I shall live, in the physical or spiritual to see the day of Africa's glory. When I am dead wrap the mantle of the Red, Black and Green around me, for in the new life I shall rise with God's grace and blessing to lead the millions up the heights of triumph with the colors that you well know. Look for me in the whirlwind or the storm, look for me all around you, for, with God's grace, I shall come and bring with me countless millions of black slaves who have died in America and the West Indies and the millions in Africa to aid you in the fight for Liberty, Freedom and Life.

The civilization of today is gone drunk and crazy with its power and by such it seeks through injustice, fraud and lies to crush the unfortunate. But if I am apparently crushed by the system of influence and misdirected power, my cause shall rise again to plague the conscience of the corrupt. For this I am satisfied, and for you, I repeat, I am glad to suffer and even die. Again, I say, cheer up, for better days are ahead. I shall write the history that will inspire the millions that are coming and leave the posterity of our enemies to reckon with the hosts for the deeds of their fathers.

With God's dearest blessings, I leave you for awhile.

Marcus Garvey

W.E.B. Du Bois to Harvey S. Firestone

In 1926 the Firestone Company was granted 1 million acres in Liberia for the production of rubber in exchange for U.S. military protection. The concession, which was supported by the U.S. State Department, was widely condemned by black leaders, who maintained it would turn the small nation into a Firestone colony. W.E.B. Du Bois wrote this letter to the president of Firestone a year before the controversial concession was made.

October 26, 1925

My dear Sir:

Early in the year 1924 I was in Liberia as special representative of the President of the United States at the inauguration of President King with the rank of Minister Plenipotentiary and Envoy Extraordinary. During that time I accompanied the resident minister, Solomon Porter Hood, and the rubber expert of the Firestone Company to look over the rubber forest with a view to deciding whether it would be worthwhile for the Firestone Company to invest in Liberia.

Since that time I have learned that arrangements have been made by the Firestone Plantations Company for raising rubber on a large scale in Liberia and making other industrial improvements. I am very much interested in this development because I have long followed the history of Liberia. I write to bring certain considerations to your attention.

It would be very easy for a great industry properly capitalized to enter Liberia and repeat there the same kind of industrial history which one finds in the Belgium, Portuguese and English colonies and to some extent in the French. There would be no doubt that such an enterprise could certainly for a time make money. But on the other hand with the awakening that is taking place in Africa and with the long struggle that the Liberians have made for independence and freedom, I do not think this method would be nearly as profitable in the long run as another method which I am venturing to bring to your attention and which I am sure would work.

I have seen parts of British and French colonial Africa and have come in close contact with those who know colonial conditions in other parts of Africa. In all these cases with the exception of the French, the procedure has been to enter the black country with an entirely white personnel; to use the natives as laborers with the lowest wage and to use imported whites as the personnel in control. This is, of course, justified by the fact that the natives are not acquainted with the modern industrial processes or industrial organization and that white persons who know them must be imported if the work is to be properly done. But the difficulty comes in the type of person who exercises this control. Usually Americans send whites used to "handling" colored labor. These get results by cruelty and brow-beating alternating with pandering to drunkenness, gambling and prostitution among the blacks. Usually no attempt is made to train the blacks for the higher positions and the result is a system of caste and of oppression and misrepresentation to the outside world leading to intense dissatisfaction on the part of the colored people. In French colonies there is the same system, mitigated only in that it is possible for black men to enter the ruling caste either through the civil service or in business and while comparatively few do this still there is the opening.

What I propose to you is that in this experiment in Liberia you give from the beginning unusual attention to the ruling industrial personnel who will conduct your venture. Of course you are in Liberia primarily to raise cheap rubber and not to reform the world; but I assume that if in raising rubber you could also in other ways help the world and particularly the black world forward a step, you would not be averse.

I suggest therefore that you choose your governing industrial personnel from the following groups:

1. White American rubber experts
2. Educated and trained Liberians
3. Colored Americans of education and experience

I am aware that this will bring protests; the white experts will not want colored colleagues and will not believe that capable ones can be found. They will want in Liberia to be like their fellows in neighboring English and French colonies, a close racial caste with all "niggers" beneath them.

If now this caste is based on fact, i.e. if it is impossible to put colored men in authority or find colored experts or train them, then there is no help for the resultant situation. But this is not entirely true. Certain it is that there are no colored men in Liberia or America who could completely man and conduct the business of a rubber plantation. But there are many who could gradually learn the profession if given the proper opportunity.

I suggest therefore that from the very beginning you seek to avoid a strict color line in your business. For instance, you will have to have a hospital and nurses. Why not take American Negroes for this work? They have proven themselves skilled in medicine and nursing, they would do a good job. Just as soon as there were properly trained colored nurses and physicians in Liberia they should, of course, be used.

But I suggest further that you do not stop there; that in addition you make it a point to give to educated black men, both African and American, a chance to work up in your industrial system. We have in America well trained young men who could do this. None of them know the rubber business. They could not expect to begin at the top, but they could begin at the bottom if allowed a chance for promotion. You would, of course, in any scheme of this kind meet at first a good deal of opposition from your white personnel, but if the proper Negroes were selected they would in the end prove their efficiency and gain the confidence of their white fellow workers. This is not merely a matter of philanthropy, it is an excellent policy. The Liberians have been trained in freedom. They are called bumptious and given a bad name by their English and French neighbors but this is merely because they have successfully resisted the encroachment of whites and have tried to rule their own land. When now a great industry dominated by white people comes into their country they are going to be sensitive. They are going to make unnecessary trouble unless they are satisfied from the first that they are going to be treated as men, without any imported color line. They themselves, because of lack of educational facilities cannot furnish much help in the higher parts of your organization, but they can furnish some persons and you can secure Negroes of the highest intelligence and training in the United States. There again you may meet some opposition from the Liberians themselves, but not much if the American Negroes prove themselves and act with discretion and sympathy toward the Liberians.

I believe that in this way you can inaugurate one of the greatest and far reaching reforms in the relations between white industrial countries like America and black, partly developed countries like Liberia if it can once be proven that industry can do the same thing in a black country like Liberia that it does in a white country like Australia: that is, invade it, reform it and uplift it by incorporating the native born into the imported industry and thus make the industry a part of the country. Only in this way can the relations between Europe and America on the one hand and Africa and Asia on the other hand be transformed and led toward mutual dependence and prosperity. If, on the other hand, you send to Africa and put in authority in your organization men who know about rubber but do not know about the aspirations of modern colored men and do not care about anything except the profit of the investment, then I do not doubt but what you may for many years carry on a successful enterprise; but in the long run, if the Negro develops as I think he is going to develop and if colored countries develop, then you and your enterprise are going to suffer just as white European enterprises are beginning to suffer in their relations with Africa and Asia.

I trust you will pardon my temerity in bringing this matter to your notice. My only excuse is my great interest in the development of the Negro race. I hope that you will perhaps let me further develop this plan if you are interested in it. I am, sir,

Very respectfully yours,

W.E.B. Du Bois

Louis-Marie Dantès Bellegarde to Arthur A. Schomburg

Louis-Marie Dantès Bellegarde (1877–1966) was a renowned philosopher and statesman who served as Haiti's ambassador to the United States, the Vatican, and the United Nations. In 1926 Du Bois dubbed him "spokesman of the Negroes of the world." He wrote this letter to Harlem bibliophile Arthur Schomburg.

Port-au-Prince
March 11, 1932

Cher Monsieur Schomburg,

J'ai reçu avec un très grand plaisir votre lettre du 9 Mars, qui m'annonce que vous préparez une exhibition d'oeuvres haïtiennes, prose, vers, histoire et essais, de façon à donner une idée complète de l'effort intellectuel réalisé par le peuple d'Haïti au cours de sa vie indépendante.

Un tel projet mérite, non seulement mon approbation, mais mes remerciements les plus vifs. Rien ne peut mieux servir la cause de mon pays, si mal connu, si décrié particulièrement aux Etat-Unis, que la démonstration que vous vous proposez de faire. Vous allez en effet montrer, de la façon la plus concluante, comment un peuple, sorti de l'esclavage le plus abrutissant, à pu vaincre toutes les hostilités qui l'entouraient et atteindre, par son propre effort, à la plus haute culture, vengeant ainsi la race noire de l'accusation d'infériorité qu'on a osé porter contre elle.

J'accepte avec joie de participer à la manifestation projetée. La date la plus convenable d'après moi est le 18 Mai,—jour anniversaire de la création du drapeau haïtien et qui est devenu fête légale de l'Université d'Haïti.

Croyez-moi, cher Monsieur Schomburg, sincèrement vôtre,

Dantès Bellegarde

[Translation]:
Dear Mr. Schomburg,

I received with the greatest of pleasure your letter of the ninth of March, telling me that you are preparing an exhibition of Haitian accomplishments—prose, poetry, history and essays—so as to give a full idea of the intellectual development achieved by the people of Haiti as an independent people.

Such a project merits not only my approbation but my most sincere thanks. Nothing can better serve the purposes of my country, which is so misunderstood and so particularly disparaged in the United States, than the demonstration you intend to make. Indeed you are going to show, in a most conclusive manner, how a people freed from the most degrading slavery has been able to overcome all the hostility that surrounded it and attain, by its own effort, the highest culture, thus avenging the black race against the accusation of inferiority that others have dared to bring against it.

I happily accept your invitation to participate in the projected event. The most agreeable date for me is May 18—the anniversary of the creation of the Haitian flag and what has become the public holiday at the University of Haiti.

Arthur A. Schomburg to Louis-Marie Dantès Bellegarde

Port-au-Prince, Haiti
May 3, 1934

Honorable Friend:

The day you resigned from the high office of Haitian representative to the American nation I had rung the door bell of the Consulate. I need not tell you the profound impression your stand gave me, similar to your address at the League of Nations. The world needs many men of your stamina, knowledge and courage to forge forward in our battles. The Haitian nation so long as she has men like Bellegarde, the Ship of State is safe. I am getting ready to bring before Xmas a number of prospective tourists to visit your country.

I am taking the liberty to hand Honorable Aquilino Lombard of the Cuban House of Representatives, a letter, he is seeking a more peaceful home to engage in agriculture and industry. I know you will advise him how to proceed in the premises.

With my high regards and admiration, hoping to see you before Xmas.

Believe me ever,

 AS
 Arthur A. Schomburg

Marcus Garvey to Norton Cruickshank

Marcus Garvey wrote this letter to a supporter he hoped would arrange speaking engagements for him during his travels to the Caribbean.

West Kensington, London, England
June 10, 1937

Dear Mr. Cruickshank,

This letter is to inform you that I shall be visiting the West Indian Islands and British Guiana on a round trip of the s/s "NELSON" sailing from Halifax on the 7th of October. I expect to arrive at Roseau, Dominica, on the 17th of October at 6 a.m. in the morning leaving at 11 a.m. My purpose of traveling to the West Indies is to address meetings at the different stops.

I am desirous of having a meeting arranged at Roseau for me to address from 8 to 10 a.m. on the day of the arrival of the ship, the 17th, which will give me one hour to reboard the ship. I have lost the addresses of friends and acquaintances in Dominica so I am asking you to do me the favour of getting this meeting arranged for me by passing the letter to someone who would be interested and seeing that the details are carried out for me. Your name was given to me by Mr. McIntyre from Grenada, who knows you well. The arrangements must be as follows:—

You should get a vocal musical programme with recitations to last about three quarters of an hour to allow me an hour for my speech. There should be an admission of 50 cents or 2/—for front seats and 1/6d or 1/—for other seats. You should have the meeting well advertised and the tickets on sale and accounted for before the meeting starts as there will be very little time at the close, in that my secretary and myself will leave immediately for the boat; so see to it that all arrangements are perfected to make my departure after the meeting. You should co-operate with everybody to make this meeting a success. This meeting should include all classes of the community. My appearance in Roseau is for the good of the country and people and is of the most friendly nature and I do hope there will be no antagonism between anyone, but that everybody will co-operate to make the meeting a success from every point of view. You should get in touch with that class of people who can really materially help. The chair should be taken by someone who is well known. Be sure to see that the people who sell the tickets account for them before the meeting and that other tickets are sold at the gate, so that there will be no difficulty in settling all business matters immediately after the meeting. You should ask responsible and respectable people to take part in the programme.

With very best wishes.
I have the honour to be,
Your obedient servant,
   MARCUS GARVEY

P.S. As stated above, I know that you will not have time to look after this meeting for me, but I am depending on you to place the matter in the hands of one who could really look after it in a proper manner.

Fredi Washington to Ademola Johnson

This letter by the actress Fredi Washington (1903–1994) is another example of her social activism. The 1930s star of film and stage advocated for black performers as head of the Negro Actors Guild.

Mr. Ademola Johnson
61 Brudnell Road
Leeds 6, England
September 23, 1949

Dear Mr. Johnson:

Please pardon the long delay in answering your very fine and stimulating letter. It is good to know that there are people like you across the sea who are aware of our organization and are interested in knowing about it. We indeed would recommend you as a member to our ranks and for this purpose you will find enclosed an application blank.

Our greatest and gravest concern in this organization is with giving assistance where we can to the indigent and unemployed actor. You may or may not be aware of the condition of the theatre in America generally, or that the Negro in this profession finds the same conditions affecting him as in industry, et cetera, so you see whether it is art or the pick and shovel, the American Negro finds himself faced with the same problem.

It is good to know that you are in England for the purpose of helping people in your country. We here by and large could do with a far better understanding of conditions in Africa, for it is only through understanding that we will ever come to the point where we can help each other.

You ask for Mr. [Paul] Robeson's address, and while we do not as a rule give it out, I am confident that he would want you to have it. You can reach him at: 22 East 89th Street, New York New York.

You are aware no doubt of the great conspiracy going on in this country against Mr. Robeson. As a matter of fact, I regret to say even the Negroes in many instances are completely unaware of the tremendous contribution he is making to democracy for all people all over the world. So you see a letter from a person like you will help to encourage him and to stimulate him to carry on the great work he is now engaged in.

With every good wish for success in your new venture.

Sincerely,

Fredi Washington

William Alphaeus Hunton, Jr., to
Ghanaian President Kwame Nkrumah

William Hunton (1903–1970) was an activist and African scholar who served as administrator of the Council on African Affairs from 1943 to 1955. Hunton, who graduated from Harvard in 1926 and received his Ph.D. from New York University, corresponded with many African leaders, including South Africa's anti-apartheid leader Walter Sisulu; Kwame Nkrumah, who in 1960 became president of the newly independent Ghana; and Kenneth Kaunda, president of Zambia from 1964 to 1991.

May 4, 1962

Dear President Nkrumah:

The award of the Lenin Peace Prize for 1961 to you, Sir, is very good news indeed. It is a most appropriate and merited recognition of your outstanding service in the cause of a proper policy regarding armaments and of international harmony based, as it must be, on the genuine freedom and progress of Africans and all mankind towards a better life. May I join with the many others in congratulating you.

I regret that since my arrival in Ghana, March 27 last, I have not had the opportunity of greeting you personally and expressing to you my great appreciation of the honour of being invited to come here to assist Doctor Du Bois in the work on the projected *Encyclopedia Africans*. Professor Boateng, Secretary of Ghana Academy of Sciences, promised to arrange an interview for me with you, but I can well understand that your crowded calendar may have made this impossible.

It is close to twenty years ago that I first became acquainted with you in New York when I was working there with Paul Robeson and others as Secretary of the Council on African Affairs. Over the years since then I have never failed to follow your path—My wife and I were among the thousands who applauded you when you visited Conakry in 1960, and again last summer, we had the privilege and pleasure of being present when you spoke in Kremlin, following your tour of the Soviet Union.

It is with much joy and satisfaction, I can assure you, Sir, that I come back to Ghana once more—this time, I trust, for a permanent stay. I welcome the privilege of being associated, however indirectly and insignificantly, with your administration. The national development, both material and ideological, that has taken place since my first visit here in December 1958, on the occasion of the First All African People's Conference, is truly extraordinary. The ideological advance is, I believe, especially remarkable and praiseworthy, and is at the same time the essential factor accounting for the great material accomplishments. For this, as well as for your great contribution to the cause of world peace, I pay homage to your wise and able leadership.

Most respectfully yours
W. A. Hunton

Charles Adjei to Lois Okudzeto

Lois Johnson, a native of Chicago, emigrated to Ghana in the early 1970s and married Raymond Okudzeto, a Ghanaian businessman. Since then she has worked in his company and been involved in numerous philanthropies. This letter was written to her by an admirer after she was ceremonially initiated as the Queen Mother of a small fishing village in Ghana's Volta region.

June 2003

Dear Mama,

Very many thanks for your letter of June 24th, 2003. I much regret the delay in replying. I much appreciate the kind sentiments expressed in your letter and wish to say once more what a pleasure it was, beyond measure, to accord traditional appreciation on your enstoolment as Queen Mother of Atorkor in April 2003.

In this connection, it is of interest to mention that the eyes of natives of Atorkor, wherever they may be, will be watching you, dare I say, with concealed curiosity, as to the performance of relevant traditional duties intrinsic to your status. That you were able to raise $3,000 within a month for the improvement of Atorkor, so soon after your enstoolment, more than proved your keenness in contributing to the development of Atorkor. Thus you have adroitly wrong-footed a lot of detractors, wherever they may be.

[. . .] Please be assured of my unflinching friendship and the keen desire for your success in your new role.

Sincerely Yours,
CDKA

P.S. Now that you are a traditional authority per se, please bear in mind that, in an atmosphere of critical coldness or bland indifference, the most carefully structured or persuasive utterance can fall lifeless to the ground! Certain things cannot be done or said unless the atmosphere is right.

Acknowledgments

No project of this magnitude is possible without the support of many special individuals. For believing in the idea from the start I thank my friend and agent, Neeti Madan, whose guidance, advocacy, and good cheer I've come to rely on. At New York University I had the benefit of early support from Catharine Stimpson, the graduate dean of the Faculty of Arts and Science, who provided seed money to launch this project. I was then awarded a generous university Research Challenge Fund grant, which provided travel and research funding that proved invaluable. Thanks to my wonderful NYU colleagues Derrick Bell, James Fernandez, Yvonne Latty, David Levering Lewis, Beth and Michael Norman, for so generously sharing their enthusiasm for the project along with their Rolodexes. I also appreciate the wonderful NYU students who at various times provided research and organizational support: Francesca Momplaisir was a great companion at the archives, Jaclyn Grodin and Vanessa Dupiton worked valiantly to keep the mountains of letters and historical data organized, and Marissa Williams proved priceless in deftly managing a host of challenging tasks heading down the stretch. I also thank my daughter Marjani, who assisted with the overwhelming task of transcribing letters, and the librarians across the country who provided invaluable support. I am especially grateful to Diana Lachatanere at the Schomburg Center for Research in Black Culture, JoEllen El Bashir at the Howard University Moorland-Spingarn Research Center, and Danielle Kovacs at the W.E.B. Du Bois Library at the University of Massachussetts at Amherst.

Kathryn Lewis did a yeoman's job securing permissions, and Donald T. Courtright and Sondra Kathryn Wilson graciously offered their assistance locating estates. I am profoundly grateful for the big-hearted support of Hamilton Fish, Taya Kitman, and all of my friends and colleagues at the Nation Institute. I am forever in their debt. And thanks to my friends who shook trees for me in search of letters. No one was more persistent than Joan Hornig.

What a pleasure it was to work with my editor, Annie Wedekind, who was as knowledgeable and encouraging as she was exacting. And a special nod to Gena Hamshaw, who adeptly guided the manuscript over the finish line.

Last but certainly not least, I thank my family for their unwavering support, especially my sister and friend Dorothy; my father, whose passion for African American history inspired this inquiry; and my husband, Michael, and daughters Marjani and Mykel who accompanied me across the country in search of letters, and reveled in each discovery.

This endeavor would not have been possible, of course, without the personal and public missives contained within these pages. In concert, they provide a multidimensional portrait of African American life over the past three centuries.

Index

Du Bois, W.E.B., 44, 128, 132n, 157, 158, 244, 285, 321, 322, 323, 326n, 338, 344, 348; correspondence with John Hope, 184–88, 191–93; correspondence with Roland Hayes, 278; efforts toward *Encyclopedia of the Negro*, 194–95; letter from Booker T. Washington, 182–83; letter from Shirley Graham, 199–202; letter from Sterling A. Brown, 202–203; letter to C.D.B. King, 335–37; letters to daughter Yolande, 19–21; letter to Harvard University, 178; letter to Harvey S. Firestone, 340–43; letter to John F. Slater Fund, 179–82; letter to Vernealia Fereira, 183–84; letter to William John Cooper, 194; letter to Woodrow Wilson, 124–25

Duff, Donald, 277

Dunbar, Alice: letter to John Edward Bruce, 188–89; *see also* Moore, Alice Ruth

Dunbar, Matilda: correspondence with her son, 11–15; letter from Robert Murphy, 29

Dunbar, Paul Laurence, 29, 188, 325, 326, 327; correspondence with Alice Ruth Moore, 65–67, 269–72; correspondence with his mother, 11–15; letter to Booker T. Washington, 272–73

E

Eastland, James Oliver, 133, 134, 135
Eastman, Max, 286
Ebony (magazine), 300–301
Eisenhower, Dwight D., 42, 133, 134
Eliot, T. S., 151, 288
Ellicott, George, 92
Ellington, Duke, 74, 307
Ellison, Ida Millsap, 29–33
Ellison, Lewis, 29

Ellison, Ralph: letter to Kenneth Burke, 303–304; letter to reader, 311; letters to his mother, 29–33; letters to Langston Hughes, 287–88, 289–90, 302

Emancipation Proclamation, 89, 109, 153, 175, 217, 218

Embree, Edwin R., 132

Eubanks, William, 324

Evers, Medgar, 43–44

Evers, Myrlie, 43–44

F

Fairfax, Jean: letter to Francis Keppel, 207–208; letter to Minnie and A. J. Lewis, 158–59

Farr, Tommy, 33

Fauset, Jessie, 276, 277

Fereira, Vernealia, 183–84

Ferguson, Charles M., 118

Ferguson, Clyde, 160

Firestone, Harvey S., 340–43

Fisk University, 51, 72, 116n, 118n, 178, 192, 198–99, 216, 301, 308

Fletcher, Marvin, 247n

Flipper, Henry O., 258

Fondren, Elnora, 208–209

Frankson, Canute, 240–47

Frasconi, Antonio, 292–96

Frazier, E. Franklin, 153

Frederick II, King of Prussia, 119n

Fugitive Slave Act, 103

G

Garfield, James A., 67n

Garland, John J., 324

Garner, Joseph, 329

his presidential bid, 169–70; letter
from Alice Walker, 170–72
Occom, Samson, 91–92
Okudzeto, Lois, 349–50
O'Neill, Raymond, 275
Operation Desert Storm, 258

Rutledge, Ed, 211
Rutledge, John, 211

S

Saar, Betye, 73
Saddler, M. W., 236–37
Sampson, Samuel, 234
Schmoller, Gustav, 179, 180, 181, 182
Schomburg, Arthur A., 188, 189n, 326n, 329n; correspondence with Louis-Marie Dantès Bellegarde, 344–45; letter from Horace Mann Bond, 204; letter from James E. K. Aggrey, 331; letter to Caterina Jarboro, 291–92; letter to Jacob Drachler, 204–205; letter to Langston Hughes, 290–91; letter to Wendell Dabney, 126–28
school desegregation: *Brown v. Board of Education of Topeka*, 46, 129, 141, 142, 175, 205, 207, 209, 210; dismissal of black teachers and principals as unintended consequence, 207–208; role of Derrick Bell, 46, 208–209
Schuyler, George, 244
Scott, Coretta, *see* King, Coretta Scott
Scott, Hazel, 135n; *see also* Powell, Hazel Scott
Scriven, Abream, 7–8
segregation: letter from Martin Luther King, Jr., to eight white clergymen, 136–52; letter from W.E.B. Du Bois to Woodrow Wilson, 124–25; in military, 227, 228, 242–43, 251, 252, 253; in schools, summary, 175; telegram from Martin Luther King, Jr., to President Kennedy, 136; *see also* school desegregation
September 11 attacks, 217
Sherley, James, 220–21, 222, 223

Short, Bobby, 307
Shuttlesworth, Fred, 138
Singleton, Mamie K., 52–53
Singleton, Richard, Sr., 52–53
Sinskey, Tony, 221
Sipple, Thomas, 234
Sissle, Noble, 306
Slater Fund, 179–82, 197n
Slaughter, Henry P., 127–28
slavery: Emancipation Proclamation, 89, 109, 153, 175, 215; legacy, summary, 3; letters between slaves, 5–9, 229; and Lincoln, 109–12; public letter from Frederick Douglass to his former master, 95–102; public letter from fugitive slaves to enslaved brothers, 103–109
Smalls, Robert, 121–24
Smith, Darr, 304–306
Smith, Elinor, 16
Smith, Ian, 162
Smith, Lillian, 147, 308
Smith, Lucy, 7
Smith, Robert Lloyd, 117, 118
Smith, William Gardner, 158
Socrates, 139, 143, 144, 200
Sojourner Truth, 110–13
South Africa, 55n, 161, 162, 209, 322
Southern Christian Leadership Conference, 79, 137, 163, 165
Spanish Civil War, 240–47
Spanish-American War, 227, 236, 237n
Spencer, Herbert, 333n
Spingarn, Amy, 283
Spingarn, Joel, 193n, 283n
Stallings, Rev. Earl, 148
Stanton, Edwin M., 235–36
Stevenson, Adlai, 133, 134
Stewart, Joseph, 116
Still, William Grant, 290
Stokes, Dr. Anson, 333
Stovall, Walter, 45n
Strachey, John, 288n
Strayhorn, Billy, 307

PERMISSIONS ACKNOWLEDGMENTS

Grateful acknowledgment is made for permission to reprint the following letters:

Charles Adjei: Reprinted courtesy of Charles D. K. Adjei.

James Emman Kwegyir Aggrey to Sadie Peterson Delaney, March 14, 1924: Letters of James Emman Kwegyir Aggrey reprinted courtesy of the Sadie P. Delaney Papers, Manuscripts, Archives and Rare Books Division, Schomburg Center for Research in Black Culture, The New York Public Library, Astor, Lenox and Tilden Foundations.

Letters of Nancy Allcorn, Mandy McCinny, and Susanah Hart: National Archives, Record 94, Records of the Adjutant General's Office, 1780–1917.

John R. Archer, Jr.: John Edward Bruce Papers, Manuscripts, Archives and Rare Books Division, Schomburg Center for Research in Black Culture, The New York Public Library, Astor, Lenox and Tilden Foundations.

Josephine Baker: Copyright © Langston Hughes Papers, James Weldon Johnson Memorial Collection of American Negro Arts and Letters, Beinecke Library, Yale University. Reprinted courtesy of the Estate of Jospephine Baker.

James Baldwin: Originally published as "My Dungeon Shook—Letter to My Nephew on the One Hundredth Anniversary of Emancipation," in *The Progressive*. Copyright renewed. Collected in *The Fire Next Time* by Vintage Books. Reprinted by arrangement with the James Baldwin Estate.

Claude A. Barnett: Reprinted with permission of the Jean Toomer Papers, Beinecke Rare Books and Manuscript Library, Yale University.

Joseph F. Beam: The Joseph Beam Papers, Manuscripts, Archives and Rare Books Division, Schomburg Center for Research in Black Culture, The New York Public Library, Astor, Lenox and Tilden Foundations. Reprinted with permission from RedBone Press for the Estate of Joseph Beam.

Derrick Bell, Jr.: The Derrick A. Bell, Jr., Papers, New York University Archives. Reprinted courtesy of Derrick Bell, Jr.

Derrick Bell, Sr.: The Derrick A. Bell, Jr., Papers, New York University Archives. Reprinted courtesy of Derrick Bell, Jr.

Louis-Marie Dantès Bellegarde: Arthur Alfonso Schomburg Papers, Manuscripts, Archives and Rare Books Division, Schomburg Center for Research in Black Culture, The New York Public Library, Astor, Lenox and Tilden Foundations. Reprinted courtesy of the Louis-Marie Dantès Bellegarde Estate.

James Hubert "Eubie" Blake: Flournoy E. Miller Papers, Manuscripts, Archives and Rare Books Division, Schomburg Center for Research in Black Culture, The New York Public Library, Astor, Lenox and Tilden Foundations. Reprinted with permission from the Estate of James Hubert ("Eubie") Blake.

Horace Mann Bond: Arthur A. Schomburg Papers, Schomburg Center for Research in Black Culture, The New York Public Library, Astor, Lenox and Tilden Foundations. Reprinted with permission of Julian Bond, the Estate of Horace Mann Bond.

Arna Bontemps: Langston Hughes Papers, James Weldon Johnson Memorial Collection of American Negro Arts and Letters, Beinecke Library, Yale University. Reprinted courtesy of Harold Ober Associates.

Letters of Arna Bontemps: Reprinted courtesy of Harold Ober Associates Inc., copyright © 1980 Arna Bontemps.

John Boston: National Archives, enclosed in Letters Received, ser. 12, RG 94. See *Freedom: A Documentary History of Emancipation*, Series I, Vol. 1, ed. Ira Berlin, Barbara Fields, Thavolia Glymph, Joseph P. Redity, Leslie Rowland (New York: Cambridge, 1885).

William Stanley Braithwaite and Edith Braithwaite: William Stanley Braithwaite Papers, Manuscripts, Archives and Rare Books Division, The New York Public Library, Astor, Lenox and Tilden Foundations. Reprinted courtesy of Hope Braithwaite, the Estate of William Stanley Braithwaite and Edith Braithwaite.

Walter D. Broadnax: Reprinted courtesy of Walter D. Broadnax.

U.S. Senator Edward W. Brooke III: Edward William Brooke Papers, Library of Congress, Manuscripts Division. Reprinted courtesy of U.S. Senator Edward W. Brooke III.

Sterling A. Brown: Reprinted courtesy of the Moorland-Spingarn Research Center, Manuscripts Division, Howard University.

John Edward Bruce: John Edward Bruce Papers, Manuscripts, Archives and Rare Books Division, Schomburg Center for Research in Black Culture, The New York Public Library, Astor, Lenox and Tilden Foundations.

Martha Bruce: John Edward Bruce Papers, Manuscripts, Archives and Rare Books Division, Schomburg Center for Research in Black Culture, The New York Public Library, Astor, Lenox and Tilden Foundations.

Roscoe Conkling Bruce: Reprinted courtesy of the Roscoe Conkling Bruce Papers, Moorland-Spingarn Research Center, Manuscripts Division, Howard University.

Clara Burrill: Reprinted courtesy of Roscoe Conkling Bruce Papers, Manuscripts Division, Moorland-Spingarn Research Center, Howard University.

Nicey E. Bush: Reprinted courtesy of the Jesse Moorland Papers, Moorland-Spingarn Research Center, Manuscript Division, Howard University.

Dr. Henry Arthur Callis: Reprinted courtesy of the Dr. Henry Arthur Callis Papers, Box 192-3, Moorland-Spingarn Research Center, Howard University.

Lois D. Cherry: Reprinted courtesy of Lois D. Cherry.

Kenneth B. Clark: The Kenneth Bancroft Clark Papers, The Library of Congress, Manuscript Division. Reprinted with permission of the Kenneth B. Clark Estate.

Myra Colson: Dr. Henry Arthur Callis Papers. Reprinted courtesy of the Moorland-Spingarn Research Center, Howard University.

Alexander Crummel: Alexander Crummel Papers, Manuscripts, Archives and Rare Books Division, Schomburg Center for Research in Black Culture, The New York Public Library, Astor, Lenox and Tilden Foundations.

Annie Davis to President Abraham Lincoln, August 25, 1864: National Archives, Manuscripts Division, Letters Received, ser. 360, Colored Troops Division, RG 94 [B-87]. See *Freedom: A Documentary History of Emancipation*, Series I, Vol. 1.

James A. Davis: Reprinted courtesy of the Estate of James and Pecola Davis.

Rev. Bernard Chris Dorsey: Reprinted courtesy of Rev. Bernard Chris Dorsey.

Dr. Frank L. Douglas: Reprinted courtesy of Dr. Frank L. Douglas.

Frederick Douglass: Frederick Douglass Papers, Library of Congress. See also *The Speeches and Writings of Frederick Douglass*, ed. Philip Foner. See also the forthcoming *Frederick Douglass Papers*, Series III, ed. John R. McKivigan, et al. (Yale University Press, 2009).

Lewis Douglass: Carter G. Woodson Collection, Manuscript Division, Library of Congress.

Dr. Charles Drew: Charles Drew Papers, Box 134-1, Moorland-Spingarn Research Center, Howard University. Published with permission of Dr. Charlene Drew Jarvis.

Shirley Graham Du Bois and W.E.B. Du Bois: W.E.B. Du Bois Papers, the W.E.B. Du Bois Library, Special Collections and University Archives, the University of Massachusetts, Amherst, with the permission of the David Graham Du Bois Trust. See *Correspondence of W.E.B. Du Bois*, Vol. I, II, and III, ed. Herbert Aptheker (University of Massachusetts Press).

Yolande Du Bois: Countee Cullen Papers, James Weldon Johnson Collection, Beinecke Library, Yale University, reprinted courtesy of the David Graham Du Bois Trust.

Matilda Dunbar: Letters of Matilda Dunbar reprinted courtesy of the Ohio Historical Society. Reprinted with permission from the Estate of Matilda Dunbar.

Paul Laurence Dunbar: Letters of Paul Laurence Dunbar reprinted courtesy of the Paul Laurence Dunbar Papers, Ohio Historical Society.

Robert Dunbar: Matilda Dunbar Papers, The Ohio Historical Society. Reprinted with permission from the Estate of Robert Dunbar.

Ralph Ellison: Ralph Ellison Papers, James Weldon Johnson Memorial Collection of American Negro Arts and Letters, Beinecke Rare Books and Manuscript Library, Yale University. Reprinted courtesy of the Estate of Fanny Ellison.

Medgar Evers: Reprinted courtesy of Myrlie Evers-Williams, the Estate of Medgar Evers.

Jean Fairfax: Derrick Bell Papers, New York University Archives. Reprinted courtesy of Jean Fairfax.

Canute Frankson: Reprinted courtesy of the Tamiment Library and Robert F. Wagner Labor Archives, New York University.

Marcus Garvey: Reprinted courtesy of the Estate of Marcus Mosiah Garvey.

Nnabu Gogoh: Reprinted courtesy of Nnabu Gogoh.

James Henry Gooding: National Archives, Letters Received, ser. 360, Colored Troops Division, RG94. See *Freedom: A Documentary History of Emancipation*, Series III.

Dr. A. T. Granger: William R. R. Granger, Jr., Letters, Manuscripts, Archives and Rare Books Division, Schomburg Center for Research in Black Culture, The New York Public Library, Astor, Lenox and Tilden Foundations. Reprinted with permission from the Estate of William R. R. Granger.

Lester B. Granger: William R. R. Granger, Jr., Letters, Manuscripts, Archives and Rare Books Division, Schomburg Center for Research in Black Culture, The New York Public Library, Astor, Lenox and Tilden Foundations. Reprinted with permission from the Estate of William R. R. Granger.

Dr. William R. R. Granger, Sr. and Jr.: William R. R. Granger, Jr., Letters, Manuscripts, Archives and Rare Books Division, Schomburg Center for Research in Black Culture, The New York Public Library, Astor, Lenox and Tilden Foundations. Reprinted with permission from the Estate of William R. R. Granger.

Maj. David Scott Harris: Reprinted courtesy of Maj. D. Scott Harris.

Thomas Allen Harris: Reprinted courtesy of Thomas Allen Harris.

J. E. Casely Hayford: John Edward Bruce Papers, Manuscripts, Archives and Rare Books Division, Schomburg Center for Research in Black Culture, The New York Public Library, Astor, Lenox and Tilden Foundations.

Langston Hughes: Langston Hughes Papers, The James Weldon Johnson Memorial Collection of American Negro Arts and Letters, Beinecke Rare Book and Manuscript Library, Yale University. Letters reprinted courtesy of the Estate of Langston Hughes, Harold Ober Associates Inc.

Zora Neale Hurston: Langston Hughes Papers, the James Weldon Johnson Memorial Collection of American Negro Arts and Letters, Beinecke Rare Book and Manuscript Library, Yale University. Reprinted courtesy of the Estate of Zora Neale Hurston.

Grace Nail Johnson: James Weldon Papers, the James Weldon Johnson Memorial Collection of American Negro Arts and Letters, Beinecke Rare Books and Manuscript Library, Yale University. Reprinted courtesy of Sondra Kathryn Wilson, executor, the James and Grace Nail Johnson Foundation.

Queen Esther Gupton Cheatham Jones: Reprinted courtesy of Renée Neblett for the Estate of Queen Esther Gupton Cheatham Jones.

Dr. James Arthur Kennedy: Reprinted courtesy of A'Lelia Bundles.

Martin Luther King, Jr., and Martin Luther King, Sr.: Letters of Martin Luther King, Jr. and Sr. Reprinted courtesy of the Estate of Dr. Martin Luther King, Jr.

Walter J. Leonard: Reprinted courtesy of Walter J. Leonard.

Urnestine Lewis: Reprinted courtesy of David Levering Lewis.

Alain Locke: Reprinted courtesy of the Alain Locke Papers, the Moorland-Spingarn Research Center, Howard University.

Thurgood Marshall: Derrick Bell, Jr., Papers, New York University Archives, with permission of the Thurgood Marshall Estate.

Claude McKay: Claude McKay Papers, Schomburg Center for Research in Black Culture, The New York Public Library, Astor, Lenox and Tilden Foundations. Reprinted with the permission of the literary representatives of the Estate of Claude McKay.

Whitefield McKinlay: Whitefield McKinlay Papers, Carter G. Woodson Collection of Negro Papers and Related Documents, Manuscript Division, Library of Congress.

Capt. Eric Mitchell: Originally published in *We Were There: Voices of African-American Veterans, From World War I to the War in Iraq*, by Yvonne Latty (Amistad/HarperCollins, 2004). Reprinted with permission of Eric Mitchell.

Francesca Momplaisir: Reprinted courtesy of Francesca Momplaisir.

Harvey Moore: Reprinted courtesy of the Jesse E. Moorland Papers, Box 126-1–126-2, Moorland-Spingarn Research Center, Howard University.

Toni Morrison: Reprinted by permission of International Creative Management, Inc. Copyright © 2008 by Toni Morrison.

Renée Cheatham Neblett: Reprinted courtesy of Renée Cheatham Neblett.

Howardena Pindell: Reprinted courtesy of Howardena Pindell.

George Pleasant: Originally published in Elizabeth Keckley's *Behind the Scenes; Or, Thirty Years a Slave, and Four Years in the White House* (New York, 1868).

Adam Clayton Powell, Jr.: Rev. Adam Clayton Powell Jr. Papers, The Abyssinian Baptist Church Archives. Reprinted with the permission of Adam Clayton Powell III.

Gen. Colin L. Powell: Reprinted courtesy of Ret. Gen. Colin L. Powell.

Craig S. Prather: Originally published in Dalton Connections. Reprinted courtesy of Craig S. Prather.

A. Philip Randolph: Bayard Rustin Papers, A Register of His Papers in the Library of Congress. Reprinted with permission of the Estate of Bayard Rustin.

George Rodgers, Thomas Sipple, and Samuel Sampson to President Abraham Lincoln, August 1864: National Archives, Letters Received, ser. 360, Colored Troops Division, RG 94 [B-57]. See *Freedom: A Documentary History of Emancipation*, Series III.

Bayard Rustin: Bayard Rustin Papers, courtesy of the Estate of Bayard Rustin.

Julia Davis Rustin: Bayard Rustin Papers, courtesy of the Estate of Bayard Rustin.

Arthur A. Schomburg: Arthur Alfonso Schomburg Papers, Manuscripts, Archives and Rare Books Division, Schomburg Center for Research in Black Culture, The New York Public Library, Astor, Lenox and Tilden Foundations.

Abream Scriven to Dinah Jones, September 19, 1858: Charles Colcock Jones Papers, Tulane University, Charles Colcock Jones Papers. See also *Blacks in Bondage: Letters of American Slaves*, ed. Robert Starobin (New York: New Viewpoints, 1974).

Bobby Short: Fredi Washington Papers, Manuscripts, Archives and Rare Books Division, Schomburg Center for Research in Black Culture, The New York Public Library, Astor, Lenox and Tilden Foundations. Reprinted with permission from the Estate of Bobby Short.

Robert Smalls: Whitefield McKinlay Papers, Carter G. Woodson Collection of Negro Papers and Related Documents, Manuscript Division, Library of Congress.

Mary Church Terrell to Robert H. Terrell, July 9, 1902: Letters of Mary Church Terrell and Robert H. Terrell reprinted courtesy of the Mary Church Terrell Papers, Box 149-2, Moorland-Spingarn Library, Howard University.

Michael Leon Thomas: Reprinted courtesy of Michael Leon Thomas.

Jean Toomer: Jean Toomer Papers, James Weldon Johnson Memorial Collection of American Negro Arts and Letters, Beinecke Rare Book and Manuscript Library, Yale University.

Sojourner Truth: Originally published in *The National Anti-Slavery Standard* (New York), December 17, 1864; and in *The Liberator* (Boston), December 23, 1864. Republished in *Narratives of Sojourner Truth*, Truth's autobiography, in 1875.

Ann Valentine: National Archives. See *Freedom: A Documentary History of Emancipation*, Series III, ed. Ira Berlin, Joseph P. Redity, Leslie S. Rowland (New York: Cambridge, 1982).

Alice Walker: Derrick Bell, Jr., Papers, New York University Archives. Reprinted courtesy of Alice Walker.

Madam C. J. Walker: A'Lelia Bundles's collection. Reprinted courtesy of A'Lelia Bundles, the Estate of Madam C. J. Walker.

Lenwood Waller to Pauline Perry, May 7, 1945: Letters of Lenwood Waller. Reprinted courtesy of Linda Waller, the Estate of Lenwood and Pauline Waller.

Booker T. Washington: Letters of Booker T. Washington. Reprinted courtesy of Tuskegee University.

Booker T. Washington III: Reprinted courtesy of Joyce Washington.

Fredi Washington: Fredi Washington Papers, Manuscripts, Archives and Rare Books Division, Schomburg Center for Research in Black Culture, The New York Public Library, Astor, Lenox and Tilden Foundations. Reprinted with permission from the Estate of Fredi Washington.

James S. Watson, James L. Watson, and Doug Watson: The James S. Watson Papers, Manuscripts, Archives and Rare Books Division, Schomburg Center for Research in Black Culture, The New York Public Library, Astor, Lenox and Tilden Foundations. Reprinted with permission from the Watson Estate.

Phillis Wheatley to Gen. George Washington, October 26, 1775: Originally published in *Pennsylvania Magazine*, April 1776 (Massachusetts Historical Society).

Leigh Whipper: Reprinted courtesy of the Leigh Rollin Whipper Papers, Manuscripts, Archives and Rare Books Division, Schomburg Center for Research in Black Culture, The New York Public Library, Astor, Lenox and Tilden Foundations. Reprinted with the permission of the Leigh Whipper Estate.

Walter White: Walter White Papers, the James Weldon Johnson Memorial Collection, Yale Rare Books and Manuscripts Library, Yale University. Reprinted by permission of Jane White Viazzi.

Roy Wilkins: Reprinted courtesy of the National Association for the Advancement of Colored People.

William T. Williams: Reprinted courtesy of William T. Williams.

Carter G. Woodson: Carter G. Woodson Papers, Carter G. Woodson Collection of Negro Papers and Related Documents, Manuscript Division, Library of Congress.

Rev. Jeremiah A. Wright, Jr.: Reprinted courtesy of Rev. Jeremiah A. Wright, Jr.

Richard Wright: Letters of Richard Wright. Reprinted courtesy of Julia Wright, the Estate of Richard Wright.

A NOTE ABOUT THE AUTHOR

Pamela Newkirk is an award-winning journalist and an associate professor of journalism at New York University. Her articles on African American art and culture have been published in numerous publications, including *The New York Times*, *The Washington Post*, *ARTnews*, *Essence*, and *The Nation*. She lives in Manhattan with her husband and two children.